LITERARY VISIONS

Ninth Edition

Part of a college-level telecourse organized around major literary genres and writing about literature, based on *Literature: An Introduction to Reading and Writing*, Ninth Edition, by Edgar V. Roberts and Henry E. Jacobs

Elizabeth Penfield
University of New Orleans

Revised by

Jose Flores
Austin Community College

Longman

New York Boston San Francisco
London Toronto Sydney Tokyo Singapore Madrid
Mexico City Munich Paris Cape Town Hong Kong Montreal

Penfield/Flores, *Literary Visions Study Guide* to accompany Roberts, *Literature: An Introduction to Reading and Writing*, Ninth Edition

Copyright ©2009 Pearson Education, Inc.
All rights reserved. Printed in the United States of America. Instructors may reproduce portions of this book for classroom use only. All other reproductions are strictly prohibited without prior permission of the publisher, except in the case of brief quotations embodied in critical articles and reviews.

1 2 3 4 5 6 7 8 9 10–STP–11 10 09 08

Longman is an imprint of

PEARSON

www.pearsonhighered.com

ISBN 10: 0-136-04101-9
ISBN 13: 978-0-136-04101-6

Contents

Acknowledgments iv

MODULE I - Introduction 1
  1 First Sight: An Introduction to Literature 1
  2 Ways of Seeing: Responding to Literature 14
  3 A Personal View: The Art of the Essay 28

MODULE II - Short Fiction 44
  4 Reflected Worlds: The Elements of Short Fiction 44
  5 The Story's Blueprint: Plot and Structure in Short Fiction 58
  6 Telling Their Tales: Character in Short Fiction 69
  7 In That Time and Place: Setting and Character in Short Fiction 81
  8 The Author's Voice: Tone and Style in Short Fiction 92
  9 Suggested Meanings: Symbolism and Allegory in Short Fiction 103
 10 The Sum of Its Parts: Theme in Short Fiction 116

MODULE III - Poetry 129
 11 The Sacred Words: The Elements of Poetry 129
 12 A Sense of Place: Setting and Character in Poetry 143
 13 Tools of the Trade: Words and Images in Poetry 154
 14 Seeing Anew: Rhetorical Figures in Poetry 166
 15 An Echo to the Sense: Prosody and Form in Poetry 180
 16 Distant Voices: Myth, Symbolism, and Allusion in Poetry 197
 17 Artful Resonance: Theme in Poetry 211

MODULE IV - Drama 227
 18 Image of Reality: The Elements of Drama 227
 19 Playing the Part: Character and Action 247
 20 Patterns of Action: Plot and Conflict in Drama 265
 21 Perspectives on Illusion: Setting and Staging in Drama 279
 22 Speech and Silence: The Language of Drama 297
 23 The Vision Quest: Myth and Symbolism in Drama 311
 24 A Frame for Meaning: Theme in Drama 325

MODULE V - Conclusion 342
 25 Casting Long Shadows: The Power of Literature 342
 26 Continuing Visions: The Uses of Literature 354

APPENDIX A - Additional Reading 365
A Love that Transcends Sadness 365
Tripmaster Monkey: His Fake Book (An excerpt from the novel) 368
The Bear and the Colt 385

APPENDIX B - Answer Key 389
Answer Key for the Self-Test 389

Acknowledgments

The year 1989 marked the beginning of a multicourse development project that had long been nurtured by the Instructional Telecommunications Consortium. Five courses were initiated that year under the leadership of INTELECOM Intelligent Telecommunications and its president Sally Beaty. One of the five courses was *Literary Visions*.

Without Sally nothing would have existed. She supplied the vision in *Literary Visions*. From that point, the thanks spread out to Interwest Applied Research: Evelyn Brzezinski, the director of Interwest's portion of the project; David Lane, the instructional designer; and Mary Lewis, the academic liaison. Together they organized, coordinated, advised, cajoled, and counseled virtually everyone involved with the project.

Credit for the fine videos and all that they entailed—multiple drafts of scripts, permissions, casting, filming, editing—goes to Gail Porter Long, the executive producer, and Beth Nardone, producer, and all the writers and directors involved, to say nothing of the creative and technical expertise of their colleagues at Maryland Public Television.

The academic integrity of the project is the result of the sound advice and teaching experience of the academic advisors. Not only did they work out the assumptions behind the course and how those assumptions might be implemented, they reviewed all the lessons for the telecourse guide and the initial scripts for the programs. Their advice was invaluable, for which thanks to all: Bob Dees, Dean, Literature and Language Division, Orange Coast College; Barbara Miliaras, Professor of English, English Department, University of Lowell; Walter Sherwood, English Instructor, Sacramento City College; Greg Ulmer, Professor of English, University of Florida; and Nova Jean Weber, Professor of English, Cerritos College.

Throughout the development of the program, Terry Britton of the Instructional Telecommunications Consortium and Vice President for Information Services at Rose State College in Midwest City, Oklahoma, provided ideas and guidance, supplying good advice and information about our intended audience, the students who will be watching *Literary Visions*. In addition, Hyman Field, early in the project, and then Hilda Moskowitz, both on behalf of the Annenberg/CPB Project, assisted and encouraged us along the way and contributed their experience and sound judgment, helping to make the course in general and telecourse in particular as good as it is.

And on behalf of everyone involved in the project, thanks also go to all of the students, ours as well as those who previewed the pilot program and materials, who therefore directly and indirectly helped shape the course.

Elizabeth Penfield
Professor of English
University of New Orleans

MODULE I

Introduction

LESSON 1

First Sight:
AN INTRODUCTION TO LITERATURE

BEFORE YOU BEGIN LESSON 1 . . .

This is the first of 26 lessons that will open your eyes—in the broadest sense of the phrase—to literature. As you know, each lesson consists of three parts: readings from your textbook, a video program, and this study guide. While you've read many textbooks and seen many television programs, you may never have worked with a document such as the study guide. So before you read the content for this first chapter, we'll give you a little information about how the guide is organized and how it can help you throughout your study of literature.

ABOUT THE LESSON: This section is designed as a "friendly" advance organizer—a motivator—for what the lesson covers. Organizers such as this help make learning more meaningful, ensure better retention, and pique your interest.

GOAL: This section—always written as a single sentence—tells you the overall purpose of the lesson. It helps you keep in mind the overriding principle guiding the lesson.

2—*Literary Visions*

WHAT YOU WILL LEARN: These are the specific objectives that you will be learning in each lesson. They form the framework for the content of the lesson. Learning these objectives will enable you to reach the lesson's goal.

LESSON ASSIGNMENT: This section presents a concise listing of the assignments and activities that you should follow to master the learning objectives and achieve the lesson's goal. "Steps" are used to reinforce the idea that learning is a process.

OVERVIEW: This section summarizes the important points of the lesson by integrating the terms, concepts, and principles within the particular readings assigned. The section is designed to help you apply the material from the text and literature selections as you prepare to watch the video. Reading this section before viewing will help the video be even more meaningful. Reading it again after viewing will reinforce learning.

VIEWING GUIDE: The Viewing Guide presents questions to be considered before, during, and after watching the video portion of the lesson. This section is designed to guide your viewing, to help you see the important points in the video. To do a thorough job of responding to these questions, you may need to watch the video more than once.

WRITING ACTIVITIES: The lesson's written assignments are presented here. Instructors may assign any or all of these activities based on the institution's course requirements and the instructor's preferences. The writing activities—separated into "formal" and "informal" activities—tap a wide variety of writing styles, goals, and foci for various interpretations of literature.

SELF-TEST: Several matching, multiple choice, and short essay questions are presented to help you review material and prepare for the typical examinations used in distance learning.

ADDITIONAL READING ACTIVITIES: This section presents other literature selections appropriate to the content of the lesson.

ANSWER KEY: Answers to the SELF-TEST items are provided at the end of this study guide.

IN CONCLUSION . . .

Keeping in mind the purpose of each section of the study guide will support your learning as you proceed through the 26 lessons. And along with the videos and your text readings, using this study guide effectively will reinforce the themes for this course:

- Language, literature, and written expression provide meaning, understanding, and order to experience.
- Literature and its genres are forms of expression that are a vital part of culture.
- The study of literature—its creation, texts, and interpretation—develops interpretive and analytical skills.
- A literary text and its reader exist within historical, social, and cultural contexts.
- The concept of "literary" changes with times and cultures and evolves from different forms—oral, visual, print, and electronic.
- Becoming a skilled reader and writer motivates a person to read and write further and to enjoy literature.

With that as an introduction, let's begin to explore the world of literature.

ABOUT THE LESSON

Print literacy, computer literacy, visual literacy, cultural literacy—these days we hear the word *literacy* used in many different contexts. This lesson explores those contexts to see what we mean by these terms and then focuses on print literacy and the particular variety we call *literature*.

Many people hear the word literature and think only of the classics—*Hamlet*, *Huckleberry Finn*, poems by Emily Dickinson—but the definition used in this course goes beyond that. Literature, as we use the term, covers well known works and some not so well known. You will be reading works by familiar authors and some not so familiar, but all qualify as literary.

This lesson looks at some of the values and standards that determine what is and what is not "literature." By the end of the course, you will know why some people value a particular work and some do not, and you will be able to apply your own informed criteria to determine your own judgment.

Your reasoned response to a work is directly related to another point. Often if you think of *literature*, your first association is the name of a particular text. But literature is more than just a text, for no text stands alone. It has an author, a setting, and an audience. The act of reading therefore goes beyond what's printed on a page and includes the author, the historical and cultural setting, and the reader. Reading literature is a communicative act. The point is not that you have to learn a lot of biographical or historical facts to understand a work but that you bring your own experience and knowledge to anything you read. The same is true of the writer.

In this lesson you'll be listening to what many writers and critics say about the experience they bring to what they read and write. Your world may resemble theirs, or it may be very different. Exploring those similarities and differences makes literature both a pleasure and a discovery.

4—*Literary Visions*

GOAL

This lesson will help you to understand the various uses of the word "literacy" and to appreciate the role of literature and writing within a cultural context.

WHAT YOU WILL LEARN

When you complete this lesson you will be able to:

1. Define *literacy* in terms of oral communication, print, and electronic communication, including the mass media.
2. Discuss *cultural literacy*.
3. Identify elements of imaginative literature that make it a distinct form of writing.
4. Recognize what the different genres of imaginative literature (novel, short story, poetry, drama) have in common.

LESSON ASSIGNMENT

Working through the following seven steps will help you complete the objectives and achieve the goal for this lesson:

Step 1: Read the OVERVIEW in this study guide lesson.

Step 2: Watch the VIDEO, following the steps in the VIEWING GUIDE in this study guide lesson.

Step 3: Reread the OVERVIEW to reinforce what you learned from the text and the video and to help you complete the Writing Activities.

Step 4: Complete any WRITING ACTIVITIES assigned in this lesson.

Step 5: Do the SELF-TEST exercises in this study guide lesson.

Step 6: Read any of the ADDITIONAL READING ACTIVITIES assigned.

Step 7: Go back to the learning objectives in the WHAT YOU WILL LEARN section of this study guide lesson and be sure you can respond to all of them.

OVERVIEW

The explanations in this lesson center on a series of questions: What do we mean by *literacy*? What is cultural literacy? What do we mean by *literature*? What do the different types of literature have in common? This lesson gives no definitive answers to these questions, but it lays the groundwork for the overall context for this course—an introduction to literature.

You will see that the explanations try to establish links between the everyday world and the world of print (particularly literature) not to oversimplify a complex subject but to emphasize that what you read affects your life. Our world is one in which writers speak to us through their texts. What they say and have said may give us pleasure or pain, may change what we think, and may even change the society in which we live. We read, interpret, analyze, and evaluate not just to be informed but to make sense of our lives and the lives around us—and to have pleasure.

What Is Literacy?

"Literal," "literacy," and "literature" all share the same root, the Latin word *litera*, meaning "letter." To be "literate" means to know one's letters, to be able to make meaning of the written symbols that make up words. Thus if you look up "literacy" in almost any dictionary, you will find a definition similar to the one found in *The American Heritage Dictionary of the English Language*—"The condition or quality of being literate, especially the ability to read and write." But look in almost any college catalogue and you will find course listings that mention "computer literacy." Look further and you may find course descriptions in departments of film or fine arts that mention "visual literacy" and journalism courses that focus on "print literacy." Obviously the meaning of literacy has changed.

If you think of the different uses of "read," you'll be able to see some similarities among the kinds of literacy. We read a newspaper by transforming symbols on a page into information. That's print literacy. But we also read a person's expression, meaning that we read what we see even though it's not print. That's visual literacy.

Now think about "reading between the lines." Imagine walking down the street and meeting a friend you haven't seen for a while. Both of you are in a hurry, and after a few minutes you go your separate ways, but not before your friend says, "We have to get together soon." By reading between the lines—reading what lies behind the words—you can tell whether an action will follow the words—whether you'll get an invitation.

Reading between the lines in this example brings us closer to an up-to-date, working definition of literacy—the making of meaning. Given this definition, the term *computer literacy*—the ability to make meaning by using a computer—makes good sense.

Not long ago in the United States, much of the information about candidates for office and issues to be voted on was transmitted by print—newspapers, flyers, advertisements. But the electronic media, especially television, changed that, making information available to people who could neither read nor write. As a result, proof of literacy was no longer required to vote. People could make meaning by watching and listening to debates and candidates; they had always been orally literate—able to make meaning through speech and hearing—and now had access to information through radio and television.

Today, even though the majority of the people in the United States are print literate, they obtain much of their information from electronic media. Yet writing still shapes their worlds, for behind the newscasts, the documentaries, and the advertisements is an army of writers turning out scripts. Directly or indirectly, we still live in a world of print.

What Is Cultural Literacy?

Given the definition of literacy as the making of meaning, it follows that *cultural literacy* is the ability to recognize and make meaning of various symbols or artifacts of a culture. But whose culture? That of African-Americans, whites, Native Americans, Aleuts, women, men, Westerners, Asians? Who are we talking about? And what kind of culture are we talking about? Ancient or modern? Popular or literary?

Simply put, someone who is culturally literate can read the cultural environment that surrounds that person. But what's simply put is not so simple. It means recognizing the major figures and events of the past and the present and the texts that feature them. We become culturally literate by studying science and the humanities, and this form of literacy is the point of higher education's general degree requirements. The study of science and the humanities and, in particular, the discipline of English takes us beyond recognition and into understanding.

Consider for example the ancient Greek myth of Icarus. According to legend, Icarus and his father, Daedalus, were imprisoned in a labyrinth on the island of Crete. To escape by the only way open to them—the air—Daedalus made wings out of feathers, warning Icarus not to fly too close to the sun since it would melt the wax that held the feathers together. But Icarus flew toward the sun; his wings melted, and he fell to the sea and drowned. The myth comes to us through the ages as part of the oral tradition that has long since been recorded in print. As you will see later in Lesson 16, Icarus also comes to us reinterpreted in 16th century art and in modern poetry. It's possible to read a modern poem about Icarus without knowing much about the myth and its various reinterpretations, but the insights gained from such a reading are limited. Knowing the myth and its reinterpretations, our insights are much more full and rewarding. That kind of cultural literacy makes the poem more meaningful.

From another perspective, the concept of slavery in the United States takes on a single dimension if all you have to go on is a history text. Add to that dimension the voices of former slaves Frederick Douglass and Sojourner Truth, the novelist Harriet Beecher Stowe, the Civil War diarist Mary Boykin Chestnut, and the 20th century speeches and sermons of Martin Luther King, Jr., and your understanding of slavery becomes richer. As a result, the impact of a novel such as Toni Morrison's *Beloved* will be all the more powerful. And your reading of a T-shirt that boasts an African American Simpson family will be all the more informed.

A reference to the television show "The Simpsons" is readily recognizable in the United States in the early 1990s, but odds are that 10 or 20 years later it will not be. What is part of today's cultural literacy may not be part of tomorrow's, a statement true of both popular and literary culture.

What Is Literature?

If you were to pick up this week's best-seller list, you might find it hard to tell what on the list is literature and what is not. Your text tells you the term *literature* refers to written (and also spoken) "compositions that tell stories, dramatize situations, express emotions, and analyze and advocate ideas" (page 3). That's true, but it doesn't help you distinguish between popular literature and the more lasting variety. Nor does it help you distinguish fiction from nonfiction.

Obviously there's a difference between your shopping list and a poem, between a how-to book and a collection of essays, and less obviously so between a predictable horror story and one by Edgar Allen Poe or Shirley Jackson. Let's start with the idea of pleasure. Poems and essays have a dimension of pleasure missing from lists and how-to books. Good literature engages the mind and the emotions longer and in a more significant way.

But what about that predictable horror story? It's certainly engaging. But would you read it again? To be worth re-reading, a work must have a certain complexity and must explore a culture's values and present insight into human experience. The 17th century English essayist Francis Bacon put it another way: "Some books are to be tasted, others to be swallowed, and some few to be chewed and digested." What books fit what category changes with the times. Today's critically acclaimed "serious" novel may be tomorrow's justly forgotten best-seller, and what sells only a few copies today may become a lasting work of literature.

A much clearer line can be drawn between fiction and nonfiction. Literary fiction depicts a world of the imagination and literary nonfiction a world of fact. Yet the concept of *genre*—or kind of form—is at work in both types. Biography, travel writing, nature writing, and essay writing are representative genres or types of literary nonfiction. Within the literature of the imagination, prose fiction, poetry, and drama are the major genres, and prose fiction can be divided further into the novel and the short story. In this course we'll concentrate on the short story, poetry, and drama, but we will also discuss the essay and one of its categories—literary analysis.

What Do Literary Genres Have in Common?

Lessons 4 through 24 explain and discuss the elements that characterize short stories, poetry, and drama, so here we will present only a brief look at what these genres have in common: structure, characterization, setting, style, symbol, and theme. While used in a special way in the context of literature, these words mean just about what you would expect.

Think of a business meeting. Its *structure* is laid out in an agenda; its *characters* are those invited to attend; its *setting* is a meeting room; its *style* is probably somewhat formal; and the person chairing the meeting sits at the head of a conference table, a position that *symbolizes* leadership. Because meetings are usually called to address a particular problem or subject, the problem's solution can be thought of as its *theme*—the statement those who vote at the meeting make about that subject.

Let's see how these terms apply to something more concrete, this telecourse. If you look at the table of contents for the study guide, you will see the course's structure—how it is put together. The people involved are the students and the teacher; they are the characters. The setting for the course may be your own home, or if you are using only part of this series, it may be the traditional classroom. The style of the course is, we hope, engaging, conversational, and informed without being esoteric or stuffy. The videos, textbook, and study guide are not just the materials for the course; together they represent or symbolize the interplay of dramatization, printed texts, and explanation that constitute a telecourse and make it different from the traditional on-campus course. As for theme, we hope you will come away from this course with the idea that literature is a vital part of your life.

Summary

All of us, unless physically impaired in some way, are orally literate; we make meaning through what we hear and what we say. Within that circle of those who are orally literate are the majority of the people living in the United States—those who are also print literate. Yet huge differences exist between someone who can barely read and write, someone who can read and write with some fluency, and someone whose life is fully engaged in reading and writing.

Language is power. Knowing how to use language and how language can be used can make the difference between an informed person and one who is manipulated by current pressures—be it advertising, political opinion, economics, or various forms of entertainment. Informed readers and writers don't believe everything they read, and they read critically, not in the sense of finding fault, but weighing, analyzing, evaluating.

When we read a work of literature, we use all kinds of literacies. We hear its words, and we see its images as well as the words on the page. And if we are culturally literate, we do not have to depend on footnotes to understand what we read. By focusing on literature and the activities of reading, writing, and thinking, this course will help you be a better reader and writer. By reading and responding to literature, you will hone your critical faculties and sharpen your reading and writing abilities. And while that sounds like and *is* work, what makes it a pleasure is what you will be reading. There's pleasure, too, as well as some pain, in growing and learning.

In his 1972 Nobel Prize lecture, the Russian novelist Alexander Solzhenitsyn stated that "Literature transmits incontrovertible condensed experience . . . from generation to generation. In this way literature becomes the living memory of a nation." Writers speak to us through their works, spanning time and culture, to share their lives and enrich ours.

VIEWING GUIDE

An important component of this lesson is the video. You will learn more effectively from it by thinking about the following questions and guidelines.

Before Viewing:

1. Reread the OVERVIEW in this study guide paying particular attention to the term *literature* and to the distinctions between print and other kinds of literacy.
2. Try to recall some of the responses you have had to particular works that can be called literature.

During Your Viewing:

1. Listen for definitions of literature.
2. Listen for what the writers give as their reasons for writing.
3. Listen for what the critics emphasize about literature.

After Viewing:

Give some thought to the following questions. You may want to write short answers in your journal or notebook.

1. Which of the dramatizations appealed to you most and why?
2. Of the writers in the video, whose view struck you as the closest to your own and why?
3. Mary Helen Washington quotes one of her colleagues as saying, "Fiction is our way of knowing." Apply that statement to a work you have read.
4. According to Mary Poovey, arcane, difficult-to-understand lectures are "only one dimension of what literature can mean to people." What are other ways people can learn what literature means to them?

5. Given what you have read in this study guide and what you have seen in the video, write a paragraph defining literature.

WRITING ACTIVITIES

After your study of this lesson, you should be able to understand the various uses of the word *literacy* and appreciate the role of literature and writing within a cultural context. Your instructor will advise you which, if any, of the following writing activities you are to complete.

Formal Writing:

The four activities are presented in order of difficulty. The first calls for an analysis of an event from the perspective of the basic terms used in studying literature. You'll find models for this activity in the "Overview." The other activities will help you better understand the concept of print and visual literacy. *Process* is the focus of Activity 2, but this isn't your ordinary how-to paper. The topic asks you to step out of yourself and observe what you do when you read. As the topic implies, *what* you read determines *how* you read it. The third activity calls for reader response, an analysis that examines cause and effect. Finally, the last activity introduces you to the kind of analysis you will work with in the course, an analysis of a person—in this case a real person who is also playing the part of the host on the show.

1. Choose an isolated event that has occurred to you recently and write a paragraph explaining its structure, characters, setting, style, symbol, and theme.
2. Think about how you read a particular text (a newspaper, textbook, novel, any kind of text) and write an essay that explains in detail how you read that text.
3. Select a work of literature that had an emotional effect on you (positive or negative) and write an essay explaining the effect and what you think caused it.
4. Write an essay in which you analyze Fran Dorn, the host on the video. What sort of person does she seem to be? What do you learn about her personal life? How does she regard literature? How does she want you to regard it?

Informal Writing:

Both activities ask you to examine and analyze your immediate environment. The first one will give you a better sense of the role print literacy plays in your life. The second looks at programming on television to see what if anything it has in common with literature. If you accept the idea that some shows on television share some characteristics with literature, this second activity also makes it possible for you to draw a distinction between popular culture and literary culture.

1. Observe your family or a close friend or yourself during the course of the day to get an idea of the roles played by the various literacies. What part is played by print literacy? Electronic literacy? Cultural literacy? Write out your conclusions in a notebook or journal.
2. Take a close look at a day's programming on one of the major television networks. What categories do the programs fit? How many shows are in each category? What category or categories are closest to literature? Write a brief summary of your findings.

SELF-TEST

Match the items in column A with the definitions or identifications in B:

A	B
1. IBM compatible	a. Print literacy
2. Genre	b. Predictable literature
3. A newspaper	c. Visual literacy
4. Theme	d. Type
5. Situation comedy	e. Popular culture
	f. Nonfiction
	g. Element common to types of literature
	h. Computer literacy

Answer the following multiple choice items:

1. Which is NOT a genre of literature?
    a. Short story
    b. Novel
    c. How-to books
    d. Poetry
2. Literature
    a. does all of the following.
    b. crosses cultures.
    c. elicits an emotional response.
    d. requires interpretation.

3. Which statement about cultural literacy is true? Cultural literacy is a(n)
   a. fixed list of things one should read.
   b. officially approved list of things one should read.
   c. index of intelligence.
   d. measure of what a culture values.
4. The reader of a literary work is a(n)
   a. active participant.
   b. literal interpreter of the author's words.
   c. member of the culturally literate.
   d. member of the same culture as the author.
5. Which element is NOT common to the genres of literature?
   a. Theme
   b. Setting
   c. Style
   d. Rhyme

In 100–250 words, answer the following short essay questions:

1. Write a paragraph or two exploring the title of this series and the title of this particular lesson. Based on those titles, what are your expectations about the course?
2. Think about the differences between hearing information and seeing it. What strikes you as the most important distinction, and what implications can you draw from it?
3. The "Overview" in this lesson uses a number of allusions to people, events, texts, and times. Select one and analyze what this allusion contributes to the paragraph containing it.

ADDITIONAL READING ACTIVITIES

If you enjoyed the ideas presented in this lesson, you may want to read further about literacy and what writers say about their writing. Here are some suggestions:

Ong, Walter. *Orality and Literacy.*
Pattison, Robert. *On Literacy.*
Plimpton, George (ed.). *Writers at Work: The Paris Review Interviews.* (A collection of eight volumes containing interviews with contemporary writers)

Postman, Neil. *Amusing Ourselves to Death: Public Discourse in the Age of Show Business*. (A critique of the ways in which the media affect our lives)

Purvis, Alan. *The Scribal Society*. (An essay examining the ways in which reading and writing shape our lives in the information age)

LESSON 2

Ways of Seeing:
RESPONDING TO LITERATURE

ABOUT THE LESSON

The previous lesson set out some broad distinctions among the types of literacy, kinds of writing, and the different genres of imaginative literature. The focus gets narrower in this lesson so that you can understand more clearly the nature of this course.

The English language is a subject we are all familiar with. Throughout the world, people speak it, read it, write it. Because it's an international language, it's also studied worldwide. Tell someone from Europe, Africa, or the Far East that you are studying English, and that person will almost automatically assume your subject is the English language. If you say no, you are studying literature, you will have some explaining to do. This lesson gives you some of that explanation.

What is literature? Why study it? What value does literature have? In what way is literature a subject? What do people do when they study literature? These are the kinds of questions about any subject of study that deserve answers at the beginning of any course. In the following pages, we'll set out some answers for you to consider.

This lesson explores the tradition of literature and its evolution, not as dusty books and yellowed pages but as resonant words of writers and their texts brought to life by informed readers.

GOAL

This lesson will help you to appreciate the tradition of literature and its evolution.

WHAT YOU WILL LEARN

When you complete this lesson you will be able to:

1. Distinguish between *popular* and *serious* literature.
2. Describe the various roles literature has historically played in culture.
3. Define the study of language and literature as a discipline.
4. Explain how literature is read.

LESSON ASSIGNMENT

Working through the following eight steps will help you complete the objectives and achieve the goal for this lesson:

Step 1: Read the OVERVIEW in this study guide lesson.

Step 2: Read Part I, pages 1–54 in the textbook, and the specific works your instructor assigns. The following are mentioned in the video and will be the focus of later lessons; but only the one marked with an asterisk (*) is discussed at length in this lesson.

Poems:
- "Dulce et Decorum Est," Wilred Owen, pages 802-803.
- "Do Not Go Gentle Into That Good Night," Dylan Thomas, page 930.
- "Woman," Nikki Giovanni, pages 1130-1131.*

Short Stories:
- "The Horse Dealer's Daughter," D. H. Lawrence, pages 471–482.

Drama:
- *The Glass Menagerie*, Tennessee Williams, pages 1643–1692.

Step 3: Watch the VIDEO, following the steps in the VIEWING GUIDE in this study guide lesson.

Step 4: Reread the OVERVIEW to reinforce what you have learned in the text and the video and to help you complete the Writing Activities.

Step 5: Complete any WRITING ACTIVITIES assigned from this study guide lesson.

Step 6: Do the SELF-TEST exercises in this study guide lesson.

Step 7: Read any of the ADDITIONAL READING ACTIVITIES assigned.

Step 8: Go back to the learning objectives in the WHAT YOU WILL LEARN section of this study guide lesson and be sure you can respond to each.

OVERVIEW

In the study guide's discussion for the previous lesson, you read about how to draw a line between what is and what is not literature. This lesson will pick up that discussion and make the line more distinct by examining the differences between popular literature and the more serious variety, between, say, a Steven King chiller and the kind of fiction you'll be reading in this course.

From that starting point, we'll go on to examine the impact literature has had over the years, a discussion that explains why we study this subject. Next, we'll very briefly trace how literature developed and how the discipline of English study came into being.

Then, to explain what we do when we study literature, we'll take a look at the roles played by writers and readers. The writers and readers in this course make up a varied group: professional writers, critics, and, of course, you, the students.

What's the Difference Between Serious and Popular Literature?

The word *serious* raises images of grim faces, earnest voices, grave subjects—all work and no play—but that's hardly what's meant by the word when it's applied to literature. Serious literature includes comic, joyful, light-hearted texts, and it covers works on small subjects as well as large ones. But this kind of literature is serious in the sense that it goes beyond entertainment to teach and delight as well. You read one of these works for more reasons than to find out what happens in the end.

But much of the reading we do is for entertainment only. Look around you in a doctor's office, an airport waiting area, or at a beach or pool side, and apart from the occasional newspaper, magazine, or report you will see mysteries, science fiction, romances, thrillers. Books like these are fun to read, and because they often use formulaic plots and characters, they are not very demanding. You can read while children splash or planes take off.

But it's a rare reader who in such a setting can command the concentration necessary to read a more challenging work, one that explores complex characters and provides insight into the individual and that person's culture. Such a work goes beyond formulaic plots and characters to develop an ordered and unified world depicted through carefully chosen words.

Think of the standard Hardy boys or Nancy Drew novel and *The Adventures of Huckleberry Finn* and you'll recognize the difference. Both are about adolescents and both are adventures, but there the similarity stops. The Hardy boys or Nancy Drew may take risks and we may get to know what makes them do so, but there's none of the complexity of Huck. Huck's risks are huge and not just his own, for he shares them with Jim, a runaway slave. Huck's adventures are more than pranks or escapades; they are quests—for freedom, for truth, for family. And though this is serious stuff, you can't overlook the humor of the book. This complexity—of *character, conflict, tone,* and *style*—brings us back to the novel again and again, each time finding something new and adding more meaning to our original understanding of the book. Meanwhile, the Hardy boys and Nancy Drew gather dust on the shelf.

Yet you cannot distinguish between popular and serious literature as you can between meat and fish, water and air, countryside and urban landscape. Perhaps a workable analogy is the difference between a child and an adult: both share many characteristics, but one is far more developed than the other. So from this point on, unless otherwise noted, we'll use *literature* in the sense of serious literature.

Why Study Literature?

A historian, psychologist, anthropologist, sociologist, artist, or teacher might all read a work of literature from distinct perspectives, but each of these perspectives would also share much in common: all of these readers would find in a text a record of a culture, insight into life, and an expression of values.

In countries that still adhere to the oral tradition, singers and priests tell of the myths and legends and events that make up that country's history. So, too, in ancient times, oral poems recounted a culture's history. These epics or sagas told of heroic deeds and figures, and many of them have come down to us in print. Much of what we know of ancient Troy and the Trojan War, for instance, we know from the epics the *Iliad* and the *Odyssey*.

But to think of literature as a record of a culture doesn't meant that the culture has to be old. Nathaniel Hawthorne's short stories and novels have much to tell us of the United States' Puritan past, and the contemporary works of writers such as Toni Morrison and Alice Walker reveal the world of the African-American to readers who grew up in very different racial and ethnic contexts. The result is not just a history; it is also literature. And it is discovery.

Literature gives us insight into its characters not available from any historical account. After all, history deals with facts, even though those facts often have to be discovered and then, always, interpreted. In literature, however, the author creates "fact," controlling the plot, the conflict, the characters, the action—what those characters say and do. And sometimes those creations are more convincing, more true, than fact. Shakespeare's Richard III is a created one who may or may not be historically accurate, but Shakespeare's Richard—not the real one—is the one who sticks in most people's minds.

Even though intelligibility imposes certain limits on a writer, as does a culture's sense of what is realistic, writers create their stories, shaping them as they wish. Thus literature can fully depict a sense of order or chaos rarely seen in the world around us. Often that order or chaos comes to us in the form of a work's *theme*, an assertion about an idea or subject dealt with in the text. In early forms of literature, these themes appeared as explicit morals. Then, a story might have pointed out the hazards of being greedy, or a play might have depicted the rewards of resisting temptation. The moral taught a lesson: "Don't be greedy" or "Resist temptation." Today, however, the moral has been supplanted by the theme, and its lesson has been replaced by an assertion that is implied rather than stated. That assertion usually expresses, questions, or reinforces a value. In the video, for instance, you will hear three critics talk about the theme each finds in Nikki Giovanni's poem "Woman." One maintains the poem shows that "women are not taken seriously by men or by society," another finds that the pairing of man and woman is "not so natural as we think," and the third implies that a woman can only be herself by rejecting a man. All three critics see the poem as exploring the traditional relationship of a woman to a man.

Relationships, individuality, courage, truth are only a few of the values you will read about in this course. The works that examine them will engage you and make you rethink your own values as well as the values of your culture.

How Did Literature Evolve?

In the lessons that introduce each of the three main genres (4, 11, and 18), you will read brief histories that relate how the genre evolved. So here we'll merely sketch the outline that the other lessons will fill in.

Poetry is the oldest of the genres, and if you think about it, you can understand why. Remember those jingles and song lyrics that you cannot get out of your mind, no matter how hard you try? They stick in your memory because of the cadences, the use of similar sounds, and, of course, rhyme. These elements combine to make the words memorable, and in pre-literate societies, memory was all people had.

Many of the forms of poetry still written today have their origins in ancient times. In the Western tradition, the *ode* and the *lyric* come to us from the ancient Greeks, and we've borrowed other forms from other countries, the *villanelle* from France, the *sonnet* from Italy, and *haiku* from Japan.

Poetry also played an important part in the development of drama. The earliest dramas, now long lost in history, probably re-enacted rituals such as the hunt or the harvest, rituals that involved song in the form of poetry and dance. You can see both poetry and dance at work in early Greek plays. In *Oedipus*, the dance is performed by the Chorus, and the play itself written in verse. And early drama was still set within a religious context. Greek tragedies and comedies were performed at the festival of Dionysus, the god of death and rebirth.

All of the dramatic forms we are familiar with in our own times that exist within the European tradition have their roots in the plays of the Greeks. The Elizabethan times were another high point in the development of theater, but comedy and tragedy, even opera and melodrama, sprang directly or indirectly from the plays put on in ancient Greece. Today's plays may be more realistic or even more non-realistic than those in Athens 2,500 years ago, but they are direct descendants.

Fiction is the most recent genre you will be studying, and within fiction, the short story is even more recent than the novel. Although narrative in verse preceded the prose narrative or novel, the audience for the novel had to wait until the printing press made the mass production of books possible. As literacy grew, so did interest in reading not just philosophical works but works of a different nature.

By the 18th century, technology combined with increased levels of education and literacy and an interest in the individual to provide fertile soil for the novel. By the end of the 19th century, both the novel and the short story were firmly in place as popular forms of entertainment.

This evolution of literary genres is almost the reverse of the order in which we will present them in this course. Here, we'll start with the short story, then move on to the poem, and conclude with drama. We begin with short fiction because it is more accessible than the other forms. And we end with drama because you will need to draw upon all you have learned about short fiction and poetry to be able to bring a play to life from the printed page.

What Does It Mean to Study Literature?

As you can see, literature has a long history, and so does the study of literature, more particularly literature written or translated into the English language. Say "English" to American college students today, and most would automatically associate the word with literature. But literature is only one of several fields within the discipline of English. Most present day departments of English also cover linguistics and a variety of writing—creative, technical, professional, sometimes even legal.

If you define the study of language as the study of creating, interpreting, and analyzing language, usually in the form of texts, you can describe what we now think of as the discipline of English. To focus on writing is to create texts, to focus on literature is to interpret texts, and to focus on language is to analyze texts. You can see this distinction in the courses listed in your college catalogue under the heading of English: writing, literature, and linguistics.

If you were to read about the kind of classes a young Aristotle or Sophocles attended, you would find much that was familiar. Students in ancient Greece and later in Rome memorized texts, wrote in imitation of them, and interpreted them. The course of study at that time and in England and Europe on into the Middle Ages was called the trivium because it encompassed three areas: grammar, logic, and rhetoric. In these earlier times, what was known as grammar included the study of literature. In medieval times, the trivium led to the B.A. degree, and the quadrivium, the four mathematical sciences (including music), led to the M.A. degree. Together the trivium and quadrivium comprised the seven liberal arts, and the literature studied was Latin and Greek.

By the 1560s, the study of English emerged first as the study of the language—its vocabulary, its syntax, its grammar—what we would now refer to as linguistics. Then in 1762 in Scotland, the discipline of English as we know it began to take shape when Hugh Blair, professor of rhetoric and *belles-lettres* at the University of Edinburgh, took the radical step of lecturing in English on English literature. The days of Latin and Greek were fading, and by the end of the 18th century, reading and public speaking in English were recognized as vital for an educated citizenry.

As the demand for education grew in the 19th century, the number of universities in the British Isles doubled, and institutions of higher education sprang up all over the United States. This growth paralleled an interest in formal instruction in the modern languages, including English and English literature.

Although scholarship in English literature has its roots in the 1500s of Tudor England, the teaching of literature did not enter the university curriculum until the late 19th century. Harvard University, for example, appointed its first professor of English in 1876; England's Oxford University, far more conservative, followed later in 1904 with the appointment of a university chair of English literature.

As the United States approached the end of the 19th century, science was making itself felt in the university curriculum. That interest combined with the notion of popular education for a democratic society and American *utilitarianism* to challenge traditional practices in education. At the university level, the study of *classical languages* waned, and interest in the *modern languages*, especially English, grew dramatically.

In 1883, the Modern Language Association was founded in the United States as the professional group for teachers of English and other modern languages. Not that there were many English teachers. At that time, only 39 of its members taught English. That's certainly not the case today. Some hundred years later, the membership has risen to over 32,000, with the great majority involved in English study. In practical terms, reading and writing had become the province of departments of English and, in higher education, English Departments focused on literary texts.

Although English as a discipline is made up of writing, literature, and linguistics, each of those areas overlaps with the others. In this introduction to literature, you will focus primarily upon the interpretation of texts, but your interpretation will analyze word choice and style and will often be expressed in writing. The course itself is one usually required or an option in the general education curriculum. For that reason, this course approaches literature from the perspective of analyzing and interpreting works of a complex structure that reveal insights into the world around us.

Within the last few years, the interpretation of literature has received much critical attention, so much so that it's now possible to identify a number of "schools" of interpretation. Your textbook gives you a brief overview of these differing ways of reading literature (pages 1854–1875), and then to show how each approach can be applied, uses Hawthorne's short story "Young Goodman Brown" as an example. The point of this course, however, is to sharpen your own critical skills, not to convert you to a particular way of interpreting texts.

How Do You Read Literature?

If you think of all the kinds of reading you engage in, you'll probably come up with quite a list. Most often, you probably read for information: how to drive to a certain address, how to program a video recorder, what happened in the city council or to your favorite team, who died, or who has what for sale. You read the newspaper, magazines, billboards, your mail, your textbooks.

Odds are, you also read for pleasure. Perhaps you're addicted to mystery stories, thrillers, romances, or science fiction. Perhaps when you flip through a magazine, your attention is caught not only by a news story but also by a poem or short work of fiction.

If you combine these two types of reading—for information and for pleasure—and then add the intellectual processes of analysis and evaluation, you will be reading the way you need to read in this course. Marjorie Perloff, one of the critics in the video, says of reading literature: "you're going to have to read it slowly, you're going to have to go back and reread . . . so that you notice all kinds of things, so that you realize that certain images are introduced that produce a certain effect that you couldn't possibly get on a first reading."

Literature is a demanding sort of reading. Although some people can read it surrounded by the noise of television and children, most need a quiet place that encourages the kind of concentration essential to good reading. Being comfortable is important too, which is why many people read in bed in the relative quiet of the night.

But no matter where you read, you need to suspend your own immediate environment and enter the world on the pages before you. Sometimes what you enter is a complete world, such as the one depicted in a full-length drama, but other times you may enter a world occupied by only an image or a feeling, as is often the case with poetry. On first reading a text, this world is what you experience. On second and third readings and beyond those, you see more and hear more, becoming aware of the parts that make up the whole.

Those parts are the elements you will study in this course. Some, such as *action*, are straightforward; others, such as *style* or *symbolism*, are more elusive. None, however, is foreign to you, and you will find that this study guide uses what you are familiar with to explain the unfamiliar. In this manner, you will learn the technical vocabulary of the discipline.

How Do You Write About Literature?

Many of the people you will hear and see in this course are the people who write essays, short stories, poems, and plays—those who make (or try to make) their living by writing. You will also hear from people who write critical analyses of what they read, who analyze theoretical issues, who pose interpretations—people for whom writing is an essential part of their professional lives.

What both groups have in common is a love for literature and language, accompanied by a healthy respect for what it takes to transform what is in their heads—what they know and think and feel—into writing. That transformation is a challenge all writers face, whether they write for a living or for class assignments. You will be facing that challenge in this course, but it is a challenge that will help you clarify your ideas.

The kinds of writing you will be doing will depend on what your instructor assigns. Probably much of what you write will be analytical essays of the kind described and exemplified in your textbook, and you will find Part 1 of the text a thorough introduction to the traditional essay on a literary topic—how to discover ideas, develop a subject, draft an analytical essay, and then revise it. Here, instead, we'll discuss some of the characteristics you share with the writers you will see in this course.

One tip you can learn from the writers you see in the video for this lesson and all the ones that follow is that you need to care about what you write. You need to relate to your subject. If you're writing a traditional analytic essay, for example, look for a way to connect with your topic. If you don't, what you write is apt to be a dry, academic exercise that holds little meaning for either writer or reader except to say, "I can do this."

Watching the video, you will also probably conclude that there is no one way to write. What you see is a great variety of habits. Some write with pens, others with pencils, and some on computer. *Where* they write contrasts as well. August Wilson writes in bars and restaurants; Steven Dixon writes in his studio; Lucille Clifton writes in her head.

No matter where or how they write, however, all these writers revise. Think of the word "revise" as two words: *re vise*, to see again. *Revision* means just that, not simply correction. This seeing again is what made Ernest Gaines take his first novel though some 20 drafts and makes Donald Hall average between 75 and 100 drafts for each poem.

And probably all the writers and critics would agree with Andre Dubus when he says: "There is something mystical about writing but it's not rare and nobody should treat it as though this is something special that writers do. Anybody born physically able in the brain can sit down and begin to write something, and discover that there are depths in her soul or his soul that are untapped."

As you progress through this course, you will find that reading literature and writing about it is one of the ways that we reach those depths, that we tap our souls.

Summary

This course concentrates on serious literature so that you may understand and enjoy works that are rich and enriching. You may find some of your reading difficult, but if you bear with it, you will also find it rewarding. Perhaps you will continue in the discipline of English, discovering more and more about the field. Short of that, perhaps, you will develop a habit of reading that will stick with you the rest of your life, nourishing and sustaining. No matter what direction you take, this course will serve as an introduction to literature, more specifically the three genres of imaginative literature: short fiction, poetry, and drama.

Along the way, you will be sharpening your skills as a reader and as a writer, for the two are inseparable. As you use your own words to analyze the words of others, you will find that writing is a unique way of knowing. Just as reading can put you in the shoes of a character, interpreting a work through your own writing can put you in the character's mind and, by extension, into the writer's mind and world.

Reading literature is an active, dynamic process. You bring to the text your own experiences, knowledge, culture, world. Reading through a work, you constantly (and often unconsciously) juggle what you know, what you have read, and what you expect against the background of the page before you. You analyze, compare, summarize, evaluate. And you enjoy what you read.

VIEWING GUIDE

An important component of this lesson is the video. You will learn more effectively from it by using the following questions and guidelines.

Before Viewing:

1. Reread the OVERVIEW in this study guide, paying particular attention to explanations of what to expect in this course.
2. Review the work assigned, paying particular attention to the ones your instructor emphasizes.

During Your Viewing:

1. Listen for the host's point about *The Wizard of Oz*.
2. Note the different ways to read different genres.
3. Note the importance of basing an interpretation upon the text.
4. Listen for the ways different interpretations can enrich meaning.
5. Listen for the different ways writers get ideas for their works.

After Viewing:

Give some thought to the following questions. You may want to write short answers in your journal or notebook.

1. List the reasons writers write.
2. Why do people interpret the same work differently?
3. Which critic made the most sense to you and why?
4. Which of the writers interests you most and why?
5. What do the quotations shown during the shots of the writers contribute to the video?

WRITING ACTIVITIES

After your study of this lesson, you should be able to appreciate the tradition of literature and its evolution. Your instructor will advise you which, if any, of the following writing activities you are to complete.

Formal Writing:

The first activity asks you to reflect upon the kind of reading you do and draw conclusions about it, thus emphasizing two of the basic kinds of thinking you will be doing in this course: reflection and analysis. Activity 2 also emphasizes the same kinds of thinking but is more difficult because it asks you to generalize about what you see in the video. These first two activities call for *expository writing*, which is also the purpose of Activity 3. There, you are asked to select an interpretation and back it up with the text of the work. The last activity is the most difficult because it calls for interpretation, evaluation, and argument.

1. Consider the reading that you do, listing as many items as you can think of that you've read in the past few days. Include all kinds of reading, even the most ordinary. What purpose does the reading serve in each case? What conclusions can you draw from your list? Write an essay that explains those conclusions.
2. The video includes a number of critics and writers talking about their reading and writing. Choose one of these two groups, either the critics or the writers, and consider what generalizations you can make based on what they say. Write an essay that explains those generalizations.
3. Three of the critics in the video present their views on Nikki Giovanni's "Woman." Select the interpretation you find most reasonable, reread the

Ways of Seeing—25

poem with that perspective in mind, and then write an essay explaining how the text supports that interpretation.
4. Work out your own interpretation of "Woman." How does it differ from that of the critics? Write an essay arguing for your interpretation of the poem.

Informal Writing:

Both of these informal activities ask you to record ideas and impressions that may well be of interest to you later in the course. With Activity 1, for example, you may find that much of what you say will apply to serious literature as well. As for Activity 2, by the end of the course, you'll be able to compare your expectations to reality.

1. If you read for entertainment, write a few pages in your journal or notebook explaining what you read and why you enjoy it.
2. Think about your reading and your previous study of literature. Given your experience, jot down in your journal or notebook what your expectations are of this course.

SELF-TEST

Match the items in column A with the definitions or identifications in B:

A	B
1. Oldest genre	a. Drama
2. Reading for information	b. Creating, interpreting, and analyzing texts
3. The discipline of English	c. Popular literature
4. Essential to writing	d. The short story
5. Evolved from ritual	e. Textbook
6. Evolved with mass production	f. Revision
7. The oral tradition	g. Assertion expressing, questioning, or reinforcing a value
8. Most recent genre	h. The novel
9. Theme	i. Poetry
10. Most mysteries	j. The beginning of literature
	k. Music lyrics
	l. Moral
	m. Grammar

Answer the following multiple-choice items:

1. *Serious* as applied to literature means
   a. no humor.
   b. large subjects.
   c. complexity.
   d. works by great writers.
2. One of the functions of literature is to
   a. record a culture.
   b. provide insight.
   c. express values.
   d. All of the above.
3. The best description of *interpretation* is that it
   a. is in the eye of the beholder.
   b. must be based on the text.
   c. depends on the writer's intention.
   d. has one correct answer.
4. To read literature well, you should
   a. reread.
   b. enter the world of the text.
   c. analyze.
   d. All of the above.
5. Which course would NOT be included in a department of English?
   a. *The Bible* as literature
   b. Film as literature
   c. The literature of popular culture
   d. Early Spanish literature

In 100–200 words, answer the following short essay questions:

1. Consider what you have read about the difference between popular and serious literature and then think about what you see on television. Does the distinction hold true there?
2. Consider what you associate with the word *literary*. To what extent do the discussion and video in this lesson support those associations?
3. At times, the line between the serious and the popular blurs and is hard to draw. Choose a work or television show and explain how it can fit both categories.

ADDITIONAL READING ACTIVITIES

If you enjoyed the topic of this lesson and what you saw in the video, you may want to read some of the following works:

Alter, Robert. *The Pleasures of Reading in an Ideological Age.*
Altick, Richard. *The Scholar Adventurer.*
Davidson, Cathy N. (ed.). *Reading in America.*
Graff, Gerald. *Professing Literature: An Institutional History.*

LESSON 3

A Personal View:
THE ART OF THE ESSAY

ABOUT THE LESSON

If you stop and think about the variety of information and entertainment that you absorb each day, you would probably be surprised at how much of it is conveyed directly or indirectly by print. The newspaper is an obvious source, what with news stories, editorials, letters to the editor, columns, advertisements, classified, and obituaries. But then there's television and radio—sources of information and entertainment. While television is a visual medium and radio an auditory one, both rely heavily on print. In fact, with the exception of talk shows, almost all of what you hear and see is scripted.

This lesson focuses on a special category of writing—the essay. The term is a broad one. It includes what you read on the editorial page and in columnists' opinion pieces, what you see in the commentary spots in newscasts, and what you hear as "human interest" stories on National Public Radio.

But before we get to the essay, let's step back a bit to see where it fits on the larger map of writing. An initial line to draw is between writing intended for a public audience and that aimed at a private one. If you also stop and think about all the forms of print that come your way—billboards, notes, shopping lists, telephone messages, letters, reports, memos, political flyers, ads, even the backs of cereal boxes—you'll be able to make this initial distinction. Most personal letters, for instance, are aimed at readers within a private circle of intimate friends and relations, one that can vary from an audience of one—as in a love letter—to many, as in a Christmas letter that goes to a number of friends.

Of course there is the occasional famous author whose personal letters get collected, sometimes in several volumes, and published for public consumption—but that is the exception. Business letters, on the other hand, are intended for the public that the writer may not even know. Again, the size of the audience varies from, say, a complaint letter you may have written that gets seen by several people at the company to the "save the _____" letter that goes to thousands in hopes of eliciting donations.

This course concerns itself with *public writing*, although you will see a number of assignments that call for *private writing* in the form of lists, notes, or personal responses in a journal or notebook. Both kinds of writing are important because of the relationship between writing and thinking. Whether public or private, writing about a subject makes you understand it better.

Beyond the distinction between public and private writing, there is another broad distinction to make between *nonliterary* and *literary* writing. News stories, reports, memos, directions, cereal box prose, and the like all fall in the nonliterary category. Essays, short stories, novels, poetry, drama, scripts for television plays, and stories, all come under the broad umbrella of literary writing.

Essays? Documentaries? But aren't those nonfiction? Yes, but they are also literary. Open up the table of contents of any survey of American or English literature and you'll find essays. So it's also necessary and useful to divide literary writing into literary *fiction* (the literature of imagination) and literary *nonfiction* (the literature of fact). The essay falls into the category of literary nonfiction; the short story, poetry, and drama fit the category of literary fiction.

In your English courses, you have probably run into this distinction in the form of literature courses and courses in composition. But labels such as those—along with the terms such as literature of the imagination and literature of fact—often do a disservice. Nonfiction draws upon the writer's imagination in much the same way that literary fiction does. And all writing—no matter what kind—is creative. Anyone, student or professional writer, who has faced a blank page knows that you have to *create* the prose to fill that page.

The great majority of the lessons in this course focus on literary fiction, specifically three genres: short story, poetry, and drama. But underpinning all those lessons is the essay, for your instructor will occasionally ask you to write an analysis of what you have read. The result will be a critical essay that as a literary form has a long and honorable tradition. This lesson examines that tradition so that you can see how what you write fits into the genre of the essay and the category of literary nonfiction.

GOAL

This lesson will help you to recognize the essay as a distinct form of literature.

WHAT YOU WILL LEARN

When you complete this lesson you will be able to:

1. Define the essay as a distinct genre of formal writing.
2. Describe the historical development of the essay in its relationship to print literacy.

3. Identify the rhetorical elements of exposition and argument and their effect on the reader.
4. Describe how the rhetorical elements of exposition and argument parallel our innate problem-solving techniques.
5. Relate the place of student writing in the essay tradition to the discipline of English.
6. Recognize student writing as an integral part of the telecourse, which is itself an audio-visual essay.
7. Identify examples of personal writing and public essays.

LESSON ASSIGNMENT

Working through the following nine steps will help you complete the objectives and achieve the goal for this lesson.

Step 1: In your text, re-read the chapter "Introduction: Reading, Responding to, and Writing about Literature," pages 1–54. The text will provide background for what you will read in the study guide, explain the key terms, and give you some information about the literary selections you will be reading.

Step 2: Read the essay by Willie Morris, "A Love That Transcends Sadness," pages 365–367 of this study guide, and any others your instructor assigns. The essay by Willie Morris will be the focus of this lesson.

Step 3: Read the OVERVIEW in this study guide lesson.

Step 4: Watch the VIDEO, following the steps in the VIEWING GUIDE in this study guide lesson.

Step 5: Reread the OVERVIEW to reinforce what you have learned in the text and the video and to help you complete the Writing Activities.

Step 6: Complete any WRITING ACTIVITIES assigned from this lesson.

Step 7: Do the SELF-TEST exercises in this study guide lesson.

Step 8: Read any of the ADDITIONAL READING ACTIVITIES assigned.

Step 9: Go back to the learning objectives in the WHAT YOU WILL LEARN section of this study guide lesson and be sure you can respond to all of them.

OVERVIEW

As you can tell by what you have already read, the word *essay* encompasses a great variety of very different kinds of writing. In discussing the essay, this lesson has three purposes: to examine the essay as a literary genre, to explain where your own writing fits within that genre, and to explore the elements that the essay has in common with literature of the imagination.

That's a lot of ground to cover, so to make it easier we will divide it into five parts. We'll start where you might suspect, with a definition, and then briefly describe the history and development of the essay. Next we'll take up the role of private writing and see how it relates to public writing, for, more often than not, what the reader finally sees in print had its origin in notes and drafts that only the writer read.

From there, we'll go on to two kinds of essays: the *critical essay* of the kind you will be writing in this and other courses, and the *general essay* that most closely parallels the literature of the imagination. Then we'll finish with a discussion of what the essay has in common with the other genres you'll be studying: the short story, poetry, and drama.

What Is the Essay?

Compared to a play or even a short story, an essay is short. How short is short? Most essays fall in the range of a few hundred to five thousand words or so. And although the focus of the essay is nonfiction, it is a genre that makes demands on the imagination, for, like works of imaginative literature, the essay has an aesthetic dimension. It is written to be enjoyed, and the writer takes a great deal of care to shape the language of an essay so that it is a pleasure to read.

The subject of an essay doesn't help define what one is, for the subjects of essays are as varied as those in imaginative literature. The same is true for tone. An essay can be humorous or serious, satiric or combative. Where the essay *does* differ from imaginative literature is in its focus. Grounded in a nonfiction subject, the essay makes a point, and that point is usually readily identifiable as its thesis—the assertion it makes about its subject. This idea of a point or thesis is similar to the idea of a theme in works of imaginative literature. Unlike the theme, however, the thesis in an essay is more explicit than implicit. It's easy to recognize.

Essays can usually be categorized by the kind of point they make. *Personal* essays concentrate on the writer's thoughts, *expository* essays on the subject under discussion, and *argumentative* essays on an assertion the writer wants the reader to accept. These categories are not rigid, and often an essay may include all three; more often than not, however, one will predominate.

The essay assigned for this lesson's reading is informal and combines the personal and the expository, leaning toward the expository. Willie Morris, the author, takes you on a visit and relates the thoughts and memories the scene brings to his mind, yet the subject stands out more than the writer.

So you can have a clearer understanding of the different aims an essay can have, let's change the subject to a work of literature. If you were to read a piece that described the thoughts that a particular experience, short story, or poem elicited, you would be reading a personal essay. Many narrative essays fall into this category, from the infamous "What I Did Last Summer" to James Thruber's account of "The Dog that Bit People." Change those topics to "What People Do on Their Summer Vacations" and "Dogs That Bite People" and the result would be an expository essay. The essay may still be written in the first person *I*, but the focus has shifted away from the writer to the subject. And if you were to change the topics once more so that they ended up "Why You Should Go to Colorado on Your Summer Vacation" and "Guard Dogs Are Better than Burglar Alarms," then the result would be an argumentative essay.

No matter what the focus of the essay—personal, expository, or argumentative—the style of writing usually places the work in one of two traditions: the *formal* or the *informal*. An essay arguing for gun control, for instance, might be formal, summoning all the pros and cons to support a reasoned position; or it might be informal, drawing upon the writer's personal experience as a friend of someone who was involved in an accidental shooting. The tone of the essay is what usually determines whether it is formal or informal, and you will learn more about tone later in this lesson.

History of the Essay

Although some of the early Greeks and Romans wrote what might be called essays, the term was coined by the French philosopher Michel Eyquem Montaigne to describe his thoughts on subjects as diverse as sleeping, liars, and friendship. He called these pieces *essais*—translates as *trials* or *attempts* because they expressed tentative thoughts as opposed to the formal, finished ideas he had written for philosophical treatises.

Montaigne published his first collection of essays in 1580, and the form soon spread to England, where Francis Bacon established himself as the first English essayist. Bacon's first collection was published in 1597 and reflected his practical advice on a number of moral and ethical subjects such as marriage and single life, studies, and negotiating.

These two writers are also representative of the two traditions of the essay, the informal and the formal. Montaigne takes a personal approach to maxims, and his tone is conversational, relaxed; Bacon takes the impersonal route, and his tone is clear, dogmatic, highly polished. Bacon's style wears a starched collar and elegant cufflinks; Montaigne's is unbuttoned and has its sleeves rolled up.

By the late 16th and early 17th centuries these two styles were brought to bear upon works of literature in the form of prefaces to longer works. These prefaces gradually evolved into the critical essay that along with essays on nonliterary subjects appeared regularly in the 18th century in what was the beginning of the magazine industry. Known as *periodical essays* because they appeared in periodicals, the essays of this time tended to be shorter and less scholarly in style than those of the previous century. Their informal style, wit, and vast range of subjects appealed to the large middle-class reading public that was growing and buying magazines.

The 19th century was a glorious time for magazines, both in England and America, and formal and informal essays flourished because of the large size of the reading public and the more modern methods of printing and distribution. Present-day American magazines such as *Harper's, Atlantic Monthly, Nation, Saturday Evening Post, Ladies' Home Journal,* and *Cosmopolitan* were founded in the 19th century.

Throughout this time and up to the present, many of the best writers in the English language also wrote essays. Some of the names associated with the formal essay are Samuel Johnson, John Stuart Mill, Ralph Waldo Emerson, and Henry Thoreau. Today we see their descendants in columnists as diverse as William Buckley and Miss Manners. As for the informal essay, the list can go on and on, starting with Montaigne and continuing to Jonathan Swift, Charles Lamb, Virginia Woolf, and Mark Twain on up to James Thurber and E.B. White—all forerunners of familiar newspaper names such as Erma Bombeck and William Raspberry.

Private Writing: Notes, Journals, and Drafts

Whether formal or informal, the essay is carefully crafted, and its polish can be intimidating. But behind most finished works are piles of crumpled pieces of paper, assorted notes and doodles, cross-outs and substitutions, or filled floppy disks. Many writers keep journals or diaries or record their thoughts on tape, as well.

Your textbook discusses the kinds of ideas and notes that may go into a journal, pages 12–14, and describes the process of transforming notes into a finished formal paper, pages 18–49. Formal papers are assigned in most courses, but private writing is also important. In this study guide, you'll find that each lesson's section on Writing Activities contains ideas for notes and journals, for that kind of private writing will help you understand what you read. Even if your instructor does not assign any of these activities, you may find that some have enough appeal for you to want to do them on your own. They are designed to work the way a writer's journal works, encouraging you to write down such things as the links you find between your own experience and what you read, a striking image or metaphor, an outline for a story, a draft for a formal essay, and so on.

Informal writing such as you will find in the lessons that follow allows you to experience the same imaginative process that a professional writer goes through and also forces you to think more critically about the particular topic under discussion. Thus you gain a dual perspective on the works assigned, viewing them not just as reader but also as writer.

Public Writing: The Critical and the General Essay

You will also see that the Writing Activities section lists topics for formal writing, the traditional short *critical essay*. It's important to realize that *critical*, in the sense it's used here, does not mean negative but rather analytical. Critical essays are not written to find fault but to explain a reasoned judgment. This form of public writing is usually a variation on the formal essay, epitomized by Bacon, and is almost as old as the essay itself. It now accounts for much of the writing assigned in college.

Within the discipline of English, the essays you write are literary analyses in the same tradition as those written by Edgar Allen Poe. If you've ever researched a paper on a literary topic, you know that any number of journals are devoted to essays of this kind. Some of those journals, such as *The Southern Review* or *The Paris Review*, invite critical essays on a broad variety of literary topics, while others, such as *American Literature* or *Shakespeare Quarterly*, focus on more specialized subjected.

The chapter in the textbook assigned for this lesson does a good job of explaining how to go about drafting a critical essay on a literary subject. All of the chapters in the textbook provide advice for writing a paper that focuses on the particular topic under discussion and all accompany that advice with a sample essay and commentary on the example. The samples are formal essays that lean toward exposition—explaining a particular interpretation—or argument—persuading the reader to adopt a particular interpretation.

Although the critical essay is most closely associated with the humanities, professional journals in scientific and technical fields frequently include critical essays in which the writer steps back from the more technical aspects of the discipline to consider issues or problems within a wider context.

Journals aimed at a general but somewhat specialized audience—think of *Discovery, Audubon, The New Yorker*—often include informal, *general essays* that follow in the tradition of Montaigne, a tradition also seen in more general magazines such as *Time, Newsweek*, and *Sports Illustrated*. One contemporary essayist, Edward Hoagland, compares the informal essay to the "human voice talking, its order the mind's natural flow, instead of a systemized outline of ideas." Yet beneath that "natural flow" lies a carefully worked out structure.

Commonalities: Structure, Point of View, Character

The informal essay may argue or explain, but often it simply expresses the author's ideas about a subject and therefore is more conversational than formal. That is certainly the case with Willie Morris's "A Love That Transcends Sadness," pages 365–367 in this study guide. The sense that the reader has of the writer as a person makes the informal essay's relation to its fictional counterpart, the short story, relatively easy to trace. Parallels also exist between the short story and the formal essay, but they are a bit more elusive.

Let's start with structure. The personal essay may be informal, but it has a well-defined structure. Like the short story, it has an identifiable beginning, middle, and end. The Morris essay, for instance, is structured chronologically. The first two paragraphs are set at a time "not too long ago" and contain a brief narrative: the author describes accompanying his friends to a nearby cemetery in search of their burial plot. Morris uses this brief narrative to establish his subject, setting, and tone.

The body of the essay is a flashback. Morris thinks about his relationship with cemeteries, tells us about the ones he dislikes, then goes on to describe his "favorites." He concludes this middle part of the essay with two personal narratives. Then he ends the essay by shifting to the present—"now"—and generalizing about his experiences.

You could go a step further and discuss structure in dramatic terms, identifying the very same parts that you will find later in the short story and drama: exposition, complication, crisis, climax, resolution. But for now, beginning, middle, and end will suffice. In the informal essay, these sections are so carefully wrought that they seem to melt into each other. The structure of the formal, critical essay is more clear-cut: introduction, discussion, conclusion.

What's usually missing from the formal critical essay is a distinct sense of the writer, the mind behind the prose. You will find that some instructors rule out the possibility of the first person singular "I" in the essays you are assigned, and others allow it with the caution that it's easy to overuse. You should ask your instructor which route you should take. The textbook takes the former route, but this study guide varies the approach. In the textbook you'll find that the sample essays avoid the first person "I," opting instead for the impersonal pronoun *one* or no pronoun at all. As a result, the focus remains clearly on the work discussed.

Not so the Willie Morris essay. The essay is presented from the perspective of the first person point of view. This choice of point of view gives you a distinct impression of the writer because you know what he thinks and why he thinks it. Now imagine a short story that is also related in the first person. You get to know that character by knowing what he or she thinks and why. When we speak of the *I* in a short story, we know the *I* is not the author but a narrator or character. It's as though the author puts on a mask—technically called a *persona*—and assumes the character of the first person narrator.

This concept of persona is also at work in an essay because in a sense the *I* in an essay is always a fiction. If, for instance, you are using first person and writing a short essay response for an examination, you have unconsciously created a persona for yourself that (you hope) will convince the instructor that you are informed, knowledgeable, and therefore deserve a good grade. The same principle was at work in ancient Greek rhetoric, for persona (or ethos) was considered one of three basic persuasive appeals. Every time you see an ad in which, say, a football star is selling a brand of cereal, you are seeing this kind of appeal used in a way that would make Aristotle shudder. A star quarterback is not necessarily a star nutritionist.

Commonalities: Setting, Atmosphere, Style, Tone

Setting can also figure as largely in an essay as in a short story, poem, or play. Morris's essay is not just about cemeteries, much of the action is *set* in cemeteries. And note that his first paragraph also sets the *atmosphere*, the emotional associations arising from the setting. His cemeteries are not those of ghosts and goblins or terror-producing slasher films but of quiet continuity, life, and adventure. He likens the quest for a plot to "picking out a Christmas tree."

If you try to think of the role setting plays in a formal, critical essay, you may be stumped. Like persona, setting does not usually figure significantly in critical essays. *Style*, however, is as important to any essay as it is to a short story. Contemporary formal essays are more apt to stress clarity over novelty and therefore go easy on narration, description, and figures of speech such as metaphor and simile. But the informal essay draws upon the same repertory of style as literary fiction.

Morris, for instance, turns nouns into verbs ("the honeysuckled air"), uses alliteration ("their patina of the past"), balances phrases ("much is taken, much abides"), and employs imagery ("this cinder of a planet out at the edge of the universe") in much the same way as a poet, dramatist, or short story writer. Yet the milder versions of these techniques can and should show up in formal essays: precise diction, carefully shaped sentences, and a sense of stylistic unity. Morris's essay weaves sentences and paragraphs together so the essay is all of one piece. That should also be true of the formal essay.

Tone is a word used to describe the overall effect of style. The tone of a formal essay is serious, but that's not to say it should be dull. Informal essays usually adopt a lighter tone, characterized by a more casual vocabulary, freer paragraph structure, and flashes of humor. Tone functions in a similar way in fiction. A writer's tone can be satirical, humorous, dramatic, stiff, conversational, or any of a number of other possibilities.

Morris's tone is serious but conversational. His occasional glints of humor and his natural sounding prose erase the dark, morbid associations we might normally link to his subject. His manipulation of tone is closer to what we find in fiction.

Commonalities: Symbol, Allusion, Theme

Morris also uses the techniques of *symbol* and *allusion* that we usually associate with literary fiction. For instance, if you stand back from the essay and think about ways in which the cemetery can be thought of as a symbol, you will probably associate it with a number of possibilities: the continuity between death and life, change, reality, humanity. And symbols exist within the text as well. Fairy Jumper, buried at the age of five with a poignant epitaph and no other family member around, can be seen to represent isolation or crushed hopes. It's interesting to note that Morris follows the description of Fairy Jumper with the narrative of his joining a man he's never seen before to help dig a grave. A symbol of isolation is followed by a symbol of community.

Rarely will you find that sort of use of symbol in the formal essay, but you will find its first cousin, *allusion*. Like symbol, allusion evokes associations. Morris, for instance, describes old remote graveyards and then quotes from Thomas Gray's poem "Elegy Written in a Country Churchyard," pages 701–704, summing up the photographs on the headstones with Gray's line "the short and simple annals of the poor." The quotation fits even if you don't know the allusion. If you do know it, however, it summons up the calm sadness of Gray's poem and its point that death makes everyone equal and that one should make the most of life. Gray also speaks of the great deeds those buried in his humble country churchyard might have achieved had they lived under different circumstances. Thus the allusion also leads naturally into Morris's description of Fairy Jumper.

In writing critical essays, you will find this sort of allusion particularly useful. It not only exercises your mind to think associatively and make connections, it also ties your ideas to the whole tradition of Western culture.

Earlier in the discussion of what is an essay, you read that one of its singular characteristics is that it makes a point. Fiction makes a point as well, but that point is usually not as clearly defined or identified as in the essay. This difference is reflected in the different terms we use for fiction and nonfiction. We call the point made by an essay its *thesis*; a point made by a work of fiction is its *theme*. On first reading, that may seem a difference without a distinction, so let's examine it more closely.

Think first about different kinds of essays. An argumentative essay should have an unmistakable thesis: solar energy isn't worth its price; recycling should be mandatory; Lawrence's "The Horse Dealer's Daughter," pages 471–482, is greatly overrated. Expository essays should also have a clear-cut thesis: solar energy operates on simple principles; public speaking need not terrify you; Lawrence's "The Horse Dealer's Daughter" explores the positive and negative values of love. Note that whether argumentative or expository these sample theses are assertions; they take a stand. They differ in what they want you to do with that stand. Whether formal or informal, the argumentative essay wants you to adopt it; the expository essay wants you to understand it.

Essays that focus on personal opinion—on the writer instead of the subject or the argument—also need to have clear theses. If you've ever seen Andy Rooney on the television show "60 Minutes," you know there's no mistaking his point, and there's no mistaking that it's his. Opinion pieces in the newspaper that let off steam to such an extent that they would convince only those readers who already agree with the writer also fall into this category, and their opinions come through clearly.

When we change the text to fiction, the point becomes much more debatable, and often even the subject is a matter of interpretation. Poe's "The Masque of the Red Death," pages 510–513, for instance, can be interpreted as being about death or ambition or pride. Your view of the story's theme will depend on what you choose as the story's subject. Yet, to switch back to the essay, there's no confusion about the subject of Willie Morris's essay. You can argue about the exact wording of its thesis, but the subject is cemeteries.

If you were to write a critical essay on the thesis of Morris's essay, your essay would have a thesis about his thesis. But if you were to write a critical essay about your view of the theme of Poe's story, your essay would have a thesis about his theme. Thesis and theme have two important qualities in common: they are assertions, and they are the central idea everything else in the work relates to. Whether essay or short story or poem or drama, all of the elements—structure, character, setting, style, symbol—all add up to thesis or theme.

Summary

As you go through this course, you will find that different genres emphasize different elements. The essay stresses the thesis, and the short story stresses structure through two of its components—plot and conflict. Also, think of poetry. Imagery and figures of speech come to mind, both directly related to style. And drama is concerned with action and its causes as expressed in dialogue.

This discussion has focused on the essay, both as a genre in itself and as a form you will be writing. But you also need to remember that no matter what form a text may take—whether it is an essay or a poem, nonfiction or fiction, formal or informal—and no matter who wrote it, you or Shakespeare, a text is just dead words on a page until someone reads it. A reader brings a world of personal experience and cultural tradition to a work, so in a very real way, its meaning is not fixed until it is read and interpreted.

Take for instance the reader or audience that most of your writing in this course will probably be aimed at—the instructor. An instructor will read one of your papers against several contexts: the sum of his or her experiences in reading, learning, and teaching about literature as well as other forms of writing; the goals of the course; the work assigned up to the point your paper was due; and any knowledge of you as a person in general and a reader and writer in particular. That's a lot of baggage to bring to a paper, and the teacher must sort it out so that only what is appropriate applies, tossing aside an aversion, say, to Hawthorne or to the size of your margins or to misspellings of pet words.

When you read a text, you also need to be an open and informed reader. And you also have to be careful that what you decode as you read is directly related to what's on the page. If you wrote a critical essay on Willie Morris's essay that concentrated on the horrible experiences you have had in cemeteries, you would be writing about yourself, not the essay.

As a writer, you learn to balance what you want to say about your subject with what the reader needs to know about it. Whether you are explaining or arguing, you will find that you draw upon patterns of thinking that you use constantly in everyday life. "Where have you been?" calls for narration; "Why did you go?" leads to cause and effect; "What was it like?" asks for definition, comparison, example, and analysis; and "What did you do?" will be answered with description. These are the patterns of thinking—narration, description, definition, cause and effect, comparison, analysis—you will be using in reading and writing about literature.

For that reason you might try using these patterns of thinking as a path into a particular work. "What's happening?" relates to narration and will take you into plot, conflict, and structure. "How can I describe the setting, atmosphere, and characters?" obviously is description. "What are the motives?" leads to examining cause and effect, and "What changes occur in the characters?" gets at comparison and contrast. Finally, the broadest question—"What's going on here; what is the author saying?"—brings you to the work's theme, the implied statement the writer is making about the subject.

These questions are examples of the kind of interior dialogue you might carry on with yourself as you read, asking yourself questions and answering them. Often such a dialogue is a good way to work out a satisfactory balance between what you want to say and what your reader needs to know. But keep in mind that your reader can only read what you put on the page and not what's in your mind. It's always best to over-explain and cut than to under-explain and leave your reader dangling.

VIEWING GUIDE

An important component of this lesson is the video. You will learn more effectively from it by thinking about the following questions and guidelines.

Before Viewing:

1. Review the chapter "Introduction: Reading, Responding to, and Writing about Literature," in the text, pages 1–54.
2. Review the work assigned, paying particular attention to what your instructor emphasizes. Try to hear the language in the essay by Willie Morris.

During Your Viewing:

1. Listen for definitions of the essay.

40—*Literary Visions*

2. Watch for who and what influenced the development of the essay and also how they did this.
3. Note the ways the camera acts as a narrator in the dramatization of the Morris essay.
4. Try to pinpoint the mood of that dramatization.
5. Listen for the points made by the critics.
6. Listen for the points made by Willie Morris.

After Viewing:

Give some thought to the following questions. You may want to write short answers in your journal or notebook.

1. Write a short definition of the essay.
2. What names would you give to the essay's major periods of development?
3. Did the dramatization of Morris's essay change your initial impression of the essay? Why or why not?
4. What similarities and differences did you find between the critics' ideas on the critical essay and the kinds of writing you have been doing for classes?
5. Did Willie Morris in the interview seem to be the same person as Willie Morris in his essay. How or how not?

WRITING ACTIVITIES

After your study of this lesson, you should be able to recognize the essay as a distinct form of literature. Your instructor will advise you which, if any, of the following writing activities you are to complete.

Formal Writing:

The first activity is deceptively easy. Odds are you have an overall impression of your experience with critical essays, but it may not be so easy to recall the specifics that are needed for a successful paper. Some latitude is possible here. You can play around a bit with details as long as you make them believable and appropriate. Activity 2 calls for an expository essay based on your "reading" of the video presentation of Morris's essay. You may find it helps to compare the visual presentation to the printed one, the written essay itself. The last two activities start you off on critical essays focused on literature. You're not flying blind here, for the textbook not only contains the story but a great deal of information about it.

1. Write an essay in which you analyze your experience writing critical essays.
2. Write an essay that defines the term "visual essay," using the video presentation of Willie Morris's piece as your primary source of examples.
3. Write an essay in which you explain whether you found the ending of "The Necklace" a surprise.
4. Write an essay in which you argue that "The Necklace" is or is not dated.

Informal Writing:

The first activity focuses on the essay by asking you to find an example of one in your own reading and then to explain why indeed it's an essay. The point here is that if you apply what you have learned to a different situation and then explain it, you will have a greater understanding of what an essay really is. As for the second activity, it concentrates on your working out the differences among various types of writing, the personal, the expository, and the argumentative. If you do this activity, it will sharpen your eye to discern the different purposes—your own and others—that writing tries to achieve.

1. Flip through a magazine you usually read or one that you would like to subscribe to, noting the different kinds of writing and looking for articles that could be called essays. Select the article that strikes you as the most interesting, and in your journal or notebook record your analysis of why it is an essay.
2. To get a clearer sense of personal, expository, and argumentative writing, open a daily newspaper to the editorial page or pages and number each contribution. You'll probably find letters to the editor, perhaps an opinion column or two, and maybe some essays by syndicated columnists. Go through each of them deciding which category it fits by thinking of its primary purpose—to let off steam, to explain, or to get you to adopt a particular opinion. Then in your journal or notebook, select one example and analyze how it does what it does.

SELF-TEST

Match the items in column A with the definitions or identifications in B:

A	B
1. Francis Bacon	a. Personal Writing
2. Information essay	b. An analytical essay
3. Literary fiction	c. Inventor of the essay
4. Critical essay	d. The short story
5. Montaigne	e. Characterized by a serious tone
6. Exposition	f. First English essayist
7. Self-expression	g. The news story
8. Argument	h. Explanatory writing
9. Formal essay	i. Literary nonfiction
10. Biography	j. Coiner of word for essay
	k. Characterized by conversational tone
	l. Characterized by humorous tone
	m. Persuasive writing

Answer the following multiple-choice items:

1. Which of the following elements do the general essay and the short story NOT have in common?
    a. Thesis
    b. Structure
    c. Persona
    d. Symbol
2. The most significant impact on the development of the essay was the
    a. shift to an interest in the individual.
    b. decline of the novel.
    c. potential of the informal essay.
    d. proliferation of magazines.
3. The essay is to literary nonfiction as a
    a. house cat is to a lion.
    b. course is to a meal.
    c. pistol is to a rifle.
    d. Chihuahua is to a Great Dane.
4. The critical essay
    a. has a negative focus.
    b. is crucial to a work's success.

c. presents reasoned analysis.
   d. questions an established theory or idea.
5. Reading is to writing as
   a. a chicken is to an egg.
   b. a store is to a car.
   c. gasoline is to a car.
   d. garden is to rain forest.

In 100–250 words, answer the following short essay questions:

1. Write a short essay of one paragraph or so exploring the meaning of the title of Willie Morris's essay.
2. If you were to represent the structure of Morris's essay with a drawing, what shape would it take? Explain what you find and whether it would mark the essay as formal or informal.
3. Examine the allusions that Morris makes in his essay. How can you categorize them? What, if anything, do they add? Are they appropriate or not? Write an essay explaining your views.

ADDITIONAL READING ACTIVITIES

If you enjoyed reading the essay and listening to the interview in this lesson, you may want to read more works by Willie Morris and perhaps some essay collections as well.

Atwan, Robert (ed.). *Best American Essays of* _____. (An annual series of essays by various authors)

Howard, Maureen (ed.). *The Penguin Book of Contemporary American Essays*. (26 essays by 26 authors, most of whom are well known)

Morris, Willie. *North Toward Home.*

_____ *Good Old Boy.*

_____ *Homecoming.*

_____ *Terrains of the Heart and Eight Other Essays on Home.*

MODULE II

Short Fiction

LESSON 4

Reflected Worlds:
THE ELEMENTS OF SHORT FICTION

ABOUT THE LESSON

Listening to everyday conversation, you are apt to hear the word story used in many different ways. The explanation too long to recount gets shortened to "It's a long story." A pointless joke is a "shaggy dog story." Little white lies and childish fantasies mean you're "telling stories." "What's your story?" demands an accounting, and "What happened?" asks for facts. "Tell me a story" is a request known to all times and all cultures. That story may be the history of a people, an animal fable, or a personal anecdote. But whether it's *The Iliad*, "Little Red Riding Hood," or the time Uncle Harry came to dinner, stories have certain elements in common: they all have character, plot, theme, and style.

None of these terms is foreign. Character and plot are both familiar words... "What a character!" you might say when describing a particularly colorful friend; "The plot thickens," you might remark when events take new turns. We talk about style, as in "hair styles" and even "lifestyles." In this lesson, we'll also talk about "prose style" so you can better appreciate how a story is written.

Character, plot, style, and other concepts covered by this lesson all contribute to the meaning you derive from a story, meaning usually expressed by the term theme. Determining the possible themes in a story is a bit trickier than figuring out character and plot, but it is like what you are getting at when people and circumstances have complicated your life. At times like that, you may want to shrug your shoulders and ask, "But what does it all mean?" If you had an answer to that question, you would have the theme of that series of events.

Although character, plot, theme, and style will be the focus of later lessons, this lesson introduces you to these terms so that you can begin to use the language of criticism to write or talk about literature. You will see these terms used again when you study poetry and drama, but you need to know them in this lesson to understand how they are all interrelated and how they apply to the short story. Because this is an introductory lesson, you will also learn about the origins of the short story and how it developed into its current form in today's books and magazines.

As in your other lessons, this study guide forms the framework for integrating the three major components used in this lesson—the text, the video, and the activities in this study guide. Specifically, your text will examine the history of the short story, define the central terms associated with it, and present the short stories to be read. In the video, you will see the development of these terms through the dramatization of one of the assigned short stories.

GOAL

This lesson will help you to recognize the short story as a distinct form of literature.

WHAT YOU WILL LEARN

When you complete this lesson, you will be able to:

1. Describe the origins of the short story as a form of literature.
2. Define what is meant by a short story.
3. Explain the major elements of the short story.
4. Give examples of these elements within a specific short story's structure.
5. Discuss how these elements are integrated within the short story.
6. Illustrate types of reader responses to a short story.
7. State why the short story may be chosen as the appropriate form for expressing an author's thoughts and feelings.
8. Give examples of short stories found in other media.

LESSON ASSIGNMENT

Completing the following nine steps will help you master the objectives and achieve the goal for this lesson:

Step 1: In your text, read "Fiction: An Overview," pages 56–70. This section will expand your knowledge about the important parts of fiction, illustrate some of the terms, and present additional background about the short story.

Step 2: Read the specific short stories that your instructor assigns. Those that follow will be the focus of this lesson, and the ones marked with an asterisk (*) will be discussed in the video.

- "First Confession," Frank O'Connor, pages 354–359
- "A & P," John Updike, pages 363–367

Step 3: Read the OVERVIEW in this study guide lesson.

Step 4: Watch the VIDEO, following the steps in the VIEWING GUIDE in this study guide lesson.

Step 5: Reread the OVERVIEW to reinforce what you have learned in the text and the video and to help you complete the Writing Activities.

Step 6: Complete any WRITING ACTIVITIES assigned in this lesson.

Step 7: Do the SELF-TEST exercises in this study guide lesson.

Step 8: Read any of the ADDITIONAL READING ACTIVITIES assigned.

Step 9: Go back to the learning objectives in the WHAT YOU WILL LEARN section of this study guide lesson and be sure you can respond to all of them.

KEY TERMS FOR STUDYING THE GENRE OF THE SHORT STORY

Listed here are the terms that will be discussed throughout the next seven lessons. You will read about some of them several times and will need to familiarize yourself with them. You may want to keep this list available so that you can make notes about the terms as you encounter them in your studying. Definitions are also provided in the text's "Glossary" (page 1955). Remember, however, that memorizing verbatim definitions is not critical when studying literature. Far more important is knowing how to apply the terms.

Action
Allegory
Antagonist
Character
  flat
  round
  stereotype
  stock
Conflict
Connotation
Denotation
Diction
Dramatic monologue
Figurative language (Figures of speech)
Flashback
Irony
  dramatic
  situational
  verbal
Myth
Overstatement
Persona
Plot
Point of View
  authorial
  dramatic or objective
  limited omniscient

Protagonist
Rhetorical devices
Sentence
  compound
  complex
  compound-complex
  simple
  loose
  parallel
  periodic
Setting
Structure
  exposition
  complication or rising action
  climax
  crisis
  resolution, denouement, or falling action
Style
Symbol
  cultural
  private
  universal
Theme
Tone
Understatement
Verisimilitude

OVERVIEW

To help you understand what a short story is, this overview briefly describes the short story's history and explains the specialized meanings of the terms used by readers and critics to discuss the short story. Starting with the short story's origins as a spoken tale, we will sketch its development up to its present day form that you see in books and magazines. What you will read here is very brief indeed—rather like what you might get if you put 3,000 years into a compactor and pushed the button. However, it should be sufficient to introduce you to this important literary genre.

History of the Short Story

In Western culture, the history of the short story is rooted—as is all fiction—in the oral tradition. In preliterate cultures, stories were told around the campfire as a way of passing on the people's history and culture. Stories told in ancient Greece celebrated the feats and lives of mythical gods and ancient heroes that reinforce Greek religion and philosophy. The more famous of these were developed into epics like *The Iliad* and *The Odyssey*. Such tales tell us about people from another time—their lives, culture, and heroes. Shorter tales used animals or everyday events to illustrate a moral or lesson. "Sour grapes" comes to us from the sixth century B.C. Greek writer Aesop; that fable is included in the textbook (page 380). The idea of the "prodigal son" is memorably related in a parable told by Jesus in the New Testament (page 399 in the text).

Today, we can see traces of the fable in cartoons and comics. Take Wile E. Coyote, a villain with a one-track appetite destined to go hungry despite his complex schemes to trap the crafty Roadrunner. Or think of Pogo, who heads a cast of forest and swamp animals whose daily exchanges parody human politics. And then there's cartoonist Gary Larson who pushes his characters into the realm of the absurd in "The Far Side." In ancient times, fables used animals to teach morality; today's comics use them to spoof modern behavior.

The parable is more difficult to spot in contemporary media, but sermons and political speeches frequently use them, and newspaper and news program "human interest stories" are often, in effect, parables—brief narratives that illustrate a moral or illuminate an admirable characteristic. The family dog that barks long and loud enough to wake the family so that all can escape the burning house, the three-year-old girl who dials 911 and saves her five-year-old brother from choking, the homeless transient who drops spare change in a blind man's cup—all these are the bases of narratives that can be seen as modern parables. As for myth, we need only to look at cartoon heroes such as Superman to recognize our version of the ancient hero who embodies what the culture values.

When we hear or read fables, parables, or myths, we get to know only a little about the main character. Whether it's a fox or a prodigal son, the character's primary purpose is to support the moral of the story. He or she reminds us, "Like the fox, I shouldn't just dismiss something I cannot have" or "Like the father, I should always forgive the person who makes a big mistake and then regrets it." But this focus of a tale or parable illustrating a moral changed as the Western world evolved. Today, modern stories reveal more about how people act and how the main character changes or doesn't change. If the tale of the fox and the sour grapes were retold today, we would probably gain insight into the narrow spirit of its furry main character rather than learn a lesson about wanting something we cannot have.

Stories such as "The Legend of Sleepy Hollow" are typical of the American short story in the nineteenth century. Its author, Washington Irving, used the short story form extensively. But it wasn't until Edgar Allen Poe established a critical theory for the form that it emerged as a separate genre, distinct from the novel in more than length. It was Poe who emphasized the idea that a short story should give a single impression and should be of a length that allowed the reader to read it within an hour. From Poe's early definition, it's only a small step to a definition of the short story as we know it today—a brief narrative that focuses on a single incident or character and treats it so concisely that the reader is left with a dominant impression.

This brief narrative is the form you will find in popular magazines such as *Sports Illustrated*, *The New Yorker*, and *Harper's*, as well as the Sunday supplement of many newspapers, various literary journals, and anthologies. Short stories also turn up frequently in television adaptations and programs such as "The American Short Story."

We have come a long way from the cave drawing that "tells" the story of a successful hunt to today's visualization of a situation comedy on television. But while the media and the purposes may differ, both have many elements in common with the short story. Yet the short story is very different. The genre of the short story that you are now learning about exists in print as a literary form and aims to do more than record or entertain.

The Vocabulary of the Short Story

Like any academic discipline, the study of literature has a history and a specialized vocabulary. You'll be glad to know, however, that the vocabulary associated with the short story and other literary genres is far closer to your own than the specialized terms of such fields as biology or economics. Even so, the terms used to analyze literature are specialized.

Fiction refers to the literature of the imagination. Specifically, it is the text that a writer creates not out of fact but out of fancy. Prose fiction depends upon narration, the "telling" of a story. The story is told by a person the author creates; we call that person the narrator and what is told is a *narrative*.

If the narrator also plays a part in the story, the author assumes a *persona* or mask to depict that character. This character may or may not resemble the author. For example, "First Confession," the story discussed in this lesson and that you will see in the video, was written by Frank O'Connor, an Irish writer who grew up in the kind of Catholic environment we see portrayed in the video. But O'Connor creates a character—the young boy Jackie—who "tells" the story by way of Jackie the adult. Having grown up in a Catholic family and attended catechism classes, Jackie faces his first confession and communion. But Jackie doesn't get along with his grandmother or his sister, and he knows his feelings are "sinful." It is Jackie, the narrator, who tells us how he felt: "I was scared to death of confession." O'Connor the author assumes a persona that is Jackie the narrator.

Besides this role of narrator, O'Connor also assumes the persona of Jackie to explore the nature of family relationships and the difference between an imagined sin and a real one. Because we see all the events in the story through Jackie's eyes, we understand it from his point of view. We will be using *point of view* as a technical term that describes the perspective from which the author presents the story to the reader.

To determine the point of view in a short story, ask first who the narrator is and what pronoun the author attaches to the narrator. Also ask yourself what role, if any, the narrator plays. For example, in "First Confession," Jackie plays two roles. He is the narrator and the main character. In telling the story in Jackie's voice, O'Connor uses the first person singular "I." Putting the answers to these questions all together, we can see that this story is told from the first person point of view.

Identifying Jackie as the narrator also tells us something else—we only know what is going on in his mind; we do not see directly into the minds of the other characters. Our direct knowledge, therefore, is limited to Jackie's point of view, though we know what he thinks others think and feel. We know everything about Jackie, a position that we call *omniscient*, but we are limited to Jackie's perspective. If you were giving a full description of the point of view in "First Confession," you would identify it as *first person limited omniscient*.

Although Jackie is the narrator and also the most important person in the story, you will see that in other stories the main character is not always the narrator. For instance, "First Confession" could have been told from the point of view of an "off-stage" narrator who plays no part in the events but tells us Jackie's story. This narrator might tell us what Jackie is thinking but would refer to Jackie as "he." Again we would know all about Jackie but be limited to his perspective. In this example, where the narrator is not a character in the story, the point of view would be *third person limited omniscient*.

We use three terms to indicate how much the narrator reveals about what goes on in the minds of the characters: *limited omniscient* (illustrated above), *omniscient*, and *dramatic/objective*. Limited omniscient, you now know, is what we call the perspective that reveals all about one character but limits us to what is going on in that character's mind. Limited omniscient is the point of view most frequently used in fiction.

In another example, imagine the narrator tells us everyone's thoughts; the point of view then would be omniscient. If "First Confession," for instance, were told from an omniscient point of view, we would know how Jackie's grandmother feels about Jackie and understand whether her actions are motivated by habit or ignorance or selfishness. We would also know whether Nora is merely self-righteous and jealous or working out an adolescent insecurity. Perhaps it is her own unhappiness with herself that she takes out on Jackie. But because O'Connor chooses Jackie to relate the story, we will never know.

But let's change the point of view again. If we had a narrator who told us *nothing* about the feelings and thoughts of any of the characters, the point of view would be termed objective or dramatic. In such a case, we would be distanced from the action. This point of view is used least frequently.

Determining whether a point of view is limited omniscient, objective/dramatic, or omniscient is always a function of how much we know about what is going on in the characters' minds; it is not necessarily related to the pronouns used in the story, i.e., to whether the story is written in first or third person. What makes the difference is how much you know *directly* about the inner workings of the characters in the story; how much we know directly determines point of view.

To use "First Confession" again, because the story is narrated by Jackie we may know what he *thinks* his sister feels, but her feelings are filtered through Jackie, who may or may not read them accurately. We are limited to his perspective; thus the point of view is limited omniscient. You will be using these terms later in the course, but they are good to know now so that you can better understand the concept of point of view and its relation to character.

The main character in a story is also sometimes called the *protagonist*. And, as you might guess, if the main character runs afoul of another person who opposes or in other ways obstructs the protagonist, that person is the *antagonist*.

Events often pit two characters against each other, and we refer to those events as actions or incidents. When the idea of motive is added to the order of the actions or incidents, the result is a *plot*. The way in which the author relates these events of the plot is what we call the story's *structure*.

To distinguish among these terms, think of the old joke about what makes a news story: "dog bites man" is an action; "man bites dog" is a news story; and "man bites dog because dog bites man" is a plot. If you were to write a story relating first the incident of the dog bite and then the man's biting the dog, the structure and plot of your story would be identical because the actions occurred in chronological order. If, however, you had interspersed stories about the dog's devotion to its owner, the man's dreams about dogs, and so on, and pieced actions together in an order that was not chronological, then the structure and plot would be different.

"First Confession," the story you will see dramatized and discussed in the video, can be seen as a study in conflict. There is conflict between Jackie and Nora, conflict between Jackie and the idea of loving one's relatives, and conflict within Jackie involving what he knows is evil compared to what he is told is so.

The nature of the conflict is often the easiest way to explore the meaning of a short story, called the *theme* or *themes*. If, for instance, Jackie's inner conflict is important to understanding the story, you can easily see evil or sin as the story's subject. To arrive at one of the possible themes for the story, ask yourself what O'Connor, the author—not Jackie, the character—is saying about evil and then put that idea in the form of a sentence that is also an assertion, an idea expressing the author's meaning. The result will be the story's theme. There are often many subjects in a story, each of which may lead to a different theme.

For example, in "First Confession," if the subjects are family strife, women, and Catholicism, then several possible themes emerge: O'Connor may be implying that conflict between generations cannot be avoided; or that Jackie's experiences with his family are enough to turn him against women for life; or that Catholicism plays an overly large and oppressive role for people growing up in Ireland. Any one of these ideas can be seen as the story's theme; however, they would have to be modified slightly to account for the story's humor.

Often authors will rely on setting, atmosphere, and symbol—in addition to conflict—to reinforce the theme or themes of the story. Setting is the physical time and place in which the action occurs while atmosphere is the emotional quality that arises from the setting. In "First Confession," the setting for Jackie's confession is what one would expect—a confessional in a church. The atmosphere is appropriately austere, quiet, and sanctified, making Jackie's contortions in the confessional all the more amusing. Also true to the humor in the story are the sweets the priest gives Jackie. We would expect communion to follow confession; and in a way it does, for Jackie and the priest have had a communion of sorts. The bullseye candies become a *symbol* representing a light-hearted version of the communion wafer. Thus, a symbol is an object that stands for or represents something in addition to its original or obvious meaning. In later lessons, we will examine specific kinds of symbols.

To understand how setting, atmosphere, and symbol work together in a short story, think about how they are used in "A & P." Start with the easiest to identify—setting. Updike—through the character of Sammy—gives you enough details so that you can see both the supermarket and the town. As supermarkets go, this one is small and its patrons tend to be shabby—the elderly and "houseslaves in pin curlers." The town lies north of Boston, and its economic base is low- to middle-income. Sammy describes the view from the front of the A & P:

> If you stand at our front doors you can see two banks and the Congregational church and the newspaper store and three real estate offices and about twenty-seven old freeloaders tearing up Central Street because the sewer broke again (365).

The beach which attracts the more affluent summer people and tourists is five miles away. Yet, Sammy tells us, "there's people in this town haven't seen the ocean for twenty years" (365).

Now consider the atmosphere this setting creates. The words Sammy uses to describe the A & P's patrons are "witch," "sheep," "houseslaves," "old party," "scared pigs in a chute." Life in this A & P, this town, seems limited, somewhat shabby, a bit depressing. To check the accuracy of your impression, see if an object or one of the characters typifies it. The three girls, for instance, are not part of the A & P scene, so that leaves us with Lengel and Stokesie. Let's look at Stokesie. Stokesie seems fairly typical of the inhabitants of the town and—by inference—of Sammy's generation. He is 22, married with two kids, and his ambition is to become store manager. In a sense, then, Stokesie is a symbol of the kind of life

Sammy has to look forward to if he stays at his job—a life of early responsibility and limited opportunity. And so, yes, the depressing atmosphere of the A & P and its surroundings is reinforced by Updike's portrayal of Stokesie.

What gives form to terms such as plot, character, conflict, and theme is *style*—the way the author gives shape and impact to the story. Style covers a variety of techniques. In "First Confession," we learn about Jackie from what he says and what others say to him—information that comes to us in dialogue. We also learn about him by what he tells us, by his description. If the story had been related by O'Connor as narrator instead of by Jackie, we would probably also learn from commentary, which is what O'Connor might say about the events in the story. But even though the story is told by Jackie, we can still discover O'Connor's *tone*—his attitude toward Jackie and the events that occur to him. O'Connor blends both humor and *irony* into his tone to convey an appreciative and amusing look at a boy's first encounter with sin and confession. The irony arises from the gap between what the reader and author know to be sin and what Jackie thinks it to be.

Thus, you can see how style gets at *how* a story is written, at the writer's technique. When we notice details that make Jackie's speech typically Irish, Sammy's typically northeastern, we are noticing differences in style. When we find ourselves shuddering with Jackie and gawking with Sammy, we are feeling the effects of style.

Short stories give us brief narratives that focus on a single character or incident and leave us with a single dominant impression. All of this is to say the obvious—they are short stories as Poe defined them. It is hard to imagine "First Confession" expanding into a novel or "A & P" as a poem. The first genre is too large and the other too concise. The form of the short story, however, fits perfectly.

Summary

To use an analogy, almost everyone knows how to drive a car just as almost everyone may enjoy reading a story, poem, or play. But relatively few people know a car from the inside out, including the names and functions of the various parts of the motor. Knowing the names and functions of the elements of literature gives you the advantage over a text that an automotive engineer has over a motor. Within the text, you can identify each element, see how each works, and appreciate how these elements interrelate to create meaning. And you can see how it's possible to get a variety of equally acceptable meanings from the text, for, as the critics in the video demonstrate, there is no "one correct way" to interpret a work.

The more you learn about literature, the more you learn about how to become an expert reader so that you can understand a text from the inside out. Almost anyone can enjoy driving a good car, but an engineer has a deeper understanding of that pleasure.

54—*Literary Visions*

VIEWING GUIDE

An important component of this lesson is the video. Your learning from the video will be more effective by following these directions.

Before Viewing:

1. Review "Fiction: An Overview" in the text, pages 56–70, paying particular attention to the following terms:

Character	Plot
Conflict	Setting
Fable	Theme

2. Review Frank O'Connor's "First Confession," pages 354–359, so that you can follow the dramatization more analytically. Think through what kind of person Jackie is, listing his character traits along with the action or quotation you base your opinions upon.

During Your Viewing:

1. Look for specific examples of the origins of storytelling.
2. Try to identify examples of conflict within the dramatization of "First Confession."
3. Summarize what each of the critics says about "First Confession."

After Viewing:

Give some thought to the following questions. You may want to write short answers in your journal or notebook.

1. How did the way Jackie was portrayed in the video production of "First Confession" agree with your idea of Jackie as you read the story?
2. How would you describe the family conflict?
3. How would you describe the conflict within Jackie?
4. What are three examples of stories told in ways other than print?
5. To what extent do you agree with the critics' views?

WRITING ACTIVITIES

Activity 1 asks you to make connections between your own world and the world presented in "A & P," which calls for a higher order of thinking. You need to compare and contrast in order to interpret why Sammy quit. The second assign-

ment is the more difficult of the two because it asks you to analyze your res
as a reader, which calls for an objective view of yourself from several perspectives—what you expected to see in the dramatization based upon your prior reading of the story, what you saw, and what you think of what the critics say about
the story.

Formal Writing:

1. Think of the experience of someone you know or your own experience with a job similar to Sammy's in "A & P." What were the customers like? How did the job affect you? What sort of future did it hold? Using your own experience, write an essay that analyzes why Sammy said, "I quit."
2. Write an essay in which you trace how your understanding and interpretation of "First Confession" developed—from the time you first read the story through your reading of the study guide, watching of the dramatization, and listening to the critics.

Informal Writing:

Your journal is a place to write down your responses to what you read and see. Some of those responses may underscore what was not clear to you, those places in the text or video where you wondered, "What does this mean?" or "I don't understand that." Other responses might note points in the story that you connect with: "I know how that feels" or "That reminds me of when . . ."

For this informal activity, you are asked to expand one of those journal entries. Think of "First Confession" and write a page or two in your journal recounting a "first" experience such as when you realized a parent or child was a person in his or her own right or when you realized that a much feared event was not so dreadful after all.

SELF-TEST

Match the items in column A with the definitions or identifications in B:

A	B
1. Theme	a. Protagonist in "A & P"
2. Edgar Allan Poe	b. Author's mask
3. Limited omniscient	c. Greek author of fables
4. Conflict	d. Events related by motive
5. Sammy	e. Articulated a theory of the short story
6. Plot	f. Opposing of characters or ideas
7. Persona	g. Series of events
8. Aesop	h. Kind of setting
9. Symbol	i. Herring snacks
10. Action	j. Author's assertion about subject
	k. Antagonist in "A & P"
	l. Point of view

Answer the following multiple-choice items:

1. Who among the following fits the role of antagonist in "A & P"?
    a. Stokesie
    b. Lengel
    c. The A & P's patrons
    d. The three girls

2. In "First Confession," which term best describes what Jackie feels at the end of the story?
    a. Resentment
    b. Relief
    c. Resignation
    d. Anger

3. The most important factor that the two stories in this lesson have in common is that the
    a. stories were written by men.
    b. point of view is first person limited omniscient.
    c. central character is a young boy.
    d. subject is initiation into adulthood.

4. Unlike the moral in a fable, the theme in a modern short story is
   a. unknown.
   b. stated by the author.
   c. created by both the author and the reader.
   d. created by the reader alone.

In 100 words or more, answer the following short essay questions:

1. What details make you think the three girls in "A & P" come from a different kind of background than the store's patrons? Write a paragraph explaining your conclusions.
2. Think about Jackie at the beginning of "First Confession" and at the end. What has he learned? What events brought about these changes? Write a paragraph in which you explain how he has changed and why.

ADDITIONAL READING ACTIVITIES

If you enjoyed reading the stories in this lesson, you may want to read the following selections by the same authors.

O'Connor, Frank. *Collected Stories.*
Updike, John. *Pigeon Feathers and Other Stories.*
_____. *Problems and Other Stories.*
_____. *Museums and Women and Other Stories.*
_____. *Trust Me.* (Short stories)

LESSON 5

The Story's Blueprint:
PLOT AND STRUCTURE IN SHORT FICTION

ABOUT THE LESSON

The lesson you just finished defined the basic elements of fiction in much the way a photograph might show you a sweeping view of a landscape. Looking at such a photograph, you would readily spot the main features of the scene—for example, two tall mountains overlooking a lake that's ringed with forest on the far side and a meadow in the foreground. This lesson zooms in on two of those features, plot—with its two components, action and conflict—and structure.

Just as it's important to keep in mind that a zoom shot is only part of a larger picture, it's important to remember that plot and structure are only two elements among many that fiction writers use to create short stories and readers use to interpret them. It's also important to know that plot and structure may be more crucial to one story than another. In some stories, characterization stands out; in others, it may be style. But in the stories you will read for this lesson, plot and structure are prominent.

You will also find that plot and structure—like all the other elements of short fiction—relate directly to your understanding of a story's themes. Knowing a story's plot and structure means that you can recall its action and see its conflicts at work. Thus, knowing plot and structure will help you understand the order of the action and grasp what the story means, what it adds up to.

What a story adds up to isn't a simple, clear-cut answer such as you get with an arithmetic problem. A good story has many themes, many meanings. Plot and structure provide us with clues to those meanings.

GOAL

This lesson will help you understand how plot arises from action, brings out conflict, and relates to structure in the short story.

WHAT YOU WILL LEARN

When you complete this lesson, you will be able to:

1. Discriminate among action, plot, and conflict in the short story.
2. Differentiate among levels of conflict within the short story.
3. Define exposition, complication, crisis, climax, and resolution.
4. List some of the ways plots are presented.

LESSON ASSIGNMENT

Completing the following nine steps will help you master the objectives and achieve the goal for this lesson:

Step 1: In your text, read "Structure," pages 275–278. The text will provide background for what you will read in this study guide, explain the key terms, and give you some information about the stories you will be reading.

Step 2: Read the specific short stories assigned by your instructor. Those that follow will be the focus of this lesson, and the Stephen Crane story—marked with an asterisk (*)—will be discussed in the video.

- "A Worn Path," Eudora Welty, pages 114–119.
- "Blue Winds Dancing," Tom Whitecloud, pages 313–317.
- "The Curse," Andre Dubus, pages 563–566.

Step 3: Read the OVERVIEW in this study guide lesson.

Step 4: Watch the VIDEO, following the steps in the VIEWING GUIDE in this study guide lesson.

Step 5: Reread the OVERVIEW to reinforce what you have learned in the text and the video and to help you complete the Writing Activities.

Step 6: Complete any WRITING ACTIVITIES assigned in this lesson.

Step 7: Do the SELF-TEST exercises in this study guide lesson.

Step 8: Read any of the ADDITIONAL READING ACTIVITIES assigned.

Step 9: Go back to the learning objectives in the WHAT YOU WILL LEARN section of this study guide lesson and be sure you can respond to all of them.

OVERVIEW

Consider how a day's events flow, how one thing follows another. It's a bit like the alphabet; one letter follows another in a fixed sequence. If, for instance, the "h" key on your typewriter were broken, you could still type a letter a person could read. The letter might look a bit odd, but anyone who read it could understand what it said. Drop out an event in your day and the rest of the events still make sense.

But the events in a short story are different because they add up to something; the events in our lives don't have to. Think of a child's tower of blocks; remove one and the whole structure falls apart. So too the events or actions in a short story are its building blocks. The author shapes the actions with a plot that involves conflict and presents them in a particular order that is the story's structure. Drop one of the actions and the rest make little sense.

So that you may more clearly understand plot and structure and see how they work in a short story, we have divided this overview section into four parts: this Introduction, and three others—Plot, Structure, and Summary. The parts that focus on the plot and structure first define them by using examples from everyday life and the stories you will read and then examine their components. In fact, what we have just described is the structure of this Overview.

Plot

One way to grasp the idea of *plot* is to distinguish between how things occur in everyday life and in the pages of a short story. Ask a small child "What have you been doing this afternoon?" and the answer you get will probably be a series of events strung together by "and": "I played with my toys and I had a cookie and I hit my brother and I helped my daddy and I walked down the street." Each of those events is an action. Each may or may not be related to another, and you can't really tell which is most or least important. And if any of us were to recount what we did on a given day, the result would be basically the same. Sure, the vocabulary, sentence structure, and the incidents themselves would be different, but we'd still be left with events that might or might not be related and might or might not be important. Many a diary entry has started with "I got up" and ended with "I went to bed." What happened in between may simply be a list.

Unlike the events in life, the events in fiction are carefully planned, selected, and arranged by the writer. A writer looking for short-story material might look over a list of incidents that happened during the day but would select only a few to reshape into fiction. In much the same way, a sculptor carves away unneeded stone to reveal the statue. But whether the writer creates fictional events out of the imagination or reality, the result is not one incident but a series of events that when put together have a beginning, middle, and end.

When we refer to this series of events in a short story, we use the term *action*. The action of a short story is therefore made up of the actions or incidents that occur in it.

In short stories that emphasize action, you will find several events that occur one after the other. In "A Worn Path," pages 114–119, you can summarize the action easily. The story begins as an old woman sets off on foot from the country for town. On her way, she gets knocked down by a dog and then pulled upright by a hunter. Once in town, she goes to a clinic, picks up medicine for her grandson, and decides to buy him a paper windmill. She then leaves the clinic to buy the present and walk home.

What's missing from this simple account above is any discussion of the causes of these actions and of the relationships among them. Once you identify these causes and relationships, you're on your way to knowing the story's *plot*—the reasons behind the sequence of events.

Phoenix, the old woman, walks to town because her feet are her only means of transportation; she falls because she is old, frail, and almost blind. We wonder why she is going to town and suspect that her mind is slipping.

After she falls, the hunter pulls her back up, but he doesn't treat her with respect. Why? The author doesn't tell us, but she gives us a lot of clues. The hunter is white and a man; Phoenix is African-American and a woman. He is strong; she is weak. He is hunting for pleasure; she is trying to stay alive.

Once in town, Phoenix again is not treated with respect, and again the reasons are only implied. We do know, however, that the attendant at the clinic mistakes Phoenix's tiredness and day-dreaming. " 'Are you deaf?' cried the attendant" (118).

At the end of the story, we discover the reason for Phoenix's trip. She walks to town to get medicine for her grandson, whose throat is permanently damaged from drinking lye. We also gather that Phoenix is her grandson's only connection with other people, and we know that she is very old, old enough to remember the "Surrender" at the end of the Civil War. Her age has brought with it diminished strength and concentration.

Once you find the causal links between the story's events, you begin to see its plot—the shape the writer has given the action. You also begin to get at the story's *subject* and *theme*. Phoenix's fight against age, poverty, and racism make her trip to the town heroic. Her love for and sense of responsibility to her grandson cause her to undertake the trip, during which she meets opposition and interaction. As the Glossary in your textbook states, "causation, response, opposition, and interaction . . . make a *plot* out of a simple series of *actions*."

The "opposition" mentioned in the Glossary is another word for *conflict*—the second element of plot. In "A Worn Path," for instance, to understand how conflict works, you would ask yourself what Phoenix has to contend with. The list you come up with might include age, physical condition, race, and economic state. Then you would examine each of those items more closely.

Taking Phoenix's trip to town as an example, you might consider why it is so difficult. Objectively, the distance is far (which is what the hunter says), but more than that, Phoenix's failing eyesight and general old age make the trip particularly hard. She is in conflict with both the natural environment and her physical state.

Now you can start to see how the idea of conflict can be further defined as internal or external. The animals that may or may not be lurking in bushes, the thorns that tear at Phoenix's dress, the log across the creek are all part of the natural environment and are therefore external forces with which she must struggle. But she must struggle within herself as well, fighting her desire to rest and, later at the clinic, wrestling her mind back to her mission.

Whether internal or external, conflict exists on many levels—from the seemingly trivial to the profound with any number of stops in between. Phoenix's encounter with the thorn bush is minor compared to her battle with age and blindness. The difference between the internal and external conflicts suggests that the major conflict is internal and that the story's focus is on character as much as action and conflict.

Examining that major conflict brings us to the question of how much longer Phoenix can walk that "worn path." The story doesn't give us an answer, but in showing us how difficult this one trip was, we suspect the worst. Long before that occurs to us, however, we have felt doubt, tension, and interest.

The story's conflicts (for any good story has many more than one) have brought together forces that seem equally strong. For example, the distance from Phoenix's house to the town is far, the way is difficult, but her will is strong and her nature determined. As we read, we do not know if she will make it. We are in doubt about the outcome of this particular fight because the forces appear almost equal.

Eudora Welty makes us feel Phoenix's struggle. She engages us with this character in part because at first we do not understand what is going on. We want to know why Phoenix hits out at bushes, why she talks to herself. These actions reveal character and create a kind of tension that engages our interest. Then "What's happening?" gives way to "What will happen?"

Thus we can trace the causal relationships involved in reading a short story. Action leads to plot that confronts conflict. For the reader, the conflict creates doubt about whether the plot will succeed; doubt leads to tension and produces interest. Without plot and its crucial component conflict, we'd have no short story.

Structure

The word "outline" recalls images of English classes and essays and seemingly simple directions, "First think of a topic, next form a thesis, then write an outline, and finally write the paper." Many of us wrote a draft, found a thesis through writing, and then made an outline, but no matter how we came up with those Roman numerals and capital letters, what we produced was an outline of the paper's *structure*.

Such an outline might describe the essay's structure as:

I. Introduction

II. Body

III. Conclusion

Similarly, a short story has a beginning, middle, and end. In "A Worn Path," Eudora Welty begins with Phoenix's journey, describes her trek and reveals her mission, and ends with her leaving the medical office. But this short account oversimplifies the story's structure.

A fuller account of the structure can be given if we break it into five components: exposition, complication, crisis, climax, and resolution.

Exposition is a term you may know from writing classes, where many essays fall into the category of expository writing—writing characterized by explanation. In a short story, exposition does much the same thing by setting out information about the characters, setting, and the action. Exposition may occur throughout a story, but many stories put much of it at the beginning.

"Blue Winds Dancing," pages 313–317, also begins with exposition. In paragraphs 1–11, we are told the essential background to the story. We learn that the main character (and also narrator) is a Native American (called an "Indian" in the story) from Wisconsin who is attending college in California. He is disillusioned with the world of whites and so longs for his home that he decides to return there.

Exposition gives us the vital background for a story, but it is *complication* that gets the plot rolling. A story's exposition may make it clear that John intends to marry Susan: but if Susan loves Bill, then we get complication. The complication presents us with the story's various conflicts. A *crisis* is the point at which the complications have piled up and the action turns. The crisis forces a *climax*. In a *resolution* or *denouement* all the loose ends are taken care of.

As you can see, the different components of a story's structure can be defined fairly easily. Keep in mind, however, that these components vary. Sometimes the climax and the crisis occur at the same point; sometimes the exposition is very short, and the resolution a matter of a few sentences. What also makes their identification a bit more difficult is their order. Sometimes the structure of the story is *formal*, which means that the order of events is chronological and the elements we've just discussed appear one after the other. But not all stories are put together that way.

Your textbook points out that some writers withhold important bits of information that you would usually expect to find in the opening exposition. And frequently, in order to build tension and interest, a story is not presented in chronological order.

Sometimes the chronology is interrupted by a *flashback*. The plot of a story can be developed almost exclusively through flashbacks, dialogue, or narration, but many short stories use all these techniques as ways of presenting their plots.

Summary

Action and plot, with its crucial element, conflict, are terms you will use not only to analyze short stories but also plays. In addition, some poems are narratives, like Frost's "Stopping by Woods on a Snowy Evening," page 637. Such poems tell a story, and therefore can also be discussed with these terms. Whether poem, play, or short story, however, all share the concept of structure.

Later, when we turn to poetry, you will meet structure again as a term used to define a poem's form—its pattern of ideas and sound—as in the structure of a sonnet or the structure of a ballad. And when we analyze plays, you will become familiar with dramatic structure, where you will again find exposition, complication, crisis, climax, and resolution.

For the time being, however, you will find the terms plot and structure help you to interpret a story so that you understand its theme. Lesson 4 introduced you to the concept of theme and showed how to identify a subject in a story and then derive a theme from it. A story's plot and in particular its conflicts help you find both subject and theme. Think of "A Worn Path" without any of its conflicts, and all you have is a woman who walks to town to get medicine for her grandson. But with the conflicts, you have meaning. If, for instance, you see the major conflict in "A Worn Path" as one between Phoenix and old age, then that conflict can serve as the story's subject.

What theme might that subject reveal? Several would work, depending upon which elements you gave most attention to. Perhaps Eudora Welty is saying that old age should be faced with courage or that even the battle with it is admirable or that society does not accept proper responsibility for the poor and aged. As you recall, it is possible to have a number of valid themes for a story just as a story can have more than one subject.

Action, plot, conflict, structure are all ways in which a writer engages a reader in a story and shapes fictional experience into meaning. We admire Phoenix, and sympathize with the Indian. Because of what these characters undergo and their conflicts, we come to a better understanding of experiences we have never had. We realize the courage old age and poverty demand; we come to know how a person's culture can work for and against that individual. Literature invites us to share the worlds of others.

VIEWING GUIDE

An important component of this lesson is the video. You will learn more effectively from it by thinking about the following questions and guidelines.

Before Viewing:

1. Review "Structure" in the text, pages 275–278, paying particular attention to the following terms:

Action	Exposition
Climax	Flashback
Complication	Plot
Conflict	Resolution
Crisis	Structure

2. Review Andre Dubus's "The Curse" to increase your understanding of the interview on the video.

During Your Viewing:

1. Look for the kind of predictable conflict you find in various kinds of formula fiction.
2. Listen for mention of the different techniques a writer can use to provide a story's structure.
3. List the major points Andre Dubus makes in the interview.

After Viewing:

Give some thought to the following questions. You may want to write short answers in your journal or notebook.

1. Which is the major conflict?
2. What do the critics see as the major conflict? The story's theme?
3. Which components of structure do you find in the dramatization (not the story)?
4. In what ways does Andre Dubus's discussion of plot fit that of the critics?

WRITING ACTIVITIES

After your study of this lesson, you should be able to analyze a story's conflict. Your instructor will advise you which, if any, of the following writing activities you are to complete.

66—*Literary Visions*

Formal Writing:

The activities are presented in order of difficulty. The first one calls for an essay based upon a model in your text—not an exact model but one that will make your writing of the essay easier. The second activity calls upon your own experience to understand the relationship between conflict and character. Conflict and characterization are also the focus of the last two activities. The comments by DeMott, Poovey, and Ulmer will help you with Activity 3. The fourth activity takes in both action and inaction, and because of that, is more complex than the third activity.

1. Using the guide and example in the textbook, pages 121–125, write an analysis of conflict in "Blue Winds Dancing." Note that although the example stresses plot, the paper focuses on conflict.
2. In your own experience, think of a time when you had to choose between what might be called "home" and "not-home." Perhaps it was a matter of going against your parent's ideas or rethinking and opting for a religious belief. How did you feel? How did you come to the decision you did? Use your own experience to analyze the conflicting values the main character is faced with in "Blue Winds Dancing" and to explain his choice. Consider as well how that choice relates to a possible theme for the story.
3. Andre Dubus says that he is "fascinated by people who act and by people who can't or won't." Analyze "The Curse" in relation to this statement. How do plot and character interact?

Informal Writing:

Each of these stories probably relates to an experience you have had. "A Worn Path" may remind you of someone you know whose courage you admire, or whose love and sense of responsibility drive them to the brink of heroism; "Blue Winds Dancing" may recall a time when you had to make a difficult decision or came to realize how much your family meant to you. Think about some point of contact your experience has with one of the stories, and write a page to two in your journal about it.

SELF-TEST

Match the items in column A with the definitions or identification in B:

A	B
1. Paper windmill	a. Formulaic structure
2. Tom Whitecloud	b. Setting out of the background
3. Climax	c. Critic
4. Tobias Wolffe	d. Author
5. The Detective Story	e. Source of conflict
6. High-Five	f. Part of resolution
7. Lye	g. Part of delayed esposition
8. Denver Bob	h. Source of potential conflict
9. Flashback	i. Indian
10. Exposition	j. Non-chronological structure
	k. Winding up of the story

Answer the following multiple-choice items:

1. The video uses the plots of detective stories, westerns, and romances to illustrate that they
    a. are examples of popular culture.
    b. are examples of formulaic plots.
    c. share the element of suspense.
    d. are easy to read.

2. Which statement about structure is NOT true?
    a. Events are often presented in chronological order.
    b. Flashbacks may provide additional exposition.
    c. The climax may coincide with the crisis.
    d. The exposition contains no action.

3. Which statement about conflict is NOT true?
    a. Conflict bears no relation to theme.
    b. Conflict can be internal and external.
    c. Conflict is essential to plot.
    d. Conflict arises from action.

4. Select four events and put them in a sequence that is a plot:
   a. Joe sneaks out of the store.
   b. Joe goes into a department store.
   c. Joe makes a phone call.
   d. Joe sees one of his neighbors.
   e. Joe sees a diamond stickpin.
   f. Joe slips a diamond stickpin into his pocket.
   g. Joe looks for his American Express card.
   h. Joe drops his keys.

In 100–125 words, answer the following short essay questions:

1. What details lead you to suspect that Phoenix's mind is not what it used to be? Is she heading into senility? Write a paragraph explaining your conclusion.
2. Toward the end of "Blue Winds Dancing," the main character asks himself "Am I Indian, or am I white?" What are the values involved in that conflict?

ADDITIONAL READING ACTIVITIES

If you enjoyed reading the stories and listening to the interview in this lesson, you may want to read more from the following selections.

Crane, Stephen. *Maggie: A Girl of the Streets & Other Short Fiction.*
_____. *The Red Badge of Courage.* (Short novel)
Dubus, Andre. *Selected Stories.*
_____. *Finding a Girl in America.*
_____. *Land Where My Father Died.*
_____. *Last Worthless Evening: 4 Novellas and 2 Short Stories.*
_____. *Times Are Never So Bad.*
_____. *Voices from the Moon.*
_____. *We Don't Live Here Anymore.*
Turner, Frederick W. 3rd. *The Portable North American Indian Reader.* (Anthology)
Velie, Alan R. *American Indian Literature.* (Anthology)
Welty, Eudora. *The Collected Short Stories of Eudora Welty.*
_____. *One Writer's Beginnings.* (Autobiography)

LESSON 6

Telling Their Tales:
CHARACTER IN SHORT FICTION

ABOUT THE LESSON

You have seen how action drives a story's plot. We're now going to take a closer look at what drives the action—the people the author has created, the characters. What these people do or do not do, how they interact with others, what they say or do not say provide the story's action.

    That action is presented to us from a particular point of view the author has chosen. And there are a side variety of choices. The author may select a narrator who is the story's main character or one who plays only a minor part or no part at all in the action. In addition, the writer must decide on a grammatical focus. Should the story be told in the first person or in the third person? Should the narrator know what's going on in the minds of the other characters or be limited to the mind of one?

    In this lesson, you will see how different answers to these questions have different effects on the story and the reader. And you will also see how important point of view is to characterization. Point of view is a kind of lens. It affects how we see the characters and how we interpret the story.

GOAL

This lesson will help you recognize and evaluate the role of character and point of view and understand how they affect the reader.

WHAT YOU WILL LEARN

When you complete this lesson you will be able to:

  1. Define terms associated with characterization and point of view.

2. Give examples of these terms within the context of the short story.
3. Discuss how various authors reveal character.
4. Discuss how differing points of view affect a story.

LESSON ASSIGNMENT

Working through the following nine steps will help you complete the objectives and achieve the goal for this lesson.

Step 1: In your text, read "Characters: The People in Fiction," pages 173–180, and "Point of View," pages 127–136. The text will give you the background for what you will read in the study guide, explain the key terms, and give you some information about the stories you will be reading.

Step 2: Read the specific short stories your instructor assigns. The ones listed below will be the focus of this lesson; any marked with an asterisk (*) will be included in the video.

- "Barn Burning," William Faulkner, pages 333–343.*
- "The Lottery," Shirley Jackson, pages 140–146.
- "I Stand Here Ironing," Tillie Olsen, pages 586–590.*

Step 3: Read the OVERVIEW in this study guide lesson.

Step 4: Watch the VIDEO, following the steps in the VIEWING GUIDE in this study guide lesson.

Step 5: Reread the OVERVIEW to reinforce what you have learned in the text and video, and to help you complete the writing activities.

Step 6: Complete any WRITING ACTIVITIES assigned in this lesson.

Step 7: Do the SELF-TEST exercises in this study guide lesson.

Step 8: Read any of the ADDITIONAL READING ACTIVITIES assigned.

Step 9: Go back to the learning objectives in the WHAT YOU WILL LEARN section of this study guide lesson and be sure you can respond to all of them.

OVERVIEW

Character and *point of view* are such common terms that it's important to distinguish between their everyday use and their meanings in the context of literature. Here and throughout this study guide, character refers to a person portrayed in a short story, poem, or play.

Another way to look at this term is to see what it is not. A character, as the word is used here, is not your cousin Freddy, whose sense of humor can make a funeral funny. Character does not mean unusual or eccentric. If Aunt Susie insists on keeping her zebra-striped Volkswagen bug and wearing dresses made out of her mother's curtains, we might well exclaim, "What a character!" In fiction, however, we would reserve that statement for a person like Phoenix in Eudora Welty's "A Worn Path," not because she is odd or colorful but because we get to know and understand her, and her courage and selflessness impress us.

Point of view can also be a confusing term. If two candidates are running a hot political race for a seat in the state senate, you might receive a call from a polling group asking for your point of view. In that case, the term would be synonymous with opinion or stand. In literature, however, the term has a different meaning, one that means the position from which the story is related.

In the paragraphs that follow, we will examine the concepts of character and point of view in detail, first defining them and then illustrating the definitions through examples drawn from the stories you've read.

Character

In fiction, some characters have become so widely known that their names now are synonymous with one of their more outstanding traits. Around Christmas time, we are all reminded that Scrooge is a character in Charles Dickens' tale *A Christmas Carol*. The rest of the year, we simply think of a scrooge as a penny-squeezing miser.

If Scrooge only possessed that one trait, we would find his character one dimensional or *flat*. But since Dickens developed Scrooge rather fully, we find his character more complex or *rounded*. The distinction between rounded and flat is the first one to make about a character.

Most stories have a number of characters. In "Barn Burning," for instance, we have the whole Snopes family—father, mother, aunt, two sons, two daughters—the De Spains, and several people without names. Of that list, only Sarty, the youngest son, and Abner, the father, emerge as fully developed, rounded characters.

How do you know this? For one thing, they are complex. You sense the boy's conflict over having to choose between his father and what is right. You also sense Abner's rage, his twisted pride. Neither character is all good or all bad. As the story opens, we see that Sarty knows the difference between good and evil, yet as the plot unfolds, we realize his attachment to his father. Sarty knows that what Abner did to De Spain's rug was wrong, but when Abner is ordered to pay De Spain 10 bushels of corn in compensation, Sarty says, "He won't git one" (339).

When we first see Abner, he is harsh, rigid, proud, angry, and an arsonist. His meanness is general, applied equally to mule or child. Yet after the incident with the rug we see him in town telling stories at the blacksmith's shop, sharing his meal with his sons, commenting amiably at the horse lot.

Of the story's two rounded characters, Sarty is the one who undergoes a change. It is this change together with the full portrayal of his nature that makes him the story's protagonist or hero. Toward the end of the story, Sarty is again faced with a moral conflict. This time, however, he follows his conscience. He has grown over the span of time covered by the story and has developed from a child into a young adult who makes moral decisions and takes responsibility for them. Sarty is a good example of a protagonist; Faulkner depicts him fully as complex and dynamic.

Flat characters lack this kind of complexity and are static. Think of Sarty's sisters. Faulkner describes them, and we even hear a bit of what they say (paragraph 50), but they do not come to life on the page. We know little about them except that they are "bovine," and they are the same at the end of the story as they were at the beginning. The sisters remain shadowy, flat.

Sarty's mother is a slightly different kind of flat character. Instead of being shadowy, she is a stock character. She is cowed by her husband and lives in fear of him. And for good reason. Capable of protesting Abner's actions, she is incapable of either preventing them or saving herself. She fits the role of the abused wife, the victim. Both of those roles are instantly recognizable. It's as though they came off a shelf; they are stock characters. Stock characters are not only static but predictable. When they are consistently predictable, they become stereotypes.

The role of rounded characters is easy to understand. These are the characters that act or react, that come into conflict with internal or external forces (and often both). They develop, they change, and they carry the theme of the story. If, for instance, Faulkner's subject is morality, we can see how Sarty embodies that subject. We may understand Faulkner to be showing us how values must be earned, how self-respect must be fought for.

Flat characters and the ready-made personalities of stock characters and stereotypes also serve a purpose. Shadowy characters further the plot but don't get in the way of the action. The characterization of the sisters, for instance, shows us that Sarty has no one to turn to, to confide in. The characters of the sisters also suggest the kind of future that may await Sarty if he doesn't fight against it. As for stock characters and stereotypes, they are a kind of character shorthand.

Whether rounded or flat, we get to know a story's characters from various sources: from what the characters say or think; from what they do; from how others respond to them; from what others say about them; and from the narrator.

Our interpretation of Sarty, for example, is made easier by knowing what he thinks, how he feels, what he says. When the story opens, we are placed in Sarty's shoes. We smell what he smells, feel what he feels. We know, therefore, that he is hungry and scared. The narrator reveals what Sarty is thinking: "He aims for me to lie, he thought, again with that frantic grief and despair. And I will have to do it" (334).

But our concept of Sarty's character is also fleshed out by what he does. When he decides to warn Major De Spain, we know how heroic his action is, for we know that it means he has chosen good over evil, even if it means turning against his own father.

What he may suffer in consequence we also know because we know how Abner treats the boy. When Abner confronts Sarty over how Sarty behaved at the first hearing before the Justice of the Peace, Faulkner tells us, "His father struck him with the flat of his hand on the side of the head, hard but without heat, exactly as he had struck the two mules at the store, exactly as he would strike either of them with any stick in order to kill a horse fly, his voice still without heat or anger" (335).

To this last bit of information we can also add what Faulkner says about the adult Sarty: "Later, twenty years later, he was to tell himself, 'If I had said they wanted only truth, justice, he would have hit me again'" (336). The final picture of Sarty that emerges is what we, the readers, glean from all these sources.

Point of View

In Lesson 4, you were introduced to the concepts of *persona* and *point of view*, so you will remember that the writer selects a persona or mask through which to tell the story. "First Confession" gave us a slightly more complicated perspective. Frank O'Connor chose the persona of Jackie as an adult recalling and reliving an incident from childhood.

The persona assumed by the author is what your text calls a "narrative voice," the person who is telling the story from a particular point in space and time. In referring to this narrative voice, we use the term *point of view*. When you try to figure out the point of view, you need to ask yourself three questions about the narrator: What personal pronoun is used? What part does this person play? What do we learn about the character's thoughts? Let's take Olsen's "I Stand Here Ironing" and see what answers we come up with.

The first thing we notice is that the story is told in the first person, I. Next, we quickly realize that the narrator is the mother and the only person we hear from in the story. Although she is not the only character, we learn about Emily, her daughter, through the mother, who is ironing. We can conclude that the mother plays a key role in the story not just as narrator but as character. As readers, it's as though we are eavesdropping as the mother thinks about her daughter.

As the story opens, we find the mother responding to someone, perhaps a counselor or social worker, who has asked her to come in to talk about Emily, "who needs help." But what at first appears to be a dialogue soon turns out to be what is going on in the mother's mind as she imagines what she might say to the counselor. The only dialogue in the story consists of lines remembered by the mother.

Given Olsen's choice of first person, her use of the mother as narrator and main character, and her method of limiting us to the thoughts of that character, we can conclude that the story's point of view is *first person limited omniscient*. The point of view is omniscient because we know what that person thinks, but the point of view is limited because we are restricted to the thoughts of only that one character.

Now think of "Barn Burning." There, we also entered the mind of one character and one character only, so again the point of view was limited omniscient. That one character is also the story's protagonist, but we learn about him in the third person. Sarty is not the narrator. In fact, the narrator is not a character in the story but an observer of the action. In this case, the point of view is third person limited omniscient.

Unlike many authors, Faulkner here does not seem to assume a persona. If you were to ask yourself what kind of person the narrator is, you'd be stumped for an answer. You know the narrator comments on the story and even reveals events that occur at some time in a future beyond the story's limits. The narrative voice in this story is hard to distinguish from Faulkner's, so we would term it *authorial*.

Also consider the narrator in "The Lottery." Again, the narrator is not part of the action, but this narrator does not comment. You get no sense of anyone telling the story. It is merely reported. Because the narrator uses "he," "she," "they," the point of view is third person, but because you have no idea what any of the characters is thinking, we call this perspective *objective* or *dramatic*.

Identifying the point of view is only part of the picture; you also need to know how a writer's choice of point of view affects the story and therefore the reader. Imagine "Barn Burning" told from the first person limited omniscient point of view with Abner as narrator. We'd have a different story. Or think how we'd feel if "The Lottery" were told from the first person limited omniscient point of view with Davy Hutchinson as narrator.

The author's point of view determines what can and can not be included in the story and what effect is has on the reader. Given the point of view in "Barn Burning," it follows that we cannot know what happens back at Abner's house in the story's last two pages; Sarty is not there to see it.

There is also a psychological effect of point of view. We find that we identify, almost unconsciously, with "I." "He" or "she," however, tends to push us away a bit. The impact of the grammatical choice—what pronoun to use—is also influenced by the degree to which we are allowed to know the characters' thoughts. We identify with Sarty, for instance, because we know how he thinks and feels. The shock of "The Lottery" comes from the cold, distanced way we are told of an emotionally devastating experience. Not knowing if the people had any tweaks of conscience makes the story more powerful.

How an author depicts a character and what point of view is used raises questions of evidence and *verisimilitude*: can we believe what the mother in "I Stand Here Ironing" says about her daughter? How realistic is the character?

Everything we know about the mother indicates that she loves Emily. Circumstances, not lack of love, separated Emily from her mother. Poverty, illness, the tugs of other family members created Emily's difficulties. Granted, we know these things because Emily's mother tells us, but we also know that she is not talking to anyone but herself and therefore has no reason to conceal the truth.

And if the mother were polishing a three carat diamond engagement ring from her first marriage while thinking about her relationship with Emily, we would know that she had chosen the ring over Emily's welfare, which would be quite out of character.

Verisimilitude has far more to do with what is probable than what is possible. We must grant a story its initial premise, no matter how outlandish it may seem. But from that point on, what's important is for a story to be true to itself. Thus a story like "The Lottery," while removed from the reality we know, is nonetheless plausible because the characters' actions are in character. The behavior of the characters in "The Lottery" suggests that the story is a modern allegory based on the ancient ritual of the scapegoat.

Summary

Character figures to some extent in poetry, particularly in what's known as a *dramatic monologue*, a form that gives us as revealing an impression of personality as Olsen's mind reading. In drama the *soliloquy* functions in a similar way, giving us a direct look into the mind of the speaker. Beyond the soliloquy, the world of drama is a world of characters who speak for themselves and need no narrator.

When you read a short story, you will find that point of view and character combine with the theme to create a sense of unity. It's hard to think of Tillie Olsen's story without hearing the mother agonize over her daughter and without recognizing the trap she has been caught in. Through a first person limited omniscient point of view, Olsen has given us a character who symbolizes all women torn between circumstances and family obligations.

We form our interpretations of a character from what the narrator tells us, from dialogue, action, and interaction. Often we know what goes on in one or more of the characters' minds, but sometimes we are kept on the outside. No matter what the source, however, we put together a picture of the people in the story that rings true to the fictional world they live in. Often that picture is true to our world as well.

VIEWING GUIDE

An important component of this lesson is the video. You will learn more effectively from it by thinking about the following questions and guidelines.

Before Viewing:

1. Review "Characters," pages 173–180, and "Point of View," pages 127–136 in the text, paying particular attention to the following terms:

Character	Point of view
Flat characters	dramatic
Rounded characters	first person
Stereotypical characters	limited omniscient
Persona	Verisimilitude

2. Review Tillie Olsen's "I Stand Here Ironing," pages 586–590, so that you can follow the dramatization more analytically. Think about the character of the mother and of the daughter, drawing up a list of their traits.

During Your Viewing:

1. Look for the different ways authors—Fitzgerald ("The Great Gatsby"), Walker ("Everyday Use"), and Faulkner ("Barn Burning")—bring characters to life.
2. Look for the character traits brought out in the dramatization of "I Stand Here Ironing."
3. Summarize what each critic emphasizes about Olsen's story.
4. Listen for mention of how the story would differ if the point of view were changed.
5. List the major points about character and guilt that Tillie Olsen makes in the interview.

After Viewing:

Give some thought to the following questions. You may want to write short answers in your journal or notebook.

1. What kind of person is the mother? The daughter?
2. In what ways are the two characters rounded or flat?
3. What do the critics find notable about the characters? How do they tie character to theme?
4. How does the point of view in the dramatization (not the story) affect the viewer?
5. In what ways does Tillie Olsen's discussion of character differ from that of the critics?

WRITING ACTIVITIES

After your study of this lesson, you should be able to identify the point of view in a story, analyze its characters, and evaluate the effect of both point of view and character on the reader. Your instructor will advise you which, if any, of the following writing assignments you are to complete.

While all of the assignments focus on characterization or point of view, they vary considerably in level of difficulty. The first one is the easiest because your text provides you with a model you can use as a guide to content and organization. The second calls for a careful reading of "The Lottery," accumulating examples you can use to characterize the Hutchinson family; you are then asked to make connections between your conclusions about the family and your view of the story's theme. The relationship between theme (in the form of conflict) and character becomes even more central in Activity 3. There you are asked to explore the implications of a statement made by the mother in the Olsen story as a key to the story's meaning. Activity 4 asks you to step outside of yourself and analyze the expectations you formed as you read the Olsen story compared to the video dramatization of it.

Formal Writing:

1. Using the study guide and the example in the textbook, pages 127–136, write an analysis of the point of view in "I Stand Here Ironing."
2. Think about the Hutchinson family in "The Lottery" (pages 140–145). What members of the family are portrayed as rounded characters? Flat ones? What traits are associated with each family member? Considering the information you have gathered, how would you describe the family? How does that description relate to the story's theme?
3. At the end of "Barn Burning" (pages 333–343) Sarty is free from his father's influence and has learned some important life lessons. Rexamine pages 342–343 before you write an analysis of the boy's conflict and how he claims his freedom.
4. Reexamine the dramatization of "I Stand Here Ironing," noting all the methods the video uses to interpret character, such as gesture, facial expression, and the like. After you have noted what those methods are and some examples, write an essay in which you analyze how the expectations you had from reading the story matched or did not match what you saw in the video.

Informal Writing:

Write your own one-page character sketch. Unlike a short story, a character sketch does not have to have a plot or a theme. It is simply a revealing glimpse of a person. You might describe a friend or member of your family or someone you've never seen before who appeals to your curiosity. List first what the person looks like and wears, and note any gestures or speech patterns that seem typical. Then choose from your list the details you need for your sketch so that the person you are describing can be distinguished from any others. You want to describe what is "characteristic."

You will also need to select a point of view. Decide how you want to present your character, how much of the person's thought you want to reveal. You will probably choose among first person, third person limited omniscient, or objective.

SELF-TEST

Match the items in column A with the definitions or identifications in B:

A	B
1. Persona	a. Used in "The Lottery"
2. Emily	b. Character in "Barn Burning"
3. Authorial voice	c. Character assumed by the author
4. First person limited omniscient	d. Used in "I Stand Here Ironing"
5. Dramatic point of view	e. Author

A	B
6. Perspective	f. Narrator's point of view
7. Shirley Jackson	g. Old Man Warner
8. "My wisdom came too late."	h. Sarty
9. Stock character	i. Mr. Summers
10. Flat character	j. Source of commentary
	k. Character in "I Stand Here Ironing"
	l. The mother
	m. Abner

Answer the following multiple-choice items:

1. The video uses excerpts from several works to illustrate
   a. how characters are presented.
   b. how characters change.
   c. different points of view.
   d. common points of view.

2. Which of the following is NOT a stock character?
   a. The dashing bachelor.
   b. The evil landlord.
   c. The bratty brother.
   d. The incompetent doctor.

3. Which statement about point of view is NOT true?
   a. It reflects a grammatical choice.
   b. It indicates a physical position.
   c. It affects the reader.
   d. It represents an opinion.

4. Which of the following actions does NOT fit the character?
   a. Bill gives to the poor.
   b. Bill visits his long-time neighbor in a nursing home.
   c. Bill is amused when small children are afraid of him.
   d. Bill is a member of four different wildlife groups.
   e. Bill has taken in eight stray cats.

5. Which of the following violates the idea of verisimilitude?
   a. Science fiction.
   b. Ghost stories.
   c. An action contrary to probability.
   d. An action contrary to fact.

In 100–150 words, answer the following short essay questions.

1. For many of us, the life of a sharecropper is something we have only read about or seen in photographs, but in "Barn Burning" Faulkner makes us feel what it's like. What details in Sarty's life make share-cropping real to us?
2. "The Lottery" is an odd mixture of fantasy and realism in that the events are fantastic but are presented realistically. What about the story rings true?
3. Sometimes if the reader only knows about a character through the eyes of another, the portrait that emerges is flat. Explain how you would evaluate Emily's character in "I Stand Here Ironing." In what ways is it rounded or flat?

ADDITIONAL READING ACTIVITIES

If you enjoyed reading the stories and listening to the interview in this lesson, you may want to read more from the following selections.

Faulkner, William. *The Collected Stories.*
———. *The Portable Faulkner.* (Stories and excerpts from novels that focus on Faulkner's fictional county and its inhabitants, including the Snopes and De Spain families.)
———. *Selected Short Stories of William Faulkner.*
Jackson, Shirley. *The Lottery.* (Collected stories)
Olsen, Tillie. *Tell Me a Riddle.* (Short story)

LESSON 7

In That Time and Place:
SETTING AND CHARACTER IN SHORT FICTION

ABOUT THE LESSON

Lesson 6 explored the concept of character and its relationship to point of view. In this lesson, we will examine how character is related to setting, how setting gives rise to atmosphere, and how both character and setting reinforce theme and affect the way you respond to a story.

We will also examine how knowing about the background of the author and the social and historical context of the story can enhance your appreciation of it. This kind of information is not essential to your interpretation of a story but often adds another dimension to your enjoyment.

In creating character and setting, the writer relies upon details to show the reader what a place looks like or how a person thinks. Faulkner, for instance, does not tell us that the Snopes family in "Barn Burning," pages 333–343, is poor—he describes what they look like. His description of their belongings that are packed into the mule-drawn wagon lets us draw our own conclusions about the kind of life they lead.

So, too, the stories you will read in this lesson rely on details to give the reader a picture of the characters and their settings. These details create a mood or atmosphere that has an emotional effect on the reader. Excitement, suspense, horror, fear, uncertainty are only some of the emotions aroused by short stories. No matter what the emotion evoked by a story, it should support the story's theme and add to the reader's impression of the work's unity. And unity is a major characteristic of the genre.

GOAL

The goal of this lesson is to help you appreciate the integral relationship of setting and character.

82—*Literary Visions*

WHAT YOU WILL LEARN

When you complete this lesson you will be able to:

1. Define setting.
2. Define how a reader's response to a character is influenced by the setting.
3. Explain the importance and significance of setting to the creation of atmosphere and mood.
4. Discuss the effect of setting on the affective response to a story.
5. Discuss how a reader's response is affected by knowledge about the background and social and historical context of a short story and its author.

LESSON ASSIGNMENT

Completing the following nine steps will help you master the objectives and achieve the goal for this lesson:

Step 1: In your text, read "Setting: The Background of Place, Objects, and Culture in Stories" pages 224–228, and "Point of View and Verb Tense," pages 134–135. The text will provide background for what you will read in the study guide, explain the key terms, and give you some information about the stories you will be reading.

Step 2: Read the specific short stories that are assigned by your instructor. Those that follow will be the focus of this lesson, and the Susan Glaspell story—marked with an asterisk (*)—will be discussed in the video.

- "A Jury of Her Peers," Susan Glaspell, pages 189–202.*
- "The Masque of the Red Death," Edgar Allan Poe, pages 510–513.

Step 3: Read the OVERVIEW in this study guide lesson.

Step 4: Watch the VIDEO, following the steps in the VIEWING GUIDE in this study guide lesson.

Step 5: Reread the OVERVIEW to reinforce what you have learned in the text and the video and to help you complete the Writing Activities.

Step 6: Complete any WRITING ACTIVITIES assigned in this lesson.

Step 7: Do the SELF-TEST exercises in this study guide lesson.

Step 8: Read any of the ADDITIONAL READING ACTIVITIES assigned.

Step 9: Go back to the learning objectives in the WHAT YOU WILL LEARN section of this study guide lesson and be sure you can respond to all of them.

OVERVIEW

The word "castle" has any number of associations. Put "Windsor" in front of the word and you can easily imagine a sunny English day, green lawns, and perhaps a formal family gathering within, where Queen Elizabeth, the Queen Mother, Prince Philip, and all the sons and daughters-in-law are waited upon by a large staff of liveried servants.

But you can take that same word and put "evil" in front of it and you have a very different image. The night is dark, threatening; the castle is gloomy, mysterious. Within, perhaps a Count Dracula lurks, waited upon by a few grotesque albeit faithful helpers. The atmosphere of Windsor Castle is formal but warm, pleasant; the atmosphere in Transylvania is frightening, suspenseful.

Setting and atmosphere are the two terms we will examine in the paragraphs that follow. As before, we will define the terms and illustrate them with examples from the stories you have read so that you can see how the stories work, how they communicate. In this way, you can see what setting and atmosphere add to character and explore how they can help you arrive at a valid interpretation of the story's meaning or theme.

Setting and Character

Imagine that you are from California and are driving through New England in the fall. It is the height of the autumn colors. Coming over the rise of a hill, you look down to see a picture-perfect New England town square, one framed in the reds, yellows, and oranges of the turning leaves. Pulling to the side of the road for a better look, you think to yourself, "That's a beautiful setting." If you think about that statement, you'll realize your comment includes not only the whole physical scene and all the objects in it but the time of day and year as well.

Setting in the short story is just as inclusive. In Susan Glaspell's "A Jury of Her Peers," pages 189–202, as in most stories, the setting is physical and temporal—which is to say located in space and time. To begin your analysis of setting, you might first ask yourself, "When and where does the story take place?"

In Glaspell's story, details such as the newness of the telephone, the horse-drawn wagon, the relative isolation of the farms, and the clothes worn by the women suggest that the time of the action is not far removed from the time your text indicates is the story's publication date, 1917.

As for the time of year, again the details of the natural setting provide the answer and give you a clue about where the story takes place. Glaspell not only makes you feel just how cold it is but tells you that the Wright's place "looked very lonesome this cold March morning" (190). For the weather to be that cold in March, the story must take place somewhere in the northern United States.

To understand a story, you do not need to know any biographical details about the author, but biographical information does enhance your knowledge of a story's context. A few facts about Susan Glaspell, for instance, would help you narrow down both the story's publication date and the setting. A little research will reveal that the short story was developed from a one-act play that Glaspell called "Trifles," published in 1916. And knowing that Glaspell grew up in Iowa, founded—with her husband—the Provincetown Players in Provincetown, Rhode Island, and wrote novels set in the Midwest further helps narrow the scene of the action.

If you were to do some more research, you would discover that during the time Glaspell was a reporter for a Des Moines newspaper, she covered a murder trial that contains many of the elements of "A Jury of Her Peers." Without knowing that fact, you would not know the short story is set in Iowa. Knowing this information is interesting, but it is not essential to your understanding of the story. In fact, knowing the story is set in Iowa is not very important. What is important is your knowing that the story takes place in isolated farming country, and that fact is revealed by the story itself.

After figuring out when and where the story takes place, you need to go a step further and see what objects in the physical environment seem important. As you reread the story, you might find yourself drawing up a list that could include the worn and broken rocking chair, the broken stove, the erratically sewn quilt, the bird cage with its fractured hinge, and, of course, the dead bird.

At this point, you start looking for ties between the setting and the characters in it. The story is presented from the third person, limited omniscient point of view, so that we see the events from the perspective of Mrs. Hale, a near-by neighbor who knew Minnie Wright before she married John. Martha Hale tells us that she feels guilty over not having visited Minnie but that she "stayed away because it weren't cheerful" (198). That line suggests that the atmosphere of the Wright's house was depressing, uncomfortable.

Almost immediately you begin to see the equation Glaspell suggests by drawing out attention to similarities. On the one hand we have the biting cold, the isolation of the Wright farm, and the harshness of Mrs. Wright's life there—a life of worn, shabby clothes and broken stove linings. Mrs. Hale calls the Wright's farm a "lonesome place" and says it "always was." More important, she also tells us that John Wright "was a hard man . . . Like a raw wind that gets to the bone" (198). John Wright appears to have little use for comfort or companionship. He has no friends. His character, the atmosphere of the farm, and the weather have cruel similarities.

Yet you know from Mrs. Hale that in the past Mrs. Wright used to be very different from her husband. Before she married him, she was warm, colorful, full of life. It is Mrs. Hale who notes the resemblance between the Minnie Foster of 20 years ago and the song bird: ". . . she was kind of like a bird herself. Real sweet and pretty, but kind of timid and—fluttery. How—she—did—change" (198).

The setting and the characters complement each other. You sense that John Wright resembles the cold cutting winds of March and the stark bareness of the house; Minnie resembles the canary, the one spot of color and song in an otherwise bleak existence.

The bleakness of Minnie's life on the farm, her lack of friends, comforts, and any love or warmth from her husband suggest a causal relationship between the atmosphere that John Wright created and a motive for Minnie's crime. Living with him has squeezed the life out of her. Pushed too far, she strangles him. You can now see a final irony in the canary's manner of death. John had "wrung his neck," a literal strangulation that parallels his metaphoric strangulation of his wife.

In a way, setting, atmosphere, characters, conflict, and irony in Glaspell's story lead you into a question, "What is justice?" That's a very real question to Minnie's "jury of her peers"—Mrs. Hale and Mrs. Peters—for they have solved the crime by examining "the insignificance of kitchen things" that their husbands find foolish. Should they reveal the evidence they have discovered or not? They know that without evidence, the state will not have a case that will stick. The two women weigh the problem. On one scale is the life Minnie has been forced to lead together with her present state, and on the other is the character of John Wright and the act of murder. Not guilty is the verdict. Mrs. Wright's peers believe justice has been served.

Setting and Meaning

Often a writer will draw a direct line of meaning between a character, a physical object, and the story's meaning. In the story by Tillie Olsen that you read earlier ("I Stand Here Ironing," pages 586–590), you "heard" a mother anguish over her relationship with her daughter. The story ends with the mother's hope that her daughter will know that "she is more than this dress on the ironing board, helpless before the iron" (590). The mother has not been so lucky and, in a real sense, life has flattened her. The connection among the iron, the mother's life, and the hardships of family responsibilities is direct.

You find a similar connection in "The Masque of the Red Death," pages 510–514, among Prospero, his "castellated abbey" with its grotesque masquerade, and the story's theme. Outside of the abbey's walls the plague of the Red Death has devastated the countryside, leaving behind an atmosphere of darkness and despair. Within the abbey's walls, however, the atmosphere is hectic, frenzied.

You see Prospero as a rather flat character, almost a stereotype of the proud, "happy and dauntless and sagacious" bold and ruthless ruler. You know him to be a prince of almost limitless resources and "bizarre" imagination. The ball Poe describes is a "voluptuous scene," rich in colors, teeming with motion and life.

Now pause a moment to trace the action. Enter a figure dressed as the dreaded Red Death, and the whole company reacts with "a buzz, or murmur,

86—*Literary Visions*

expressive of disapprobation and surprise—then, finally, of terror, of horror, and of disgust." Prospero, however, overcomes a "strong shudder either of terror or distaste" and responds with rage. When no one follows his order to "Seize him and unmask him" prior to hanging the uninvited visitor, Prospero "maddening with rage and the shame of his own momentary cowardice" chases after the masked figure with dagger drawn. The masked visage turns and Prospero is instantly felled by the very sight. The masked stranger is, of course, the Red Death.

When and where does the action occur? The story is presented to us from a dramatic point of view—a perspective that does not give us much insight into the characters other than through their actions. Generally, it is a time of plagues—some point prior to the 1800s—for we know the costumes were similar to those "since seen" in *Hernani,* Victor Hugo's 19th century play. The story opens with brief exposition that tells us about the plague, the Prince, and his seclusion, and then moves swiftly to focus on the night of the ball. The story—like the night and the ball—ends at midnight. The exact place and period remain vague.

What stands out, however, are the details, and it is those details that give the story its mysterious and threatening atmosphere. The strange seven rooms, each with its own color, decor, and feverish indirect light, possess a nightmarish quality echoed by the dress and appearance of the revelers. And then there's the black and red seventh room, the one that contains the sinister ebony clock whose chimes each hour still even the merriest masker. We know that the guests shun that seventh room, which is also the one where the Red Death reveals himself.

Yet it seems natural that the figure of the Red Death is drawn to that room, for its colors are the colors of blood and death. At this point in understanding the story, you start to combine what you know of Prospero with the setting, atmosphere, and action. You know Prospero has chosen to isolate the abbey from the death that stalks outside its walls, and he has created the bizarre decoration within and staged the ball. With this setting Prospero seems to mock the real disease outside the walls. It's as though he is saying, "Look at me! Here's my version of the Red Death, rich colors and textures at the heart of a ball. I can even mask death!" What he had intended to be an atmosphere of grotesque gaiety turns into one of horror and suspense.

What does it all mean? Any number of themes are possible. Perhaps Poe is suggesting that no one can outwit death, but you could just as well substitute "outwit" with "conquer," "be immune from," "mock," "taunt," "challenge," or any number of other possibilities. No matter what the interpretation, we have seen how a fantastic setting creates an atmosphere of suspense and excitement, even terror. We have been entertained.

Setting and Author

Even if we had not known who wrote "The Masque of the Red Death," we might have said that it read like one of Poe's short stories, for Poe's name is synonymous with tales of terror. Many of us have seen screen adaptations of Poe's stories or heard them read in such a way that they raised goose-bumps. Knowing a bit about his life and times, however, adds another dimension to the story.

At the time "Masque" was written, little was known about the transmission of disease, so that the idea of escaping by shutting oneself off from it was commonplace. Imagine reading the story and not knowing about the bacterial origin of disease. The story comes a bit closer to reality and Prospero's abbey is not that far removed from the "pest houses" of the time.

As for Susan Glaspell's story, your initial reading of it would have been different if you had known that she was an early advocate of equal rights for women. Although that information is not necessary to enjoy and understand the story, rereading with that fact in mind makes the attitudes of the men stand out and highlights the story's irony—that it is the kitchen-bound women, those who deal only with trifles, who solve the murder. The men—concerned with the larger picture—are blind. What's more, from the point of view of fellow wives, justice has been served.

Knowing historical or biographical information colors your reading of a story, just as reading through the eyes of a critic instead of your own may reveal additional meaning. It's important, however, that you bring your own knowledge and experience to what you read. A woman may read the Glaspell story very differently from the way a man reads it. So, too, growing up knowing—directly or indirectly—a kind of family life that is similar to the Wright's bleak existence will make the story have a greater impact. What's important is being able to use your experience and the information in the story to arrive at an interpretation that you can then support. You'll note that both the study guide and the text constantly refer to summary or quotation to back up statements.

Summary

By looking at how setting intertwines with character and theme, we can understand how it creates atmosphere and meaning. Later, when we come to drama, you'll find another dimension to setting—in the set of a play.

For now, notice how point of view can guide what you know or don't know not just about characters but about setting as well. As you have learned, setting refers to everything physical or temporal in a story—from the most cosmic time framework to the most insignificant object. Recognizing the importance of setting can give you additional insight into stories you have read in earlier lessons.

Reconsider "A Worn Path" (You know it is told from the third person limited omniscient point of view so that we know what goes on in the mind of Phoenix. We can then understand that a seemingly meaningless object such as the paper windmill can imply a whole world of joy and surprise. An artifact that is part of the story's setting gives us additional information about its main character.

Objects in a story hold significance for both the characters and the reader. The physical objects or details of a story's setting have one other effect—they create a sense of *verisimilitude*. With verisimilitude, even a fantastic scene such as Poe's masquerade seems believable to us. But from that point on, we expect that world—whether it is Poe's nightmarish red death or Faulkner's Mississippi—to be believable.

VIEWING GUIDE

An important component of this lesson is the video. You will learn more effectively from it by thinking about the following questions and guidelines.

Before Viewing:

1. Review "Setting" in the text, pages 224–228.
2. Review Susan Glaspell's "A Jury of Her Peers," pages 189–202, so that you can follow the dramatization more analytically. Jot down the details of the setting that strike you as important.

During Your Viewing:

1. Look for the connections between a "wish you were here" postcard and a writer's use of setting in a short story.
2. Look for the objects in the set used for dramatization. Also pay attention to their placement.
3. Listen for the links between character and setting that the critics make.
4. Note what was happening in the America of 1916.

After Viewing:

Give some thought to the following questions. You may want to write short answers in your journal or notebook.

1. What is the importance of the time of year in the Glaspell story?
2. What similarities can you find between the setting and characters?
3. What do the critics see as the most important characteristic of the setting and character?
4. What elements of Glaspell's setting are not included in the dramatization? What reasons can you think of for not including them?

In That Time and Place—89

WRITING ACTIVITIES

After your study of this lesson, you should be able to analyze a story's setting. Your instructor will advise you which, if any, of the following writing activities you are to complete.

Formal Writing:

The first activity is the easiest because the model in the text can serve as a guide and the critics' comments give you a head start. Activity 2 turns to the link between setting and theme—a connection made accessible by the comments of the critics and the visual impact of the dramatization.

1. Using the study guide and the example in the textbook, pages 288–293, write an analysis of the interior setting of "A Jury of Her Peers."
2. Mary Helen Washington points out in the video that the effect of the setting in "A Jury of Her Peers" is "a tremendous sense of . . . isolation." Write an essay exploring the various kinds of isolation the story suggests.

Informal Writing:

The two activities differ in their focus. The first—and probably the easier of the two—focuses on your own experience and asks you to analyze a setting that holds meaning for you. A familiar setting is also the subject of the second activity, but here the focus is fictional and you are asked to see with another's eyes.

1. Think of a place that holds particular meaning for you. Perhaps it is a room or an outdoor spot. In your journal, describe that place in detail so a reader can see it as you do. As you write your description, include the meaning the various artifacts or natural elements hold for you. What you end up with will be an analysis of the links between you and that place, another way of looking at character and setting.
2. If you would prefer to play with your imagination, put yourself in the position of a human-thinking, extra-terrestrial being who visits Earth (you choose where), knows nothing about our culture, and tries to make sense of some particular setting. What, for instance, would such an alien think of an urban traffic jam? Your medicine cabinet? The Super Bowl? Pick a setting and write an interpretation from the alien's point of view.

SELF-TEST

Match the items in column A with the definitions or identifications in B:

A	B
1. "He had come like a thief in the night."	a. A setting
2. "I know what stillness is."	b. Created by setting
3. "Trifles"	c. Noted by the host
4. A post card	d. Masquerades
5. Cherry preserves	e. Held by the Prince
6. Arabesque figures	f. Source of conflict
7. A drawn dagger	g. The Red Death
8. Atmosphere	h. Played at the ball
	i. A play
	j. Said by Mrs. Peters
	k. Noted by Mrs. Hale
	l. Held by the musician
	m. A request

Answer the following multiple-choice items:

1. The video compares a play's set to a short story to illustrate
    a. similarities.
    b. differences.
    c. theme.
    d. irony.

2. Which artifact is NOT part of the settings of the two stories studied in this lesson?
    a. Moby Dick
    b. A quilt
    c. An ivory clock
    d. A rope

3. Which statement about setting is false?
    a. Setting bears no relation to theme.
    b. Setting bears no relation to point of view.
    c. Setting gives rise to atmosphere.
    d. Atmosphere gives rise to setting.

4. Which of the following is NOT covered by the concept of setting?
   a. Time
   b. Season
   c. Trait
   d. Manufactured artifacts
5. Which of the following does NOT enrich your understanding of the story's setting?
   a. Biographical information about the author
   b. Historical information about the times
   c. Precise identification of the point of view
   d. Precise knowledge of the time in which the story is set

In 100–250 words, answer the following short essay questions:

1. Trace the clues that the women notice in "A Jury of Her Peers" so that you can put together an account of the murder.
2. Poe concludes "The Masque of the Red Death" with the statement: "And Darkness and Decay and the Red Death hold illimitable dominion over all." What does this final description of the story's setting imply about its theme?

ADDITIONAL READING ACTIVITIES

If you enjoyed reading the stories and listening to the interview in this lesson, you may want to read more from the following selections:

Clark, Walter Van Tilburg. *The Ox-Bow Incident.* (Novel about a lynching)
Dixon, Stephen. *Fourteen Stories.*
_____. *Love and Will.*
_____. *Fall and Rise.*
_____. *Garbage.*
_____. *Movies: 17 Stories.*
Poe, Edgar Allen. *The Complete Tales and Poems.*

LESSON 8

The Author's Voice:
TONE AND STYLE IN SHORT FICTION

ABOUT THE LESSON

All the elements of fiction that you have studied up to this point can fit under the large umbrella of style—the way the writer chooses to present a story's plot, structure, characters, point of view, and setting.

Language is the means by which the author presents these elements; thus, to analyze a writer's style is to look at how the author uses language. In this lesson, we will examine some of the components of language that determine style—word choice or *diction*, sentence types, and *rhetorical devices* that are also known as *figurative language*. And we will see how style in turn relates to tone, the means by which the reader's perspective or attitude toward the story is shaped.

To pin down these two terms—style and tone—think of how you tell a joke, not a one-liner but a joke that involves a bit of narrative. Odds are your language is specific but informal and that you build to a punch line that caps the narrative. If the joke is a good one and you've told it effectively, your listener responds with laughter. Why? Because of style and tone. Your style was conversational and fit the voices in your story; your tone was humorous.

Just as the effect of a joke is apt to be greater than the sum of its parts, so too with style. Although you can analyze a writer's style by labeling all the components and their effects, you still may not be able to account for the story's full impact. But being able to recognize the techniques the writer uses and to discuss the various effects they achieve can help you make a case for your interpretation of a short story. You're in somewhat the same situation as a first-year medical student in a physiology course: you need to know the parts, but you can never forget the whole body.

GOAL

This lesson will help you to understand how style and tone are created by an author and will demonstrate how style and tone contribute to the effect of stories on the reader.

WHAT YOU WILL LEARN

When you complete this lesson, you will be able to:

1. Identify the major elements and characteristics of style.
2. Describe how style contributes to tone.
3. Give examples of how style affects the reader.
4. Give examples of how tone affects the reader.

LESSON ASSIGNMENT   All

Completing the following nine steps will help you master the objectives and achieve the goal for this lesson:

Step 1: In your text, read "Tone and Style: The Words That Tell the Story," pages 324–331. The text will provide background for what you will read in this study guide, explain the key terms, and give you some information about the stories you will be reading.

Step 2: Read the specific short stories that are assigned by your instructor. Those that follow will be the focus of this lesson, and those marked with an asterisk (*) will be discussed in the video.

- "The Hammon and the Beans," Américo Paredes, pages 482–485.
- "Tripmaster Monkey," Maxine Hong Kingston, Appendix A in this study guide, pages 368–384.*

Step 3: Read the OVERVIEW in this study guide lesson.

Step 4: Follow the steps in the VIEWING GUIDE in this study guide lesson.

Step 5: Reread the OVERVIEW to reinforce what you have learned in the text and the video and to help you complete the Writing Activities.

Step 6: Complete any WRITING ACTIVITIES assigned in this lesson.

94—*Literary Visions*

Step 7: Do the SELF-TEST exercises in this study guide lesson.

Step 8: Read any of the ADDITIONAL READING ACTIVITIES assigned.

Step 9: Go back to the learning objectives in the WHAT YOU WILL LEARN section of this study guide lesson and be sure you can respond to all of them.

OVERVIEW

Style and writing are often used as synonyms. In school, most papers are written in an academic style, which is to say that they are more formal than informal. You may have been told to avoid contractions, keep the first person to a minimum, and back up your assertions with examples and details.

Yet when you wrote lab reports, you probably shifted gears. The first person probably disappeared altogether, the vocabulary became even more formal and impersonal, and the active voice may have given way to the passive. "Today, I ran a test to find out what salt was made of" becomes "On Feb. 10, 1990, an experiment was conducted to determine the properties of salt." The result is a scientific style and a distancing between the reader and the writer.

Now think of the style you see in a newspaper, whether a school or national one. The paragraphs are short, the sentences are breezy, the words are often easy to understand, and the structure is clear-cut. Within the first few paragraphs, the writer quickly communicates who did what to whom and where, when, and why. What you read is a journalistic style.

Tone is a result of style. It is the attitude the writer creates toward the subject and audience. With the academic papers mentioned above, the tone is explanatory and analytical. A scientific style, however, has a more objective and removed tone, and a journalistic style has a you-are-here tone, factual and vivid.

Another way to think of tone is to associate it with tone of voice, for the two are closely related. Depending upon the tone of your voice, the word sure can take on a variety of meanings. The simple question, "Have you had a good day?" can be answered with a "Sure" that indicates the day was good, bad, or so-so.

In the sections that follow, we will take a look at style and tone to see how they work in short fiction. We'll examine some terms used to identify style and tone, and we'll apply the terms to some of the short stories you have read so that you can see them in action.

Words

Diction is an important element of style, for it refers to the writer's choice of words. Anyone can make up a vocabulary list, but to go beyond vocabulary and into diction, you have to be able to use those words wisely. Good writers use diction that is appropriate to their purpose.

Think about the words you can use to describe the place that you live in. Is it your domicile, residence, or home? Writing a legal document, an attorney would probably use "domicile." Yet a person conducting a voting poll would choose "residence." "Home" is probably the word you would use. These words represent three different levels of diction: *formal, neutral,* and *informal.*

Slang and colloquial words, as you might expect, fall into the category of informal diction. Slang, however, dates quickly. "Cool," "awesome," and "righteous" soon go the way of "hubba, hubba" and "23 skidoo." Colloquial diction is not as fleeting because it is part of everyday speech.

Connotation and *denotation* are also qualities associated with diction. A word's denotation is its dictionary meaning; its connotation is the emotional overtones a word has picked up as it has been used over the years. Your textbook makes a similar distinction, that "denotation refers to what a word means, and connotation to what the word suggests" (page 327).

A place where you read, for instance, can be called a library, study, den, or family room. The differences among the words lie more in their connotation than their denotation. "Library" suggests a formal room with many bookcases. A "study," however, seems far less grand and evokes the image of a sparsely furnished, serious sort of place. "Den" brings to mind a comfortable lair—something private and personal. A "family room," on the other hand, suggests a casual, multi-purpose area where reading is just one of the activities that may go on.

In modern times, you can also categorize an author's diction according to its level of generalization, all the way from the concrete to the abstract. Within most short stories, you'll find ready examples of both kinds of language. Again, what is important is appropriateness.

Sentences

In addition to choosing words that suit the story, the writer must also shape sentences that are appropriate. The terms *simple, compound, complex,* and *compound-complex* probably sound vaguely familiar for they are the names of sentences defined by the kinds and numbers of clauses they contain. Identifying the sentence types is not hard if you keep in mind that a clause is a group of words with a subject and a verb. Once that's straight, all you need to do is make the distinction between an independent clause that can stand alone as a complete sentence and a dependent or subordinate clause that cannot stand alone.

A *simple sentence* is one that has one independent clause and no dependent clause. A simple sentence can be used to show what feelings a character is having in prose. For example, a feeling of dullness or emotionless can be displayed in a direct simple sentence.

Like the simple sentence, the *compound sentence* lacks dependent clauses, but it differs in that the compound sentence contains two or more independent clauses. In an example of this sentence type, a string of actions can be listed without any sense of relationship among them: He picked up his hat, she said goodbye, and he left.

The notion of relationship enters with the *complex sentence*. Unlike the simple or the compound sentence, the complex sentence contains one or more dependent clause along with one independent clause. In this sentence type, a causal relationship can be revealed, The independent clause tells us why a character feels the way he or she might, and the postponed dependent clause adds emphasis to that meaning: A bad taste arose in her mouth because of all the lies she had told during the night. Grammatical relationships are more complicated in the *compound-complex sentence*, for it has two or more dependent clauses and two or more independent clauses.

Another way to look at sentences is to classify them by rhetorical types. A loose sentence is one that starts with the main idea and follows with phrases or clauses that add to its meaning.

In a *periodic sentence,* the main action is withheld until the end of the sentence. The effect is to arouse our interest in what comes next and to hold the main idea in suspense. Often you will find that writers use *parallelism* to emphasize a statement or idea.

Rhetorical Devices

Your textbook mentions several types of parallelism that are rhetorical devices—figures of speech used to emphasize or enhance a word, statement, or event. *Cumulatio* is a term used to describe the building up of details through a parallel pattern of words or phrases.

Far less frequent but always striking is *chiasmus*—a figure of balance and reversal. The concept is easy to remember if you think of an often quoted line from John F. Kennedy's inaugural address: "Ask not what your country can do for you—ask what you can do for your country."

Other rhetorical devices are far more familiar to you. *Understatement* and *overstatement*—also known as *meiosis* and *hyperbole*—frequently turn up in cliches. Sitting by the side of a swimming pool, reaching for a glass of iced tea on a hot day, you might say you're "dying of thirst." Reverse the situation to see how understatement works. Imagine not having had any water for two days, being offered a glass, and replying "I don't mind if I do."

Both of those examples are also ironic in that the words are at odds with the situations. The term for this device is *verbal irony*. The *double-entendre* or double meaning is a form of verbal irony. For instance, in *Hamlet* when Hamlet's mother remarks that the prologue to the play Hamlet has planned is "brief," he responds "As woman's love," a comment on his mother's hasty mourning for Hamlet's father—and her speedy remarriage.

Or, for another example of double-entendre, think of what you usually associate with the idea of a lottery and then think of the story by that name. The lottery in the story is a very different kind from the one the title alone suggests, for the standard association with the word "lottery" is positive. What Mrs. Hutchinson wins, however, runs contrary to the usual association.

Situational irony is well illustrated in "The Hammon and the Beans," by Américo Paredes (pages 482–485). The center of the story is Chonita, a "scrawny" little girl of nine who is a child in the Mexican-American community at the Texas-Mexico border during the 1920s. This period closely followed the "border troubles" of the previous decade. The theory of the Mexican military uprisings was the optimistic idea of creating a new country and a new society in the region so that the Mexicans living there could find freedom and economic development. That dream, by itself, illustrates a social and political irony of situation.

As a symbol of the story's immense situational irony, little Chonita does not have any chance at all of betterment. She begs food from the soldiers at Fort Jones. She tries to speak English, and the children who listen to her mock her pitiful performance despite her cheerful attempts. In addition, we learn that she is the daughter of an executed thief and the step-daughter of a drunkard. This kind of home life would be enough to prevent her ever from rising, but that isn't all. Assuming that she ever could have the opportunity for a decent education, she would then have to get away from her impoverished community and create a totally different life. The story makes plain that such success is never even a remote part of what life might hold in store for her.

There is a still more crushing layer to the story's ironic situation, for it is Chonita's fate to die without ever reaching adulthood. The character Dr. Zapata, whose name recalls the Mexican military leader Emiliano Zapata, explains that Chonita dies from "Pneumonia, flu, malnutrition, worms, the evil eye" (page 484, paragraph 23). In brief, she dies of the poverty and neglect that are the heritage of her Mexican identity in the society of the 1920s. With presumably great intelligence and the ability to develop, Chonita's life is cut short. Through her birth, she receives the gift of life, but she receives nothing else—not love, not sympathy, not education, not opportunity, not even good clothing, and not health. In her situation, she never has even the slightest chance at growth and opportunity Without the love of a nurturing family and the care of a supportive larger society, Chonita symbolizes the irony that life without powerful encouragement is a mockery.

Rhetorical figures in general, and *metaphor* and *simile* in particular, are more frequently used in poetry than in prose.

Summary

Style and tone are essential elements in any work of literature. And once you get used to reading analytically, you can easily spot their components. You have seen how diction plays a role in the short stories you have read, and in later lessons you will see how crucial it is to poetry. Diction is important in drama as well, but connotation, denotation, and rhetorical devices are the building blocks of poetry.

Later too you will come to a different view of dramatic irony—for in the genre of drama it takes on a different dimension. For example, in the play *Oedipus the King,* Oedipus was abandoned as a small child and left to die. The reader of the play knows that death was intended because the child's feet were bound together. His name was given to him because of the resulting disfigurement, for Oedipus means "swollen foot." As a reader, to know the meaning of the name adds an extra dimension of irony, but the irony is even greater for a theater audience that watches Oedipus limping across the stage; every step reminds the audience of the king's origins.

For the time being, though, think about how style and tone have worked together in the earlier stories you have read. The powerful effect that reading "The Lottery," pages 140–146, has on the reader comes from understatement and irony. Remember the line, "someone gave little Davy Hutchinson a few pebbles"? (page 145)

Think also of "First Confession," pages 354–359, where the comic and the serious combine to give the story impact.

VIEWING GUIDE

An important component of this lesson is the video. You will learn more effectively from it by thinking about the following questions and guidelines.

Before Viewing:

1. In your text, review "Tone and Style: The Words That Tell the Story," pages 324–331. As you read, pay particular attention to the following terms:

Complex sentence	Overstatement
Compound-Complex sentence	Parallelism
Compound sentence	Periodic sentence
Connotation	Simple sentence
Denotation	Style
Diction	Tone
Irony	Understatement
Loose sentence	

The Author's Voice—99

During Your Viewing:

1. Look for the everyday use of the word "style" and the literary use. Note the differences.
2. Listen for mention of how style relates to plot, structure, character, setting, and point of view.
4. List the major points Maxine Hong Kingston makes in the interview.

After Viewing:

Give some thought to the following questions. You may want to write short answers in your journal or notebook.

1. What characteristics of style can you identify?
2. What do the critics see as the story's tone? The story's theme?
3. What examples of irony do you find in the dramatization (not the story)?
4. In what ways does Kingston's discussion of style fit that of the critics?

WRITING ACTIVITIES

After your study of this lesson, you should be able to analyze how style and tone contribute to your understanding of a story. Your instructor will advise you which, if any, of the following writing activities you are to complete.

Informal Writing:

The first activity calls upon your eye for detail and contrast, and your observations are directed to what is ironic. By noting irony in your own world, you will be more attuned to it in literature. The result of your observations will be a writer's journal—the stuff of which short stories are made.

The second activity is highly structured and difficult, but the result will probably surprise you and be more than worth your efforts. By using imitation—an exercise as old as ancient Greece—you will be able to express your ideas in the style of a well-known author.

1. Declare one of your days "Irony Day" and with pad and pencil in hand note all the examples of irony that you run across. You might start by looking in the paper to see what you can find there. Then as your day wears on, be on the lookout. Perhaps you spot a street person dressed in rags who is wear-

ing a battered top hat. Perhaps the mice have eaten the cat food. There will no doubt be many such cases of irony.

2. If you would like to play with the idea of style, choose a paragraph or group of 20 lines or so from one of the stories you have read that struck you as having a distinct style. You are going to try to imitate that style but in your own words. To do that, write out each sentence double-spaced. Then for the first sentence, plug in a word of your own choosing that is the same part of speech as the original. For instance, Truman Capote once wrote, "I live in Brooklyn. By choice." You might have turned that into, "She sings in church. Off key." As you work your way through the text, you will probably have to revise what you first put down, but the end result should be an original passage in the style of a well-known author.

SELF-TEST

Match the items in column A with the definitions or identifications in B:

A	B
1. Connotation	a. Author
2. Parallelism	b. Emotional meaning
3. Loose sentence	c. Overstatement
4. Verbal irony	d. Characteristic of speech
5. Maxine Hong Kingston	e. Informal low style
6. Denotation	f. Critic
7. Abstract word	g. Found in chiasmus
	h. Dictionary meaning
	k. Dictionary meaning
	i. Character in "The Hammon and the Beans"
	j. Level of diction

Answer the following multiple-choice items:

1. The video opens with a personal narrative to illustrate
    a. difficulty of choice.
    b. necessity of material goods.
    c. appropriateness of choice.
    d. importance of china patterns.
2. Which is NOT always an element of good style?
    a. Choice
    b. Appropriateness
    c. Correct grammar
    d. Diction
3. Which statement about tone is false?
    a. Tone is integrally related to style
    b. Tone can vary within a short story
    c. Irony is a kind of tone
    d. Parallelism is a kind of tone
4. Which pair does NOT fit?
    a. Compound sentence and complex sentence
    b. Understatement and overstatement
    c. Parallelism and chiasmus
    d. Situational irony and dramatic irony
5. Style and tone affect the reader's response to
    a. all of the following.
    b. characterization.
    c. setting.
    d. point of view.
    e. theme.
    f. conflict.
    g. structure.

ADDITIONAL READING ACTIVITIES

If you enjoyed reading the stories and listening to the interview in this lesson, you may want to read more from the following selections.

Atwood, Margaret. *Bluebeard's Egg & Other Stories.*
_____. *Dancing Girls & Other Stories.*
_____. *The Handmaid's Tale.* (Novel set in a post-nuclear future)
Hemingway, Ernest. *Short Stories of Ernest Hemingway.*
_____. *The Sun Also Rises.* (Novel depicting the expatriate generation of the 1920s)
Williams, Joy. *The Changeling.*
_____. *State of Grace.*
_____. *Escapes.*

LESSON 9

Suggested Meanings:
SYMBOLISM AND ALLEGORY IN SHORT FICTION

ABOUT THE LESSON

When you studied setting, you saw how it related to character and theme. In "The Masque of the Red Death," pages 510–513, for instance, the setting was related to the character of the Prince and the theme of the story; Prospero tried to exert his power over death by walling off the abbey, and he designed rooms for the masked ball as though to mock death. In this lesson, you will be studying somewhat similar relationships. With *allegory*, the connections are direct; with *symbolism*, less so.

This lesson will also examine the idea of myth, because myth, allegory, and symbolism are integrally related. We will be introducing some new terms, defining them, explaining the concepts of myth, allegory, and symbolism, and then analyzing how they work in short stories.

Because examples help clarify explanations, we will illustrate concepts by using not only the short stories assigned in this lesson but also others you have read. You may remember that in the introductory lesson for the story, Lesson 4, we examined symbolism briefly in "A & P," pages 363–367. After this lesson, you will be able to re-read that story and others with greater appreciation of the author's use of symbol, and you will be able to see how writers use myth and allegory to give their works an additional dimension.

GOAL

This lesson will help you recognize the role and effect of symbolism and allegory in short fiction.

WHAT YOU WILL LEARN

When you complete this lesson, you will be able to:
1. Define symbolism and allegory and their relationship to each other.
2. Distinguish among *private, cultural,* and *universal* symbols.
3. Identify examples of symbolism within various short stories.
4. Discuss reasons for using symbolism and allegory within literature.

LESSON ASSIGNMENT

Completing the following nine steps will help you master the objectives and achieve the goal for this lesson.

Step 1: In your text, read "Symbolism and Allegory: Keys to Extended Meaning," pages 380–385. The text will provide background for what you will read in this study guide, explain the key terms, and give you some information about the stories you will be reading.

Step 2: Read the specific short stories assigned by your instructor. Those that follow will be the focus of this lesson, and those marked with an asterisk (*) will be discussed in the video.

- "Young Goodman Brown," Nathaniel Hawthorne, pages 385–393.
- "The Chrysanthemums," John Steinbeck, pages 411–417.
- "The Horse Dealer's Daughter," D. H. Lawrence, pages 471–482.(*)

Step 3: Read the OVERVIEW in this study guide lesson.

Step 4: Watch the VIDEO, following the steps in the VIEWING GUIDE in this study guide lesson.

Step 5: Reread the OVERVIEW to reinforce what you have learned in the text and the video and to help you complete the Writing Activities.

Step 6: Complete any WRITING ACTIVITIES assigned in this lesson.

Step 7: Do the SELF-TEST exercises in this study guide lesson.

Step 8: Read any of the ADDITIONAL READING ACTIVITIES assigned.

Step 9: Go back to the learning objectives in the WHAT YOU WILL LEARN section of this study guide lesson and be sure you can respond to all of them.

OVERVIEW

The concept of *symbol* is not that abstract once you set it in familiar surroundings. For example, if someone from a non-Western country asked you to name a typical American food, you might think of hamburgers, hot dogs, apple pie, ice cream, even french fries. What you picked would be a food that is not just popular in our culture but one that in many ways represents us, symbolizes our culture. The hamburger, for instance, embodies efficiency, informality, and luxury.

Luxury? In many nations beef is an expensive rarity, yet in our culture it is so commonplace that we take it for granted. For us, the hamburger is an inexpensive meal; for many others, it represents a standard of living beyond their reach.

If we broil that beef patty, put it in a bun, add lettuce and tomato, we have a protein-rich meal that can be prepared quickly and requires little in the way of dishes and utensils. And it can be eaten on the run, as our various fast-food franchises prove. From that perspective, the hamburger also represents our fast pace of life and the value we place on efficiency. In many ways, the hamburger symbolizes the United States.

If you had been asked to name a typical American kind of movie, you might have thought of the old-time Western. And if you think about the stereotypical Western, you probably find yourself thinking about heroes and villains, symbolized by white hats and black hats. Push yourself a bit further to examine the system of symbols, and you'll be able to see the Western as *allegory*.

On one level, the typical Western is a straightforward narrative—bad guys threaten town, good guy defends town, good guy defeats bad guys. But the same story works on an allegorical level, with each element symbolizing an abstract quality that adds up to an illustration of an idea or philosophy—evil threatens order, good defends order, good triumphs, order is restored.

The sections that follow will define myth, allegory, symbolism, and the terms associated with them, illustrating those concepts with examples from stories by Hawthorne, Lawrence, Steinbeck, and stories you read earlier. To see how these concepts are related, we will examine the Hawthorne and Steinbeck stories in detail, analyzing them first from the perspective of myth, then allegory, then symbol. In the Summary section, we will see what they all add up to.

Myth

Ancient myths originated from the primitive beliefs of cultures and attempted to explain both the natural and the supernatural. These myths therefore centered on fundamental subjects such as religion, creation, nature, death, and the meaning of existence. The mythology of the ancient Greeks and Romans is familiar to us. For example, Mercury—the Roman messenger of the gods—is our name for quicksilver and the Ford Motor Company's name for a car.

All ancient cultures developed mythologies, and certain subjects recurred in them no matter how far apart geographically or culturally those societies happened to be. The term used for these shared subjects is *archetype*. The idea of the archetype is related to the idea of the *collective unconscious,* a term used by Karl Jung, a psychologist, to describe what he saw as the ancient memory shared by humankind. In literature, motifs such as the hero, the virgin, the temptress, and the devil are archetypes. We can see them at work within the Christian tradition as Samson, the Madonna, Delilah, and Satan.

Myth is also used in a broader sense to mean any real or fictional story, recurring idea, or character type that appeals to the imagination of a people because it represents that culture's ideals or expresses intense emotions shared by that society. We are using myth in this sense when we speak of the myth of the Wild West.

Whether ancient or modern, a particular myth can be invoked by an *icon*—an artifact or attribute that immediately establishes the identity of character or myth. Thus winged feet identify Mercury, a small bow and arrow signal Cupid, and a black 10-gallon hat indicates the stereotypical Western's bad guy.

Recognizing an icon can help you interpret a story. In Hawthorne's "Young Goodman Brown," pages 385–393, we see that the staff of the "fellow-traveler" Brown meets in the forest "bore the likeness of a great black snake, so curiously wrought, that it might almost be seen to twist and wriggle itself like a living serpent," (page 386). For anyone raised knowing the story of Eden, the snake is a ready icon for the devil.

From the story's outset, then, we know that Brown's guide is Satan in human form, an interpretation further supported by the fact that the staff is later described as a "writhing stick," (page 388). Hawthorne further emphasizes this identification when he describes the staff's coming to life and identifies it as "perhaps ... being one of the rods which its owner had formerly lent to the Egyptian Magi" (page 388).

Your textbook's notes then refer us to the Bible, Exodus 7:10–12, where we learn that when Moses and Aaron were pleading to the Pharaoh of Egypt to "Let my people go," God caused Aaron's staff to turn into a serpent to impress the Pharaoh with His powers. In Hawthorne's story, we don't know whether Satan has stolen the rod or merely mocks God by performing his own "miracle." This ambiguity suggests another possible subject for the story, that of reality and illusion.

We do know that in the Christian tradition Satan is the embodiment of evil, evil that is represented by different figures in other traditions and is therefore an archetype. John Steinbeck's "The Chrysanthemums," pages 411–417, presents us with others. The tinker who repairs pots and pans is a version of the Wanderer—an archetype that turns up in forms as varied as the Ancient Mariner of Coleridge's poem and Johnny Appleseed of American legend.

Once you trace the character of Elisa Allen, you will recognize a more familiar archetype. Recall how Steinbeck first describes her. She is working in her garden and appears "blocked and heavy in her gardening costume, a man's black hat pulled low down over her eyes, clodhopper shoes, a figured print dress almost completely covered by a big corduroy apron with four big pockets to hold the snips, the trowel and scratcher, the seeds and the knife she worked with. She wore heavy leather gloves to protect her hands while she worked" (page 411).

Note that while Steinbeck tells us that Elisa's "face was lean and strong and her eyes were as clear as water," (page 411) the image that he first establishes is of a bulky figure with almost no feminine characteristics. She is engrossed in her garden work, "Her face was eager and mature and handsome; even her work with the scissors was over-eager, over-powerful. The chrysanthemum stems seemed too small and easy for her energy" (page 411). "Strong" is the word Steinbeck associates with her.

Later in the story when she is talking to the tinker about her flowers, she speaks of her "planting hands" that go about their work with an almost mystical energy (page 414). At this point in the story, Steinbeck has established Elisa as almost larger than life and identified her to such a degree with her garden and its growth that the two seem one, both giving and receiving sustenance from each other. She is a life-force.

If we see Elisa from the standpoint of myth, we can find a ready identification with the archetype of the Earth Mother. In the Greek mythology with which we are familiar, this archetype takes the form of Demeter, goddess of the harvest and fertility. The *allusion* fits. Elisa is described as larger than life, pulsing with energy, the grower at one with the earth. So now we have two archetypes in "The Chrysanthemums"—the Wanderer and the Earth Mother.

Archetypes are also at work in "The Horse Dealer's Daughter," pages 471–422, but of a different kind—the Maiden and the Rescuer. In a sense, Mabel is a damsel in distress, a sort of Cinderella figure who is ignored and to all extents abandoned by her family. She lives a loveless life and faces a bleak future. The doctor is the Rescuer, the person who saves Mabel—both literally and figuratively. She is not only restored to life but a life of love.

Allegory

If we could continue with "The Horse Dealer's Daughter" and find a corresponding archetype or abstract meaning for every significant event and character, we would have an *allegory*, but we can't. To explore the possible meanings behind Lawrence's use of myth, we must hold off until we look at symbolism. That's not the case, however, with "Young Goodman Brown."

The narrative in "Young Goodman Brown" works on two levels. On one level—a literal one—here is a young Puritan raised in an atmosphere that stresses original sin. He goes to sleep one night and dreams that he leaves on a journey—one that brings him into the forest—where he joins up with the stranger he had pledged to meet. Once in the forest, he sees many of his fellow townspeople, agrees to accompany the stranger farther, and finds himself deep in the wilderness at a ceremony that celebrates evil. As the stranger declares, "Evil is the nature of mankind" (page 392).

Brown sees his wife, Faith, at the ceremony, cries out to her to "Look up to Heaven, and resist the Wicked One!" and then finds himself alone "amid calm night and solitude" (page 392). The next morning, Brown is a changed man full of distrust and sternness that stay with him all the years to his death. Even his "dying hour was gloom," (page 392).

Although the narrative functions on a literal level, it also works on an abstract level, one in which each event, character, and action represents another and becomes part of a pattern. Faith, the name of Brown's wife, is the first indication that the story has an allegorical meaning. And then we know that the stranger's staff, as we noted earlier, is an icon identifying him as the devil.

Each of the townspeople represents another lost soul, and we see Brown "doubting whether there really was a Heaven above him" (page 389). Faith appears and Brown calls out to her, but she vanishes, leaving behind only a pink ribbon. When Brown cries "My Faith is gone!" (page 389), the line works on both literal and figurative levels.

The ceremony itself is an inversion of the Puritan one and appears to be one of confirmation and communion, for converts are being brought forth. But Satan, not God, is the object of worship, and evil, not good, is predominant. Young Goodman Brown has seen the face and expression of evil, and it marks him for life.

Now consider the point of view Hawthorne has chosen for the story, third person limited omniscient. We are told the story by a narrator who plays no part in it but tells us what Brown saw and how he responded. Hawthorne, through this narrator, suggests that Puritan religion emphasized sin to such a degree that it could overwhelm people, who then could see sin and only sin no matter what good was there.

Symbolism

Once you start reading the story as an allegory, you begin to see other correspondences in which an event or object represents or *symbolizes* another. The journey symbolizes a journey into evil or the unknown; the forest can be seen as hell; the stranger's resemblance to Brown suggests original sin; Faith's pink ribbons represent innocence, goodness. What makes symbols a bit difficult is that they are not clear-cut. Unlike the icon or the allegory that work in a one-to-one relationship, symbols may function on many levels.

In Lesson 7, for instance, we discussed the setting of "A Jury of Her Peers" and showed how it is used to reinforce an idea; the cold and empty kitchen echoes the cold and empty marriage. From that comparison of the real setting to the real marriage it is just a short step to symbolism. Imagine the kitchen as a metaphor for the marriage. Explore that metaphor and you'll see other larger points of comparison. The kitchen can be seen as symbolizing not just the Wrights' marriage but the harshness of farm life, the crippling effect of not being able to talk about things that matter, and the slave-like existence of wives.

The kitchen is used as a private symbol, one that takes on these meanings only in the context of the story. This is why the author of your textbook uses *authorial* and *contextual* as synonyms for *private* when discussing symbols.

If you think about "The Chrysanthemums," you can see how myth relates to symbolism. Consider the archetype of the Earth Mother, Elisa's attachment to her flowers, her gift of them to the tinker, and her reaction to seeing them flung by the roadside. These details suggest that Elisa sees the flowers the way a mother would see a child. And, of course, Elisa and her husband have no children.

Chrysanthemums also have a symbolic meaning within our culture, where they are the flower commonly associated with death. If we decide to explore the idea of the flowers as a *cultural symbol*, we would look first to see if the story has any other references, direct or indirect, to death.

The first image to come to mind is that of the cast-aside flowers, tossed out by the tinker to die by the roadside. But we also note that the time of year is December and that the surrounding foothills prevent the sun from shining on the farm. Both the time of year and lack of sunlight suggest death and therefore support the idea of the chrysanthemums as a cultural symbol.

But now we seem to be at an impasse. On the one hand we have Elisa, an archetype of the myth of the Earth Mother, giver of life; and on the other, the chrysanthemums are a cultural symbol representing death. And don't forget, those chrysanthemums are also a private symbol for Elisa's children. How does it all add up?

If we view the story ironically, we can see how the myth and the dual symbolism work together. Here we have a modern-day Earth Mother who, lacking true children, can only raise something with a life-span so short that its death is almost synonymous with life—a flower.

Another interpretation relies on the myth of Persephone, daughter of Demeter. When Persephone is raped by Dis, the god of the Underworld, the act brings on winter. You can see the analogy—Elisa is figuratively raped by the tinker, and the result is despair, the winter of emotions.

The idea of winter brings to mind another archetype—that of the cycle of life and death—a universal symbol. From this perspective, life and death are part of a natural recurring sequence, irreversibly linked. Given that link, it's not surprising we find a farm but no sunshine and a gardener who cultivates a flower associated with death.

Universal symbolism is also at work in "The Horse Dealer's Daughter." Mabel's life changes (to put it mildly) when the doctor rescues her from the pond. From that point on, she not only regains her life but finds it a full one. The pond therefore takes on a significance that suggests it functions as a symbol.

But what might the pond symbolize? If you think about water, you'll begin to associate all sorts of properties with it. It is life-giving. Science tells us that all life emerged from the sea, and we begin our lives in the amniotic fluid of the womb. We also know that without water there is no life. In Christian terms, water is a symbol of purification, for baptism is a symbolic washing away of sin.

Now think of "The Horse Dealer's Daughter." Mabel wades into the pond to end her life but ironically it is there she finds it. The pond therefore can symbolize a kind of baptism, a washing away of her past life, as well as a rebirth—an affirmation of what we realize later is powerful love. The pond is the catalyst in the story's action, and its symbolic meaning foreshadows the reaffirmation of life that brings Mabel and the doctor together.

Summary

An archetype can best be seen as a special kind of symbol—one that stands for a recurrent subject that crosses cultural boundaries and can be found in most systems of myth. In "The Lottery," pages 140–146, for instance, you can easily spot the archetype of the scapegoat. Mrs. Hutchinson symbolizes that which takes on our problems and is eliminated along with the problems as well.

You can see many other symbols and myths at work in that story, such as the ritual of sacrifice and the ceremonies associated with fertility. Artifacts such as the black box take on significance because black is the color our culture associates with death. And death by stoning raises Biblical associations, as in "He that is without sin among you, let him first cast a stone."

Or one can read "The Lottery" against the political background of the days of Senator McCarthy and his allegations of communist conspiracies. From that perspective, the story becomes an allegory of our need to find someone to blame, the degree of acceptance such actions can achieve, and the guilt we incur in pinpointing that blame.

Because myth, allegory, and symbolism are part of our history and everyday culture they are often used in literature to enrich the meaning and effect of a work. The discussion in this lesson focuses on myth, allegory and symbol as they are used in the short story, but keep in the back of your mind that they are also used extensively in poetry and drama.

VIEWING GUIDE

An important component of this lesson is the video. You will learn more effectively from it by thinking about the following questions and guidelines.

Before Viewing:

1. Review "Symbolism and Allegory" in the text, pages 375–380, paying particular attention to the following terms:

Allegory	Myth
Archetype	Private symbol
Cultural symbol	Universal symbol

2. Review D. H. Lawrence's "The Horse Dealer's Daughter," pages 471–482, so that you can follow the dramatization more analytically. Think about the story's setting, characters, action, and conflict in terms of symbol and myth, jotting down what has possible symbolic value.

During Your Viewing:

1. Listen for the various symbolic meanings of water.
2. Look for visual examples of personal, cultural, and universal symbols.
3. Listen for reasons writers use symbols.
4. Listen for what the critics have to say about symbolism in "The Horse Dealer's Daughter."
5. Listen for Majorie Perloff's explanation of what brings the two characters together.
6. Listen for N. Scott Momaday's discussion of the horse as symbol.

After Viewing:

Give some thought to the following questions. You may want to write short answers in your journal or notebook.

1. What is the major conflict in the Lawrence story?
2. How do myth and symbolism relate to that conflict?
3. What do the critics see as the story's theme? How do myth and symbolism relate to the theme?
4. What reasons can you find for selecting the scenes from the Lawrence story that were shown in the video?
5. In what ways does the writer's discussion of symbolism and allegory fit that of the critics?

WRITING ACTIVITIES

After your study of this lesson, you should be able to analyze how symbol, myth, and allegory can contribute to your understanding of a story. Your instructor will advise you which, if any, of the following writing activities you are to complete.

—*Literary Visions*

Formal Writing:

Each of the three activities that follow calls for an analysis of one of the lesson's key terms in relation to a short story. By writing about the term, you can better understand how it functions in the short story.

    The first activity calls for a video recorder so that you can review the first part of the video. The result is a paper that traces how the video explains symbolism and therefore it serves as summary. The next activity is slightly more difficult in that it calls for analysis—a higher order of thinking. At the same time, the model in the textbook makes organizing the essay an easier task. Activity 3 takes up some points made by Marjorie Perloff and asks you to apply what you have learned to "The Horse Dealer's Daughter." The last activity is the most difficult because you are on your own, analyzing how symbols are used to mark changes in character.

1. The first part of the video functions as a visual essay that explores the symbolic meaning of water. Write an essay in which you match the images in the video with the explanatory narrative so that you summarize the process by which the video explains the central term.
2. Using the study guide and the example in the textbook, pages 417–431, write an analysis of allegory in "Young Goodman Brown."
3. Reread the first few pages of "The Horse Dealer's Daughter," through paragraph 95. What symbolic possibilities do you find for the characters? The setting? Select one of your ideas and write an essay explaining the symbolism you find, relating it to the overall theme of the story.
4. In Steinbeck's story, Elisa changes from a lumpy figure dressed in boots and a man's hat to a nicely-dressed pretty woman. Consider how she is described at each point, her actions, and the possible meaning of the change. What symbols are at work here? Write an essay in which you explore the meaning of the change and how Steinbeck uses symbol to point to that meaning.

Informal Writing:

These two activities will give you practice in creating an allegorical structure and in exploring the meanings of a cultural symbol. In Activity 1, working out an allegory on your own will help you see the larger context that characters are involved in and therefore will also help you think more abstractly about what you read. As for Activity 2, thinking through the symbolic significance of an element of United States culture will sharpen your awareness of symbolism and how it functions.

1. Think about a subject you know well—say the role of parent or student or job-holder—and sketch out an allegory based on that subject. If you consider working in a fast-food restaurant as allegory, for instance, you might see

yourself as Mercury, speeding from one spot to another, delivering food to the gods. The patrons, then, would take on the characteristics of various gods from Greek mythology.

2. If you prefer, think of something associated with your culture—in the U.S. that might be football, Thanksgiving dinner, rap music, blue jeans, a Fourth of July parade—and explore its symbolic value by seeing how many associations you can discover. As you think of words or images, write them down in your journal. After you've run out of ideas, re-read your notes and summarize them in a single sentence.

SELF-TEST

Match the items in column A with the definitions or identifications in B:

A	B
1. Salem	a. Narrative formed by a pattern of symbols
2. Icon	
3. Private symbol	b. Young Goodman Brown
4. "He would marry and go into harness"	c. "Writhing stick"
	d. Symbol that occurs in many mythologies
5. Archetype	
6. "A curious vehicle, curiously drawn"	e. Caravan
7. Allegory	f. The bird in "A Jury of Her Peers"
8. Universal symbol	g. Mabel's brother, Joe
9. "... he had not the power to break away."	h. U.S. flag
	i. Halo
10. Cultural symbol	j. Setting for "Young Goodman Brown"
	k. The doctor
	l. Winter
	m. Setting for "The Chrysanthemums"

Answer the following multiple-choice items:

1. The video uses a glass of water to illustrate
   a. archetype.
   b. myth.
   c. symbol.
   d. allegory.

2. Which statement about symbols is NOT true?
    a. Symbols are related to myths.
    b. Private symbols take meaning from their immediate contexts.
    c. Colors are cultural symbols.
    d. Seasons are cultural symbols.
3. Which statement about myths is NOT true?
    a. Many myths share similar subjects.
    b. Many myths explain extraordinary events.
    c. Myths are ancient.
    d. Myths arise from shared beliefs.
4. Which statement about allegory defines it best?
    a. Allegory builds on a pattern of symbols.
    b. Allegory is an ancient form of narrative.
    c. Allegory deals with one-to-one relationships.
    d. Allegory operates on two levels.
5. Which symbol is a universal one?
    a. The "herring snacks" in "A & P."
    b. The rooms in "The Masque of Red Death."

In 100–200 words, answer the following short essay questions:

1. Think about the character of Young Goodman Brown. What kind of person was he before his journey? After? In what ways is his journey a spiritual one? Put what you know about Brown together with what you know about his journey, and write a paragraph that analyzes the effects of that night in the forest.
2. Consider how Steinbeck describes the tinker in "The Chrysanthemums." How does that description and the description of his actions suggest that he may be an archetypal figure?
3. "The Horse Dealer's Daughter" ends with the doctor telling Mabel, "I want you," he said, "with that terrible intonation which frightened her almost more than her horror lest he should *not* want her," (page 482). How do you explain Mabel's fear?

ADDITIONAL READING ACTIVITIES

If you enjoyed reading the stories and listening to the interview in this lesson, you may want to read more from the following selections.

Hawthorne, Nathaniel. *Tales and Sketches.*
Lawrence, D. H. *The Prussian Officer and Other Stories.*
Steinbeck, John. *The Long Valley.*
_____. *Short Novels of John Steinbeck.*
Trilling, Diana (ed.). *The Portable D. H. Lawrence.*

LESSON 10

The Sum of Its Parts:
THEME IN SHORT FICTION

ABOUT THE LESSON

You first met the concept of *theme* in Lesson 4, the lesson that introduced you to the short story. All the other lessons mentioned theme, either directly or indirectly. What you will cover in this lesson, therefore, is nothing new.

This lesson is both a review and a summary. We will take a look at the elements of the short story that we have covered so far and then see how all of them tie into the concept of theme. We will also review the essay that you studied in Lesson 3 so that you can better understand the difference between a *thesis* in an essay and a theme in a short story.

Because the video for this lesson will present some scenes from earlier dramatizations, you will see that most of your assigned reading is a review. To help you apply what you have learned, however, we have also included two stories you have not read before.

Imagine the elements of the short story as blocks the author uses to build an arch. On the one side, you might have *plot, conflict, character,* and *point of view;* on the other, you might have *setting, style, tone,* and *symbol.* If that were the case, theme would be the keystone—the topmost, wedge-shaped block that holds all the others together. Theme is what brings all the other elements together in the short story and—as you will see later—in the poem and play.

GOAL

This lesson will help you appreciate how the various elements in a work of fiction combine to present its meaning.

WHAT YOU WILL LEARN

When you complete this lesson you will be able to:

1. Explain the relationship between a story's *action* and *meaning*.
2. Differentiate between *theme* in a story and *thesis* in an essay.
3. Differentiate between *subject* and theme in the short story.
4. Recognize that there may be more than one theme in a story.
5. Determine the theme(s) of a story.
6. Give examples of common subjects used in short stories.

LESSON ASSIGNMENT

Completing the following nine steps will help you master the objectives and achieve the goal for this lesson:

Step 1: In your text, read "Idea or Theme: The Meaning and the Message in Fiction," pages 432–437. The text will provide background for what you will read in the study guide, explain the key terms, and give you some information about the stories you will be reading.

Step 2: Read the two new stories that will be mentioned in this study guide lesson and review the works below that you studied earlier. The ones marked with an asterisk (*) will be featured in the video.

- "Everyday Use," Alice Walker, pages 108–114.*
- "A Worn Path," Eudora Welty, pages 114–119.
- "A Jury of Her Peers," Susan Glaspell, pages 189–204.
- "The House on Mango Street," Sandra Cisneros, pages 228–229.
- "First Confession," Frank O'Connor, pages 354–359.*
- "The Chrysanthemums," John Steinbeck, pages 411–417.
- "Araby," James Joyce, pages 262–265.
- "I Stand Here Ironing," Tillie Olsen, pages 586–590.
- "A Love that Transcends Sadness," Willie Morris, Appendix A in this study guide, pages 365–367.

Step 3: Read the OVERVIEW in this study guide lesson.

Step 4: Watch the VIDEO, following the steps in the VIEWING GUIDE in this study guide lesson.

118—*Literary Visions*

Step 5: Reread the OVERVIEW to reinforce what you have learned in the text and the video and to help you complete the Writing Activities.

Step 6: Complete any WRITING ACTIVITIES assigned in this lesson.

Step 7: Do the SELF-TEST exercises in this study guide lesson.

Step 8: Read any of the ADDITIONAL READING ACTIVITIES assigned.

Step 9: Go back to the learning objectives in the WHAT YOU WILL LEARN section of this study guide lesson and be sure you can respond to all of them.

OVERVIEW

You are already familiar with the general idea of a story's theme and the specific idea of an essay's thesis, so in a way this lesson is a review. What is somewhat new, however, is a closer look at how each of the elements that you have studied relates to a short story's theme.

In this Overview, we will first review the meaning of the terms thesis and theme, in both your own writing and the writing of others. Then the next sections will examine all the elements of a short story to see how they relate to theme; each section will focus on one of those elements. We will conclude with another look at your own writing about literature. The conclusion will also explain some of the pitfalls involved in interpretation.

Although no story would exist without an author, no story would come to life without a reader. You—the reader—are an active participant in the understanding and interpretation of a work of literature—whether it is a short story, poem, or play. In arriving at your interpretation, you will find that you explore the relationship between a story's action and meaning.

Thesis and Theme

Subjects and assertions are part of our everyday life. When we talk or write, we talk or write about something—a subject. If you meet your neighbor as you walk out to pick up your morning newspaper, you may find yourself engaged in a conversation about the weather. The weather, then, is your subject. Make a value judgment about that weather and you've stated an assertion, an arguable opinion or stand.

Whether the statement is "It's a beautiful day" or "This is the worst rain I can remember," you've taken a position on the subject. Your position—your assertion—cannot be confused with a fact, such as "It rained 3.2 inches last night." The exact amount of rain can be easily verified, but you must make the case for your assertion.

You can see how the same distinctions are at work in an essay. Willie Morris wrote an essay called "A Love that Transcends Sadness," pages 365–367 of this study guide. That's a fact. The essay is about graveyards. That's a fact and a statement of the essay's subject. Morris finds history, peace, and memories in graveyards. That's an assertion because some readers may disagree with you and say he finds something else. The essay's thesis is what Morris asserts about his subject.

But the thesis is not something tangible. You cannot take it out and put it under a microscope. Instead, it is what you—the reader—deduce as the major point of the work. And because it is your view, it is arguable—an interpretation, not a fact. Good essays or good short stories have a number of plausible meanings, so a number of different interpretations are possible, although often a better case can be made for one than for another.

When you write a paper about an essay or a short story, you are presenting and explaining your interpretation of the work. In the case of Morris's essay, you have formulated your own thesis about his thesis. Let's say your instructor has asked you to write an informal essay about "A Love that Transcends Sadness." Your first thought might be, "I liked it." That's an assertion. Now think about why you liked it, and you're on your way to your thesis and an essay that supports it.

If you take your initial assertion and combine it with your answers about why you liked the essay and what you perceive as the essay's thesis—what Morris asserts about graveyards—you will have your own working thesis for your paper. You might come up with the idea that "Willie Morris's fondness for graveyards has changed the way I think about them." If you state that idea as your working thesis, then to develop it into a paper, you would need to explain how you had thought of graveyards before reading the essay, what Morris's view is, and how that view changed yours. Your thesis explores his.

Interpreting a short story works much the same way. But because the main idea in a work of fiction is usually a bit harder to identify than one in an essay, we use a different term—theme. The concept, however, is similar.

You may recall that examining the nature of the conflict is often the easiest way to explore the meaning of a short story. In the last lesson, it was easy to spot a number of conflicts in "Young Goodman Brown," pages 385–393, but let's take just one: faith versus doubt. Because doubt is the idea associated with the main character, you might select it as the story's subject. Ask what Hawthorne is saying about doubt, and you may come up with "Doubt may grow to the point where it colors a person's whole life." What you then have is a theme.

Notice that last sentence said *a* theme. Although a story's theme is related directly to its meaning, the two are not synonymous because a story usually has more than one theme. If it were possible to express all the possible themes in a short story, then your list of themes would indeed reflect the story's meaning. But we never go that far with interpretation. We settle instead for a theme that corresponds to a meaning. Your interpretation, therefore, is what you see as the story's meaning but it is not the same as all the story might mean. If you want to have a better sense of the range of interpretations a story can span, take a look at the different meanings given to "Young Goodman Brown" in your textbook.

And though the meaning of a work will differ, you will find as you read more works of literature that any number of subjects appear again and again: love, death, family, coming of age, truth, justice, reality—the list goes on and on because human experience is the rich source from which writers draw their subjects.

Plot, Structure, and Theme

If you think back on "A Worn Path," pages 114–119, you'll remember the *action*: Phoenix sets out for town, encounters trouble on her way, arrives at the clinic, picks up some medicine, and leaves to go to a store before heading home. That's a bare outline of the story's action, the sequence of events that take place.

Examine those actions in terms of *motive, causation, opposition, response,* and *interaction,* and you have plot. Phoenix takes the trip because she is the only person in charge of her grandson who needs the medicine to live; she walks because she is too poor to do anything else; her trip is difficult because she is old and black; she irritates the attendant at the clinic because she appears to be daydreaming, yet we know that it is only her age, for she is slipping into senility.

Once you have an understanding of plot, you can see the conflicts at work on many different levels. On the surface, the conflict is external and immediate: Phoenix must get to town and back. Beyond that, however, you can see other conflicts. For instance, think of the battle she wages with herself to control her mind and what that battle predicts for the future. When you think about Phoenix edging into senility and that she must take this trip time and time again, the conflict is internal and continuing.

Your view of the story's conflict will determine what you find as its subject and theme. If you see the struggle as internal, the subject might be old age, and the theme might be that old age makes it impossible to meet responsibilities. If you see the struggle as external, the subject might be poverty, and the theme might be that poverty is hardest on the aged.

No matter what you perceive to be the story's theme, you have arrived at it by thinking about the action, plot, and conflict. In doing that, you have also considered—to a lesser degree—character and setting, even perhaps point of view, tone, style, and symbolism.

Character, Point of View, and Theme

When you think about how the characters in a short story relate to its theme, you have to keep in mind the point of view chosen by the author—for that point of view is the lens through which character is revealed.

Start by asking yourself what personal pronoun is used, and the answer will lead you to the *narrator*. Then ask what part the narrator plays in the story, which will reveal the extent to which the narrator is involved in the action. Finally, ask what you learn about the characters' thoughts so that you can tell whether the point of view is *dramatic* or *omniscient*. You need to know the answers to these questions so that you can evaluate what you get to know about a character.

For instance, "I Stand Here Ironing," pages 586–590, uses the first person "I," and the narrator is involved in the action and is the only source of information about all the events and characters in the story. The narrator—the mother—reveals all that is going on in her mind. The point of view therefore is first person limited omniscient, limited because we are limited to the mind of the narrator.

Now you can start to flesh out what you know about the mother, what kind of person she is, what motivates her, what worries her, how she feels about her life and her daughter. You also become aware of what she has had to fight to raise her daughter—poverty, divorce, illness, family responsibilities. In considering character and conflict, you may find yourself wondering to what extent the mother is to blame for the daughter's problems, in which case you're on your way to exploring the subject of responsibility so that you can arrive at a theme.

When you consider that you can trust the mother as a narrator and that she loves her daughter and that she has had any number of circumstances working against her, you can see how you can come up with a theme such as "Both mother and daughter are victims of their circumstances, circumstances over which they had no control."

That, of course, is just one interpretation of the story's theme. A feminist or a Marxist or a Freudian or a working mother would see the story differently. But no matter what your perspective, to interpret the story you must consider character and point of view.

Character, Setting, and Theme

You have already seen how point of view and character interact to help you determine a story's theme, so adding one other element will be relatively easy. When you consider setting along with character, you still think about point of view, but your focus shifts so that it emphasizes both character and setting.

The entire action of Tillie Olsen's story, for example, takes place as the mother irons clothes—a routine, hot, monotonous chore associated with housework and drudgery. The connection between the act of ironing and its housework setting is obvious and can reinforce an interpretation of the story's theme.

If you think about "A Jury of Her Peers," pages 189–202, you can see a similar connection. Martha Hale, Mrs. Peters, and Minnie Wright know what it's like to be a wife living in a rural community, and they know the harshness of the winters and of the role of women. They also know how important love is. Mrs. Peters—as the sheriff's wife—knows the importance of the law, but all three women recognize that the law should not take precedence over justice.

122—*Literary Visions*

By looking at items the men find insignificant—a broken stove, a quilt, a sewing basket—Mrs. Hale and Mrs. Peters discover the motive that would hang Mrs. Wright for the murder of her husband. The clues are part of the setting and therefore crucial to the reader's interpretation of what actually went on.

In the time Mrs. Hale and Mrs. Peters spend in the Wrights' farmhouse, they not only discover what went on but understand what drove Minnie Wright to murder. They change from observers to participants in the action, from people who did not know Minnie Wright to people who can read her mind and heart, from women who were defined by their husbands to women who take independent action.

From understanding the characters of all three women and their setting it is only a short step to a subject and theme. If, for instance, you see justice as the subject, you might come up with a theme that sees justice served by the spirit instead of the letter of the law.

Style and Theme

If you were to select style as the element you wanted to explore in relation to theme, you would probably look at style by narrowing it down. For instance, you might analyze style by examining one of its elements—such as *irony*. Or you might look at the style a writer uses to present character and then tie that analysis to the story's theme.

The irony in "A Jury of Her Peers" has many facets. On one level, it is ironic that only those who pay attention to "trifles" are able to solve the crime. On another, it is ironic that a sheriff's wife covers up evidence. And, of course, there's the title—in a very real way, Minnie Wright was judged by a "jury of her peers."

Because irony is often used to give a story impact, it is a technique of style that links up directly with theme.

Symbolism, Allegory, Myth, and Theme

Lesson 9 explored the various symbols and *archetypes* at work in "The Horse Dealer's Daughter," pages 471–482, so here we'll examine one of the new stories you have read for this lesson, "Everyday Use," pages 108–114. If you think about the characters, setting, and conflict, you can quickly identify what stands out, and that process of identification is the first step in thinking about *symbolism, allegory, and myth.*

On one level, the conflict is between the mother and her two daughters—Maggie and Dee. But then think about what's at stake. Dee, now renamed Wangero, has returned to her rural home with the kind of attitude one might expect of a museum-goer, not a daughter. From Dee's perspective, her mother is quaint, her sister ignorant, their household items decorative artifacts. And Dee wants those artifacts to decorate her new apartment, but her mother has promised the quilt, the object that Dee most wants, to Maggie, who will use it.

"You just don't understand," Dee states to her mother. What doesn't she understand? "Your heritage," says Dee. Immediately, the reader sees the conflict between the family's heritage (as symbolized by the quilt, bench, and butter churn) and their different ways of life. Dee has chosen a new African name, moved to the city, adopted a new way of life. Maggie and her mother have stayed behind.

Among the various possible symbols, the quilt stands out as the most important. It represents the family's heritage in that it is made of scraps of clothing worn by generations of family members, including a bit of a uniform worn in the Civil War. And, of course, the quilt is sewn by family hands, used on family beds. It has seen history, and it is history.

For Maggie and her mother, that history is alive. For Dee, it is as dead as her name. She does not accept "Dee" because it is not part of her heritage. Yet her mother points out that Dee is named for her aunt, who was named for her grandmother and great-grandmother. She could trace it further, but that's enough heritage for her.

By analyzing these symbols, we can see a number of possibilities for a theme. Perhaps the author is suggesting that the Dees of this world make the mistake of rejecting the new in favor of the old. Or perhaps Walker is suggesting that to understand the African-American heritage, we have to include the present as well as the past. She may also be saying that poverty and a lack of sophistication and education cannot be equated with ignorance. Or she may be telling us that dignity or self-respect rise from and are vitally connected to *all* of one's heritage—not a selected part of it.

And, of course, the mother is a kind of "Earth Mother," an archetype for strength and wisdom and love that recurs in myth after myth, no matter what culture. Push your interpretation a bit further and you can see parallels between "Everyday Use" and the Parable of the Prodigal Son that make it possible to read the Alice Walker story as a modern allegory.

Summary

This lesson gives you a good chance to review the various elements of the short story because they all tie in to theme. When you study poetry and drama, you will be dealing with theme as well, though, as you will see, theme in poetry can be a bit more slippery. In texts with a narrative focus—which includes some kinds of poetry as well as drama and the short story—a theme usually stands out clearly even though you may have to wrestle a bit to express that theme as fully as you wish.

As you have seen, the concept of theme is central to working out an interpretation of a short story. Conflict, character, setting, point of view, style, symbol, myth—all contribute in greater or lesser degrees to a story's theme, to your reading of what the work means.

124—*Literary Visions*

Having said that, it's also necessary to point out some pitfalls in interpretation. Although a story may have a number of valid themes, your interpretation of the theme is not a matter of "anything goes." There are boundaries to legitimate interpretation, and if you cross those boundaries, you are apt to be reading your own story and not the author's.

To give you an example, if you are an avid gardener who has just grown a prize-winning chrysanthemum, you might be tempted to read Steinbeck's story "The Chrysanthemums," pages 411–417, from only the perspective of your own experience. In that case, you would over-identify with Elisa and the flowers to the exclusion of the larger meanings of the story. Your view of the subject would be quite literal, and you might state the theme as "A true gardener is never appreciated." Obviously, the story means more than that.

When you write an analysis of a short story, whether it is an essay or an essay response to a test question, you are presenting your interpretation of a short story's theme. What you have to say about that theme, your assertion about it, is your thesis. And you have to back your assertion with evidence you draw from your own experience and from the text.

VIEWING GUIDE

An important component of this lesson is the video. You will learn more effectively from it by thinking about the following questions and guidelines.

Before Viewing:

1. Review "Idea or Theme: The Meaning and the Message in Fiction," pages 432–437, paying particular attention to the following terms:

Action	Conflict
Allusion	Irony
Character	Myth
Plot	Style
Point of View	Symbol
Setting	Tone

2. So that you can follow the dramatization more analytically, review Alice Walker's "Everyday Use," pages 108–114; Tillie Olsen's "I Stand Here Ironing," pages 586–590; Frank O'Connor's "First Confession," pages 354–359; and Sandra Cisneros's "The House on Mango Street," page 228. Think through the possible subjects in each of the stories, listing the subjects so that you can take the next step to theme.

During Your Viewing:

1. Look for the predominant elements in the story that tie into theme.
2. Listen for the various possibilities of the story's themes.
3. Look for the important elements in "Everyday Use." Think about how each contributes to what you see as the story's theme.
4. Summarize what each critic has to say about theme.
5. List the major points Sandra Cisneros makes in the interview.

After Viewing:

Give some thought to the following questions. You may want to write short answers in your journal or notebook.

1. What are the possible subjects explored in "Everyday Use"?
2. Which strikes you as the most important?
3. What do the critics see as the story's subject? Theme?
4. Which elements of the short story are highlighted in the dramatization?
5. Note that the dramatization changes the story's presentation of Mrs. Johnson's thoughts, externalizing them as dialogue. What reasons can you think of for this change?
6. In what ways does Sandra Cisneros's discussion of theme fit that of the critics?

WRITING ACTIVITIES

After your study of this lesson, you should be able to analyze a story's theme. All of the writing activities review stories you have read earlier. Your instructor will advise you which, if any, of the activities you are to complete.

Formal Writing:

The first activity calls for an analysis of theme so that by writing about the term you can better understand it. The next two activities ask you to compare and contrast stories that deal with a common subject. As a result you will be analyzing the stories and drawing your own conclusions about their different approaches to similar material.

The fourth question is drawn from a statement made by Sandra Cisneros. It asks you to examine a conflict that may not be obvious in a number of the stories you have read. Once you see it, however, you may wonder why it didn't strike you on first reading.

126—*Literary Visions*

1. Using the study guide and the example in the textbook, pages 486–492, write an analysis of the theme in one of the short stories not discussed in this lesson.
2. "A & P," pages 362–367 and "First Confession," pages 314–319 can be read as sharing a common subject: coming of age. Write an essay that compares and contrasts the way the stories treat this subject.
3. "Barn Burning," pages 333–343; "Everyday Use," pages 108–114; and "I Stand Here Ironing," pages 586–590, all deal with the general idea of the family. Examine what each story suggests about the family, and write an essay that explains the similarities and differences you find.
4. Sandra Cisneros speaks of herself as a "translator" whose writing enables her to "cross bridges from [her] community into the community of power." Select one of the stories you have read that deals with two communities—one in power and one on the outside—and analyze that conflict in relation to what you find to be the story's theme.

Informal Writing:

So that you may better understand what Alice Walker is getting at with the concept of *heritage*, the first activity asks you to think about your own heritage and to analyze how and what it means to you. The activity also calls for your addressing an audience you do not know so that you may write somewhat objectively about the objects that represent your heritage.

Activity 2 gives you practice in examining the world around you in terms of subjects and themes so that you may analyze not just the facts of events but their meanings.

1. Think about the objects that represent your heritage. What are they? What exactly do they represent? Are all the memories associated with them pleasant? How so? In your journal, write a few pages as though you were writing a letter to your great-grandchildren that explains your heritage to them.
2. If you prefer, skim through the newspaper for a story that has some appeal to you. You may be interested in an international event, a national election, or something much closer to home such as a zoning battle or debate over the placement of scattered site housing. Read the news account of the issue that interests you, and then in your notebook or journal, sketch out a rough draft of the same issue as it might be presented in a short story. What are the possible subjects? What are some of the themes?

SELF-TEST

To review Lessons 4–10, match the items in column A with the definitions or identifications in B:

A

1. "First Confession" and "Araby"
2. Conflict
3. Setting
4. "The Lottery" and "Everyday Use"
5. Irony
6. "The Masque of the Red Death" and "Portable Phonograph"
7. "I Stand Here Ironing"
8. Archetype
9. Private symbol

B

a. Always functions on two levels
b. Related to myth
c. Written by English men
d. The setting in "Araby"
e. Initiation stories
f. Focus on family relations
g. Includes time
h. Essential to plot
i. Is a monologue
j. Emphasize theme thruogh irony
k. Quilt in "Everyday Use"
l. Emphasize theme through setting

To review the entire section on the short story, Lessons 4–10, answer the following multiple-choice items:

1. Which story does NOT fit thematically?
    a. "Barn Burning"
    b. "A & P"
    c. "I Stand Here Ironing"
    d. "First Confession"

2. Which statement about theme is NOT true? A theme is
    a. an assertion.
    b. synonymous with meaning.
    c. derived from a subject.
    d. related to the elements in the short story.

3. Which relationship is correct? A theme is to a short story as a
    a. pronoun is to a point of view.
    b. parable is to a theme.
    c. thesis is to an essay.
    d. subject is to a theme.

4. Which story does NOT fit thematically?
   a. "A Worn Path"
   b. "The Chrysanthemums"
   c. "I Stand Here Ironing"
   d. "Everyday Use"

5. To support your interpretation, which do you NOT need to do?
   a. Deal with the concept of theme
   b. Explore multiple meanings
   c. Cite evidence from the text
   d. Identify with the theme

So that you can see how well you can apply what you have learned about theme to a short story we have not discussed, answer the following short essay questions:

1. At the end of "Araby," pages 262–265, the main character states, "Gazing up into the darkness I saw myself as a creature driven and derided by vanity; and my eyes burned with anguish and anger" (page 265). What has he learned?
2. What details in the setting of "Araby" stand out and bear a significant relationship to your interpretation of the story? In a paragraph or two, explain the relationship between the details you select and your interpretation of the theme.
3. "Araby" contains a number of *allusions*—both direct and indirect—to Christianity. Choose one group of allusions and write an essay that explores their relationship to your interpretation of the story's theme.

ADDITIONAL READING ACTIVITIES

If you enjoyed reading the stories and listening to the interview in this lesson, you may want to read more from the following selections:

Cisneros, Sandra. *The House on Mango Street.* (Short story collection)
_____. *Woman Hollering Creek.* (Short story collection)
Joyce, James. *Dubliners.* (Short stories)
Walker, Alice. *The Color Purple.* (Short novel that won the Pulitzer Prize and American Book Award in 1982)
_____. *In Love and Trouble.* (Short stories)
_____. *You Can't Keep a Good Woman Down.* (Short stories)

MODULE III

Poetry

LESSON 11

The Sacred Words:
THE ELEMENTS OF POETRY

ABOUT THE LESSON

If someone were to say to you "I want you to meet a friend of mine who is a short story writer," you probably wouldn't have a distinct image spring to mind. Substitute the word "poet," and it may well produce a mental picture of a long-haired, gloomy-looking, pale, aging person with a vague and far-away look in his eyes. Yet the poets you will be seeing in the videos on poetry will shatter that image, replacing it with real people—black and white, male and female, young and old, plain and fancy.

What all the poets have in common, however, is a love of language—its words, its meanings, its rhythms, its sounds, even its shapes. And although the poets' subjects vary and the forms they choose to present their ideas differ, they share a common literary history and draw upon common techniques.

This lesson will provide a capsule view of that history and introduce the major characteristics of poetry. The six lessons that follow will explore the various techniques poets draw upon to create their unique view of the world they live in.

Throughout these lessons, we will explore the reasons behind poetic techniques, and we will study how these techniques may affect readers. Now and then, you will be asked to explicate a poem in writing. An explication is a formal analysis of a text, and for poetry that means taking a very close look at the relationship between form and content. You should keep in mind that the relationship between the two is as strong and intimate as that between Siamese twins. They are integrally linked and depend upon each other to exist.

The tight relationship between form and content often scares people away from poetry. At one extreme is the reader who reads a poem the same way as a newspaper. Looking only for information, this person misses the essential characteristics that make a poem a poem—its musicality, its rhythms, its images. But at the other extreme is the reader who reads a poem as though it were written in code. Searching for hidden clues and obscure meanings, this person misses what makes reading poetry a pleasure. Between these extremes is the reader who hears what is on the page and finds delight in the poet's construction of images and sounds, and finds correspondences between the world of the poet and his or her own. That is the ideal reader.

GOAL

This lesson will help you to recognize poetry as a distinct form of literature.

WHAT YOU WILL LEARN

After you have finished studying this lesson, you will be able to:

1. Recognize the evolution of poetry in Western thought.
2. Discuss why economy of language is important in poetry.
3. Explain the major characteristics of poetry.
4. Analyze how a poem's title, subject, speaker, imagery, setting, theme, and form affect the reader's response to a poem.
5. State why poetry may be chosen as the appropriate form for expressing an author's thoughts and feelings.
6. Give examples of poetry and poetic forms found in other media.

LESSON ASSIGNMENT

Completing the following nine steps will help you master the objectives and achieve the goal for this lesson:

The Sacred Words—131

Step 1: In your text, read the chapter "Meeting Poetry: An Overview," pages 624–633. The text will provide background for what you will read in the study guide, explain the key terms, and give you some information about the poems you will be reading.

Step 2: Read the specific poems your instructor assigns. The following works will be the focus of this lesson, and those in the video are marked with an asterisk (*):

- "Schoolsville," Billy Collins, pages 624–625.
- "Dover Beach," Mathew Arnold, pages 694–696.*
- "Dulce et Decorum Est," Wilfred Owen, pages 802–803.*
- "We Real Cool," Gwendolyn Brooks, page 857.
- "Nikki-Rosa," Nikki Giovanni, pages 920–921.*
- "Do Not Go Gentle Into That Good Night," Dylan Thomas, page 930.*
- "next to of course god america i," e. e. cummings, page 666.*
- "Résumé," Dorothy Parker, page 1162.*
- "Revolutionary Petunias," Alice Walker, pages 1186–1187.*
- "The Day Zimmer Lost Religion," Paul Zimmer, page 1194.*

Step 3: Read the OVERVIEW in this study guide lesson.

Step 4: Watch the VIDEO, following the steps in the VIEWING GUIDE in this study guide lesson.

Step 5: Reread the OVERVIEW to reinforce what you have learned in the text and the video and to help you complete the writing activities.

Step 6: Complete any WRITING ACTIVITIES assigned in this lesson.

Step 7: Do the SELF-TEST exercises of this study guide lesson.

Step 8: Read any of the ADDITIONAL READING ACTIVITIES assigned.

Step 9: Go back to the learning objectives in the WHAT YOU WILL LEARN section of this study guide lesson and be sure you can respond to all of them.

KEY TERMS FOR STUDYING THE GENRE OF POETRY

Listed here are the terms that will be discussed throughout the next six study guide lessons. You will read about some of them several times, and some of them you already know from your study of the short story. Review these terms to familiarize yourself with them. You may want to keep this list available so that you can make notes about the terms as you encounter them in your studying. If you want more information about a term as you study, you should use the index and the glossary in the textbook. Remember, however, that memorizing strict definitions is not critical when studying literature. Rather, understanding how they are applied to the genre is more important.

Allusion

Character
Connotation
Denotation
Diction
    abstract and concrete
    formal and informal
Dramatic monologue
Explication
Figurative language
    metaphor
    personification
    simile
Forms of poetry
    closed form
    ballad
    couplet
    quatrain
    sonnet
        Shakespearean or English
        Petrarchan or Italian
    tercet
    open form
        free verse
Imagery
Myth
Persona
Poem

Prosody and Meter
    number of feet
        dimeter
        trimeter
        tetrameter
        pentameter
    type of feet
        anapestic
        dactylic
        iambic
        pyrrhic
        spondaic
        trochaic
Setting
Stanza
Rhetorical figures
Rhyme
    exact
    slide or slant
Rhythm
Sound devices
    alliteration
    assonance
    caesura
    onomatopoeia
Symbol
    cultural
    private
    universal
Theme
Tone
Verse

OVERVIEW

Many of the concepts crucial to the understanding of a poem are ones you have already studied in relation to the short story, so in a way you will be examining the same concepts but as applied to a very different form, that of poetry. And while it is easy to see similarities, it is also easy to underrate the differences. A poem is far more than a short story caught in a compactor.

To emphasize and analyze just what makes a poem a poem, this overview will take a quick look at how poetry has developed over the years, the elements that poems share with short stories, and the qualities that distinguish poetry from other forms of writing. So that you can more easily adjust to the kind of reading that poetry demands, we will also spend some time explaining how to read a poem.

As you read, it may help to keep in mind the distinction between verse and a poem. The word *verse* has two meanings: one, to refer to a line as a unit of poetry; the other, to refer to any work that uses rhythm and rhyme. Working from this second meaning, we can distinguish between verse and a *poem*. Those works that fall into a category containing limericks, jingles, and the like we can call verse; works of high and lasting quality we can call poems. Most of the works you will be reading in these lessons will be poems.

The Development of Poetry

Within Western culture today, verse turns up in many forms that you would not necessarily associate with poetry. Bumper stickers, graffiti, rap music, greeting cards, advertisements, and T-shirts can be—and often are—outlets for verse. Together with traditional forms of poetry such as the lyric, ode, and sonnet, they share a common literary history.

That literary history is still alive today in oral societies in which, on ceremonial occasions, the history of the tribe or culture is sung or chanted as a poem. The person who sings or recites is usually regarded as sacred and powerful. Rhyme and rhythm punctuate the history, emphasizing important events and people.

From such origins as these, *epics* such as *The Iliad* and *The Odyssey* developed to celebrate the acts and lives of gods and heroes of ancient Greece. Similarly, *Beowulf*, the earliest known English epic, draws upon tales and legends to record heroic conflicts and triumphs. Much later, John Milton, writing in the 17th century, chose the epic to document the fall of man in *Paradise Lost*.

Shorter poetic forms may well have had their origin in the spells and prayers of primitive tribes. Embedded in such forms is the belief in the power of language and its emotional effect. The idea of compressed, powerful, moving language is embodied in the lyric, and the jump from the *lyric poems* of the ancient Greeks to the Bible's *Songs of Solomon* to William Blake's 19th century *Songs of Innocence* and *Songs of Experience* is not as great as one might think.

Another popular form is the short, precise lyric that is the *sonnet*. Associated with Petrarch, a 14th century Italian, the sonnet made its way to England where it was modified into what we now recognize as the English or Shakespearean sonnet. Poets such as Edna St. Vincent Millay and Robert Frost used the same form to present 20th century ideas.

Whether a short *epigram* or a *couplet*—a rhymed pair of lines—or the longer traditional *ode*—an elaborate, complex type of lyric—the poetry of the ancients is also the poetry of the present. Today's poets still use these forms as well as new ones. Much of the poetry you see in magazines and books is written in a non-traditional form.

Poems that have a specific and often traditional pattern of lines reinforced by rhythm and rhyme are classified as having a closed form. Couplets, odes, sonnets, ballads, and many lyrics are written in a closed form. Poems written in an open form—also known as *free verse*—do not employ a fixed pattern to convey their meaning. At the same time, these poems are poems. Although they do not have a set pattern of rhyme or rhythm, they share other characteristics with poems written in traditional styles. They have power, unity, rhythm, and imagery, and they rely on diction and various poetic devices to convey meaning. The poems you will read for this lesson represent both types of poetry.

Shared Characteristics

Many of the poems you will be reading have elements in common with short fiction. Like a short story, a poem is somewhat open-ended in that there is rarely one correct interpretation. Instead, a poem invites the reader into a world of images, and the reader interprets the poem by examining those images and the meanings they convey. Like a short story, a poem will have a subject and several possible *themes*.

What is being said in a poem depends on the poet's *persona*, the voice assumed by the poet to relate the poem. In "Résumé," for example, the persona is that of a world-weary person who finds the various ways of committing suicide as bad as the life that drives someone to think of ending it.

"The Day Zimmer Lost Religion" appears to merge poet and persona with the choice of the title and the use of first person. The *character* that emerges was once an altar boy, for he tells us that "I mumbled Latin / At the old priest and rang his obscure bell" (line 9–10). He also went to a Catholic school "Where God reigned as a threatening, / One-eyed triangle high in the fleecy sky" (lines 13–14). (Note that when you are quoting lines of poetry, you need to mark the end of the line with a slash mark.)

The Zimmer we see now, however, knows that he can miss Mass without being personally accosted by Christ (stanza 1). And that knowledge has made him realize that faith is not faith when it rests on threats. Christ never came for Zimmer when he missed Mass because Christ knew "that / I was grown up and ready for Him now" (lines 20–21). The threat of Hell no longer works because Zimmer has reached the point where he thinks for himself. That first missed Mass was the day Zimmer "lost religion" but found himself.

The poem portrays a character who is in *conflict* with the religious beliefs he was brought up with. In that sense, the poem uses Zimmer as a *private symbol* representing anyone who has faced a similar situation when faith is tested by reason and reality.

Setting and *atmosphere* also play a part in some poems. "We Real Cool" is set at a pool hall called The Golden Shovel. The persona is that of a young man speaking for himself and his friends. They have dropped out of school, "We / Left school," and spend their time drinking, staying out late, thumbing their noses at society: "We / Sing sin. We / thin gin. We / Jazz June" (page 857). The atmosphere in which they exist is "cool" by their standards, but the last lines, "We / Die soon," undercuts their coolness with reality.

Although setting, atmosphere, conflict, symbol, and character play a part in some poems, they do not figure as largely or as frequently as they do in the short story. Even theme does not stand out as clearly in poetry, though all of the poems you will be reading in this section do have themes.

The Nature of Poetry

Rhyme, rhythm, strange sounding devices like *onomatopoeia*, and a distinctive form are what most people think of when they think of poetry, but what makes a piece of writing a poem goes much deeper than that. Certainly, a poem consists of one or more *stanzas*—separate groups of lines—so that it *looks* different form a piece of prose, but looks are still surface distinctions. What distinguishes a poem from other kinds of writing is economy of expression, vividness of imagery, power of emotion, and use of sound. The result for the reader is pleasure, pleasure that comes from hearing the poem and understanding it. We are moved by its sound, images, and ideas.

Prosody is the study of sound and rhythm in a poem. The pattern of strong and weak stresses placed on the pronounced syllables in a line of poetry is created by the poet's choice of *meter*—a term that refers to the type and number of metrical units, which are called feet, within a line. The syllables that are heavily and softly stressed are determined by the way you naturally pronounce the word. Take the name Richard Nixon. You pronounce it RICHard NIXon, not richARD nixON.

What you have in this example is two trochaic *feet*—two units of two syllables, each with strong followed by weak stresses. If the former president's name were a single line of verse, it would be called trochaic dimeter, *trochaic* for the type of foot and *dimeter* because there are two feet in the line. The point here is not to confuse you with terms but to show that a certain amount of natural rhythm is built into our language.

You can take a sentence as seemingly unpoetic as "The man walked down the road to find his dog" and find that once you mark the strong and weak stresses, you reveal a pattern that is five iambic feet or iambic pentameter. Lesson 15 will take up prosody in detail. For now, you only need to start tuning your ear to the natural rhythms of the language of a poem so that you can hear its musical pattern.

Rhyme is much more familiar, for most of the songs we have grown up with employ rhyme. For example, think of nursery rhymes such as "Little Miss Muffet / Sat on a tuffet," "Ring around the rosie, / A pocket full of posies," "Now I lay me down to sleep. / I pray the Lord my soul to keep," and jump-rope chants. All use exact rhyme of the moon/June variety, a rhyme that helps emphasize words or images.

Imagery is central to poetry. Poets use imagery to convey a description or impression by appealing to our senses. Consider "Schoolsville," a poem in which the poet assumes the persona of a college English teacher who is thinking about all those students who have sat in all those classrooms over the years and imagines that they populate a town called "Schoolsville." We might be struck by the lines

> The girl who signed her papers in lipstick
> leans against the drugstore, smoking,
> brushing her hair like a machine. (page 625)

The poet has created an image that appeals to our vision so that we, too, can see this girl and draw an impression of what she is like.

The visual image the poet gives us is made more vivid by his use of *figurative language,* in this case the *simile* "brushing her hair like a machine." The unlikely analogy between the motions of the girl and those of a machine not only gives you a good deal of information about the regularity and speed of the girl's brushing but also makes the description stick in your mind.

By using figurative language, poets manage to "say" a great deal in very few words. It is one way a poet achieves the economy of expression that is characteristic of poetry. Paul Zimmer, for instance, describes a vengeful Christ who is going to get him for missing Mass: Zimmer "waited all day for Christ to climb down / Like a wiry flyweight from the cross" (page 1194).

With this image, Zimmer brings to mind all the crucifixes we may have ever seen, but by using a simile to yoke the idea of a crucified Christ with that of a boxer, Zimmer also humanizes Christ and at the same time conveys one way religion is seen by the eyes of an adolescent.

Poets use economy, imagery, and sound to convey their ideas and feelings to the reader. Those three qualities distinguish poetry from other forms of literature and also give it its power.

Often you will find that years after you have read a poem and long after you have forgotten who wrote it, you will still remember a line, an image, a metaphor. Once you have read Dylan Thomas's "Do Not Go Gentle Into That Good Night" and then see a parent grow older and weaker, you may well recall the line "Rage, rage against the dying of the light" (page 930).

How to Read a Poem

Your text (pages 629–631) gives you some good and full advice on how to read a poem, so what follows here is more a supplement than a rerun.

Let's start with the problem. Rarely does a poem "tell" you its theme; instead, it suggests many ideas that you draw upon to interpret the poem's meaning. This suggestiveness is another characteristic of poetry, and it can make a theme somewhat elusive. Yet if you work your way through the poem using your own knowledge of language and life, you will be able to understand its multiple meanings.

As for a solution, revise the way you read so that you read the poem more carefully than the way you read prose, but read the poem naturally, not in a sing-song way. Let the rhythm of the poem, the natural sound of the language, and the poem's structure guide your reading. And always read poetry aloud so that you may more clearly hear the pattern of rhythm and rhyme. After you've read a poem aloud a few times, start making notes. It's often best to put off analysis until you've read the poem several times because its full effect does not usually come through on first reading.

As for your notes, the text suggests that you write a paraphrase of the poem. You will find it much easier to do that if you examine the poem sentence by sentence. Watch out for semicolons, though; the clauses on either side of the semicolon need to be treated as whole sentences.

You might try starting with a paraphrase and then working from both your paraphrase and the poem itself to reexamine your initial ideas about the poem's title, persona, setting, subject, and form. You might do well to check a good dictionary for the meanings of any word that strikes you as a key one. What's a good dictionary? Any of the hardback kind such as *Webster's New Collegiate* or *Random House* would qualify. When you look up a word, remember that many poems use the full range of a word's meaning, so read through the entire entry.

To figure out a rhyme scheme, mark the last word in the first line as *a*, and then look at the last words in subsequent lines, marking any that rhyme with the first also as *a*. Then go to the next line, marking the last word *b*, and so on. Any word that does not rhyme, simply mark with an *x*. When you have worked your way through the whole poem, you will have revealed its rhyme scheme.

Using your own knowledge of the English sentence, your experience in reading short stories, your imagination, your paraphrase, and your dictionary, you will be able to interpret any poem that comes your way. And you should be able to write an explication that presents your interpretation to a reader, who, in many cases, will be your instructor.

Summary

You may be asking yourself how you will ever find the time and patience to read the group of poems assigned for each lesson if you read each one as closely and carefully as the previous section suggests. The simple answer is that you don't have to. Your instructor will point out the poems you should pay particular attention to. Others that the instructor does not emphasize may be included in the video; you need only to be generally familiar with them.

Keep in mind, however, that although economy, sound, form, and imagery are important to the understanding of a poem—and you can best appreciate those elements if you can identify and analyze them in depth—the whole of the poem is always greater than its parts. The themes you explore in a poem are the result of your interpretation of the work's ideas.

Why not state those ideas clearly and simply? Why should the reader have to read so carefully? Isn't there an easier way to say things? Well, yes. But what would be said would not be as powerful or as pleasurable. In response to questions like these, the poet Edwin Arlington Robinson said, "Poetry is language that tells us, through a more or less emotional reaction, something that cannot be said." Ezra Pound put it another way, "If you can say it in prose, then use prose to say it." As for reading poetry, Emily Dickinson said, "If I feel physically as if the top of my head were taken off, I know that it is poetry."

VIEWING GUIDE

An important component of this lesson is the video. You will learn more effectively from it by using the following questions and guidelines.

Before Viewing:

1. Review "Meeting Poetry: An Overview" in the text, pages 624–633, paying particular attention to the following terms:

Atmosphere	Free Verse	Simile
Character	Imagery	Stanza
Conflict	Meter	Symbol
Explication	Persona	Theme
Figurative Language	Rhyme	Verse
Forms of poetry	Setting	
ballad		
epic		
lyric		

2. Review the poems assigned, paying particular attention to the ones your instructor emphasizes. Try to hear each poem's sound.

During Your Viewing:

1. Listen for the different rhythms in the poems that present the different views of the United States.
2. Listen for the different rhythms in the poems that deal with death.
3. Look for the images that accompany these poems.
4. Summarize what each critic stresses as a characteristic of poetry.
5. Listen to what the host has to say about the development of poetry.
6. Listen for what James Dickey has to say about "The Life Guard" and "Performance."

After Viewing:

Give some thought to the following questions. You may want to write short answers in your journal or notebook.

1. What differences do you find between the images you found in the poems and the visual images presented in the video?
2. How do the critics' views of poetry differ?
3. Which critic's comments do you find most compatible with your own and why?
4. What surprised you about the development of poetry?
5. How did James Dickey differ from your image of a poet?
6. How did Dickey's reading of the poems differ from the way you might read prose?

WRITING ACTIVITIES

After your study of this lesson, you should be able to discuss what makes poetry a distinct form of literature. Your instructor will advise you which, if any, of the following writing assignments you are to complete.

Formal Writing:

The first assignment will test how well you can grasp the main points in a poem and summarize them in your own words. The other three assignments are more difficult because they call for analysis, not just summary. By analyzing instead of summarizing, you bring your own knowledge and experience to bear upon the work, thus achieving a higher level of understanding than mere restatement can bring.

1. Using the model in the textbook (pages 645–646), write a *paraphrase* of one of the poems assigned.
2. Using the model in the textbook (pages 647–652), write an explication of one of the poems assigned.
3. Choose two of the assigned poems that focus on the same subject and write a paper that compares and contrasts the poets' themes.
4. Write an essay that explores why "Performance" is an appropriate title for Dickey's poem and the expectations the title sets up in the reader. Are they fulfilled? Why or why not?

Informal Writing:

The two assignments have different purposes. The first calls for a personal essay that traces your attitudes toward poetry. Writing this essay will make you more aware of your tastes and how they developed. Think back to your earliest experiences with verse and then try to trace the development of your present attitude toward verse and poetry. Write a personal essay or a journal entry in which you explain how you view verse and poetry together with how that view developed.

The second writing suggestion calls for you to imitate the form of a poem but to use your own experience. Because the form is there for you to follow, this assignment will give you practice in the techniques of writing poetry. If you would prefer, use "Nikki-Rosa" as a close model and write your own poetic account of your own "childhood remembrances." Try to keep the same sentence structure and approximate line length as Giovanni's poem.

SELF-TEST

Match the items in column A with the definitions or identifications in B:

A	B
1. Verse	a. Pattern of strong and weak stresses
2. "Nights dark as a blackboard"	b. Study of sound and rhythm
3. One of the oldest forms of poetry	c. Sonnet
4. Private symbol	d. The speaker in the poem
5. Meter	e. Economy of expression
6. A rhymed narrative of four-line stanzas	f. Any work that uses rhythm and rhyme
7. Persona	g. Poems lacking a set pattern of rhythm and rhyme
8. Open form	h. Receives meaning from within the culture
9. One of the major characteristics of poetry	i. Ballad
10. Prosody	j. Simile
	k. Study of sound
	l. Receives meaning from within the work
	m. Epic

Answer the following multiple-choice items:

1. Identify the simile from the lines below:
   a. "O My Luve's like a red, red, rose"
   b. "A rose is a rose is a rose"
   c. "Life's a beach"
   d. "Life's a roller coaster ride"

2. Which term best defines prosody?
   a. The study of rhyme
   b. The study of meter
   c. The study of sound and rhythm
   d. The study of rhythm

3. Of the following poetic forms, which is the most recent?
    a. Lyric
    b. Free verse
    c. Epic
    d. Ballad

4. Poems and verse are
    a. rhymed.
    b. closed forms.
    c. of equal quality.
    d. of unequal quality.

5. Which characteristic is NOT essential in poetry?
    a. Imagery
    b. Economy of expression
    c. Sound
    d. Rhyme

In 100–200 words, answer the following short essay questions.

1. Reread "next to of course god america i" from the perspective of who is speaking and where. Then write a short essay that explains how the poem's setting relates to its theme.
2. Reread "Do Not Go Gentle Into That Good Night," looking at the images of light or its opposite, dark. Write an essay that examines the ways Thomas uses the image.

ADDITIONAL READING ACTIVITIES

If you enjoyed reading the poems and listening to the interview in this lesson, you may want to read more works by James Dickey. He is the author of three readily available collections of poems:

Dickey, James. *Buckdancer's Choice.*
_____. *The Central Motion: Poems, 1968–1979.*
_____. *The Early Motion: Drowning with Others & Helmets.*

LESSON 12

A Sense of Place:
SETTING AND CHARACTER IN POETRY

ABOUT THE LESSON

The lesson you just finished pointed out that short stories and poems share a number of elements, *persona, character,* and *setting* among them. In this lesson, we'll take a more concentrated look at how those elements can operate in poetry.

As you watch the video, you'll see how the host and the critics work through the clues that a poem provides. They look for the answers to the standard journalistic questions—Who? What? When? Where?—and then put those answers together to gain a better understanding of the possible themes of the poem.

We'll be emphasizing how to bring your own experience and knowledge to bear in interpreting a poem, but it's also important to keep in mind that the poem's meaning is integrally related to its form. *Rhyme, rhythm, imagery,* and *figurative language*—concepts fresh from Lesson 11—all support and emphasize the impressions of character and setting that the poet creates.

GOAL

The goal of this lesson is to help you appreciate how character and setting function in a poem to produce the poem's meaning.

WHAT YOU WILL LEARN

When you complete this lesson you will be able to:

1. State the purposes for setting and character in poetry.
2. Demonstrate how to find setting and character.
3. Show how clues and information about the setting affect a poem's meaning for a reader.

144—*Literary Visions*

4. Describe how the clues and information about the character affect a reader's response to a poem.
5. Discuss how a reader's response is affected by knowledge about the background and historical and social context of a poem and poet.

LESSON ASSIGNMENT

Completing the following nine steps will help you master the objectives and achieve the goal for this lesson:

Step 1: In your text, read the chapter "Character and Setting: Who, What, Where, and When in Poetry," pages 686–694. The text will provide background for what you will read in the study guide, explain the key terms, and give you some information about the poems you will be reading.

Step 2: Read the specific poems your instructor assigns. Those that follow will be the focus of this lesson, and those marked with an asterisk (*) will be discussed in the video.

- "Stopping by Woods on a Snowy Evening," Robert Frost, page 637.*
- "Dover Beach," Matthew Arnold, pages 694–695.*
- "My Last Duchess," Robert Browning, pages 697–698.*
- "Song," C. Day Lewis, page 707.
- "The Passionate Shepherd to His Love," Christopher Marlowe, page 709.
- "The Nymph's Reply to the Shepherd," Sir Walter Raleigh, page 711.
- "Theme for English B," Langston Hughes, pages 1083–1084.*

Step 3: Read the OVERVIEW in this study guide lesson.

Step 4: Watch the VIDEO, following the steps in the VIEWING GUIDE in this study guide lesson.

Step 5: Reread the OVERVIEW to reinforce what you have learned in the text and the video and to help you complete the Writing Activities.

Step 6: Complete any WRITING ACTIVITIES assigned in this lesson.

Step 7: Do the SELF-TEST exercises in this study guide lesson.

Step 8: Read any of the ADDITIONAL READING ACTIVITIES assigned.

Step 9: Go back to the learning objectives in the WHAT YOU WILL LEARN section of this study guide lesson and be sure you can respond to all of them.

OVERVIEW

When you studied *character* in the short story, you learned about rounded, flat, stock, and stereotypical characters. In poetry, however, characterization works a bit differently. First, not all poems are narratives. And then there's the fact of poetry's compressed form, its economy of language. That means that characters do not receive the degree of development that they would in a short story. The same is true for setting. Often it is implied or suggested instead of described or depicted at some length.

In the sections that follow, we will explain how these elements function within the context of poetry, and we will take a close look at two other terms that are intimately related: *persona*, which is linked to character; and *atmosphere*, which is linked to setting.

Character

Way back in Lesson 4, you learned that prose fiction depends upon narration, the "telling" of a story. Some poems also tell stories, and, like the writer of fiction, the poet creates a narrator—a person who tells the story. If the narrator plays a part in the poem, the poet assumes a *persona* or mask to depict the character. You will recall from earlier lessons that the persona may or may not resemble the author. In fact, it's best to assume the two are different.

Think of Browning's dramatic monologue, "My Last Duchess." Robert Browning is certainly not the Duke of Ferrara, nor is he a murderer who is arranging his next marriage. Another extreme example is "The Passionate Shepherd to His Love." Reading the poem, we know that the "I" in the poem is a fiction made up by the author, Christopher Marlowe. And the fiction is an obvious one. Shepherds, as we may imagine them, are rough and ready caretakers of sheep, not courtly, educated people.

To explain this seeming contradiction between shepherds in life and in poetry, it helps to know about a type of poem known as pastoral. In Latin, the word for shepherd is *pastor*, and poems celebrating shepherds and rustic life were written as early as the third century B.C. Often these poems fell into three categories: a dialogue between two shepherds, a lament or elegy for a dead friend, or a monologue about love or praise.

The pastoral was a popular form among the ancient Greeks and Romans. Later during the Renaissance in England—a time that spanned (roughly) the 14th through the early 17th centuries—the pastoral received special attention as one of the many ancient poetic forms rediscovered in classical literature. When Marlowe and Raleigh were writing in the late 16th century, *pastoral* had come to be used as an adjective. Thus we have pastoral lyrics, elegies, dramas, even epics.

As the genre developed through the years, it acquired certain characteristics, focusing not only on rural life but doing so in the language and sometimes the dress of the court. Are we really expected to believe shepherds—ancient, Renaissance, or modern—are like this? Obviously, no.

What we have in this contradiction is a *convention,* a widely used and accepted literary device or technique. A shepherd speaking in the language of the highly educated is unrealistic, but we are asked to accept it as a convention. Think of drama and the use of the soliloquy, a convention you are probably more familiar with. When, for instance, Hamlet starts his famous "To be or not to be," we accept as a convention the idea of speaking one's thoughts aloud on stage. On the sidewalk, we call it crazy.

We can then see "The Passionate Shepherd to His Love" as part of a long-standing literary tradition, a pastoral love lyric in the form of a monologue. In it, Marlowe takes on the persona of a shepherd who is trying to persuade his love to live with him in rustic bliss. We find the shepherd to be a fairly persuasive and clever fellow, for he carefully paints only the best picture of the life they would lead.

In doing so, the shepherd's appeal fits another literary tradition, that of a category of common *motifs* or subjects. The argument put forward by the shepherd can be summarized as "Let's make the most of what we have today—youth, love, and a beautiful setting." It therefore fits the general category of works associated with the idea of *carpe diem,* literally meaning "seize the day." Underlying this idea is the unspoken reason that we do not know what tomorrow may hold, that death is certain and may be near.

Like the pastoral, carpe diem poems have a long history. In fact it was the Latin poet Horace who, as far as we can tell, first used the phrase. As might be expected with the rediscovery of classical literature, the motif was taken up later in English love poetry of the 16th and 17th centuries, and it finds full expression in the poem by Marlowe. Sir Walter Raleigh's "The Nymph's Reply to the Shepherd" strikes a nice counterpoint to the carpe diem idea. In this poem, the poet takes on the persona of the woman addressed by Marlowe's shepherd. In contrast to her would-be lover, we see her as an ironic realist who can spot a line when she hears one. She quite correctly finds the flaw in the shepherd's logic: love and youth do not last long.

In the poems by Browning, Arnold, Marlowe, and Raleigh, it is easy to distinguish the poet from his persona. It is less easy in poems such as those included in this lesson by Frost, Hughes, and Merrill. The line between poet and persona becomes particularly hard to find in the Hughes poem, "Theme for English B."

If you were to work with only general knowledge about Langston Hughes, you would probably know that he was African-American, probably from the South, spent time in New York, and was interested in both jazz and classical music. You might also know that as one of the major figures in the Harlem Renaissance, the rediscovery of African and African-American culture that took place in New York in the 1920s and '30s, Hughes was vitally concerned with the issues of race.

So far, this picture sounds as though it might fit the speaker in "Theme." But that's not a safe assumption. For one thing, Hughes was born in Joplin, Missouri; the speaker was born in Winston-Salem, North Carolina. Hughes was graduated from Lincoln University in Missouri, an African-American institution; the speaker is enrolled in a freshman class at Columbia University in New York. And whereas the interests and emotions expressed in the poem by the speaker may be close to what Hughes felt in 1959 as he looked back on his days in New York, the reader cannot assume that is so.

Robert Frost may have paused on a snowy evening to think about life, and James Merrill may have conducted experiments in a laboratory, but we don't know that. Even if we did know for certain that one of these experiences were real, we would still be reading a fictional recreation of it. The speaker in a poem is always a fiction. A poet takes a feeling or experience, distills it into images, and shapes it to convey a feeling or idea. The result is a fictional moment in the shape of a poem.

Setting

In Lesson 7, you studied the importance of setting in a short story; and in narrative poetry setting is equally important. Remember that *setting*, as the word is used in literature, covers both the physical and the temporal in that a narrative is located both in space and time. Thus to begin your analysis of setting, you might first ask yourself, "When and where does the poem take place?"

The setting for Marlowe's poem is an ideal one. The time is May—early spring—and nature is full of flowers and the melodious songs of birds. The countryside is gentle and inviting, offering "shallow rivers" with waterfalls and "valleys, groves, hills, and fields." Even the "steepy mountain" yields pleasure. What does one wear in such a natural, pleasure-provoking place? Natural fibers of course—a dress of leaves, a "gown . . . of the finest wool," a "belt of straw and ivy buds." Nature also supplies ornament in the form of coral, gold, amber. No wonder each morning will be greeted with song and dance.

Marlowe's shepherd paints a picture of nature in the ideal. His world has no ants, no bears, no rain, no cold. There is also no sense of the passing of time. This is a world that is always May. And because it is ideal, it could be England or Italy, ancient times or 16th-century.

Contrast the world Marlowe creates with that of C. Day Lewis's "Song." The world Lewis depicts is one of hardship, poverty, uncertainty. Like Raleigh's poem, "Song" is an ironic parody or take-off on Marlowe's "Passionate Shepherd," but the similarity stops there. Whereas Raleigh's "Nymph's Reply" satirizes the carpe diem mentality and the conventions of the pastoral lyric, Lewis's poem attacks the degrading conditions of English life in the 1930s.

Lewis's lover can only offer in the "peace and plenty, bed and board / That chance employment may afford." This 20th century lover is no shepherd living on the bounty of nature but a dock worker dependent upon a paycheck. In this modern urban wasteland, the canals are polluted "sour." As for song birds, the best this couple can hope is to overhear music from human throats singing madrigals.

The result of such a life is not Marlowe's "cap of flowers" but a "wreath of wrinkles." And "toil," not a leafy "kirtle," is what will "tire thy loveliness," a nice turn on the word *attire*. The future this couple faces is not one of timeless pleasure but one of poverty so great that they will not have enough to eat. This hunger, then, can "cheat fond death of all but bone."

Lewis uses the setting to emphasize his theme. By parodying the pastoral lyric, Lewis sets up a contrast between the ideal and the real, as though to say these days and conditions are ones no one would want to seize.

In contrast, Robert Browning uses setting to bring out character. Through his dramatic monologue, the Duke of Ferrara reveals himself to be ruthless, prideful, and materialistic. The painting of his last duchess is one he calls attention to, not because of its subject or the story behind the painting but because of the painter. The portrait is not a reminder but a possession, a treasure.

The same attitude comes out as the Duke leads the Count's emissary down the stairs. He points to a statue of Neptune, emphasizing that it is a "a rarity" that Claus of Innsbruck cast specially for him. Like the emissary, we are supposed to know that Calus of Innsbruck is a famous (albeit fictitious) sculptor. The Duke is the kind of name-dropper who can make you nod assent even when you've never heard of the person.

The duchess, like the portrait and the sculpture, was a possession, an addition to the Duke's collection, something to increase his status. Her failing was that she treated him with the same kindness and courtesy with which she treated everyone; she acted "as if she ranked / My gift of a nine-hundred-years-old name / With anybody's gift."

As a result, the Duke "gave commands; / Then all smiles stopped together." Without the slightest trace of irony, he adds, admiring the portrait, "There she stands / As if alive."

It's interesting to note that the Duke reveals his character quite inadvertently. That someone might be horrified by what he relates doesn't even occur to him. After all, what does he care about others?

The Duke's title, the setting, and attitude suggest that the time is 16th-century Italy. Even without the footnote in your text, there's enough in the poem to remind you of the Borgia family that made intrigue, art collecting, murder, and power plays synonymous with their name. In fact Lucrezia Borgia was Duchess of Ferrara from 1480 to 1519.

Summary

All of the poems assigned for this lesson deal with setting and character. But as you continue reading poetry, you should keep in mind that you will be reading some poetry that has no narrative line whatsoever. Some poems simply (although it's not so simple) create an image or convey a feeling. For those that do depend on character and setting, you need to know how those elements relate to theme.

In this lesson you have taken a look at the who, where, and how at work in a number of poems, and we have occasionally brought out a theme, the what of a poem. "Song," for instance, is an attack on the bleak prospects a worker faced in the 1930s, and "The Nymph's Reply" is an ironic criticism of the shepherd's appeal and, more generally, of the carpe diem approach to life.

Using these discussions as models, you will be able to discover the themes of the other poems assigned and the ways in which character and setting support those themes. But try not to let *what* is said overshadow *how*. Poems are poems, and their sounds and rhythms are integrally related to their meaning.

For example as you read "My Last Duchess" aloud, you will notice that—The poem is composed of couplets, yet because so few lines are end-stopped (a natural pause at the end of a line), the rhyme is not obvious. Lines that are not end-stopped are known as enjambed lines or enjambment.

Listening for the stressed words, hearing the rhymes and sounds of the words, can help you better understand the meaning of the poems. If you read Marlowe's poem aloud, you can hear the light, skipping rhythm, the same rhythm that is at odds with the words in Lewis's "Song." In "Song," that rhyme scheme and meter become ironic, further emphasizing the poem's central irony, which is unlike the pastoral; here the future is at best dim.

VIEWING GUIDE

An important component of this lesson is the video. You will learn more effectively from it by thinking about the following questions and guidelines.

Before Viewing:

1. Review "Character and Setting" in the text, pages 686–694.
2. Review the poems assigned, paying particular attention to the ones your instructor emphasizes. Try to hear each poem's sound.

During Your Viewing:

1. Listen to the sound of the poems as they are read.
2. Listen for the Duke's tone of voice.
3. Listen for what the critics have to say about the setting for "My Last Duchess."
4. Listen for the speaker's tone in the Hughes poem.
5. Note the physical and historical setting in the poems by Hughes and Arnold.

After Viewing:

Give some thought to the following questions. You may want to write short answers in your journal or notebook.

1. How would you characterize the speaker in Hughes's poem?
2. How would you characterize the speaker in "Dover Beach"?
3. What relation do the critics find between character and setting and a poem's theme?

WRITING ACTIVITIES

After your study of this lesson, you should be able to analyze how character and setting combine to produce a poem's meaning. Your instructor will advise you which, if any, of the following writing activities you are to complete.

Formal Writing:

The first three activities are presented in order of difficulty. The first points you to a model and asks for the kind of analysis you do everyday as you talk to people. The next suggestion is more difficult because odds are you're not that used to analyzing setting. You will find, however, that because this assignment asks you to read a poem closely and then write about it, the act of putting your thought into words will lead to a firmer understanding of the two concepts under discussion—setting and theme. If you like to examine small details and figure out how they relate to each other and add up to a larger picture, you will like Activity 3. Working out a rhyme scheme and pattern of stresses calls for patience and attention to detail, but it will train your ear and make you a more-aware reader of poetry. And analyzing the video's version of "My Last Duchess" in Activity 4 will make you more aware of how interpretations of a poem can differ.

1. Using the study guide and the model in the textbook, pages 718–725, write a character analysis of the speaker in one of the poems assigned.
2. Write an essay that analyzes the relationship between setting and theme in one of the poems assigned.
3. Using the information in the study guide choose one of the poems assigned and work out its rhyme scheme and pattern of stresses. Then write an essay in which you analyze what you find in relation to the poem's content, particularly as it relates to character and setting.
4. Write an essay in which you explore how the dramatization of "My Last Duchess" in the video conveys the character of the Duke of Ferrara.

Informal Writing:

This activity forces you to interpret the character in a poem and at the same time emphasizes poetry as spoken word. Because you will be giving a dramatic reading, you will find yourself paying close attention to the small details of the poem, such as its punctuation, stresses, and rhyme. The activity also has the added advantage of preparing the way for drama, the third genre you will be studying.

Imagine that you have been asked to "play the part" of a character in a poem that you have read but have not seen dramatized. Before you give a dramatic reading, however, you have to work out the characterization of the speaker in the poem so you'll know how to act it out. Select a poem that would be suitable for this activity, and in your journal or notebook write a few pages that explain how you see the character—the tone of voice you would use and the lines or words you would stress.

SELF-TEST

Match the items in column A with the definitions or identifications in B:

A	B
1. Twentieth-century England	a. Motifs
2. Common subjects	b. Common literary form
3. Enjambed lines	c. Lines that are not end-stopped
4. Pastoral	d. Setting
5. Carpe diem	e. Poet
6. The Sea of Faith	f. Common literary motif
7. Convention	g. Sculptor
8. Opposite to what you expect	h. Irony
9. Claus of Innsbruck	i. Setting for "Song"
10. Physical and temporal aspects	j. Stressed words
	k. Lines that are end-stopped
	l. Accepted literary device
	m. Setting for "Theme for English B"
	n. Figurative language

Answer the following multiple-choice items:

1. Which element exists in all poems?
    a. Persona
    b. Character

c. Setting
   d. Theme

2. The poem by Christopher Marlowe is an example of a pastoral
   a. epic.
   b. drama.
   c. lyric.
   d. elegy.

3. Which best completes the following statement: The speaker of the poem is
   a. a fictional character.
   b. the poet.
   c. a character in the poem.
   d. a literary tradition.

4. To understand character and setting in a poem, you must
   a. know its historical context.
   b. know biographical information about the poet.
   c. pick up the clues within the poem.
   d. identify the rhyme and meter.

In 100–300 words, answer the following short essay questions:

1. Paraphrase what is going on in "The Conjurer" and then write an essay in which you explain the setting and what may be about to happen.
2. Think about the characterization of the speaker in "The Nymph's Reply to the Shepherd" and write a paragraph or two describing the kind of person she is. Make sure your support your points with evidence.
3. "Dover Beach" can be said to have both a literal and a symbolic setting. Describe the two and in a short essay analyze their relationship.

ADDITIONAL READING ACTIVITIES

If you enjoyed reading listening to the interview in this lesson, you may want to read works by Maxine Kumin, as follows:

Kumin, Maxine. *Our Ground Time Here Will Be Brief.* (Poems)
_____. *To Make a Prairie.* (Essays)
_____. *In Deep.* (Essays)

LESSON 13

Tools of the Trade:
WORDS AND IMAGES IN POETRY

ABOUT THE LESSON

Earlier, in Lesson 11, you were introduced to the nature of poetry and the characteristics that differentiate poetry from other forms of writing—economy of expression, vividness of images, power of emotion, and use of sound. If you think about each of those qualities, you will quickly realize how much each one depends upon the poet's choice of words. The choice of words is to poetry as air is to life.

You first examined diction—the writer's choice of words—when you studied style in the short story. There, you learned about the role diction plays in prose and the terms associated with it: formal, neutral, and informal levels of diction; abstract and concrete words; denotation, a word's dictionary meaning, and connotation, what the word suggests. This lesson will take you one step further in the study of diction by explaining how it functions in poetry.

Knowing the meanings of words and their associations will help you visualize a poem's images and feel more deeply its emotional appeal. You will discover that poets shape their images to invite your participation in poetry through your senses so that you can enjoy poetry emotionally as well as intellectually.

Understanding the patterns and images that are created by the poet's choice of words will not only make it easier for you to relate your own experience to that in the poem but will also help you arrive at a fuller understanding and appreciation of the poem itself.

GOAL

This lesson will help you to understand the integral relationship of diction and imagery.

WHAT YOU WILL LEARN

When you complete this lesson you will be able to:

1. Recognize the various levels and types of diction working in a poem.
2. Give examples of formal and informal, concrete and abstract diction.
3. Give examples of different kinds of poetic language, from street language to courtly poems.
4. Define the "imagery" of a poem.
5. Give examples of imagery in a poem.
6. Give examples of how word choice and connotation affect a poem's interpretation.

LESSON ASSIGNMENT

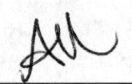

Completing the following nine steps will help you master the objectives and achieve the goal for this lesson:

Step 1: In your text, read the chapters "Words: The Building Blocks of Poetry," pages 653–661, and "Imagery: The Poem's Link to the Senses," pages 726–732. The text will provide background for what you will read in the study guide, explain the key terms, and give you some information about the poems you will be reading.

Step 2: Read the specific poems your instructor assigns. Those that follow will be the focus of this lesson, and the ones marked with an asterisk (*) will be discussed in the video:

- "Snow," Louis MacNeice, page 641.*
- "Jabberwocky," Lewis Carroll, pages 663–664.*
- "Richard Cory," Edwin Arlington Robinson, page 675.
- "Preludes," T. S. Eliot, pages 735–737.*
- "In a Station of the Metro," Ezra Pound, page 747.*
- "Homage to My Hips," Lucille Clifton, page 811.*
- "The Soul Selects Her Own Society," Emily Dickinson, page 1037.*
- "The Windhover," Gerard Manley Hopkins, page 1140.*
- "right on: white America," Sonia Sanchez, page 1171.*
- "Sonnet 29," William Shakespeare, page 1175.*
- "The Red Wheelbarrow," William Carlos Williams, page 1193.*

Step 3: Read the OVERVIEW in this study guide lesson.

Step 4: Watch the VIDEO, following the steps in the VIEWING GUIDE in this study guide lesson.

Step 5: Reread the OVERVIEW to reinforce what you have learned in the text and the video and to help you complete the Writing Activities.

Step 6: Complete any WRITING ACTIVITIES assigned in this lesson.

Step 7: Do the SELF-TEST exercises in this study guide lesson.

Step 8: Read any of the ADDITIONAL READING ACTIVITIES assigned.

Step 9: Go back to the learning objectives in the WHAT YOU WILL LEARN section of this study guide lesson and be sure you can respond to all of them.

OVERVIEW

If someone said you had a problem with diction, you might well associate the word with acting or elocution and think your pronunciation was being criticized. And if the context for the comment were a debate or a play rehearsal, your assumption would probably be correct.

Yet when the word is used in connection with writing instead of speech, it has a different meaning and refers to your choice of words. In your own writing for classes, you may have seen "diction error" noted in the margin if you used the wrong word, such as the common mistake of *affect* instead of *effect* or *lay* instead of *lie*. Conversely, you may have seen "Good word choice!" written by a sentence in which you used a particularly apt word. What was being praised was your diction.

This lesson will explore the vital link between diction and poetry by examining connotation and denotation, types of imagery, levels and types of diction, and, finally, syntax—the way words are put together. In each section, we will look at how poets use words to create images and how imagery relates to theme.

Denotation and Connotation

Sometimes when you are reading the editorial page of the newspaper or an occasional essay in one of the weekly news magazines, you will come across an essay that depends primarily upon definition to make its point. In writing about the justice of a guerrilla war in Africa, for instance, the writer would hone in on the word *war* and examine it from every angle. Such an essay may start with the dictionary definition of *war*, the word's *denotation*, and then go on to explore the various emotional meanings or overtones associated with the word, its *connotation*.

Most of the reading you do is probably informational—news stories, flyers, business mail, and the like. When you read those kind of texts, you are working primarily with the words' denotational value, their standard dictionary meaning. Yet the connotational value is always there.

Think of the political campaigns of the 1990s. Sometimes after a candidate gave a speech, election volunteers and staff would wander through the audience giving the talk a positive "spin." And within the talk itself, the candidate may have dropped an unpopular term such as *increased taxes* in favor of a more positive form such as *increased revenues*.

In poetry, denotation and connotation work together to create patterns and images—both negative and positive. And they are crucial to your understanding and enjoyment of a poem. Your textbook explains how Robert Graves uses the two words *nude* and *naked*—words that share the same denotative meaning—in such a way that he explores their difference in connotation (page 660). Here, we'll take "Richard Cory," a shorter and simpler poem, to see how denotation and connotation combine to create an image and reinforce the poem's emotional impact.

The poem's effect depends on the contrast between the illusion and reality that is Richard Cory. From the outside, he appears to be enviable in almost every way, a handsome, rich, polite "gentleman." Yet the last stanza presents us with a reality that turns the opinion the townspeople have had of him into illusion: Cory "Went home and put a bullet through his head." Hardly the act of a contented person.

The characterization of Richard Cory that you find in the poem sets up a context for rereading it. To illustrate that idea, you may remember reading a newspaper and hitting a word you didn't know. You looked it up, and once you knew its meaning, you found it a useful word. You also probably find that now that you know the word, you hear it frequently. The same is true for a poem—your initial familiarity with it alerts you to key words that then link up with others.

To see how this effect works in poetry, reread "Richard Cory," looking for any word associated in any way with the image of royalty; you will find "crown," "imperially slim," "richer than a king," "schooled in every grace." And you will also notice the opposite. If Richard Cory is royalty, we see the townspeople in direct contrast, more vassals than citizens, living on bare essentials and working without hope: "So on we worked, and waited for the light."

What else do you associate with royalty? Crown jewels, coronation robes, gold, and pageantry. So you also notice that Cory is "quietly arrayed," that he "glittered when he walked." With descriptions such as those, it makes sense to choose the elevated and slightly archaic phrase "in fine" rather than the more common "in brief."

The diction the poet uses to depict Richard Cory creates an image of a noble and majestic person, one of whom the townspeople said, "we thought that he was everything / To make us wish that we were in his place." This image combines with the reality of the last stanza to lead you to a theme. In fact, the cliché "All that glitters is not gold" is almost unavoidable.

On the other hand, perhaps you want to examine the title a bit more closely and see if together with the diction it can lead to a different theme. Working again with the overall image of Cory as royal, you might find yourself thinking of kings named Richard. If you know Shakespeare's "Richard III," you know Shakespeare's Richard would not be described as "a gentleman from sole to crown," but that description does fit Richard Coeur de Lion, also known as Richard the Lion Hearted and Richard I. Coeur and Cory might lead you to a dictionary to check the etymology for *core* and find that it comes from Latin *cor*, meaning *heart*. Working with this information and its associations, you can see your way clear to a theme that focuses on our inability to know another's heart.

As you can see when you are working closely with the diction of a poem, a good dictionary is crucial, "good" defined as a large hardback such as Webster's *New World* or the *Random House Dictionary*. Dictionaries like those will give you a word's etymology as well as its multiple meanings. And for poems written before 1900, you may want to look up key words in the *Oxford English Dictionary* which will give you a history of changes in the meaning of a word.

Types of Imagery

When you read "Richard Cory," Robinson's diction creates a picture of Cory in your mind because the imagery in the poem is primarily visual. But poets create images to appeal to all of the senses—sight, hearing, touch, taste, smell.

When in his poem "Preludes" T.S. Eliot writes, "The winter evening settles down / With smell of steaks in passageways," the olfactory image immediately connects with our own noses and experiences. And anyone who has ever lived in a city can feel and hear what happens when a "gusty shower wraps / The grimy scraps / Of withered leaves about your feet / And newspapers from vacant lots." Those lines give us an image that draws upon our sight, touch, and hearing. We see the scene, hear the sounds made by the shower, leaves, and newspapers, and we feel the leaves and papers around our ankles. Thus the image is visual, auditory, and tactile.

In contrast to the images of the evening, Eliot's second stanza presents images of the morning. If you have ever passed the open door of any bar when it is being swept out, you can relate to the olfactory image conveyed by the "faint stale smells of beer." Eliot depicts an earlier urban world of beer and sawdust-strewn streets and muddy feet, of coffee stands where people go through the empty motions or "masquerades" that carry them through life. He imagines the lives these people live by giving us a visual image "of all the hands / That are raising dingy shades / In a thousand furnished rooms."

For the speaker in the poem, these images add up to "The notion of some infinitely gentle / Infinitely suffering thing." And if you take another look at the imagery in the poem, you will see that all the images share certain qualities—

drabness, lack of hope, depression. The person who lives out a life in this environment is indeed an "Infinitely suffering thing."

As for the last three lines, there the "your" could refer to the reader or to an imagined companion (who may or may not be the reader) who is accompanying the speaker though the streets of the city. Whoever that "you" may be, the last three lines suggest several actions: ignore the world Eliot describes, keep up the "masquerade," enjoy your life that is very different from the ones depicted, or simply carry on with your own life. The final image—"The worlds revolve like ancient women / Gathering fuel in vacant lots"—suggests that the kind of life depicted in the poem has always been with us and has always been depressing.

Types of Words

Like most matters of usage, the choice of what type of word, specific or abstract, general or concrete, is a matter of its context, of appropriateness rather than of rules. Imagine the effect of the last line of "Richard Cory" if it were "Went home and committed suicide."

Or, for that matter, try rereading "The Red Wheelbarrow" without the words *red* and *white*. It is the colors and their contrast as much as the wheelbarrow and the chickens that make the image memorable. Think, too, of the image Hopkins creates of the falcon he depicts in "The Windhover." This falcon isn't a generic falcon but one Hopkins makes you see in flight by using specific and concrete words. The bird is "riding" the air currents, "striding high there" in the sky, banking as he "rung upon the rein of a wimpling wing." The falcon's "ecstasy" is Hopkins' as well, as he watches "the mastery of the thing!"

To Hopkins, this bird that rides the air and masters its environment with such grace is the concrete representation of abstract terms such as "beauty," "valour," and "pride." The specific falcon makes the general terms come alive, as though bird and abstraction were joined together in this instant, and in that sense they "buckle" or are buckled together. By using both the abstract and concrete, Hopkins creates an image that gives life to what might have turned up in a journal entry as a rather flat statement: "This morning I saw a falcon riding the air in such a way that it was beautiful, brave, and proud."

Levels of Diction

Much of what you read and write falls into the category of *neutral* diction—that is, diction that fits in the middle between formal or high and informal or low. If you were writing a character sketch of your mother, you would probably refer to her as "Mother;" yet if you were writing her a letter, she might be "Mom." The most formal word for mother is "mater," but it is so little used that using it today would sound affected, phony.

In fact, today it is relatively unusual to use formal language in writing, with the exception of legal documents and the like. You will notice, for instance, that

160—*Literary Visions*

the poems you have been reading that use a fair amount of formal diction were written before this century. Most of the modern and contemporary poetry you read relies upon neutral diction, although you will also find a number of examples that illustrate informal diction, even slang, idioms, and dialect.

Sonia Sanchez's "right on: white America" makes its point with informal language, though if you read the poem closely you'll see that she mixes diction levels. Convert lines 11–15 into prose by ignoring the line breaks and slashes and using conventional punctuation and capitalization and you have a perfectly correct middle diction sentence: "This country might have needed shootouts daily once" (page 1171). Yet what follows is not the neutral "are not" and "any more" but the informal and dialect "ain't no mo."

By using both neutral diction and the speech patterns and diction usually associated with minorities, Sanchez emphasizes the differences between the two races, white and African-American. America, she suggests, is not only white but is still persecuting people of color. Having wiped out the Indians, "white America" is now turning its attention to African-Americans. "Black" in the last line then has two meanings, the race and the idea of hopelessness. The "tomorrows" are "blk" in both senses of the word. And by abbreviating "black," Sanchez also suggests "bleak."

Syntax

Although some contemporary poets use formal language, we are almost forced to turn to earlier poems to find obvious examples of formal language. And even there, much of what strikes us as formal isn't linked to word choice as much as to syntax—the way words are put together. If you reread Shakespeare's Sonnet 29 looking for formal words, you may be misled by "beweep," "bootless," and "haply." These words now strike us as lofty and formal, but that impression is misleading. At the time the poem was written, they would have fallen into the middle category.

What gives us a sense of the sonnet's elevated language is more a matter of syntax than diction. The word order in examples such as "I all alone beweep my outcast state," and "Yet in these thoughts myself almost despising" inverts what we would expect: "All alone I beweep" and "almost despising myself." The result of the inversion is to slow down our reading of the poem to a somewhat majestic pace and leave us with the impression of formal language.

Unusual word order is a technique poets often use to emphasize an image, idea, or sound. Two others to watch for are *parallelism* and *repetition*. Shakespeare uses both in his Sonnet 29. Read lines 1–4 again, listening to the repetition of "and" that draws out the pain of his "outcast state."

And read lines 6 and 7 with an ear for parallelism and contrast: "this man's art and that man's scope;" "most enjoy contented least." The first example balances "this" with "that" and "art" with "scope." The second contrasts "most" with "least." The exact parallelism is upset by Shakespeare's inverting the second

Tools of the Trade—161

term. We would expect exact syntactical parallelism—a superlative followed by a verb form, "most enjoy"—but instead we have the reverse, "contented least."

These techniques are also very much alive in contemporary poetry. As you listen to Lucille Clifton read her poems, you will hear the same poetic devices.

Summary

When you read a poem, you may find it easier to understand if you read it first only to get a general sense of its sound and sense. Then, after reading it a few more times to familiarize yourself with it, you may find it helpful to break down the poem into sentences. At this point, you would need to look up any words you do not know so that you understand their denotation. From there, see what emotional impact the words have and what images the diction creates. Odds are, you'll find a pattern among the images. Ask yourself what senses the images appeal to and what the images have in common.

If character and setting are important to the poem, see what images are associated with them. On the other hand, some poems lack any narrative line, so you need to take a particularly hard look at diction and imagery to understand what the poem is about.

What you are looking for when you analyze a poem's diction and imagery is a pattern, for that pattern provides you with one way to understand the many meanings of a poem and to work out your own interpretation. In using diction and imagery to arrive at your interpretation, you will be able to understand and appreciate the poem's emotional impact. Robert Frost put it another way: "A poem . . . begins as a lump in the throat, a sense of wrong, a homesickness, a lovesickness . . . . It finds the thought and the thought finds the words." For a poem to be successful, the words the thought finds must be the right ones, a matter of diction.

VIEWING GUIDE

An important component of this lesson is the video. You will learn more effectively from it by thinking about the following questions and guidelines.

Before Viewing:

1. Review "Words: The Building Blocks of Poetry," pages 653–661 and "Imagery: The Poem's Link to the Senses," pages 726–732 in the text, paying particular attention to the following terms:

Connotation	auditory
Denotation	gustatory
Diction	olfactory
Imagery	tactile
abstract	visual
concrete	Syntax
general	parallelism
specific	repetition

2. Review the poems assigned, paying particular attention to the ones your instructor emphasizes. Try to hear each poem's sound.

During Your Viewing:

1. Listen and look for the images in "In a Station of the Metro."
2. Listen for the images in "The Windhover."
3. Look and listen for the types of images depicted in "Snow" and "Preludes."
4. Summarize what the critics have to say about Dickinson's and Sanchez's diction.
5. Summarize what the critics say about the differences between the two love poems.
6. List the major points Lucille Clifton makes about language.

After Viewing:

Give some thought to the following questions. You may want to write short answers in your journal or notebook.

1. Which poem do you think has the most powerful images and why?
2. What type of imagery do you find the most appealing and why?
3. What relationship do the critics see between diction and imagery?
4. In what ways do the visual images in the video reinforce those in the poems?
5. In what ways do Lucille Clifton's views of imagery and diction fit those of the critics?

WRITING ACTIVITIES

After your study of this lesson, you should be able to analyze the diction and imagery in a poem. Your instructor will advise you which, if any, of the following writing activities you are to complete.

Formal Writing:

The first two activities are less complex than the second two. Activity 1 gives you practice in exploring the connotation of words, since many of the poet's words are made up. Activity 2 calls for a full discussion of the pattern of imagery in a poem of your own choosing and therefore requires both a sound understanding of imagery and your own interpretive reading. The last activity calls your attention to the effect of imagery and diction in the selection of Lucille Clifton's poem.

1. Summarize the narrative in "Jabberwocky" and then discuss how Carroll manages to convey meaning despite so many nonsense words.
2. Choose a poem not covered so far in this course and, using the study guide and the example in the textbook (pages 758–763), write an analysis of its imagery.
3. Lucille Clifton uses the word "celebratory" to characterize her poetry. Write an essay explaining what her poetry celebrates and how.

Informal Writing:

Both of these suggestions give you practice in choosing the most appropriate words to create specific images. The first activity also gives you practice in making the abstract concrete and in analyzing an image. The second allows you to compose images according to a set pattern. It will also give you practice in spotting syllables, practice that will be good preparation for the later lesson on prosody.

Writing in your journal or notebook, choose an abstract word such as "truth," "beauty," "honor," "love," "friendship," and write out the statement: "(Insert your abstract word here) is." Then make the word concrete through a series of brief images. Choose the image you like best and write a paragraph that explains why. If you would prefer, try your hand at haiku. The form is strict: three lines totaling 17 syllables, line one composed of five syllables, line two of seven, and line three of five again. For examples, refer to the poems by Ezra Pound (page 747).

164—*Literary Visions*

SELF-TEST

Match the items in column A with the definitions or identifications in B:

A

1. Tactile image
2. Abstract diction
3. Formal diction
4. Auditory image
5. Slang
6. Visual image
7. Connotation
8. Specific diction
9. Olfactory image
10. Parallelism

B

a. Prevaricate
b. "Petals on a wet, black bough"
c. "The jaws that bite, the claws that catch"
d. "The showers beat / On broken blinds"
e. "Elusive little flames play over the skin"
f. Low or informal diction
g. Meaning in addition to that in the dictionary
h. Middle or neutral diction
i. "Quinquereme of Nineveh from distant Ophir"
j. "We thought he was everything"
k. "Gardens . . . / Where blossomed many an incense-bearing tree"
l. "He took his vorpal sword in hand"
m. Dictionary meaning

Answer the following multiple-choice items:

1. The diction level in a poem
    a. varies.
    b. stays the same.
    c. depends on the author's level of education.
    d. depends on the reader's level of education.

2. A poem's pattern of imagery
    a. appeals to only one sense.
    b. appeals to all senses.
    c. relates to the title.
    d. supports the theme.

3. Which statement about imagery is NOT true?
   a. An image may appeal to more than one sense.
   b. An image conveys an emotional impact.
   c. Imagery is one of the important characteristics of poetry.
   d. Imagery is present only in poetry.
4. Which statement about diction is NOT true?
   a. A poem often contains abstract and concrete words.
   b. A poem often covers a range of diction levels.
   c. Words convey meaning through their connotations.
   d. Words must have dictionary definitions.
5. If you analyze a poem's syntax, you are examining its
   a. imagery.
   b. word order.
   c. type of diction.
   d. diction level.

In 100–200 words, answer the following short essay question.

1. Louis MacNeice's "Snow" uses both abstract and concrete words—diction that sharply contrasts. What other contrasts do you find in the poem? What purpose do they serve?

ADDITIONAL READING ACTIVITIES

If you enjoyed reading the poems and listening to the interview in this lesson, you may want to read more from the following selections.

Clifton, Lucille. *Good Woman: Poems and a Memoir, 1969–1980.*
_____. *Next: New Poems.*
_____. *Two-Headed Woman.*

LESSON 14

Seeing Anew:
RHETORICAL FIGURES IN POETRY

ABOUT THE LESSON

When you studied the short story, you saw how style and tone contributed to a story's overall effect and meaning. This lesson will examine some of the same terms—tone, metaphor, and irony—and supplement them with others that are particularly applicable to poetry.

The general heading for metaphor, simile, and the new terms is one that you learned about in Lesson 11—the introduction to the elements of poetry. That heading is *figures of speech*. Most of the words or expressions a writer uses that are out of the ordinary, unusual, and vivid fall into this category. Occasionally you will see the term *rhetorical device* or *poetic device* instead of figure of speech, but these names share virtually the same meaning. Often the terms are used synonymously.

The use of figures of speech and all the terms included in that category come down to us from the ancient Greeks and have been filtered through the Romans. From those times through the 18th century, figures of speech were thought of as ornamentation, something aesthetically and intellectually pleasing but not essential. More recently, however, figures of speech have been viewed as the very essence of poetry, as devices that help distinguish poetry from other forms of writing.

You can understand this difference more clearly if you think about the idea of decorating a Christmas tree. Imagine that you are part of a Christian family in search of the perfect Christmas tree. You find one that's just the right height, shape, and color. You bring it home and set it up. Then the trimming begins. Christmas bulbs, lights, ornaments, popcorn and cranberry strings, angels, stars, odd-looking objects made by children long grown up all decorate the tree, making it a very different tree from the one you bought.

Now, if you think about all those ornaments, you'll see that they aren't just objects added to enhance the tree but are an integral part of something original—*your* Christmas tree. By choosing this bulb and that light and placing one here, another there, you have created a Christmas tree that holds particular meaning and aesthetic pleasure for you and your family. And that is how figures of speech function—not as external decoration but as essential bearers of meaning and pleasure.

And in a sense, a decorated Christmas tree has its own tone. If you think of tone as the attitude the tree-trimmer creates toward the tree and the tree's audience, you can see that if the ornaments and strings are home-made, the effect of the tree will probably be warm, homey. But imagine a tree decorated with all the disposable objects in our culture—the throw-away lighters, paper plates, plastic forks, TV dinner trays, Styrofoam cups, and the like. The result would be irony. Where we should have a symbol of everlasting love and rebirth of the spirit, we have the short-lived and material.

Scholars have argued that all figures of speech are forms of metaphor. And when you think about it, all language is metaphoric in that we use words to represent objects, people, ideas. We are using a word to stand for the thing itself. The term metaphor as we will use it in this lesson, however, refers to a particular kind of figure of speech—a comparison.

Figures of speech and tone are very much a part of our everyday lives. In poetry, however, they are particularly important, for they contribute to the conciseness and vividness that make a poem a poem.

GOAL

The goal of this lesson is to help you to recognize how figures of speech and tone function in poetry.

WHAT YOU WILL LEARN

When you complete this lesson you will be able to:

1. Discuss why all language is metaphoric.
2. Give examples of figures of speech, including metaphor, simile, and personification.
3. State reasons why poets depend on figurative language.
4. Describe the effect of figures of speech on the tone of a poem.
5. Discuss the effect of tone (and especially irony) on the meaning of a poem.

168—*Literary Visions*

LESSON ASSIGNMENT
Working through the following nine steps will help you master the objectives and achieve the goal for this lesson:

Step 1: In your text, read the chapters "Figures of Speech or Metaphorical Language: A Source of Depth and Range in Poetry," pages 760–768, and "Tone: The Creation of Attitude in Poetry," pages 800–808. The text will provide background for what you will read in the study guide, explain the key terms, and give you some information about the poems you will be reading.

Step 2: Read the specific poems your instructor assigns. The following works will be the focus of this lesson, and those marked with an asterisk (*) will be discussed in the video.

- "The Death of the Ball Turret Gunner," Randall Jarrell, pages 639–640.*
- "Sonnet 130," William Shakespeare, page 749.
- "Conjoined," Judith Minty, page 783.
- "Metaphors," Sylvia Plath, page 1099.*
- "Sonnet 18," William Shakespeare, page 787.
- "London, 1802," William Wordsworth, page 790.
- "Dulce et Decorum Est," Wilfred Owen, pages 802–803.*
- "My Papa's Waltz," Theodore Roethke, page 828.
- "Woman," Nikki Giovanni, pages 1130–1131.*
- "Snapshot of Hue," Daniel Halpern, pages 1132–1133.*
- "The Secretary Chant," Marge Piercy, pages 1163–1164.*
- "Oranges," Gary Soto, pages 1178–1179.*

Step 3: Read the OVERVIEW in this study guide lesson.

Step 4: Watch the VIDEO, following the steps in the VIEWING GUIDE in this study guide lesson.

Step 5: Reread the OVERVIEW to reinforce what you have learned in the text and the video and to help you complete the Writing Activities.

Step 6: Complete any WRITING ACTIVITIES assigned in this lesson.

Step 7: Do the SELF-TEST exercises in this study guide lesson.

Step 8: Read any of the ADDITIONAL READING ACTIVITIES assigned.

Step 9: Go back to the learning objectives in the WHAT YOU WILL LEARN section of this study guide lesson and be sure you can respond to each of them.

OVERVIEW

When you studied diction and imagery in the previous lesson, you were also, indirectly, learning about tone and figures of speech. In "Richard Cory," page 675, Robinson's word choice created a contrast between the townspeople's image of Cory as someone superior and fortunate and the reality of an unhappy, desperate person driven to suicide. The resulting tone is ironic, and the imagery that gives rise to the contrast between the illusion and reality is a form of metaphor. To say that Cory was "imperially slim" is to compare his physical appearance to that of royalty. Comparisons such as those in "Richard Cory" are at the heart of all figures of speech.

Metaphor, simile, and *personification* are the most obvious forms of comparison, and they are also the most important figures of speech for you to learn, for they will help you understand the meanings and effects of a poem. For these reasons, the three terms are discussed in the first section of this lesson. Next, terms of lesser importance are discussed.

At first, you may find the less important terms bewildering and confusing, but you will also probably find that their meanings become clearer as you see them at work and use them yourself. As always, you will find that as you write about literature and use the terms associated with it, the specialized vocabulary becomes more useful and meaningful.

Tone comes next. You will see that the discussion of tone in poetry builds upon the discussion of tone in the short story. In fact, in any number of poems, you may find tone easier to identify than in some short stories because poetry is a much more succinct form.

Remember, however, that "succinct" does not necessarily mean "simple." More often than not, the meanings in a poem are so varied and complex that an analysis of the work is longer than the poem itself. But that shouldn't scare you off. A good poem more than repays your efforts to understand it.

Major Terms: Simile, Metaphor, and Personification

Simile, metaphor, and personification are all figures of speech that give words and images greater impact and meaning. By joining the unfamiliar with the familiar, the concrete with the abstract, the striking with the mundane, these figures of speech bring vividness and additional layers of association and meaning to a poem.

The word *simile* comes from the same root as our word *similar*. Both come to us from the Latin word *similis,* meaning a likeness. As you can see, the closeness of the two words makes the more unfamiliar one—simile—easy to remember. You can also recognize overused similes in everyday speech, where they often turn up as clichés: "She eats like a horse;" "He eats like a bird."

The word *metaphor* comes from the Greek and literally means to carry over. Unlike a simile, where one object is being compared with another, a metaphor equates the two. On a very basic level, you can tell a simile by the words "like" or "as;" you can tell a metaphor by forms of the verb "is." Like similes, metaphors turn up in conversation: "My date was an angel;" "My date was a moose."

If you had a series of disappointing first dates, you might conclude that while love at first sight devours or nibbles some people, it has escaped you. You would then be using *personification*—the device that takes an inanimate object or abstract word or phrase (love at first sight) and gives it the qualities associated with a living thing (a creature that devours, nibbles, or flees).

A good way to understand how metaphor and simile function is to look at how they are used in very obvious ways. In 17th century English poetry, for instance, metaphor was carried to the extreme in what was known as the `conceit`, a form of extended metaphor that is intricately complex and designed to evoke the reader's surprise by comparing elements that have little if anything in common.

Shakespeare, however, makes fun of the conceit in his Sonnet 18, page 787 and Sonnet 130, page 749. In Sonnet 130, he interprets the conceit literally and plays with some standard metaphors, asserting in lines 1–12 that the comparisons are quite false. His concluding couplet, however, is serious—he thinks his love is as "rare" as anyone "belied" with false comparisons.

As for a specific comparison, Shakespeare takes up a common one in Sonnet 18, that one's love is like a summer day. Not so, says Shakespeare. His love is far better than that. Summer days are subject to "rough winds" and time—they change. But his love, as expressed in this poem, shall live "So long as men can breathe, or eyes can see."

Shakespeare's sonnet concludes with personification: "So long lives this, and this gives life to thee." With this last line the speaker in the poem implies that the sonnet, which is inanimate, becomes a living thing that gives life to his love.

One other point to remember is that metaphor and personification can be implied as well as explicit. Shakespeare does not state directly that his sonnet takes on life but implies it with diction, "gives life." So, too, if you think back on "Richard Cory," you can see that the diction and imagery Robinson associates with Cory imply a metaphor—that Cory is royal.

Minor Terms: More Comparisons

Shakespeare's idea that a poem is alive is not only personification but *paradox*—a seeming contradiction—and therefore arresting. On the surface the statement cannot be true, but beneath the surface it is. After all, there has been much debate over the identity of the person in Sonnet 130—the object of the speaker's love—but the sonnet itself is here for us to read. The poem is indeed more alive than the person. The personification has turned out to be justified.

Apostrophe is related to personification, and it is the term used when the speaker in the poem addresses an inanimate object as though it were alive. Unlike personification, however, apostrophe can also apply to any direct address to a dead or absent person, animal, or thing. In "London, 1802," page 790, William

Wordsworth uses apostrophe in this manner in line 1 by speaking to the dead poet Milton. Apostrophe, too, can be thought of as a form of paradox; Milton is dead but addressed as though he were alive.

Another form of paradox is *synesthesia*, the mixing of senses. You would be using synesthesia if you described a beautiful fall day (sight) as "delicious" (taste). Or if you were to say that a friend's tie is so loud it screams, you would be joining what an object looks like with a term associated with sound. On the other hand, if you saw yourself drowning in silence, that too would be synesthesia. You can see this technique at work in Wilfred Owen's "Dulce et Decorum Est," pages 802–803, when he describes the soldiers as "Drunk with fatigue" and refers to "smothering dreams."

Association is also the key to two terms easy to confuse—*metonymy* and *synecdoche*. Metonymy is from the ancient Greek, meaning a change in name and it refers to one word substituted for another closely related to it. We use metonymy when we substitute the trademarked name of a product for the product itself, as in Band-Aid, Kleenex, or Xerox. When we refer to the church to mean the whole Christian religion, we are using metonymy the same way it is used in poetry. In "London, 1802," for example, Wordsworth uses metonymy with the words "altar, sword, and pen" to stand for the clergy, the military, and the writers.

Synecdoche is frequently thought of as a form of metonymy in that it substitutes a part for the whole or the whole for a part. The substitution must be an important one. For instance, you might characterize a large room full of talkative people as 100 tongues, not 200 lips.

Both metonymy and synecdoche have an effect similar to paradox in that they cause the reader to slow down and think, to savor the meanings and images they add. However, they are less familiar to you than other commonly used figures of speech—*understatement* or *meiosis*, *overstatement* or *hyperbole*, *anaphora* or *repetition*, and the *pun* or *paronomasia*.

Overstatement comes naturally to us in everyday speech. "Thanks a million" and "I never have any fun" are examples of overstatement that we hear frequently. It is also a common device in poetry. When Marge Piercy describes "The Secretary Chant," pages 1163–1164, she is relying upon hyperbole to emphasize the extended metaphor that compares the human secretary and the inanimate machines she uses. Through overstatement, she implies all that is demeaning, routine, and mechanical about working in an office.

Understatement is also a standard figure of speech in conversation. "It was nothing," you might find yourself saying about an action that was quite the opposite. Again, the device is common to poetry, as in Nikki Giovanni's "Woman." Stanzas 1 through 4 depict the needs and desires of the speaker who is attempting to define herself in relation to a man. The last stanza, however, sees her giving up trying to define herself in relation to the man and instead defining herself as herself—as "woman." Then comes the understatement: "and though he still refused / to be a man / she decided it was all / right." The single word as the last line underscores the understatement.

Emphasis is also the effect of *anaphora*, the ancient Greek's term for repetition of a word or phrase. Anaphora not only emphasizes the repeated words but also can lend rhythm to the language.

As for puns, one need look only as far as the nearest bumper sticker or T-shirt: "Life is a beach"; "Black holes are out of sight"; "Don't Californicate Colorado." In poetry, the play on words may not be so obvious, as in the play on sound in Piercy's "File me under W / because I wonce / was / a woman." Think, too, of the second to the last line in Shakespeare's Sonnet 130:

> And yet, by heaven, I think my love as rare

"My love" could refer to the object of his love or to the feeling he has for her. And "she" in the last line could refer to any woman—a noun—or to this particular woman—the subject for the verb "belied."

As you can see, puns in poetry are a high form of wordplay that add an extra dimension of meaning and depth. Like metonymy, synecdoche, anaphora, understatement, and overstatement, puns emphasize as well as add to what is being said.

Tone

Your study of style in the short story also included tone—the means by which the reader's perspective or attitude toward a work is shaped. *Tone* in literature is close to the common meaning of *tone of voice*. The tone of a poem, for instance, can be light-hearted, humorous, sarcastic, bleak, serious, scholarly, objective, sardonic, informal, ironic, and an almost limitless number of other possibilities. You can also clarify your understanding of tone if you keep in mind that it is the emotional coloring that is created by the author's diction. The writer's choice of words, images, and figures of speech determine a poem's tone.

In Sylvia Plath's "Metaphors," page 1099, for example, we have just what she says—"a riddle in nine syllables." And as befits a riddle, the diction is concrete; its words come from everyday usage—"melon," "fruit," "load," "cow," "apples," and the like. The diction level is the same as the old stand-by, "What is black and white and read all over?"

What distinguishes the poem from the standard riddle is its imagery, which is presented in the form of metaphors, nine or ten of them, depending on how you count. The speaker is

> An elephant, a ponderous house,
> A melon strolling on two tendrils.

She is also a "loaf," a "fat purse," "a means, a stage, a cow in calf." It is as though she has "Boarded the train there's no getting off." In short, she is pregnant; the nine syllables that make up the riddle are the abbreviations for the nine months, and that's the answer to the riddle. As you might expect with a riddling poem, the tone is playful, whimsical.

In contrast, consider the tone of "The Death of the Ball Turret Gunner," pages 639–640. This five line poem depicts the horrors of war by describing the short life and messy death of a World War II gunner. "Hunched" in the belly of a bomber, the gunner "woke to black flak and the nightmare fighters." What was left of him was "washed . . . out of the turret with a hose." The tone is somber, quiet.

The short span of the gunner's life is described as though he went straight from his mother's womb into the belly of the bomber:

> From my mother's sleep I fell into the State
> And I hunched in its belly till my wet fur froze.

The seemingly quiet images ("sleep" and "hunched") contrast ironically with the gunner's violent death. And other ironies abound. The narrator is the dead gunner, perhaps because no one else is either interested or able to tell his story. Consider too that a very real person is reduced to something that can only be hosed out. The understatement of that last line is also ironic, the horror of the death running counter to the flatness of the statement. The irony in the poem is both verbal and situational.

Irony figures largely in poetry as it does in fiction. Back in Lesson 8, you examined irony and its various forms—situational, dramatic, and verbal. As you can see, these types of irony are also present in poetry. For dramatic irony, think of "Richard Cory," (page 675), or "The Death of the Ball Turret Gunner," (pages 639–640). For situational irony, think of "The Secretary Chant," (pages 1163–1164), or "Snapshot of Hue," (page 1132), or "My Papa's Waltz," (page 822).

Sometimes irony only plays a part in a poem, as in Shakespeare's sonnets. But often irony becomes a poem's dominant tone, and you could make a case for that with "Woman," (pages 1130–1131), "The Secretary Chant," (pages 1163–1164), "Dulce et Decorum Est," (pages 802–803), and "Conjoined," (page 783). Some poems, however, are simply not ironic, such as Gary Soto's "Oranges," (pages 1178–1179). To decide what part, if any, irony plays, you have to keep careful track of diction, imagery, and figures of speech.

Summary

In the previous lesson, you learned about diction and imagery; this lesson put both of those terms in a larger context. Just as a writer's choice of words forms images, those images are built on various types of figures of speech and result in the poem's tone. Thus, as a reader, you can move from (1) comprehending individual words to (2) images to (3) the devices that create the images to (4) the poem's tone. Your understanding then starts with the specific—the words—and moves beyond the literal to the abstract—the figures of speech. Understanding the figures of speech, particularly metaphor, simile, and personification, allows you to grasp the poem's tone. As a result, you understand the poem emotionally and intellectually.

But there are still two more steps to take—understanding the sounds and the themes. *Prosody*—the study of sound and rhythm—is the subject of the next lesson; theme is a matter you have probably been mulling over as you read, for it is what the figures of speech and tone add up to—what you interpret as the poet's major assertion about the subject of the poem. In Shakespeare's "Shall I Compare Thee to a Summer's Day?" for instance, you can tell that the sonnet is a love poem and that Shakespeare is saying that his love will be made immortal through the power of his poetic words.

Many of the poems you have read have themes that are not so readily graspable. If you are having difficulty arriving at a theme for a poem, try starting first with the subject. "Oranges" deals with a boy's first date; "My Papa's Waltz" with the relationship between father and son; "Conjoined" with marriage; and so on. Once you have grasped the subject, then ask yourself what the poet is saying about that subject. Then you will be on the way to theme.

VIEWING GUIDE

An important component of this lesson is the video. You will learn more effectively from it by thinking about the following questions and guidelines.

Before Viewing:

1. Review "Figures of Speech or Metaphorical Language: A Source of Depth and Range in Poetry," pages 760–768, and "Tone: The Creation of Attitude in Poetry," pages 800–808 in the text, paying particular attention to the following terms:

   Major terms:

   Metaphor
   Personification
   Simile
   Tone

   Minor terms:

   Anaphora
   Apostrophe
   Irony
   Metonymy
   Overstatement
   Paradox
   Pun
   Synecdoche
   Synesthesia
   Understatement

2. Review the poems assigned, paying particular attention to the ones your instructor emphasizes. Try to hear each poem's sound as you focus on the images and tone.

During Your Viewing:

1. Look for the visual representations of figures of speech, particularly metaphor and tone.
2. Listen for definitions of figures of speech.
3. Listen for the reasons that poets use figures of speech.
4. Listen for what the critics on the video say about the role of the reader in interpreting figures of speech.
5. Listen for what the critics on the video say about the use of metaphor.
6. Summarize what Gary Soto says about metaphor and tone.

After Viewing:

Give some thought to the following questions. You may want to write short answers in your journal or notebook.

1. In the poems covered in the video, what metaphors do you find the most effective and why?
2. What differences in tone do you find among the war poems?
3. How does Gary Soto's life figure in his poetry?
4. How would you describe the tone of Soto's two poems?
5. To what extent does Soto's opinion of metaphor differ or agree with those of the critics?

WRITING ACTIVITIES

After your study of this lesson, you should be able to analyze a poem's figures of speech and tone. Your instructor will advise you which, if any, of the following writing activities you are to complete.

Formal Writing:

The first two activities are the easiest because the textbook provides models for you to follow. And both take the information you have read and seen and ask you to apply it to a poem you are familiar with so that you can work out for yourself how metaphor or tone functions.

176—*Literary Visions*

The third activity is slightly more difficult but only because no model is provided. Like the first two, it uses information you have read and seen and asks you to apply it to a poem you already have some knowledge of. Writing about it, however, will make you know the poem all the better.

The fourth suggestion is the most challenging. You will need to look at each metaphor in the poem individually and as part of a pattern, figuring out the qualities the metaphors share. Though the hardest, this activity offers the most reward in that you will be working with what is implied, not just what is said. That calls for a higher order of thinking and, therefore, is more intellectually engaging.

1. Choose one of the poems that deals with what it means to be a woman and, using the example on pages 795–798 in the textbook as well as what the host and critics in the video have to say, write an analysis of the poem's metaphors.
2. Choose one of the poems that deals with war and, using the example on pages 835–838 in the textbook as well as what the host and critics in the video have to say, write an analysis of the poem's tone.
3. Reread Gary Soto's "Oranges" and review the interview with him on the video as well as the host's comments. Then write an essay explaining the poem's central metaphor and what it contributes to the theme of the poem.
4. As you know, metaphors can be both explicit and implied. Reread "The Secretary Chant" and write a paper that examines the poem's explicit metaphors and the central metaphor (the one that runs through the whole poem) they imply. Consider the relationship between the implied metaphor and your interpretation of the poem's theme.

Informal Writing:

The point of the first activity is to tune your ear for figures of speech by making you more aware of how frequently they occur in non-literary contexts. The activity calls for identification only, but in determining what are and what are not figures of speech, you will come to a greater understanding of them. The second suggestion for writing requires that you use first your imagination and then your analytical and critical skills. By creating metaphors and similes, you will be exercising your skills and imagination in much the same way as poets. And by analyzing what is good about what you have created, you will be practicing your critical faculties.

1. Arm yourself with a note pad and pen or pencil so that as the day progresses you can write down examples of figures of speech that you hear and see. Use the list in the Viewing Guide, page 174, and listen for these rhetorical devices in conversation and on television and radio. Also, look for them as

you pass billboards or bumper stickers or as you leaf through a magazine or newspaper. Advertisements are likely places, too. The only category of writing that is off limits for your search is literature. Try to find at least one example for each figure of speech covered in this lesson.
2. If you would prefer, choose a word that holds particular meaning for you and work out several metaphors and similes that are appropriate. While no rules apply about what word to choose, you'll find it easier to come up with metaphors and similes if the word is real to you. It might be a person's name or something as impersonal yet distinct as the rain outside your window. After you have a few examples, select the one you find to be the best and write a paragraph explaining why you find it most appropriate.

SELF-TEST

Match the items in column A with the definitions or identifications in B:

A	B
1. Metaphor	a. The living word
2. Synesthesia	b. "My Last Duchess"
3. Synecdoche	c. Implied metaphor
4. Apostrophe	d. Equation of two seemingly dissimilar things
5. Personification	e. "They look like rosebuds filled with snow"
6. Simile	f. "Writers do it with sytle"
7. Metonymy	g. Whole subsituted for part
8. Conceit	h. Meiosis
9. Pun	i. Mixing of two senses
10. Situationoal irony	j. Paradox
	k. O Muse
	l. Extended metaphor
	m. "Altar, sword, and pen"

Answer the following multiple-choice items:

1. Figures of speech are
   a. mere ornament.
   b. unrelated to meaning.
   c. characteristic of poetry.
   d. rarely found in everyday speech.
2. A poem's tone is the end result of
   a. theme.
   b. setting.
   c. persona.
   d. diction.
3. You can identify an explicit metaphor by its
   a. imagery.
   b. vividness.
   c. use of "is."
   d. use of "like."
4. "Two hundred head of cattle" is an example of
   a. metaphor.
   b. metonymy.
   c. synecdoche.
   d. paradox.
5. "Champagne laughter" is an example of
   a. simile.
   b. apostrophe.
   c. personification.
   d. synesthesia.

In 100–250 words, answer the following short essay questions:

1. Reread Sylvia Plath's "Metaphors," paying particular attention to line 4. Write a paragraph explaining how you interpret the line.
2. Look up *conjoined* in your dictionary and working with the definition of the word and Judith Minty's central metaphor in her poem of the same name, write a paragraph or two that explains what the author is saying about marriage.
3. Consider the character, setting, and title of "My Papa's Waltz" and write a paragraph or two on what you find to be the poem's tone.

ADDITIONAL READING ACTIVITIES

If you enjoyed reading the poems and listening to the interview in this lesson, you may want to read more from the following selections.

Soto, Gary. *Black Hair.* (Poems)
_____. *Small Faces.* (Poems)
_____. *Living Up the Street.* (Essays on growing up in a Chicano world)

LESSON 15

An Echo to the Sense:
PROSODY AND FORM IN POETRY

ABOUT THE LESSON

Anyone who has ever seen or heard a poem knows that its language sounds different from that in a short story, and anyone who has ever listened to the lyrics of a song knows that rhyme can be an important element of that difference.

Rhyme turns up in all sorts of guises—in jump rope chants, children's games, rap music, graffiti, greeting cards, tombstones, slang, limericks, and, of course, serious poetry as well as verse we learned in childhood. In American culture, we are all aware of poems that begin "Ring around the rosie," or "Roses are red / Violets are blue," or "There once was a lady from . . . ."

But not all poems rhyme. Some are written in free verse and others in the form that Shakespeare made famous in his plays, *blank verse*—also known as unrhymed iambic pentameter. There's something about the words blank verse that make the term seem far more understandable than the more foreign-sounding *unrhymed iambic pentameter*. But there's a way to remember the various names for the patterns of unstressed and stressed syllables that make up a poem's meter, and that's what this lesson will explain.

Why bother learning all about rhyme and meter? Imagine you have developed a peculiar pain in your side and have set up an appointment with your doctor to have it looked at. But also imagine that you do not know the word for pain nor any of the adjectives that might go with it. Is it constant? Burning? Dull? Sharp? You would be at a loss to explain.

Without the vocabulary that accompanies prosody—the study of poetic sounds, rhythm, and meter—you would be equally at a loss to analyze a poem. In large part, the effect of a poem depends upon the poet's use of the sounds of language, for those sounds complement, reinforce, and emphasize the poem's meaning.

To follow the sound of a poem, read it aloud so that you are using your eyes not just to see but also to hear, listening to the sound of words as you read them. Read as you would normally, though perhaps more slowly, pronouncing the words in a natural way. Syllables are what matter in prosody, but only the syllables that are pronounced. For instance, when you say "I learned a lot," you pronounce *learned* as one syllable, not two, because you slide the *learn* into the d. You would never say "I learn-ed a lot." The study of prosody is one of those happy times when spelling takes a back seat to how words sound.

Sound is as important to poetry as water to a garden. Sure, a poem has to have an idea just as a garden cannot grow without seeds, but without sound and rhythm there is no poetry. It also follows that just as not all poetry rhymes, not all that rhymes is poetry. Back in Lesson 11 we drew a distinction between verse and a poem, and that distinction rises again here.

GOAL

This lesson will help you to hear and recognize how sound, rhythm, and form contribute to poetry.

WHAT YOU WILL LEARN

When you complete this lesson, you will be able to:

1. Describe what creates rhythm in language and in a poem.
2. Give examples of the sounds, rhythms, and standard poetic feet found in poetry.
3. Discuss the purpose of sounds and rhythm in a poem.
4. Demonstrate how to scan a poem for rhythm.
5. Identify the different types of rhyme.
6. Annotate a poem's rhyme scheme.
7. Describe common stanza forms and other characteristic forms of poetry.
8. Identify a poem's form and explain how the form supports its content.
9. Discuss how the musicality of a poem affects the reader's response.

LESSON ASSIGNMENT

Working through the following nine steps will help you master the objectives and achieve the goal for this lesson:

Step 1: In your text, read the chapters "Prosody: Sound, Rhythm, and Rhyme in Poetry," pages 841–856, and "Form: The Shape of the Poem," pages 897–915. The text will provide background for what you will read in the study guide, explain the key terms, and give you some information about the poems you will be reading.

182—*Literary Visions*

Step 2: Read the specific poems your instructor assigns. The following poems will be the focus of this lesson, and those marked with an asterisk (*) will be discussed in the video.

- "We Real Cool," Gwendolyn Brooks, page 857.
- "Macacity: The Mystery Cat," T.S. Eliot, pages 861–862.
- "At a Summer Hotel," Isabella Gardner, page 863.
- "The Bells," Edgar Allan Poe, pages 870–873.*
- "Miniver Cheevy," Edwin Arlington Robinson, pages 876–877.
- "Sonnet 73," William Shakespeare, page 878.*
- "March for a One-Man Band," David Wagoner, page 882.*
- "The Eagle," Alfred Lord Tennyson, page 899.
- "Ballad of Birmingham," Dudley Randall, pages 927.*
- "Do Not Go Gentle Into That Good Night," Dylan Thomas, page 930.
- "Old Men Pitching Horseshoes," X.J. Kennedy, page 965.
- "I Heard a Fly Buzz—When I Died," Emily Dickinson, page 1033.*
- "Pied Beauty," Gerard Manley Hopkins, pages 1139-1140.*

Step 3: Read the OVERVIEW in this study guide lesson.

Step 4: Watch the VIDEO, following the steps in the VIEWING GUIDE in this study guide lesson.

Step 5: Reread the OVERVIEW to reinforce what you have learned in the text and the video and to help you complete the writing assignments.

Step 6: Complete any WRITING ACTIVITIES assigned in this lesson.

Step 7: Do the SELF-TEST exercises in this study guide lesson.

Step 8: Read any of the ADDITIONAL READING ACTIVITIES assigned.

Step 9: Go back to the learning objectives in the WHAT YOU WILL LEARN section of this study guide lesson and be sure you can respond to each of them.

OVERVIEW

Your study of diction, imagery, tone, and metaphorical language showed you what these elements contribute to a poem's economy of expression, vividness of imagery, and power of emotion. The other distinctive feature of poetry is the use of sound, and that is the subject of this lesson. To make the complex subject of sound in poetry easier to comprehend, this lesson breaks up sound into its components. Keep in mind, however, that all these components are closely interwoven.

What's involved in the sound of a poem? We'll start with the obvious—*rhyme*. Everyone is used to the "June/moon" variety, but we will be looking at another kind as well, *slant rhyme*. Slant rhymes are inexact but close; they are words that almost rhyme, such as "June/lone."

Next comes a section that will examine various devices that make up part of a poem's sound effects: repeated vowel and consonant sounds, forced pauses, words that are pronounced in such a way that they suggest their meaning. We will also take a look at the overall emotional effect these sounds have on the reader.

What binds sound devices and rhyme together is *meter*, the pattern of stresses distributed over pronounced syllables. Meter gives a poem its distinctive gait, its musical interplay of strong and weak stresses.

Finally, we'll take a look at some standard poetic forms. Some of these you have met before. The poems by Shakespeare that you read in Lessons 13 and 14 were sonnets. In these forms and others, we'll be exploring how form and content interrelate to convey meaning.

Analyzing the prosody of a poem can be not only interesting but revealing. Sometimes a pattern of repeated sound or a variation in the meter or the pattern of the rhyme can give you insight into the meaning of a poem in a way that thinking about its content never can. After all, the sound, rhythm, rhyme, and form of a poem are what give it its music as well as its meaning.

Rhyme

Rhyme is the most easily identifiable sound element in poetry, and it usually occurs at the end of a line, though some poems also have *internal rhyme*. Isabella Gardner's "At a Summer Hotel," page 863, for instance, rhymes "gold" with "bold" as an internal rhyme in line 3: "My girl is gold in the sun and bold in the dazzling water." The result is emphasis and a linking together of ideas.

The rest of the rhyme in Gardner's poem, however, is *exact*. But that's not true of all rhyming poems. You also need to be on the lookout for *slant rhyme*, which you may have come across by a different name—slide, near, half, or off rhyme—rhyme that is close but not exact.

Exact rhyme not only gives the poem a musical quality, it can link ideas, emphasize them, and give a sense of completeness. Yet exact rhyme is not as obvious as it may look. Some of its uses turn out to be subtle, as you will see. Let's take another look at Isabella Gardner's "At a Summer Hotel" to see how exact rhyme works in both obvious and subtle ways.

We start, however, with an obvious rhyme scheme. The poem is written in such a way that every two lines rhyme. If you were working out the rhyme scheme, marking the last word in the first line as "a," noting the last word in line 2 as "a" as well because it rhymes with line 1, you would reveal a rhyme scheme of aa, bb, cc.

But now the subtleties start. Because line 1 runs into 2, and lines 4 and 5 into 6, the rhyme is muted. This technique, as you may remember from "My Last Duchess" in Lesson 12, is called *enjambment* or a *run-on line*. Lines 2 and 3, on the other hand, are *end-stopped*. The effect of enjambment is to undermine the obviousness of exact rhyme. The same sort of undercutting exists in the content of the poem. Here we have what appears to be a calm scene and a beautiful young girl, but somewhat overshadowing that calmness and beauty are her mother's uneasy memories of what happened to "Europa Persephone Miranda." The obvious is not always obvious.

Then there's the matter of where the stress falls on a syllable in a rhyme. If it falls on the last syllable, it is called *heavy-stress rhyme, accented*, or *rising rhyme*. Gardner's first and second lines are good examples of rising rhyme: "child" and "wild." The rising rhyme emphasizes the words. But listen to the next two sets of rhymes: "water" and "daughter"; "veranda" and "Miranda." These are examples of *unstressed* or *family rhyme*. The effect of falling rhyme is weak. A type of rhyme often used in humorous verse, falling rhyme in "At a Summer Hotel" has the effect of blunting the bleak images raised by "Europa Persephone Miranda."

Slant rhyme—the other important kind of rhyme—turns up more frequently than it may seem, in part because we tend to not notice it. It's easy, for example, to read Emily Dickinson's "I Heard a Fly Buzz," page 1033, and not hear the slant rhyme in "room" and "storm" and "firm" and "room." Yet imagine what the poem would sound like if it were written with the same rhyme scheme as "At a Summer Hotel." That would be too clear-cut, too tidy. As is, the rhyme scheme for the Dickinson poem is as unpredictable and seemingly random as death itself, the subject of the poem.

As with exact rhyme, slant rhyme can also be run-on (enjambed) or end-stopped, rising or falling. And as you would think, if falling slant rhyme is combined with enjambed lines, the rhyme itself is even less noticeable.

Individual Sound Devices

We use our language so much and for so many purposes that we often let the meaning of a word overwhelm its sound. For instance, a famous writer once said that the most beautiful word in the English language is *syphilis*. Yet our associations with the word are so strong that we fail to hear anything remotely pleasant about it.

Often, however, poets will select a word that coordinates meaning with sound. Words like "buzz," "mumble," "mutter," "hiccup" have sounds that imitate what the word represents. The use of such words is called *onomatopoeia*. You can hear this device at work in David Wagoner's "March for a One-Man Band," page 882, when he describes the sounds made by the musician. We're used to drums that go "boom," but Wagoner also gives us the "tweedledy" of a flute, "honk" of a cornet, "tweet" of a whistle ("whistle" itself being onomatopoeic), and the "crash" of a cymbal. We also hear the musician "click" his heels and "wheeze."

Less obvious but just as effective is Isabella Gardner's use of onomatopoeia in "At a Summer Hotel." Listen to the narrator of the poem describe her daughter: "She drowses on the blond sand and in the daisy fields my daughter / dreams." The sound of the word "drowse" imitates what the word represents, that sleepy, nodding stage just before sleep.

But take another look at that line of Isabella Gardner and you'll see another sound device at work—*alliteration*. Alliteration is a term that refers to repeated initial sounds. With the sentence above from the Gardner poem, notice how the poet picks up the "d" sounds from "drowses" in "daisy" and "dreams."

The term alliteration is also used for repeated consonant sounds, no matter where they occur in a word. Go back to that same sentence and listen to all the "s" sounds; the "s's" of "drowses" are repeated in "daisy," and "fields." Notice that the "sh" of "she" and the "s" of "sand" are not included. That's because the "sh" sound in "she" and "s" in "sand" are different from drowses' "s" sound, which is closer to a "z." Sound—not spelling—is what counts.

If the sound repeated is one of vowels, the device is called *assonance*. Let's take the first two lines from "At a Summer Hotel":

> I am here with my bountiful womanful child
> to be soothed by the sea not roused by these roses roving wild.

At first glance, you recognize two familiar devices: first, alliteration in the "s's" of "soothed," "sea," and the last "s" sound in "roses"; then, the "z" sound of the "s's" in "roused" and "roses" (the first one); and the "r's" of "roused," "roses," and "roving"; finally, the exact rhyme of "child/wild." But if you listen carefully you can also hear another similarity—the sound "iful" in "bountiful" and "womanful." Notice that we pronounce the "a" in "woman" as if it were a short "i," as though we were saying "womin." Again, it is sound, not spelling, that counts.

In standard speech, our syllables cluster in groups, in part for emphasis, but also in part because of the nature of the English language and our need to breathe. Your text calls these clusters of syllables *cadence groups*—a term that is probably unfamiliar to you. Yet your ear is so accustomed to cadence groups in American English that when you hear another language spoken, it sounds as though it is being spoken very fast. Most of the time, however, what we perceive as fast speech is simply a difference not of speed but of cadence groups. Different languages group syllables differently.

The cadence—the rhythm of language—is also tied to the pause, another aspect of sound. In poetry, we are forced to pause by the placement of punctuation. Commas—as you would suspect—force a shorter pause than periods, and semicolons and colons are in between. The pause itself is called a *caesura*, and it plays an important part in the rhythm of a poem. Taken from the Latin word meaning "to cut," a caesura makes the reader hesitate for a beat, cutting the rhythm of a line.

To illustrate, reread "At a Summer Hotel." You'll remember that you worked out the rhyme scheme as aa, bb, cc—all exact rhyme. Yet the rhyme is not emphasized because you are not forced to pause at the end of each line. Only three of the six lines are end-stopped by caesurae (the plural of caesura). Compare this effect achieved by enjambment with what you find in "Macavity: The Mystery Cat," pages 861–862, where a caesura occurs at the end of each line, emphasizing the rhyme.

If "Macavity" uses the caesura heavily, Gardner goes to the other extreme in her last line, omitting commas where we would expect them to separate the three names, "Europa Persephone Miranda." Yet by omitting the comma, Gardner implies that the three figures are almost one, representing innocence about to be violated. By omitting the commas, the poet not only implies that the three have one identity but also an identification between them and the daughter. The image the poet portrays of the daughter is also one of innocence and beauty.

When you read a poem, you will find that the punctuation not only guides you through its sense but contributes to its rhythm. If you reread David Wagoner's "March for a One-Man Band," you'll notice that the only pause comes at the end of the poem in the form of a period. And when you consider that the poem describes a one-man band playing "the Irrational Anthem"—complete with sound effects—it makes sense for the poem to romp along in a breathless way.

"One-Man Band" is also a fine example of *cacophony*, a word that in ancient Greek meant harsh-sounding and comes from the two words meaning *bad* and *voice*. What with the poem's booms, blats, toots, honks, thumps, crashes, rimshots, clicks, and wheezes, the result is a jumble of sound that grates upon the ear.

The opposite of this effect is *euphony*, stemming from the two Greek words for *sweet* and *voice*. The combined effect of the sounds in "At a Summer Hotel" is euphony. And that effect fits the action, a proud but somewhat apprehensive mother watching her beautiful daughter—half child, half woman—laze about the beach.

Onomatopoeia, alliteration, and assonance combine with rhyme to create the musical quality of a poem in somewhat the same way that repeated notes make up the melodic line in music. And just as notes in music are accompanied by a beat, caesurae, enjambed or end-stopped lines, and variation in the strength of the stresses on pronounced syllables all work together to set the rhythm of a poem.

Meter

You are probably used to the word *scan* as used in two contexts: to examine carefully, as in "To figure out how to get home, I scanned the map carefully"; and in American English just the opposite meaning, to glance at quickly, as in "I overslept, rushed through breakfast, and just scanned the morning paper." In the study of poetry, *scan* used a third way, meaning to work out the rhythm of a poem by analyzing its beat. To do that, you need to examine the syllables in each line, listening for strong and weak stresses, marking them by using a slash mark (/) for heavy stresses and a short accent mark (˘) for the weak ones. It's not as hard as it may seem, for the stresses are built into our language.

What is *not* a part of everyday language, however, is the vocabulary used to identify the different patterns. You need to know this vocabulary so that you can correctly label the units of strong and weak syllables, units that are called *metrical feet*.

To help you learn this vocabulary, we'll concentrate only on those feet most common to English poetry. There are four standard ones and two that turn up as variations:

STANDARD FEET				
Name	Number of Syllables	Sound	Mark	Example
Iamb	two	weak, strong	˘ /	MaRIE
Trochee	two	strong, weak	/ ˘	RICHard
Anapest	three	weak, weak, strong	˘ ˘ /	MaryLOU
Dactly	three	strong, weak, weak	/ ˘ ˘	Eleanor

Another way to remember the standard feet is to associate each with names or phrases:

> JoHÁN něs BRÁHMS...is a double iamb
> RICHarěd NÍXŏn..is a double trochee
> Go to HÉLL, MaryLÓU ....is a double anapest
> ÉLeanor RÓOsevelt...is a double dactyl

STANDARD FEET				
Name	Number of Syllables	Sound	Mark	Example
Spondee	two	strong, strong	/ /	George Bush
Pyrrhic	two	weak, weak	˘ ˘	(see below)

Most poems are controlled by one dominant meter, though it's rare to find a poem that is all one meter. Poets vary the primary meter to add emphasis and rhythmic variety. The four standard feet—iambic, trochaic, anapestic, dactylic— are ones that you will hear in the poems you read, although occasionally you will run across a pyrrhic or spondaic foot. For instance, if you were to scan the first line of Robinson's poem, "Miniver Cheevy," pages 876–877, you would mark it like this:

> Mín ĭvěr Chéevy, chíld ŏf scórn

Starting at the beginning of the line, you can see that the first foot could be a dactyl. If that were so, you would scan the rest of the line as two trochees and an extra strongly stressed syllable, "scorn." While it's not impossible to end a line

188—*Literary Visions*

with a leftover strong syllable, it's unusual, so try breaking out the feet another way. If you start with a trochee, you would read the rest of the line as three iambs. That seems to work. In fact, it's often safe to assume that the number of stresses in a line is equal to the number of feet. here, you have one trochee and three iambs. To mark off the feet, use a single straight line (|) between them. The line would then look like this:

Mǐní | vĕr Chee | vy, chíld | ǒf scorn

To check your reading of the meter—your *scansion*—got to the next line and try iambic meter, again noting the breaks between feet:

Grĕw léan | whǐle hĕ | ăssaíled thĕ séa | sŏns

    The result is four iambic feet and a leftover weakly stressed syllable. Unlike strong stresses, it's not unusual to have a line end with a surplus weak syllable. So far, then, the meter looks as though it's going to be iambic. Try line three: four iambs. Line four? A surprise—two iambs and a surplus weak stress. The pattern of strong stresses that emerges is 4, 4, 4, 2.

    At this point, you have to dig into some more vocabulary, but again only the terms that are most common. The names for the number of feet in a line come from the Greek, not the more familiar Latin, which is why they sometimes seem confusing.

Number of Feet	Prefix	Example	Metrical Term
two	di-	dioxide	dimeter
three	tri-	tripod	trimeter
four	tetra-	tetracycline	tetrameter
five	penta-	pentagon	pentameter

    Back to "Miniver Cheevy." You can now say that the predominant meter in the first stanza is three lines of iambic tetrameter followed by a fourth of iambic dimeter. And from your study of rhyme, you can go a step further and point out that lines 1 and 2 are rising rhymes, while 3 and 4 are falling ones.

    As for the effect of the rhyme and meter, listen to the poem again. You'll hear that the iamb sounds natural, the rising rhyme emphasizes words, and the falling rhyme sets a mildly ironic tone. Then there's the matter of surprise. The first three lines prepare you for tetrameter but instead the line is truncated into dimeter. The effect is somewhat ironic, as is the poem as a whole.

    Because of its specialized vocabulary and its dependence upon sound, meter is often the most difficult aspect of poetry. Although you will not need to figure out the meter of every poem you read, you will need to be able to scan a poem

An Echo to the Sense—189

and for a full analysis, you will need to relate meter to meaning. For those reasons, you may find the following summary and list of *general* rules helpful:

1. The most common feet are iambic, trochaic, anapestic, dactylic.
2. The most common number of feet are pentameter and tetrameter.
3. The number of strong stresses *usually* equals the number of feet (watch out for the occasional pyrrhic or spondaic foot).
4. There are varying degrees of strong and weak stresses, so try first to sort out the obvious extremes.
5. It's more common to end with a surplus weak stress than a strong one.
6. Watch for obvious differences in line length—they usually indicate differences in meter—and see if they form a pattern.
7. Figure out a working ideas of the meter by scanning five or so lines chosen at random.
8. When in doubt, try iambic.

If you stat looking at meter in poems that immediately appeal to your ear, you'll find the terms and the sounds easier to deal with. But no matter what poem you read, these seven statements will be useful guides as you practice your scansion. Remember, though, they are not hard and fast rules. At the same time, they will see you through most of the poetry you read.

Common Poetic Forms

Way back in Lesson 11, you heard the terms *open form* or *free verse* and *closed form*. Poems written in free verse do not adhere to a set meter; those that are written in closed forms not only have a distinct meter but often also follow a traditional form that sets up a certain rhyme scheme. In this section, we'll take a closer look at these two types of poetry and their effects. Although we won't be going into much detail for the closed forms, we will examine two of the more common ones—the ballad and the sonnet—and point out some of the interesting features of two others—the haiku and the villanelle.

"Ballad of Birmingham," page 927, is a contemporary version of the same form, and in it you'll see not only that same xaxa rhyme scheme (the "x" means that the first and third lines do not have a consistent rhyme scheme) but also that the meter varies between lines of iambic tetrameter and iambic trimeter. That meter, the rhyme scheme, the four-line stanzas or *quatrains*, and the focus on a dramatic event define the classic ballad form—one of the oldest forms of poetry. Its meter and rhyme reveal why it is often sung to music.

At least as well known a form is the sonnet, probably because of Shakespeare's artistry. To him we owe the English sonnet, which takes the traditional 14 line, iambic pentameter form and sets it out as three quatrains and a concluding couplet.

In Sonnet 73, page 878, for example, Shakespeare gives us a separate image in each of the quatrains, and each has its own rhyme scheme: abab; cdcd; efef. Each of the images is a metaphor. The narrator first pictures himself to his lover as autumn, then as twilight, and then as a dying fire. The images lead up to a capping couplet (gg), summing up the images of approaching death with the word "this" and the thought that his aging makes love all the stronger, for his life will not last.

The Shakespearean or English sonnet is a variation on the Italian sonnet. The difference lies in the rhyme scheme and presentation of ideas. Instead of consisting of three quatrains and a concluding couplet, the Italian sonnet is broken into 8 lines, the octave that rhymes abba, abba, and 6 lines, the sestet that usually rhymes cde, cde. The content follows the form, with the first part usually presenting an idea, problem, or question and the second part commenting or answering.

The appeal of forms such as the sonnet and the ballad to the reader or listener is self-evident—they combine form and content in such a way that the one reinforces the other to the point where they cannot be separated. But what is the appeal to the poet? The video interview with X. J. Kennedy addresses this question directly, but let's also take a look at how very strict forms can be followed so artfully that the reader barely notices that the form exists.

Another equally tight form is the villanelle, a pattern we borrowed from the French. The rhymes in the form make it particularly challenging, for the degree of repetition is hard to disguise. Let's see how a poet works it out.

Reread Dylan Thomas's "Do Not Go Gentle Into That Good Night," page 930, a poem you read for Lesson 11. By now, you know the poem's general content—a son's plea to his father who is approaching death. The two lines that are repeated are addressed directly to the father: "Do not go gentle into that good night" and "Rage, rage against the dying of the light."

These two lines frame the first stanza and come together as a couplet in the last. If you trace those lines, you'll find that the first one is introduced in line 1 and then reappears as lines 6, 12, and 18. The second occurs first in line 3 and then surfaces again as lines 9, 15, and 19. In short, those two lines serve as 8 of the poem's total of 19 lines. That would appear to be a lot of repetition but it isn't. Thomas manages to give the lines different meanings; they appear as statements, pleas, commands, and petitions.

Now look closely at the rhyme scheme. You'll see it is built on only two rhymes—"night" and "day"—and forms the pattern aba, aba, aba, aba, aba, and abaa. You have five stanzas of three lines each, also called tercets, and a concluding sixth stanza of four lines, a quatrain. Again, however, the reader doesn't get a sense of repetition, in part because the imagery is so striking that it blunts the rhyme and in part because of enjambment, which you will recall as the carrying over of a line.

Finally there's the matter of meter. Although predominantly iambic pentameter, the meter has a great deal of variation, variation provided by the spondee of "Do not" and "Rage, rage." There are others as well, but the point is made.

If the closed form can be worked with so well that its limitations aren't evident, so too free verse can be so free that it may not appear to be poetry at all. On first listening, for example, Leonard Adame's "My Grandmother Would Rock Quietly and Hum," read in the video component of this lesson, may sound more prose than poetry, but listen more carefully. You will not find a predominant meter but you will find cadence. And where the closed form is built upon the unit of the metrical foot, free verse is built upon the stanza.

You'll see, for example, that each stanza in the poem stands on its own, presenting an image or picture of the narrator's grandmother. The lines within each stanza are composed of clusters of syllables that have cadence. Listen carefully and you'll hear it. And listen to the last three lines, each of which ends with a weak stress, fading as is the grandmother.

Summary

As you have seen, the initial distinction to make about prosody is whether the poem is a closed form or a free one. Unliked closed verse forms, free verse lacks both rhyme and a dominant meter. Instead of being based on the metrical foot, free verse is based upon the stanza. Two common stanza forms are the quatrain (four lines) and the tercet (three lines), and they are found in both free and closed forms. In this lesson, you studied two of the more popular closed forms, the sonnet and the ballad.

Next, you need to analyze the poem's use of sounds. Grouping the various components of sound devices into categories makes them easier to understand and fix in your mind. For rhyme, you only need to remember exact and slant rhyme and that both can occur inside a line or at the end.

As for most of the sounds associated with parts of words and individual words, they are covered by the terms alliteration, assonance, and onomatopoeia. Those sounds can create the harshness of cacophony or the smoothness of euphony.

Rhyme and sound devices contribute to the musicality of a closed form poem and also make up parts of its basic unit of rhythm, the metrical foot. The rhythm of a line is driven by the metrical foot's pattern of weak and strong stresses and by forced pauses or caesurae.

A poem's meter is identified by the number and type of metrical feet that form the dominant sound pattern of its lines. The most frequently occurring foot in English is the iamb; the other common feet are the trochaic, anapestic, and dactylic. However, you will find the pyrrhic and spondaic foot used as variations. As for the number of feet, the most frequently occurring ones are pentameter (5) and tetrameter (4), although trimeter (3) and dimeter (2) are also commonly used.

As the poems you have read illustrate, all these sounds are integrally related to meaning. Listen to Poe's "The Bells," pages 870–873, and you will hear how sound supports tone—silver bells "tinkle," alarm bells "shriek," iron bells "toll."

Meter, rhyme, and similar sounding units of words can be used to emphasize, to link ideas, to surprise, to soothe, to excite.

The mechanics of scansion are time-consuming, and if you use your head more than your ears, they can be frustrating. But if you start with poems that have a fairly regular form, you can work your way into those that are more metrically challenging. And if you keep relating form to content, you'll steer clear of two dangers: one is allowing the mechanics to overshadow meaning; the other is separating form from content.

VIEWING GUIDE

An important component of this lesson is the video. You will learn more effectively from it by thinking about the following questions and guidelines.

Before Viewing:

1. Review the chapters "Prosody: Sound, Rhythm, and Rhyme in Poetry," pages 841–856, and "Form: The Shape of the Poem," pages 897–915, paying particular attention to the following terms and their application:

Alliteration	Metrical
Assonance	Number of feet
Cacophony	dimeter
Caesura	pentameter
Euphony	tetrameter
Feet	trimeter
anapest	Onomatopoeia
dactyl	Rhyme
iamb	exact
pyrrhic	slant
spondee	
trochee	

2. Review the poems assigned, paying particular attention to the ones your instructor emphasizes. Try to hear each poem's sound.

During Your Viewing:

1. Listen for examples of rhythm.
2. Listen for examples of onomatopoeia in "March for a One-Man Band."

3. Listen to the stresses in the examples of meter and try to hear how the sound supports the meaning.
4. Summarize what Benjamin DeMott has to say about varying the meter in the poem by Shakespeare.
5. Summarize what William Vesterman has to say about free verse.
6. State why traditional meter and rhyme appeal to X. J. Kennedy.

After Viewing:

Give some thought to the following questions. You may want to write short answers in your journal or notebook.

1. What creates rhythm in a poem?
2. What draws some poets to rhyme?
3. What do devices such as alliteration and onomatopoeia contribute to the sound of a poem?
4. What views do Kennedy and the critics hold in common?
5. Which poem *sounded* best to you and why?

WRITING ACTIVITIES

After your study of this lesson, you should be able to analyze a poem's sound, rhythm, meter, and form. Your instructor will advise you which, if any, of the following writing activities you are to complete.

Formal Writing:

The first two activities walk you through the mechanics of figuring out sound patterns and rhyme and meter. Your text describes how to number lines, mark the meter and the like on pages 882–896, but note that the description is for a full analysis of both sound devices and meter. Obviously, if you are working on Activity 1 below, you can ignore the directions about meter. If, however, you do choose to work on meter, you'll see that the marking system in your text differs from the one described in the study guide. The one here is slightly simpler and therefore easier to use. Both activities call for you to relate form to meaning, but neither asks for an extended discussion.

If you have found that working with sound and meter comes easily to you, you'll find Activity 3 more rewarding than 1 or 2 because it assumes you have worked through the sound, rhyme, and meter, and builds on that knowledge to

Literary Visions

lore the relationship between form and content. Activity 4 will reveal one reader's interpretation of a poem's meter.

1. Choose any poem you wish that you think would work well and, using either the samples in your text on pages 851–852 or the marking system in this study guide, work out the pattern of either alliteration or assonance. Write a paragraph to accompany your analysis in which you state your conclusions about the effects of the poet's use of the sound device.
2. Pick a poem that is an example of closed form and, using the samples in your text on pages 853–856, work out its meter and rhyme scheme. Write a paragraph to accompany your analysis in which you state your conclusions about the effects of the poet's use of rhyme and meter.
3. Choose one of the sonnets by Shakespeare, or one of the ones in chapter 20 by Milton, Shelley, or McKay and write an essay in which you analyze the relationship between its form, including sound and meter, and meaning. To do that, first work out your interpretation of the poem and then its form. Your essay will examine how the form of the poem—including sound, rhyme, and meter—supports what you find to be its theme.
4. Select one of the poems read on the video and using a clean copy of the poem and a pencil, mark the syllables stressed by the reader. What conclusions do you reach about the poem's meter? About variations?

Informal Writing:

Both of the activities call for practice in prosody and in analysis, and both take you though the creative process of writing a poem. The first deals with a short closed form that you must first analyze and then illustrate. Writing a poem to fit the form will give you a sense of the creative process that Kennedy describes in that you will find the words and the sounds lead you to ideas. The second activity is both simpler and more difficult. It's simpler because you do not have to make up the content; it's harder because to turn prose into poetry, you have to come to terms with the subtleties of free verse.

1. Your text gives you two examples of a humorous form known as the double dactyl (page 904). Read the examples of the form carefully so that you can deduce what it is. In your notebook or journal, write down the "rules" for a double dactyl and make up an example of your own.
2. If you would prefer to explore an open form, you can go on a hunt for "found poetry," prose written by someone else that you can turn into free verse. Knowing the look of a stanza of free verse gives you a good idea of how a stanza functions, so look around for a chunk of prose that sets out ideas or images or statements. The newspaper is a good source, particularly reports of speeches, classified ads, even obituaries. You want a chunk probably not

more than 50 words but no less than 15. After you have found a suitable piece, cut it out or copy it (noting your source), rewrite it as free verse, and then write a paragraph explaining why you made the line and stanza breaks where you did. Your completed activity will consist of three parts: the original prose version, your free verse version, and your analysis.

SELF-TEST

Match the items in column A with the definitions or identifications in B:

A

1. Sonnet
2. Iambic
3. Pentameter
4. Alliteration
5. Onomatopoeia
6. Pyrrhic foot
7. Ballad
8. Rhyme scheme
9. Cacophony
10. Slant rhyme

B

a. Strong followed by weak stress
b. Pattern of rhyme
c. Sound of word imitates what word stands for
d. Similar initial sounds
e. Inexact rhyme
f. Similar vowel sounds
g. Two weak stresses
h. Weak followed by strong stress
i. Has 14 lines
j. Harsh sounds
k. Five feet
l. Two strong stresses
m. xaxa rhyme scheme

Answer the following multiple-choice items:

1. The iambic foot is
   a. composed of three syllables.
   b. composed of two weak stresses.
   c. the most unusual in English.
   d. the most common in English.
2. A caesura is a
   a. pause.
   b. stress.
   c. form of punctuation.
   d. traditional form of poetry.

3. Which of the following does NOT affect a poem's sound?
   a. Meter
   b. Rhyme
   c. Assonance
   d. Stanzas

4. Which of the following statements is false?
   a. Poems use natural cadences.
   b. Slant rhyme is inexact.
   c. Assonance can be a form of slant rhyme.
   d. Poems have regular meter.

5. In scanning a closed form poem, which of the following is NOT included?
   a. The predominant meter
   b. The rhyme scheme
   c. All syllables
   d. All weak and strong stresses

In 100–300 words, answer the following short essay questions:

1. Read Tennyson's "The Eagle," page 899, working out the patterns of weak and strong stresses. What do you find to be the meter? What variations do you find? What is the overall effect of the meter? Write an essay that makes a case for your answers to these questions.
2. Analyze the rhythm of Gwendolyn Brooks's "We Real Cool," page 857, relating it to the poem's meaning and title.

ADDITIONAL READING ACTIVITIES

If you enjoyed reading the selections and listening to the interview in this lesson, you may want to read more works by X. J. Kennedy. He is the author of a number of readily available collections:

Kennedy, X. J. *Cross Ties: Selected Poems.*
_____. *The Forgetful Wishing Well: Poems for Young People.* (A collection of 70 poems)
_____. *Brats.* (More poems for young readers and good fun)

LESSON 16

Distant Voices:
MYTH, SYMBOLISM, AND ALLUSION IN POETRY

ABOUT THE LESSON

Back in Lesson 9 you examined the role of symbolism, allegory, and myth in short fiction—so you already have a head start for studying symbolism and myth in poetry. Your study of connotation from Lesson 13 will also help you understand how allusion, symbolism, and myth can function in a poem. Connotation, you may remember, involves a word's emotional and psychological effects, not just its dictionary meaning. Allusion, symbolism, and myth also add layers of meaning.

Poetry's compactness, its characteristic compression, makes its words and phrases carry more than their own weight. When does a word mean more than a word? When it's an allusion. The lesson you just finished included Dudley Randall's poem "Ballad of Birmingham," page 927. If you were British, you might think that the reference to Birmingham placed the poem in England, but the note below the title sets the scene as Alabama in 1963 and adds the detail of the bombing of a church. Those three allusions or references—to Birmingham, 1963, and bombing—immediately connect the poem with the fight for racial equality that took place in the United States in the early sixties, a time of protests, beatings, and even murder.

The poem begins with a narrative between a child and mother, the child asking permission to take part in a freedom march and being told instead to go to the church to sing in the choir. The child goes, the mother thinks she is safe, and then the bomb strikes. The poet sets up this one ironic, mindless act of violence so that it symbolizes all the evils and ironies encountered by the Civil Rights Movement.

The poets you will be reading in this lesson draw upon allusions and symbols—including those drawn from myth—to add more meaning and power to their words. And while any given poem encompasses more meaning through allusion and symbols, the basic meaning is still there. You can be moved by

"Ballad of Birmingham" without knowing much about the Civil Rights Movement, but having that information adds more meaning to the poem.

GOAL

This lesson will help you to understand myth, allusion, and symbolism as used in poetry.

WHAT YOU WILL LEARN

When you complete this lesson you will be able to:

1. Recognize the use of allusion and symbolism in poetry.
2. Distinguish among myths, allusions, and symbolism in poetry.
3. Demonstrate how the same myth can recur through history.
4. Discuss how a poet's use of myth, allusion, and symbols contributes to the effect of a poem.
5. Describe the role of culture in the reader's response to an allusion.

LESSON ASSIGNMENT

Working through the following nine steps will help you master the objectives and achieve the goal for this lesson:

Step 1: In your text, read the chapters "Symbolism and Allusion: Windows to a Wide Expanse of Meaning," pages 940–947, and "Myth: Systems of Symbolic Allusion in Poetry," pages 983–991. The text will provide background for what you will read in the study guide, explain the key terms, and give you some information about the poems you will be reading.

Step 2: Read the specific poems your instructor assigns. The following works will be the focus of this lesson, and those marked with an asterisk will be discussed in the video.

- "Let America be America Again," Langston Hughes, pages 1078–1080.*
- "Buffalo Bill's Defunct," e.e. cummings, page 908.
- "The Second Coming," William Butler Yeats, pages 974–975.*
- "Odysseus," W.S. Merwin, page 992.

- "Penelope," Dorothy Parker, page 993.
- "Musee des Beaux Arts," W.H. Auden, pages 998–999.
- "Icarus," Edward Field, pages 999–1000.*
- "To a Friend Whose Work Has Come to Triumph," Anne Sexton, page 1001.*
- "Landscape with the Fall of Icarus," William Carlos Williams, page 1002.*

Step 3: Read the OVERVIEW in this study guide lesson.

Step 4: Watch the VIDEO, following the steps in the VIEWING GUIDE in this study guide lesson.

Step 5: Reread the OVERVIEW to reinforce what you have learned in the text and the video and to help you complete the Writing Activities.

Step 6: Complete any WRITING ACTIVITIES assigned in this lesson.

Step 7: Do the SELF-TEST exercises in this study guide lesson.

Step 8: Read any of the ADDITIONAL READING ACTIVITIES assigned.

Step 9: Go back to the learning objectives in the WHAT YOU WILL LEARN section of this study guide lesson and be sure you can respond to each of them.

OVERVIEW

This lesson will start with a brief explanation of allusion, using some of the poems you have read previously to explain the meaning and function of the term. We will take a look at several kinds of allusions—historical, religious, and literary.

Then, because you have already studied symbolism, myth, and the connotative value of words, what will follow will be a quick review before we move on to new material. The review will make connections between what you know that is based on general knowledge and what you have learned about symbol and myth.

The three sections following the review will explore how symbolism and myth work together in poetry, first looking at ancient myth, then private myth, and finally cultural myth. As you read these sections, you will see that allusion, symbol, and myth are closely bound in that all are ways in which the poet makes connections between the poem and the reader's experience and knowledge.

Allusion

Listen to any presidential speech or to any Fourth of July orator and you will find the address dotted with references to major historical and political events. All those are *allusions*. John F. Kennedy's inaugural speech refers to the beliefs for which "our forebears fought," just as in the Gettysburg Address, Lincoln's opening reference is to the nation of "our fathers" that was "conceived in liberty and dedicated to the proposition that all men are created equal." With these allusions, both presidents invoked the revolutionary spirit and values on which the United States of America is based. And the allusions therefore added power and emotion to the speeches.

You can see allusion at work to a different end—satire and irony—in e.e. cummings' poem "next to of course god america i," page 665, which you read for Lesson 11. When you read cummings' poem, you were probably struck by the number of bits and pieces of patriotic songs that the poem included: "Land of the pilgrims," "dawn's early," "my / country 'tis of." The allusions are obvious because the songs they refer to are part of our cultural heritage. But think of the problems someone from China would have with the poem.

Another form of allusion that occurs frequently in poetry is the literary allusion. You hit one of these in "Dover Beach," pages 694–695, when Arnold remarks about the "eternal note of sadness" that "Sophocles long ago / Heard ... on the Aegean." The reference is to the Greek playwright—noted for his tragedies—and even more specifically to lines from his play *Antigone*. The meaning of the allusion comes through clearly if you know the kinds of plays Sophocles wrote, but the link is even stronger if you know the lines from *Antigone*.

These examples illustrate historical (or political), religious, and literary allusions, but there are as many categories as there are categories for ideas. What is important is twofold—to spot an allusion and then to make the connection between the allusion and the poem. Proper names and place names are obvious candidates for allusion; phrases or key words are more subtle and therefore easy to miss. Reference books can help you here. Start with the easiest reference tool to come by—your dictionary. If this doesn't help, try an encyclopedia. If you suspect that a word or phrase is an allusion and neither a dictionary nor an encyclopedia helps, a dictionary of quotations will probably save the day. You'll find all the quotations' key words listed at the back of the book.

Review: Symbolism and Myth

Recall from Lesson 9 the discussion of the hamburger as a symbol of American culture. Or think of how a country's flag functions as a symbol. The stars and stripes in the U.S. flag symbolize not just the present 50 states and 13 original ones but also more than that—the flag represents beliefs and values. A country's flag represents all that the country stands for—which is why it is honored by salute, respectful silence, song, and in many other ways.

Thus a *symbol* is anything—an object, person, place, idea, or situation—that stands for itself and also gathers to it a larger meaning. A hamburger is a hamburger, but it can also symbolize the values of American culture, particularly efficiency and inventiveness. So, too, a flag represents a country's history and also symbolizes its values.

The idea of a flag has now become a *universal symbol;* all countries have one. A particular country's flag is a *cultural symbol* in that it holds meaning only for the people of that particular country. As for a private *symbol,* think of a flag that a small boy might make. Its colors and design would probably make sense only to him. Your textbook points out that both universal and cultural symbols have agreed upon meanings. Private symbols, however, hold particularized meanings that arise from their contexts.

Think again of "next to of course god america i." The allusions to the various patriotic songs are cultural symbols that the poet gives a private twist to. In the mouth of the speaker their cultural symbolism is subverted. Instead of symbolizing the good qualities of patriotism, they become empty phrases that symbolize the speaker's own emptiness.

The poem also taps into *myth*. You will recall that myth can take several forms. Ancient myths grew up in all cultures to account for natural and supernatural phenomena—floods and wars, life and death, creation and other worlds. But myth can also refer to a recurring idea or character type that holds meaning for a people because it represents that culture's ideals or expresses strong emotions shared by that society.

Remember that to call a system of belief a myth is not to make a value judgment, and it is certainly not an attack. To use the label *myth* is merely to call attention to the shared beliefs—both religious and secular—of a particular group.

Cummings' poem attacks one aspect of the myth of patriotism, the belief that anyone who makes patriotic noises is indeed a patriot. So, too, Wilfred Owens' poem "Dulce et Decorum Est," pages 802–803, that you read for Lesson 14, is not an attack on war but on a myth, particularly popular in wartime, that it is "sweet and fitting to die for one's country." Owen shows us that in war, death may be unavoidable, but it is hardly "sweet."

Myth and Symbol: Ancient

Five of the poems listed for this lesson reexamine the myth of Icarus, so we'll start by reviewing the original myth. Originally one of the ancient legends of Crete, the myth of Icarus was absorbed into ancient Greek mythology, and it is in that form that it has come down to us today.

Icarus was the son of Daedalus, a famous Athenian carpenter and craftsman who had killed a rival and sought safety under the protection of Minos, king of the island of Crete. There, Daedalus built the famous Labyrinth that housed the Minotaur, a beast that fed on human flesh. Because of an act against the king, Daedalus, with his son, was put into the Labyrinth.

Known for his ingenuity and skill, Daedalus planned their escape by constructing wings of feathers and wax so that he and Icarus could fly to safety. He warned Icarus not to fly too close to the sun or else the wax would melt. But Icarus did fly too close to the sun, and with the inevitable result—the wings melted, he fell into the sea, and he drowned. His flight and his fall are the most important features of the myth.

What has intrigued people over the centuries is not the truth or falseness of the tale or of Icarus's actions but what those actions symbolize. Several subjects suggest themselves: a father-son generational conflict, the attraction of danger, the ecstasy of flight, the danger of pride. Let's see what the five poets focus on and what subjects they explore.

None of the poems focuses on the relationship of Daedalus and Icarus, and only three concentrate on Icarus.

Anne Sexton's Icarus is quite different. She devotes only one line to his fall and spends the rest on his heroic curiosity. Here we have a young boy initially excited by "that strange little tug at his shoulder blade." She follows his flight out over the Labyrinth, over "the plushy ocean." She describes him as "innocent" and notes

> ... how casually
> he glances up and is caught, wondrously tunneling
> into that hot eye.

Instead of contending with the sun, Sexton's Icarus is "acclaiming the sun," praising it. This Icarus can be said to symbolize the wonder, innocence, and heroism of youth.

Then there's Edward Field's Icarus, an Icarus who not only survives his fall but is transformed into a suburban drone with "sad, defeated eyes *that* had once / compelled the sun." Aging, defeated, every night he tries again to fly, and even though he only tries for the ceiling, he "Fails every time and hates himself for trying." Fields suggests that for a hero a living death of despair and isolation is worse than drowning. His Icarus can be seen to symbolize the numbing tedium that can follow triumph.

Instead of focusing on Icarus and his flight, the poems by Auden and Williams both center on his fall as depicted in Brueghel's painting which is reproduced in the color insert (I-7). As you can see, Icarus also seems to play a minor part in the painting. In fact, you have to look hard to find him, and when you do, all you see are legs and a splash. Daedalus flies overhead at the top of the painting, just left of center, catching the eye of the farmer on the lower field. On the upper field, a farmer—the largest and most central figure—continues his plowing, unaware of Icarus's fall. To the right, a ship sails away from the fallen figure.

Williams recreates this scene in his poem with each stanza presenting one of the painting's images. The first three stanzas center on the land scene—spring, a time of planting and promise. The scene is "concerned with itself." The last two stanzas tell of Icarus's death, but first as "a splash quite unnoticed." The last two lines objectify the death through understatement: the "splash ... was / Icarus drowning."

Williams appears to be reinterpreting the painting for us, emphasizing the idea that humans and nature are so concerned with the immediate that they do not even notice tragedy. And that "immediate" is the natural cycle of life. Perhaps Williams is suggesting that our natural concerns—working, planting—blind us to the unusual, the symbolic, the tragic.

Auden's focus is more easily apparent. He finds in Brueghel's painting a comment on suffering. The first 13 lines of the poem connect the "Old Masters" of painting with the idea of suffering, noting that they portrayed a world indifferent to it. The poem then narrows down to Brueghel's painting and how the figures in it may have heard or seen Icarus's fall but simply went on about their business. Auden finds in the myth—as depicted in the painting—a symbol of our inhumanity, our indifference to the suffering of others.

All five poets deal with the same myth. For Sexton, Icarus is the central figure; his flight and what it symbolizes is most important. For Fields, Icarus—his flight and his fall—becomes a symbol for the failed hero. Williams and Auden focus on Icarus's fall; what is important is the casual indifference to it.

Myth and Symbol: Private

Occasionally you will read works by writers who have created their own myths—myths that either coexist with or borrow from other myths. Because these private myths are just that and are not shared by a culture, they may be hard to track down and to understand.

You will find, for example, that your textbook provides a lengthy introduction to William Butler Yeats's "Second Coming," pages 974–975. Not only are the religious and literary allusions noted, but you are given a short summary of Yeats's theory of cycles which form part of his mythology. The poem is a good example of private myth combined with the mythos of various religions.

For people who either grew up in or have adopted the Christian culture, the title of the poem should present no problem. In the Bible, the *New Testament* predicts all kinds of disasters followed by the second coming of Christ. Yeats takes this belief, examines the world around him, applies his theory of 2,000-year cycles, and hypothesizes a second coming not of Christ but of a monster.

From this perspective, you can read the first stanza symbolically. One event—the birth of Christ—has now lost most of its meaning: "The falcon cannot hear the falconer." We are now so distanced by time and history that "the center cannot hold." As a result, "mere anarchy is loosed upon the world."

The second stanza predicts the future. Things have gotten so out of control, Yeats implies, that "Surely the Second Coming is at hand." And here Yeats's beliefs take over, for just as the first cycle originated from good, so this one will originate from evil, starting another 2,000-year cycle that is the reverse of the previous one. Yeats then imagines the form this evil may take.

Yeats draws upon Egyptian mythology for the image of the monster, finding an appropriate figure in the Sphinx, a figure of evil, cruelty, bestiality. He believes his image is fitting and knows "That twenty centuries of stony sleep / Were vexed to nightmare by a rocking cradle." Humankind has brought this new vision upon itself. What will it be? Something worse than what Yeats has imagined:

> And what rough beast, its hour come round at last,
> Slouches toward Bethlehem to be born?

The creature is an anti-Christ, a complete reversal of all that Christianity has stood for.

While you do not need to know where Yeats draws his images from or what he symbolizes with his figure of the gyre, knowing certainly enriches your understanding of the poem. But what if there are no footnotes? No helpful explanations of the private mythology? To research the writer's philosophy by reading biographies and criticism probably requires more time than you have, but you can find useful summaries in resources such as *The Oxford Companion* series which has volumes devoted to English, American, and World literature.

Myth and Symbol: Cultural

For an example of a cultural myth, we'll take a look at what is known as the American Dream. The myth has a number of forms, but it is based on the concept of democracy—liberty and justice for all—and its promise that any citizen can be a success.

You can hear this idea of success echoed in the cliché, "Anyone can grow up to be President." You might also think of rags to riches stories or self-help books with titles along the lines of *How to Make a Million Dollars, How to Be a Social Success,* or *Dress for Power.* In its most crass expression, the American Dream is pure materialism, the idea of happiness defined as a fancy suburban home, a two-car garage, and a swimming pool. In its noblest expression, the American Dream is the Bill of Rights and the Constitution.

Has the result been liberty and justice for all? Is the American Dream real? Not according to Langston Hughes. In "Let America be America Again," pages 1078–1080, Hughes speaks for all who have been denied access to that dream—the poor white, the African-American, the Native American, the immigrant, the farmer and worker who live in financial bondage. He speaks also for those who came to this country "To build a 'homeland of the free.' "

The America the poet seeks is one where "opportunity is real, and life is free, / Equality is in the air we breathe." That America, the poem implies, is the ideal one (the reader might think of the Bill of Rights and the Constitution), a "dream that / Lies deep in the heart of me." Without freedom and opportunity, Hughes implies, self-respect and success are impossible.

We get a different view of success in cummings' poem, "Buffalo Bill's Defunct," page 908. Cummings' plays on the popular image of Buffalo Bill, the army scout, buffalo hunter, and western frontiersman who went on to organize a Wild West show that toured the United States and Europe. The show was a great success, making Buffalo Bill famous and rich.

Cummings opens his poem with the lines that have now become known as its title. What's interesting is that cummings does not say Buffalo Bill is dead but uses the word *defunct*. The word is a synonym for dead but is more formal, less emotional. Then the poem presents a portrait of Buffalo Bill the showman, summing him up in the lines "Jesus / he was a handsome man." The last three lines turn away from the image. The narrator says, "and what i want to know is / how do you like your blueeyed boy / Mr. Death."

In this poem we have a portrait of someone who had freedom and opportunity and took advantage of both to develop an image of the hero of the Wild West. A successful showman, Buffalo Bill created a larger than life persona that almost wiped out the far more ordinary life of the real person, William Cody. What did all that success come to? Cummings implies that to Mr. Death, one person is just as defunct as another. Success means nothing.

On the other hand, there's no disputing the "life" of the myth Buffalo Bill created. We seem to be left with irony—the success that was real died; the myth that was illusion lived on.

Summary

As you have seen, myth and symbol are closely allied. Both can be private, cultural, or universal. The universality of myths lies in their metaphorical, not literal, truth and in their recurring motifs which back in Lesson 9 we referred to as archetypes.

Just as writers of short fiction often used archetypes—the hero, the victim, the devil—to explore the meaning of events and the nature of characters, poets use individual myths to reexamine and reinterpret their meaning. Both kinds of writers are rethinking ideas. All five poets used the myth of Icarus to say different things to us.

So, too, Howe, Hughes, and cummings take different parts of a cultural myth, and their perspectives give them different views. If you are familiar with Arthur Miller's play *Death of a Salesman* or Martin Luther King, Jr.'s "I Have a Dream" speech, then you can see what writers in other genres have to say about the American Dream.

Because poetry is so compact, allusions, symbols, and myths all add important additional layers of meaning. These devices allow the poet to tap into the reader's experience and knowledge and draw them into the poem. By using allusions, symbols, and myths, poets (and other writers as well) enrich their texts with the collective wisdom of various cultures.

206—*Literary Visions*

VIEWING GUIDE

An important component of this lesson is the video. You will learn more effectively from it by thinking about the following questions and guidelines.

Before Viewing:

1. Review "Symbolism and Allusion: Windows to a Wide Expanse of Meaning," pages 940–947, and "Myth: Systems of Symbolic Allusion in Poetry," pages 983–991, in the text.
2. Review the poems assigned, paying particular attention to the ones your instructor emphasizes. Try to hear each poem's sound.

During Your Viewing:

1. Listen to what Marjorie Perloff and Mary Poovey say about the differences among the Icarus poems.
2. Look for the connection the video makes between the myth of Icarus and the poem by Yeats.
3. Listen for definitions of myth.
4. Listen for definitions of the American Dream.
5. List the major points Marge Piercy makes in the interview about her use of myth.

After Viewing:

Give some thought to the following questions. You may want to write short answers in your journal or notebook.

1. What are the major categories of myth?
2. What is a good working definition of myth?
3. How do myth and symbol work together?
4. How necessary is it to know all the allusions in a poem?
5. What role does myth play in Marge Piercy's poetry?

WRITING ACTIVITIES

After your study of this lesson, you should be able to analyze how allusion, symbol, and myth function in a poem. Your instructor will advise you which, if any, of the following writing activities you are to complete.

Formal Writing:

Both Activities 1 and 2 ask you to analyze the elements under discussion; information and models in the text will be helpful guides. Applying your new knowledge of poetic devices to a poem that has not been discussed and then writing out the result will reveal the extent of your understanding. Your drafts may reveal gaps in your knowledge; you can fill them before writing your final version. The third activity is more difficult—but potentially more rewarding—because you can review and combine the information from Lessons 15 and 16. The last activity explores the effectiveness of the dramatizations of the Icarus myth.

1. Choose a poem that uses symbolism and allusion from among those that you have read for this lesson and the earlier ones and, using the information in the text as a model (pages 976–980), analyze the poem's use of these two devices.
2. Select one of the poems that focuses on the legend of Odysseus and, using the information in the text as a model (pages 1016-1022), analyze the poet's use of myth.
3. Consider the Brueghel painting and the poem by William Carlos Williams, and write an essay that examines the form of Williams's poem. You will find information in Lesson 15 helpful for this activity.
4. Write an essay in which you discuss the dramatization of the Icarus poems that strikes you as the most effective, analyzing your response to it.

Informal Writing:

Both activities focus on personal experience but call for the same kind of imaginative and analytical thinking that goes into creating a poem. Both activities also ask the writer to "read" his or her immediate environment. From that point, Activity 1 asks the writer to discover a symbol system, and Activity 2 calls for the creation of a myth. Both ask the writer to explain the results so that the teacher can see the connection between the subjects analyzed and the topics under discussion in this lesson.

1. If, like many people, you have a favorite outfit, one that from head to toe makes you feel comfortable or elegant or attractive or whatever, the odds are that the clothing and accessories that make up that outfit have some symbolic value for you. Granted they may be private symbols, but they are symbols just the same. Each of the items may have a personal history that holds various memories for you. In your journal or notebook, jot down the items that make up that outfit, and note what makes each item special. If the result is a great deal of information, you may want to narrow your focus to one or two items. Your notes will serve as the basis for an essay that analyzes the symbolism of your clothes.

208—*Literary Visions*

2. If you would rather explore myth, think about an object, fad, or style in popular culture, preferably one that you do not like. Some people, for example, can't stand certain kinds of music or find some clothes or hair styles outlandish. Others have no use for some of the machines that others find indispensable—the computer, the mountain bike, the video game. In your journal or notebook, compose a myth that explains the origin of the subject you select.

SELF-TEST

Match the items in column A with the definitions or identifications in B. The quotations are general statements, not sentences taken from poems.

A

1. Archetype
2. The American celebration of the 4th of July
3. A gyre
4. "Having a teenager is to know the sufferings of Job."
5. Daedalus
6. Spring
7. Odysseus
8. "I caught a fish as big as Moby Dick."
9. Pieter Brueghel

B

a. Part of private mythology
b. Literary allusion
c. Father of Icarus
d. Universal symbol
e. Political allusion
f. Husband of Penelope
g. Symbol that occurs in many mythologies
h. Cultural symbol
i. Brother of Icarus
j. Religious allusion
k. Flemish painter
l. Private symbol

Answer the following multiple-choice items:

1. Poets use allusions to
   a. appear learned.
   b. avoid the obvious.
   c. enrich their ideas.
   d. test the reader.

2. The Statue of Liberty is a(n)
   a. private symbol.
   b. allusion.
   c. cultural symbol.
   d. myth.
3. Which statement about myth is NOT true?
   a. A myth involves a value judgment.
   b. A myth may adapt itself to another myth.
   c. Some poets make up their own mythology.
   d. Some motifs are common to most mythologies.
4. Which statement about the use of myth in poetry is NOT true?
   a. A myth can be used as a symbol.
   b. A myth is a form of allusion.
   c. A myth can contain universal truths.
   d. A myth has only one meaning.
5. To enjoy a poem, the reader has to
   a. know the allusions.
   b. understand the symbolism.
   c. know about the poet.
   d. hear the rhythms.

In 100–300 words, answer the following short essay questions:

1. Using the myth of Oedipus (you'll have to first find out what this myth is all about), explain the progression with the stanzas of John Updike's poem "On the Way to Delphi" (page 1012) and analyze his central imagery and use of allusion.
2. Analyze W.S. Merwin's portrayal of Odysseus in the poem by that name, comparing Merwin's Odysseus to the one of legend.

ADDITIONAL READING ACTIVITIES

If you enjoyed reading the poems and listening to the interview with Marge Piercy in this lesson, you may want to read more from the following selections, which include both poems and fiction.

Piercy, Marge. *Available Light.* (A collection of poems)
_____. *Circles on the Water.* (Selected poems)
_____. *Braided Lives.* (A novel about growing up in Detroit in the 1950s)

210—*Literary Visions*

_____. *Going Down Fast.* (A novel about the effect of a university on an inner-city neighborhood)

_____. *Woman on the Edge of Time.* (A novel about a Chicano woman committed to a mental hospital)

LESSON 17

Artful Resonance:
THEME IN POETRY

ABOUT THE LESSON

Imagine an aerial photograph of a major interchange for a vast, wide highway—at least a six-laner. From above, this kind of interchange would look like its label, a cloverleaf—the four-leaf kind, with each leaf feeding into or out of the main highway. In much the same way, the elements of poetry interact with theme. Character, setting, diction, imagery, tone, metaphorical language, prosody, form, myth, allusion, and symbolism all feed into and out of a poem's theme—the major thoroughfare of meaning.

Much of what you will study in this lesson is not new. You have already learned about theme in short fiction, and all the lessons so far on poetry have brought in theme, either directly or indirectly. What will be new is the perspective, for here we will focus only on poetry, much of it new to you, and on theme, examining how all of the other elements you have studied in poetry relate to it.

It is probably helpful to start off with a distinction among four terms: *interpretation, subject, theme,* and *meaning*. When you read a work (short story, poem, or play), you think through an interpretation of it—your analysis of what the work is about (its subject) and what it means. If you were to write out that interpretation, the result would probably run to several pages of commentary. Now if you were to take that analysis and boil it down to one sentence that expressed your view of what the author is asserting, you'd have a theme.

Another reader might find a different subject in the same work and therefore would probably have a slightly or even completely different interpretation which would result in a different theme. And the same would be true of a third reader, a fourth, and so on. The richer the work, the more there is to explore and to say.

Now even if we added up all those interpretation and listed all the themes that all the readers came up with, we probably would not do justice to everything a work could mean. But imagine for a moment that such a thing were possible; the result would be the meaning of the work. Meaning encompasses everything involved in a work—its themes, the means by which they are conveyed, and the overall effect on the reader.

As an informed reader, you open up your mind and your senses to the world the writer portrays, suspending any judgment of a work until you've finished it and reviewed it. Then you're in a good position to interpret it. And to enjoy it.

GOAL

This lesson will help you to appreciate how the various elements of poetry combine to present the meaning of a poem.

WHAT YOU WILL LEARN

When you complete this lesson you will be able to:

1. Describe how poetry expresses theme.
2. Differentiate between subject and theme in poetry.
3. Determine the theme(s) in various poems.
4. Describe how elements of poetry combine to reinforce the poem's theme in such a way that they are more than the sum of their parts.
5. Give examples of traditional subjects for poetry.
6. Recognize that there may be more than one theme in a poem.

LESSON ASSIGNMENT

Working through the following nine steps will help you master the objectives and achieve the goal for this lesson:

Step 1: In your text, read the chapter "Words: The Building Block of Poetry," pages 653–685. The text will provide background for what you will read in the study guide, explain the key terms, and give you some information about the poems you will be reading.

Step 2: Read the specific poems your instructor assigns. The following works will be the focus of this lesson and the ones marked with an asterisk (*) will be discussed in the video.

- "Naming of Parts," Henry Reed, pages 674–675.
- "To His Coy Mistress," Andrew Marvell, pages 968–969.
- "Ethics," Linda Pastan, page 1162.
- "The Sun Rising," John Donne, pages 860–861.*

- "Patterns," Amy Lowell, pages 1149–1152.*
- "Bells for John Whiteside's Daughter," John Crowe Ransom, pages 1166–1167.
- "Auto Wreck," Karl Shapiro, pages 1175–1176.*
- "Not Waving But Drowning," Stevie Smith, page 1177.*

Step 3: Read the OVERVIEW in this study guide lesson.

Step 4: Watch the VIDEO, following the steps in the VIEWING GUIDE in this study guide lesson.

Step 5: Reread the OVERVIEW to reinforce what you have learned in the text and the video and to help you complete the Writing Activities.

Step 6: Complete any WRITING ACTIVITIES assigned in this lesson.

Step 7: Do the SELF-TEST exercises in this study guide lesson.

Step 8: Read any of the ADDITIONAL READING ACTIVITIES assigned.

Step 9: Go back to the learning objectives in the WHAT YOU WILL LEARN section of this study guide lesson and be sure you can respond to each of them.

OVERVIEW

This lesson is both a review and a look at new material. To set your focus on theme, we'll start with a discussion of how theme is treated differently in short stories and poetry, making a few suggestions about working with theme in poetry.

The five parts that follow will deal with the five groups of elements you have studied: speaker, character, and setting; diction and imagery; tone and metaphorical language; prosody and form; and myth, allusion, and symbolism. Each of these sections will build upon the ones before it.

Each of these five sections will review the topics under discussion by reminding you of a poem that played a key role in an earlier lesson. Each section will also cover poems not assigned in the previous lessons so that you can follow the steps involved in working out first a subject and then a theme.

Unlike the lesson on theme in the short story, this lesson and accompanying video will examine works that you have not read before so that you can apply what you have learned to new material. As you read, you will find that while all of the elements you have studied relate to a poem's theme, not all are equally important. In some poems diction may be vital, and in others the key may be setting or figurative language or another element. But because poetry is poetry, prosody and form always play crucial roles in interpretation.

Theme: Short Fiction and Poetry

When you studied the idea of theme in the short story, you learned how all the other elements related to theme, and the same general idea is true for poetry. However, the theme of a poem is sometimes more difficult to identify because poetry depends more heavily on imagery and figurative language and because it is a concise form that also depends on rhythm and sound. The form of poetry and the kind of language it uses often make the theme less direct than it is in short fiction.

Even so, although the theme of a poem may be more difficult and less direct than that of a short story, it is not impossible to understand. What you learned about interpreting the theme of a short story will carry over to poetry; in addition, you have already learned a good deal about theme from the earlier poetry lessons.

Sometimes readers are intimidated by the idea of finding a theme in a poem, but that feeling should vanish when you consider that poems are made up of familiar words, syntax, images, comparisons, and allusions. As a reader, you bring your own world—your knowledge and experience—to bear upon the world the poet has created on the page. These two worlds overlap to a huge extent. Knowing that will keep your focus on the familiar, so that what is unusual will not throw you off.

When you read, try to let several possible meanings wash over you until you reach the end of the poem. Then put together your knowledge and experience to interpret the poem, to figure out which of the meanings you have thought about makes the most sense. Then you can sort out which of the various elements of poetry play the most important parts in conveying that meaning and how rhythm and sound reinforce it.

Once you've gone this far, you can probably shape your interpretation in the form of a thesis that is your interpretation of one of the poem's themes. Your thesis will probably change and sharpen as you work out the poem's details, but you will be well on your way to a solid understanding of the poem's theme.

Speaker, Character, Setting, and Theme

Just as the narrator in a short story can be an observer or part of the action, the same is true of the speaker in a poem. Think of when you studied character and setting in poetry and analyzed Browning's poem, "My Last Duchess," pages 697–698. There you noted the speaker and the setting and how in that poem, the setting told you a good deal about the Duke, and it became apparent that he had his wife murdered because she treated him no differently from the way she treated anyone else. Her portrait has become what she never was willing to be—a possession that reflected the Duke's power and status. As a whole, the poem points to the folly of human vanity, and if you were to select pride as its subject—what the poem is *about*—then your idea of a theme—what the poem says about the subject—might assert that Browning uses the figure of the Duke to symbolize how pride defeats itself. If you were the emissary, would you give a good report of the Duke?

Karl Shapiro's "Auto Wreck," pages 1175–1176, is a radically different poem, but one in which character and setting play an equally important role. Unlike "My Last Duchess," where the character of the speaker dominates the setting, in "Auto Wreck" the reverse occurs—the setting dominates the characters.

To analyze how setting, character, and speaker relate to theme, let's start by identifying what's what in the poem. The poem breaks into two stanzas, the first describing the wreck and the second the witnesses' response to it. Throughout the poem, the focus is on the aftermath of the event and in particular its meaning. The narrator is the person who describes the accident; the "we" in the poem the narrator refers to may be general (we who were watching) or it may refer to a friend who also witnesses the accident.

The focus in the first stanza is on the scene itself, in particular the arrival of the ambulance, the loading of the injured, and the departure of the ambulance. Then liens 15 through 21 describe the activities of the police who are cleaning up the scene. From that point on, the poem concentrates on the impact of the accident on the witnesses, building first to the question "Who shall die?" and then moving to a more important though "unspoken" question, "Who is innocent?"

The last seven lines refer to other kinds of deaths that have "cause" or "logic," both absent from this accident that "Cancels our physics with a sneer." Here we have no "denouement," no neat explanation and exit.

The title proclaims the poem's subject, and the poet's use of setting suggests a theme: Because accidents overthrow our sense of order, they not only maim those directly involved but witnesses as well. Or to put it another way, accidents permit no logic—no one is "innocent"; no one can avoid being a potential victim. To support this theme further, you might note how lines 21–27 use metaphor and simile to equate the accident's witnesses with its victims, suggesting that all are casualties.

Diction, Imagery, and Theme

Shapiro's choice of words such as "occult," "denouement," "expedient," and "wicked" all support the interpretation above by implying that logic does not exist. So, too, when you studied "Richard Cory," page 675, you analyzed how Robinson used diction to create an image of Cory the royal personage, an image quite counter to the reality. By contrasting the reality of suicide with the image of Cory's "ideal" life, Robinson suggests any number of themes that are variations on the idea that appearances can be deceiving. Contrast also undergirds Henry Reed's "Naming of Parts," pages 674–675, for when you look at the language of the poem and analyze the contrasts, the diction appears to be drawn from two very different worlds: the world of war and the world of nature. Each of the five stanzas describes first a military rifle drill and then concludes with images drawn from "neighboring gardens."

Who is speaking? Are there two voices here or one? Is this a drill sergeant saying one thing and thinking another? Or has the poet ignored the convention of quotation marks so that we have the drill instructor speaking and a soldier thinking? The latter seems the better choice because the first suggestion does not seem probable; an unemotional "just the fact" type may stop to smell the flowers, but it's doubtful that he would think of war and nature at the same time.

Separating the two worlds of diction, you will find that the drill instructor appears to be merely going through the motions. Several of the parts he refers to are parts the soldiers "have not got," thus making the drill all the more empty. What appears to be important is that everything have its proper name; what is missing is a sense of purpose, of life. The emphasis is on the mechanical. The most important part is the bolt that is slid back and forth to load the rifle, an action called "easing the spring."

The same phrase can apply to the garden. There, the bees, like the bolt, move to and fro, "assaulting and fumbling the flowers," carrying the pollen that makes future springs possible. The contrast between the world of the drill and the world of the garden is obvious—a loaded rifle may bring death, a loaded bee may bring new life.

The last stanza appears to be in the voice of the soldier who satirizes the drill instructor. Given these two contrasting worlds—one mechanical, the other natural; one associated with death, the other with life—what is missing is "the point of balance." The poem concludes with a summarizing comparison, "the bees going backwards and forward, / For today we have the naming of parts." The two worlds continue, each oblivious to the other.

So what is being said here? Perhaps the poem merely points out that there is a gulf between the world of war and the world of nature. Or if you follow through on the dullness of the lecture and the busyness of the bees, maybe the poet is implying that when bored, a young man's thoughts turn to sex. On a deeper level, the poet may be implying that we have lost our "point of balance" or that the world of war is unnatural. Any of these interpretations and others can be supported by analyzing Reed's diction and imagery.

Tone, Metaphorical Language, and Theme

Reed's poem may have reminded you of Wilfred Owen's "Dulce et Decorum Est," pages 802–803, a poem that also deals with war. Set during World War I, Owen's poem depicts the realistic, ugly side of combat, when exhausted soldiers are "Bent double, like old beggars under sacks." Through metaphor and simile, Owen describes what it's like to be numbed by fatigue and then gassed, what it's like to see a man die from mustard gas poisoning. The poet contrasts this reality to the high-sounding patriotic belief propounded by the person he is addressing: that it is noble and fitting to die for one's country. The contrast creates irony and underscores the theme, which could be put succinctly as "War is hell, and only a fool would think otherwise."

Let's examine Stevie Smith's "Not Waving But Drowning," page 1177, for a similar tone and also analyze how setting, diction, tone, and figurative language can lead to a theme. The poem is short and seemingly simple. The subject is easy enough, the death of a man by drowning. But look again at the three stanzas and you hear three voices—a nameless narrator who tells us "Nobody heard him, the dead man, / But still he lay moaning"; people who knew the dead man who tell us "Poor chap, he always loved larking" and speculate on why he drowned; and the dead man himself.

The poem is built on an implied metaphor that leads to paradox. But first let's look at what is happening on the literal level. The first stanza tells us the drowning man appeared to be waving but in reality was signaling for help. In the next stanza, his friends speculate that the water was so cold that he had a heart attack. The third stanza reveals the truth and raises the literal to the metaphoric in that the dead man tells us "I was much too far out all my life / And not waving but drowning." His death was like his life in that he was always floundering about in the cold, always signaling for help, and always misread. His death becomes a metaphor for his life.

And think of the paradoxes—his "accidental" death was no accident but a logical end to the kind of life he led; his friends thought he loved to have fun ("he always loved larking") but his life was "too cold always"; his life was a kind of death; and, of course, there is the paradox of the dead man speaking. The situation is ironic, and the poet treats it with verbal irony. For example, if you were to look up *lark* in your dictionary, you'd find it has several meanings, two of which apply here: to frolic or play, or to play a "merry prank." If the latter meaning is what the poet intends, then it suggests the additional irony that the people on shore thought his waving was a joke of some kind.

The tone, setting, diction, paradox, and implied metaphor suggest several possible themes—that "accidents" are sometimes "logical" or that appearances can be misleading. Obviously there is a relationship here between the theme in Smith's poem and those by Shapiro ("Auto Wreck") and Robinson ("Richard Cory").

In John Donne's "The Sun Rising," pages 860–861, setting, diction, and figurative language work together to create a very different tone and theme. Here we have a bedroom scene where the sun awakens two lovers. The speaker reprimands the sun for this interruption and, using the rhetorical device of apostrophe, addresses the culprit directly.

Calling the sun a "saucy pedantic wretch," the speaker redirects its attention to those who live by the clock or routine—schoolboys, apprentices, the king's huntsmen, ants. Love, he states, "no season knows nor clime." Hyperbole or overstatement continues with his claim that love knows no "hours, days, months"— an idea finished off with a metaphor that scorns such divisions as "the rags of time."

Stanza 2 focuses on the object of the speaker's love, though still in the guise of addressing the sun. Hyperbole dominates the imagery in this stanza. His love's eyes are so beautiful that they can blind the sun, and all the spices and gold of the

Indies and all the power and significance—the kings of the world—are embodied in her form.

The speaker summarizes this idea in the third stanza with "She is all states," and then refers to himself as "all princes, I." As for the rest of the world, "Nothing else is." This stanza then directs the reader's attention to the two lovers and their love, a love so cherished and rich that "All honor's mimic, all wealth alchemy." The stanza concludes with the idea that the lovers are a microcosm of the world; if the sun shines on them, it shines "everywhere" because "This bed thy center is, these walls, thy sphere."

The subject of the poem is obviously love, but the setting narrows that topic by emphasizing physical love. The rhetorical devices of apostrophe and hyperbole create a tone that is both joyous and triumphant—one that celebrates this love. Putting together the setting, subject, figurative language, and tone, you can arrive at several possible statements of the poem's theme, all of which will be variations on the idea that Donne uses the poem to glorify and rejoice in the passionate side of love.

Prosody, Form, and Theme

The tone, setting, character, diction, imagery, and figurative language of a poem are all affected by its form and prosody. You may recall, for example, how Robinson's poem "Miniver Cheevy," pages 876–877, depicted a bitter person who had dreams of grandeur that he never did anything about. He "scorned the gold he sought, / But sore annoyed was he without it." The tone of the poem is ironic, and its meter underscores the irony by ending each stanza a foot short. Each stanza's last line, like Miniver himself, falls short of expectations.

A very different effect is created by the same technique in John Crowe Ransom's "Bells for John Whiteside's Daughter," pages 1166–1167. In five quatrains, Ransom portrays the life and death of a small girl, the "Bells" of the title referring to funeral bells. If you were to scan those quatrains, you would find a mixture of metric feet but a pattern of three lines of four feet (with an occasional five foot line), followed by a three foot line. In each stanza, the first and third lines usually contain a slant rhyme and the second and fourth lines rhyme exactly. One other pattern stands out—falling rhyme in the first and third lines and rising rhyme in the second and fourth. The only variation is stanza 3 where the rhyme is exact and rising in all four lines.

Stanza 3 is also the only stanza that does not mention the little girl directly. Instead it focuses on the geese she used to herd, geese who are personified as mourning the child's death and "cried in goose, Alas." This is also the only stanza that does not contain a slide rhyme in lines 2 and 3.

The images we are given of the live little girl are those of action. And it is the contrast between her "speed" in life and her stillness in death that is brought out in the first and last stanzas to frame the poem. Stanza 1 refers to the narrator and friends (the "we" in the poem) being astounded by her "brown study," her looking as though she were deeply absorbed in thought.

Stanzas 1 and 4 depict images of the child as playful, imaginative, busy, waging war with her shadow and herding geese. Now, however, in stanza 5 the bells toll and people gather

> ... sternly stopped
> To say we are vexed at her brown study,
> Lying so primly propped.

Like the last line of each stanza, the child's life has been cut short. That incompleteness is echoed by the falling rhyme, but the finality of the death is represented by the rising rhyme. And like the poem's meter, the little girl's life had been full of variety.

That variation in meter is evident in virtually every line, and the differences that variety achieves can be seen in the first lines of the first and last stanzas. The poem's first line begins with an anapest, followed by a dactyl, then two trochees; the meter is light, the "s" sounds and short vowels contributing to its liveliness. These effects are appropriate as the line introduces the reader to the little girl as she was in life, vital and quick. In contrast, the first line of the last stanza opens with an iamb followed by four trochees, as regular a metric line as one can find in the poem's four and occasional five foot lines. The alliteration of the "b's" and assonance of the open "o's" and "e's" slow the rhythm to that of a dirge, as is only appropriate since the line describes the tolling of the bells and the gathering of the mourners.

The tone of the poem conveys the sadness and astonishment the death caused. Ransom uses "vexed" to communicate the idea that those who are attending this death keep going over and over it, trying to understand it, trying to match the stillness of the body before them with the vivid image of the live child. It's as though they find this death absurd—in the sense of clearly unreasonable—and are waiting for her to awaken.

What the poem conveys then is the sense of stunned disbelief we are apt to feel when confronted with the sudden death of someone who had been very much alive. That is certainly one of its themes and one that is supported by diction, imagery, tone, form, sound, and meter. As for figurative language, you will find that Ransom uses understatement to describe the child's death and overstatement to describe her life.

Myth, Allusion, Symbolism, and Theme

Once you have established a theme for Ransom's poem, it's easy to examine it for symbolism. For instance, if the theme is that one initial reaction to sudden death is that it is unbelievable, absurd, then it's possible to see that the death of the child in the poem stands for or symbolizes all such deaths.

And if you remember reading the Icarus poems in Lesson 16, you saw how the different poets found separate uses for the myth of Icarus, with each interpretation focusing on a different aspect of the myth and therefore giving rise to diverse symbols. That myth was simply one illustration of the kinds of allusions and myths that poets draw upon to link the experiences of the poem with those of the reader.

Here, we'll study Andre Marvell's "To His Coy Mistress," pages 968–969, a 17th century poem that also brings allusion, myth, and symbol to bear on theme. Its subject is one that you are familiar with from Lesson 12, the idea of `carpe diem` or seize the day. The speaker in the poem is addressing a woman he is attracted to, pressing her to give in to his advances. "Coy," at the time of the poem, meant shy or unresponsive; it did not have its present connotation of coquettishness, of playing hard to get.

The poem is written in three verse paragraphs, each supporting an assertion. The three lines of argument can be summarized as "If x were so, then I would do y;" "But x is not;" and "Therefore let us do z." Each of the verses is packed with allusions that focus on the key idea of time.

The first verse paragraph states that if "we had but world enough, and time," his lady's refusals would be no problem, for he would devote himself to loving her at the rate she deserves, allowing thousands of years for her to "show her heart." The speaker says that she "Shouldst rubies find" by the Ganges, and with those lines invokes the exotic image of India and its holiest river, the Ganges. He also alludes to a belief of his own times, when rubies were believed to be charms for preserving virginity. And with the reference to the English river—the Humber—the speaker not only places himself at the opposite end of the world from his love's Ganges but also contrasts his modest Englishness with her sacred exoticism.

The allusions also help set the scale of time the speaker would be willing to accept if time had no meaning. He "would / Love [her] ten years before the flood," and she could refuse him "Till the conversion of the Jews." Thus the poet uses the Christian mythos to describe the span of time for his courtship. Within that mythos, the flood occurred in pre-history and was God's punishment for human misdeeds; the conversion of the Jews is an event that precedes the end of the world.

The second verse paragraph starts with allusion to Chronos—the god of time in Greek mythology—who was depicted as riding across the heavens in a chariot drawn by winged horses. There is a literary allusion packed in here as well as it is to the 14th century Italian poet and scholar Petrarch. In the *Trionfi*, Petrarch sets out a hierarchy in which Death conquers Chastity; Fame conquers Death; Time conquers Fame; and Eternity conquers Time. Thus the speaker uses this allusion to make his case that the fame that she may deserve—and the time he would take to do it justice—will be vanquished by time, which in turn is defeated by eternity: "And yonder all before us lie / Deserts of vast eternity."

Given the idea that youth and desire are circumscribed by time, the speaker arrives at his conclusion—"Now let us sport us while we may." He proposes that "like amorous birds of prey," they "our time devour" rather than letting themselves "languish in [time's] slowchapped power." If they were to "sport," he says, even though they could not make the sun "stand still," they would make it "run."

With that final allusion, again the poet draws on Greek mythology. According to legend, Zeus, king of the gods, stopped the sun to create a night three times longer than usual, the better to enjoy his affair with the moral Alemena. The speaker suggests that although they will not be able to imitate Zeus, they will be able to make time fly.

Although the theme of the poem can be stated simply as "Let us take advantage of youth and desire because both fade quickly," the tone is more complicated than such a pitch would suggest. The speaker is no happy-go-lucky shallow seducer, but a witty, serious, playful, educated, sexy, arguer. The tone, therefore, is also both serious and playful, erotic and repulsive, witty and persuasive.

Note too all the figurative language at work in the poem. Metaphor, simile, personification, overstatement, paradox, understatement, and puns abound. As for prosody and form, they reinforce all the other elements. Written in couplets, all exact and rising rhyme, the poem also mixes end-stopped with enjambed lines. Thus the rhyme is both obvious and subtle, obvious when endstopped but subtle when enjambed. And so it imitates the actions of time, always present, always ticking, but not obviously so.

The meter is iambic tetrameter, which sets a conversational rhythm akin to common English speech, but the variations are interesting and call attention to key ideas. The third verse paragraph, for instance, begins with a trochee, the stress falling upon the first syllable "Now." And the last line starts with a spondee, as though to emphasize further Zeus's feat.

And listen to the sounds of those last six lines. All those "s's" create euphony, a sweetness of sound that comes from alliteration. *Seduction*, of course, begins with an "s."

Summary

"To His Coy Mistress" is part of the tradition of carpe diem poems, poems that celebrate the present—and love in particular—because life is short and death is a "vast eternity." As you would expect, other common subjects and motifs turn up with some regularity in poetry, no matter when the poems were written or by whom. Fear of death, love of life, mutability—the changing nature of the world—are only some of the recurring motifs in poetry.

Almost all of the poems you have read for this lesson deal with the subject of death—sudden death, accidental death, violent death, ironic death, leveling death, instruments of death. Yet the sameness of general subject means little when you consider the range of themes the poems cover.

In a way, all literature deals with both the universal and the unique, focusing on common subjects but providing original perspectives. Short fiction uses a brief narrative to create for us a dominant impression of a single incident or character. Poetry uses economy, sound, emotion, and imagery to convey a feeling, idea, or event. And, as you will see, drama uses dialogue and action to explore the same motifs that occur in short stories and poems. The most common denominator among the three genres is theme.

VIEWING GUIDE

An important component of this lesson is the video. You will learn more effectively form it by thinking about the following questions and guidelines.

Before Viewing:

1. Review the following chapters: "Words: The Building Blocks of Poetry," (pages 653–685), "Character in Setting: Who, What, Where, and When in Poetry," (page 686), "Imagery: The Poem's Link to the Senses," (pages 726–727), "Tone: The Creation of Attitudes in Poetry," (page 800) and "Symbolism and Allusion: Windows to Wides Expanses of Meaning," (page 940) in the text, paying particular attention to the following topics.

Character, setting, action	Rhyme, syntax, and form
Diction	Speaker
Images and rhetorical figures	Symbol and allusion
Rhythm and meter	Tone

2. Review the poems assigned, paying particular attention to the ones your instructor emphasizes. Try to hear each poem's sound.

During Your Viewing:

1. Listen to the rhyme and meter in the poems that are read aloud.
2. Listen for what the critics suggest as possibilities of the poems' themes.
3. Notice how the critics work out their interpretations.
4. Summarize what each critic has to say about theme.
5. List the major points Donald Hall makes in the interview.

After Viewing:

Give some thought to the following questions. You may want to write short answers in your journal or notebook.

1. What similarities do you find among the poems read in the program?
2. How do those poems differ?
3. What points do the critics make that you would like to know more about?
4. How important is theme to Donald Hall?
5. In what ways does Hall's discussion of theme fit that of the critics?

WRITING ACTIVITIES

After your study of this lesson, you should be able to analyze the theme of a poem. Your instructor will advise you which, if any, of the following writing activities you are to complete.

Formal Writing:

Only the first activity is based upon a model in the textbook, but even so it is not a simple one. You would be best off picking a poem you like that is relatively short (say, under 30 lines). Then try to isolate its most important feature, perhaps metaphor or symbolism or prosody or imagery. You can then use that feature as the key to the poem's theme. As for Activities 2 and 3, they are patterned after the ones in Lesson 10 on theme in the short story. If you wrote an essay based on one of those activities, you have a head start on method and organization. Exploration and evaluation are the goals of the fourth essay, the assignment with the greatest latitude.

1. Using the study guide and the example in the textbook (pages 1073–1079) write an analysis of the theme in one of the poems not discussed in this lesson. Like the example in the textbook, your essay should focus on one of the techniques in the poem, relating it to what you interpret as the theme.
2. "Dulce et Decorum Est," pages 802–803, and "Naming of Parts," pages 674–675, share a similar subject—life in the military. Write an essay analyzing how contrast and irony support the poems' themes.
3. "Auto Wreck," pages 1175–1176, and "Not Waving But Drowning," page 1177, all deal with violent death. Examine what each poem suggests about violent death and write an essay that explains the similarities and differences you find.
4. Donald Hall emphasizes the importance of multiple themes in a work. Analyze one of his poems to determine the extent to which he practices what he believes.

Informal Writing:

The first activity calls for a close reading of a poem and identification of what makes it work, both in light of the reader's experience. The second one should appeal to anyone who enjoys poetry, for it calls for imagination coupled with the knowledge of poetic techniques.

1. Choose one of the poems you have read for this course that connects most directly with your own experience. In an informal essay, explain what those connections are and identify the techniques and elements in the poem that reinforce its theme.

2. If you would prefer, rethink one of your experiences in terms of poetry. The purpose here is to recast an experience into poetic form, but you do not have to write the poem itself—just the notes for it. That you do by drafting ideas for some of the elements your poem might contain. For instance, what diction would be appropriate? Metaphors or similes? Other figurative language? Images? Allusions? Write a short description of what happens in the poem, note down the subject, and write out one of the poem's themes. Then give samples of some of the elements your poem might include.

SELF-TEST

Match the items in column A with the definitions or identifications in B:

A	B
1. "Miniver Cheevy" and "Richard Cory"	a. Use a similar metric technique
2. "Miniver Cheevy" and "Bells for John Whiteside's Daughter"	b. Are examples of free verse
	c. Are written by the same poet
3. "Ethics" and "Not Waving but Drowning"	d. Are written in couplets
	e. Focus on violent death
4. "Naming of Parts" and "Bells for John Whiteside's Daughter"	f. Emphasize theme through setting
	g. Involve more than one speaker
5. "To His Coy Mistress" and "My Last Duchess	h. Avoid symbols
	i. Used as a common motif
6. "Naming of Parts" and "Not Waving But Drowning"	j. Use allusion to emphasize theme
	k. Were written by women
7. "Auto Wreck" and "My Last Duchess"	l. Deal with the same myth
	m. Use diction to emphasize theme
8. Carpe Diem	
9. "Auto Wreck"	
10. "To His Coy Mistress" and "Ethics"	

Answer the following multiple-choice items:

1. Which poem's subject does NOT fit?
    a. "Dulce et Decorum Est"
    b. "Auto Wreck"
    c. "Naming of Parts"
    d. "Death of the Ball Turret Gunner"

2. Which poem's theme does NOT fit?
   a. "Dulce et Decorum Est"
   b. "Auto Wreck"
   c. "Naming of Parts"
   d. "Death of the Ball Turret Gunner"

3. Which statement about theme is true? A theme in poetry is
   a. a statement of fact.
   b. synonymous with meaning.
   c. derived from a subject.
   d. unrelated to the elements in the short story.

4. To support your interpretation of a poem, which do you NOT need to do?
   a. Deal with the concept of theme
   b. Explore multiple meanings
   c. Cite evidence from the text
   d. Identify with the theme

5. Short fiction and poetry
   a. have no similar elements.
   b. have dissimilar subjects.
   c. depend upon prosody.
   d. differ in form.

So that you can see how well you can apply what you have learned about theme to a poem we have not discussed, answer the following short essay questions in 100–300 words:

1. In Linda Pastan's "Ethics," page 1162, what question is posed and what is the speaker's concluding response to it? Based on that response, what would you state as the poem's theme?
2. Consider the settings in the poem. Describe them and relate them to the theme you proposed in response to question 1.
3. What does the allusion to a Rembrandt painting add to the poem? What relationship does it have to the theme you have identified?

ADDITIONAL READING ACTIVITIES

If you enjoyed reading the poems and listening to the interview in this lesson, you may want to read more works by Donald Hall:

Hall, Donald. *The Happy Man.* (Poems)
　　_____. *The One Day: A Poem in Three Parts.*
　　_____. *Contemporary American Poetry.* (An anthology of post-World War II poetry edited by Hall)

226—*Literary Visions*

_____. *Kicking the Leaves.* (A collection of Hall's essays)
_____. *To Keep Moving: Essays 1959–1969.*
_____. *The Oxford Book of American Literary Anecdotes.*
_____. *Ox-cart Man.* (A children's story book for ages 5–7)
_____. *The Oxford Book of Children's Verse in America.* (Edited by Hall and aimed at children 11 and up)
_____. *String Too Short to be Saved: Recollections of Summers on a New England Farm.* (Essays by Hall)
_____. *Fathers Playing Catch with Sons: Essays on Sport.* (Mostly baseball)

MODULE IV

Drama

LESSON 18

Image of Reality:
THE ELEMENTS OF DRAMA

ABOUT THE LESSON

If you wanted to study drama at a college or university, you would probably find yourself faced with a choice—Should you take a course offered by the English Department or Theater Department? If you looked into this decision a bit more, you'd find that both courses cover similar plays, so what's the difference? It's a big one. A Department of Theater (or Drama or Theater Arts) looks at a play as a production, with the emphasis on performance; a Department of English looks at a play as a text, with the emphasis on analysis and interpretation.

But wait a minute. How can you interpret a play without thinking about performance? After all, it is a *play*, intended to be performed. And how can you discuss performance without thinking about interpretation? How a part is played, a set designed, or a scene directed depends on how the play is interpreted. The boundary between these two academic perspectives appears to be drawn in invisible ink.

The difference becomes clearer if you think of emphasis instead of exclusive territory. If you take an English course, you will be reading and analyzing plays as writing, as literature, but always with the idea that they are meant to be performed. And if you enroll in a theater course, you will be studying performance but always with the idea that performance is based on a reading—an interpretation—of the text. The two approaches reinforce instead of exclude each other.

In the best of all possible worlds, you would probably study drama from both perspectives. So, too, in the best of worlds, you would be able to read a play and then see it produced on the stage by professionals. But few of us have that opportunity. Live professional productions of plays are relatively inaccessible for most of us, and film and television adaptations are accessible but are not the same thing as seeing a performance on the stage. *The Glass Menagerie*, for instance, is often shown on television in both film and dramatic versions. In the very best of all possible worlds, you would be able to read the play, see it performed live, and then see a version of it on television. The result would be a triple perspective that would deepen your understanding of the work.

The seven lessons that follow guide you through the process of interpreting plays and augment your analysis with professional productions of various scenes from the dramas you will be reading. Although you will not see a whole play as performed by a professional stage company, the scenes you will see in the videos will come close to staged performances.

There's an important distinction here. Think about how you watch a movie or television drama and you'll realize that the camera mediates between you and the written script. What you see is what the focus of the director and the camera allow you to see. It's as though the camera is a silent or visual narrator; it controls your view of what's on the screen and guides your interpretation. In the medium of film or television, a writer's script is interpreted first by the director, who sets out the controlling interpretation, and then by the film editor. The result is the sequence of camera shots that you see on the screen, and it does not change from one viewing to another.

A director for a stage production has far less control. The stage performance is live, not frozen on film, and you may look at anything you wish. If halfway through a performance, your attention is diverted because a minor actor decides to upstage the leads or because a stage prop falls off a table, there is nothing the director can do to keep your focus on what he or she has determined should receive the most attention. There are no close-ups here, no camera angles. Nothing mediates between you and the action—what is happening on stage.

Then too, there's the interaction with the audience. An appreciative, attentive group of play-goers can bring out the best in the actors, and a good production can create a sense of community among those who witness it.

The performances you will be seeing of *Oedipus the King* and *Hamlet* are videotaped versions of staged performances; *The Glass Menagerie* is a film adaptation. The videos and film cannot recreate the interaction between players and audience. Nor are the scenes enacted shot as though the camera were looking through your eyes as you sat in the audience. But the performances will come close to recreating the experience of being in the theater.

All of the scenes you will see are produced as they might be for the contemporary American theater. The sets are what you might expect. For instance, the scenes from *Oedipus the King* are not presented as they might have been for an audience of 6th century Athenians. There are no masks, no platform boots. Instead, you will see actors in the costumes of the time playing the scenes against sets appropriate to the play.

The videotaped performances are closer to the original written plays than the film adaptation. In the video dramatizations, not as much has been cut as in film, and the *realism* of the medium lies between that of film and that of live theater. Film is a much more realistic medium than the videotapes you will see here.

As you work your way through these lessons, you'll also notice another difference. Instead of continuing with the elements of drama, your textbook presents the plays by type—first Tragedy, then Comedy, then Realistic and Nonrealistic drama. This study guide, however, continues with a format similar to the ones you used for the study of the short story and poetry. The elements of drama are first introduced and then presented in separate lessons: Character and Actor; Action and Plot; Setting and Staging; The Language of Theater; Myth and Symbolism; and Theme.

Thus when you study drama, you will be able to draw upon what you learned about the short story and poetry to see how the various components work to convey meaning. Presenting information in the same format should make it easier for you to learn.

You will see that this lesson mentions *Oedipus the King*, *Hamlet*, and *The Glass Menagerie*, the three plays that will be discussed in the seven lessons that follow. You do not have to read them for this lesson, but you will find the lesson easier to follow if you read the scenes that will be shown in the video and mentioned in this study guide (see Lesson Assignment, Step 2). You will see that the scenes noted from *Oedipus the King* in this lesson and in those that follow refer to two translations—the one by Thomas Gould in your text and a more accessible and dramatic one by Robert Fagles (Penguin Classics edition) that is used in the videos.

On the assumption that your instructor will probably assign these three plays, we have spread out the reading so that you read one play for each lesson, which means that the lessons that come later will be able to draw upon all three. This method allows us to illustrate a dramatic device or element with more than one example.

You will also notice a huge difference in what is covered. The textbook offers a wide selection of different types of plays from different historical periods and countries. We have opted instead for a narrower but more focused view: three plays from three different periods and countries, but all examples of serious drama. We have chosen serious drama because it is usually what people think of when they think of plays. And for good reason. These plays, like the short stories and poems you have read, concentrate on the human condition and deal with questions that go beyond the boundaries of time and culture.

"Who am I?" becomes the central and ironic question that Oedipus pursues, but it is also crucial to Hamlet and to *The Glass Menagerie*'s Tom Wingfield. And that is only one of the universal questions these dramas explore.

GOAL

This lesson will help you to recognize drama as a distinct form of literature.

WHAT YOU WILL LEARN

When you complete this lesson you will be able to:

1. Define the major characteristics of drama.
2. Describe similarities and differences among short fiction, poetry, and drama in terms of dramatic action, structure, and forms.
3. Explain why performance is critical in drama.
4. Explain why audience is critical in drama.
5. Recognize the different types of drama.
6. Describe the origins of drama.
7. Discuss how the characteristics of drama affect a viewer's response.
8. State why drama may be chosen as the appropriate form for expressing an author's thoughts and feelings.
9. Give examples of drama found in other media.

LESSON ASSIGNMENT

Working through the following nine steps will help you master the objectives and achieve the goal for this lesson:

Step 1: In your text, read the chapter "The Dramatic Vision: An Overview," pages 1204–1225, and the introductory pages of "The Tragic Vision: Affirmation through Loss," pages 1265–1281, and "The Comic Vision: Restoring the Balance," pages 1496–1504. The text will provide background for what you will read in the study guide, explain the key terms, and give you some information about the plays you will be reading.

Step 2: Read the specific plays your instructor assigns. The lessons that focus on drama (18–24) will deal with three plays:

Image of Reality—231

[Handwritten note: Read 1 play — #19 – #24 if applicable to your play]

- *Oedipus the King,* Sophocles, Gould translation in Roberts, pages 1281–1318; Fagles translation—Sophocles. *The Three Theban Plays,* translated by Robert Fagles. New York: Penguin Books, 1982.
- *Hamlet,* William Shakespeare, pages 1322–1421.
- *The Glass Menagerie,* Tennessee Williams, pages 1643–1692.

This lesson, 18, will deal briefly with all three plays. Lesson 19 will concentrate primarily on *Hamlet,* Lessons 20 and 23 on *Oedipus the King,* and Lessons 21 and 22 on *The Glass Menagerie.* Lesson 24 will review all three. Your instructor may want you to use the Penguin Classics edition of *Oedipus the King.*

The following scenes provide a context for the study guide discussion and video performances, and the speeches marked with an asterisk (*) will be shown in the video. For *Oedipus the King,* video performances will be based on the Fagles translation; the corresponding lines in the Gould translation in your text are listed in parentheses.

- *Oedipus the King,* Fagles: Lines 97–126 (Gould: Lines 57–64)*
- *Hamlet,* Act I.ii.67–86*
- *The Glass Menagerie,* Scene 1, Speeches 1, 6–10, 28–38*

Step 3: Read the OVERVIEW in this study guide lesson.

Step 4: Watch the VIDEO, following the steps in the VIEWING GUIDE in this study guide lesson.

Step 5: Reread the OVERVIEW to reinforce what you have learned in the text and the video and to help you complete the Writing Activities.

Step 6: Complete any WRITING ACTIVITIES assigned in this lesson.

Step 7: Do the SELF-TEST exercises in this study guide lesson.

Step 8: Read any of the ADDITIONAL READING ACTIVITIES assigned.

Step 9: Go back to the learning objectives in the WHAT YOU WILL LEARN section of this study guide lesson and be sure you can respond to each of them.

KEY TERMS FOR STUDYING THE GENRE OF DRAMA

Listed here are the terms that will be discussed throughout the next seven lessons. You have already read about all of them in your study of the short story and poetry. Consequently, you may want to refer back to either Lesson 4 (short story) or Lesson 11 (poetry) to refresh your memory. And you may want to keep this list available so that you can make notes about the terms as you encounter them in your studying. Definitions are also provided in the text's "Glossary." Remember, however, that when studying literature it is more important to know how to apply the terms within the genre rather than to memorize strict definitions.

Action
Anagnorisis or Recognition
Antagonist
Atmosphere
Character
    flat
    rounded
    stereotype
    stock
Conflict
Connotation, Denotation
Diction
Figurative language (figures of speech)
Hubris or Pride
Imagery
Irony
    dramatic
    situational
    verbal

Myth
Peripeteia or Reversal
Plot
Prosody and Meter
Protagonist
Rhyme
Setting
Structure
    exposition
    complication or rising action
    climax
    crisis
    resolution, denouement, or falling action
Symbol
    cultural
    private
    universal
Theme

OVERVIEW

Our word *drama* comes from the ancient Greek word *dran*, meaning *to do*. And that etymology is a good capsule definition, for drama is concerned with doing, with action and its consequences. In drama, it is action that reveals character and brings about conflict. But unlike the action in a short story, the action in a play is enacted before you—as dialogue either printed on the page or spoken on the stage.

Long before print and long before recorded history, what we now recognize as drama had its origins in ritual. The first part of the explanation that follows sketches out the little we know of drama's beginnings as ritual and describes the forms in took during its early development by the ancient Greeks.

Next we will discuss the different kinds of drama and illustrate them with references drawn from stage, television, and film, giving a succinct history of the various forms. From there, we'll take a look at the elements that drama shares with the short story and poetry and then move on to the characteristics that distinguish drama from the other genres.

And finally, because this course emphasizes the interpretation and analysis of plays, we will explain how to read a play. After all, for many of us the nearest play is on the bookshelf or in the library rather than on the stage. The videos, however, will bring a bit of the stage to you.

The Origins of Drama

Anthropologists have studied various rituals associated with primitive cultures, rituals centered on cyclical or important events—the hunt, the harvest, the summer and winter solstices, and the like. No matter what event was celebrated, what was important was its religious significance, the surrounding ritual, the reinforcing of shared values, and the elevated form of language.

These characteristics are present in early Greek religious rites, and over the years, ritual evolved into drama. What we know about the origins of drama is based on information that has come down to us from the ancient Greeks, in particular the works of three great 5th century Athenian tragedians—Aeschylus, Sophocles, and Euripides—and the philosopher Aristotle, who later described what he saw in the theater in his *Poetics*. From these beginnings in Greece, we can link the western tradition of drama to religion, ritual, and communal experience.

For instance, the festival of the greater Dionysia was held in late March or early April—a time appropriate to the god Dionysus's association with death and rebirth. In Athens, one of the features of the celebration was the singing of hymns, religious songs in verse consisting of parts sung by a chorus and lead singer. In 534 B.C., an Athenian by the name of Thespis changed the form of the hymn by adding an actor. With the interplay of the lead singer, the actor, and the chorus came the possibility of dramatic action and therefore conflict. Religious ritual then evolved into the dramatic form we see represented by the plays of Aeschylus, Sophocles, and Euripides.

By Sophocles's time (ca. 496–406 B.C.), such celebrations had become extensive and sophisticated. Poetry, song, dance, and spectacle were the means of celebration, and a sense of mystery and wonder were the result. The festival of Dionysus spread over five days, with two days of poetry contests and religious festivities leading up to the last three days that were devoted to dramatic competition. And the language of drama was verse—language elevated to poetry.

This competition took place in the Great Theater of Dionysus, a theater far closer to an American college football stadium than a Broadway playhouse. In fact, the only element in common between the theater of the Greeks and that of today is the vocabulary, and even there the meaning is slightly different. To ancient Athenians, the orchestra was a place for actors and chorus, not for expensive seats. And it was a place where the chorus danced and sang, not a reference to people playing instruments. Yet the theater of the Greeks is easy to visualize. Imagine some 14,000 people, sitting on hard benches that line a semi-circular amphitheater built into the side of a hill. Each row of benches is sharply raked so that each seat has a clear view of the action below, and the shape of the cut-away hillside provides natural amplification of the words and song spoken below.

Looking down from above, you would see that the best view is reserved for the priest of Dionysus, whose throne looks out on the level area—the orchestra—where the chorus sings and dances and where part of the dramatic action takes place. In the center of the orchestra stands the altar of Dionysus, and to the left and right are aisles leading away from the theater that were used by spectators as well as the actors and chorus.

Just beyond the orchestra is the *skene* or scene building that usually represented the front of a temple or palace. The area directly in front of the skene is a level platform—the proskenion, same as our proscenium stage—and it is here that most of the play's dramatic action occurs.

At dawn the competition begins. By nightfall, the audience would have watched five or six plays—a cycle of three tragedies, each related and dealing with a familiar myth or legend—followed by a satyr play that provided some comic relief, then one or two comedies. All in all, that's a lineup that makes watching a contemporary play seem like an intermission.

In keeping with the idea of competition, Greek playwrights were chosen prior to the festival. Those who wrote tragedies were responsible not only for a cycle of the three plays but also for the satyr play. A satyr play? Isn't a satyr a figure with the head and body of a man and the legs of a goat and known for general lechery? Yes, but you also have to remember that Dionysus was a god associated with wine and fertility; the satyrs were part of his court and known for lustiness, drinking, and dancing.

At the end of the festival of Dionysus, prizes were awarded to the best writers of tragedy and of comedy. Sophocles may have set a record for awards, having won some twenty first prizes for his tragedies.

As you can imagine, with that large an audience and none of the technical assistance we have today—no lights, no microphones, no special effects—the drama was presented with broad strokes. Masks froze all facial expression, Frankenstein-like platform boots gave the actors additional height, gestures were broad and stylized, the scenery static, and the plot straightforward. And, of course, the plot was familiar. Audiences knew the plot of *Oedipus the King* because the legend was part of their culture; what kept them in their seats was watching how Sophocles unfolded the story, seeing and hearing how he used dramatic irony to play off Oedipus's ignorance against the audience's knowledge, and, of course, listening to the beauty of the play's language.

The subject of the play's language brings up the question of translation, for different translators emphasize different points in the play. Thomas Gould, the author of the translation in your text, brings out the stateliness of the language:

> Oedipus: My children, ancient Cadmus newest care,
> why have you hurried to those seats, your boughs
> wound with the emblems of the suppliant?
> The city is weighed down with fragrant smoke,
> with hymns to the Healer and the cries of mourners. — (lines 1–5).

Robert Fagles, the translator for the dramatizations in the videos, emphasizes the action, the tension in the language, in the same opening address:

> O my children, the new blood of ancient Thebes,
> why are you here? Huddling at my altar,
> praying before me, your branches wound in wool.
> Our city reeks with the smoke of burning incense,
> rings with the cries for the Healer and wailing for the dead. — (lines 1–5)

As you can see from these opening lines, the Fagles translation is more accessible, more immediate and detailed—less stiff. For those reasons, it lends itself well to performance, which is why it is the translation used in the video.

Sophocles's greatness lies in his ability to combine the earlier dramatists' emphasis on religion with their later focus on the individual. In so doing, he reinforced several of the beliefs upon which Greek culture was based: know thyself; nothing in excess; and punishment is near. Seeing these concepts exemplified in the dramatization of *Oedipus the King,* hearing them reinforced by the choral odes, and finding their expression in the character and fate of the king, the Greek audience was moved and enlightened. The drama strengthened their sense of communal experience by reinforcing the values of their culture.

The Types of Drama

If you were to turn to the entertainment section of your newspaper, you would see all sorts of advertisements for movies. Scanning down the pages, you would find serious films and comedies and some that fall somewhere between. And then there's the television schedule that provides an even greater variety of fictional shows—situation comedies, soap operas, cartoons, improvisational comedy, dramatic series, adaptations of plays, novels, and short stories, even the occasional opera or musical comedy. All of these kinds of films and shows had their origins or counterparts in early Greek drama.

The early Greek form of *tragedy* centered on a hero courageous enough to take on forces beyond human control. But what makes the hero great also causes suffering and the person's eventual downfall. As exemplified in *Oedipus the King*, fate or the gods play important roles in the hero's suffering and eventual disintegration.

But as drama became more concerned with humanity and less with the gods, the nature of tragedy changed. By the first century A.D. and the time of the Roman playwright Seneca, tragedy had shifted its focus to the individual, and ghosts and portents figured largely in plots that revolved around the idea of revenge.

In the years that followed the decline of the Roman civilization came the rise of Christianity, which emphasized the religious over the secular at the expense of drama. What resulted was a long period in which plays were suppressed and folk arts and music prospered. Mimes and singers wandered from town to town, performing for their keep, but the Dark Ages were dark indeed for the performance of plays.

It was during these medieval times in England and on the continent that religious music and song took another turn, one ironically similar to that taken by the ancient and pagan Greeks. But instead of evolving into tragedy, in medieval times music and song kept their religious center, giving rise to religious drama. As the music that accompanied medieval religious services became more elaborate, the priests added spoken instead of sung lines, eventually developing dramas that told of the lives of saints in miracle plays or illustrated the path to salvation in mystery plays.

By the late Middle Ages, probably around the late 14th century, this type of drama also led to another form—the dramatic allegories, such as *Everyman*, concerned with vice and virtue and known as the morality play. Today we can see the tradition of the religious play in a direct descendent such as the play depicting the last events in the life of Christ that is performed every ten years at Oberammergau, in Germany. Less pure forms can also be found in the occasional Biblical film or televised drama.

But the golden age of Greek tragedy was not to be equaled until the 16th and 17th centuries when the Renaissance with its interests in the classics and in the individual gave us playwrights such as England's Shakespeare, Spain's Calderon, and France's Corneille. Their plots dealt with love, honor, revenge, duty—the same topics that appear in serious plays of the 19th and 20th centuries.

Whether the plays of these later periods are indeed tragedies in the same sense as the Greek plays is arguable, but there's no questioning their thoughtful examination of universal topics. Plays such as *Death of a Salesman*, pages 1424–1486, and *The Glass Menagerie*, pages 1643–1692, are first cousins to television shows and films that deal with contemporary concerns such as drug abuse and crime but do so within a larger framework of universal values such as loyalty or family conflict.

Comedy has followed a somewhat similar route, from the Greeks to the Romans to the Renaissance to the 19th and 20th centuries. But it has also taken some specialized byways. The commedia dell'arte of the 16th century added improvisation and a wealth of stock characters to comedy. And the 17th century—with playwrights such as the French dramatist Moliere—highlighted human frailties and specialized in the comedy of manners. Farce and satire add to the rich, broad vein of comedy, so that by the 20th century the term can be applied to plays as different as the often perplexing *Waiting for Godot* and a readily accessible Neil Simon production.

And of course the subjects of comedy are as varied as the events of life. We can see remnants of the ancient Greek political satire in cartoon strips such as "Doonesbury," while the *commedia dell'arte* lives on in improvisational comic routines and in slapstick. The quick turns of plot that provided much of the humor in the plays of 18th and 19th century England continue today in altered form within the TV sit-com.

Then there are all the plays that fall somewhere between tragedy and comedy, into that broad category called *tragicomedy*. Evolving from a mixture of the classic traditions of tragedy and comedy, tragicomedy flourished during the 16th and 17th centuries and surfaced again in changed form as the 19th century melodrama—the grandparent of our present day soap operas.

What about real operas? Just as the early Greek religious songs evolved into drama, music not only led to the medieval mystery, miracle, and morality plays but also to opera. The opera developed in 16th century Italy and had its origins in the musical intermezzo, the musical entertainment that filled the time between acts of plays that were imitations of the classical forms. Drawn to the musical and theatrical possibilities inherent in the intermezzo and to the classic tragedies, the Italian writers first drew upon mythology for their plots.

In time, opera acquired both a tragic and comic tradition and eventually spun off what we know as the musical comedy. The 18th century English play *The Beggar's Opera* is probably the first musical comedy in that it uses folk tunes and popular ballads to portray contemporary life. Today, one could argue that plays such as *My Fair Lady, Guys and Dolls,* and *South Pacific*—which represent the modern musical comedy—are an important American contribution to the theater. And one could also argue that the revues and vaudeville that preceded the modern musical comedy have been seen in the television variety show—the string of skits and songs and dances usually centered on a popular music or comedy star.

Of course, much of what we see on television has nothing to do with drama. The news shows, game shows, documentaries, exposés, and sports coverage provide dramatic and comic moments, but these shows are not rooted in fiction. Dramatic action arises or does not arise from events beyond the control of the director or scriptwriter. But in plays, and in fiction in general, the writer creates the events that lead to dramatic action and conflict.

Shared Characteristics

You have already studied characterization in short fiction and in poetry, so characterization in drama will not be anything new. In fact, drama uses many of the terms you learned in connection with the short story—rounded and flat characters, static and dynamic characters, stereotypes or stock characters, and, of course, protagonist and antagonist.

To separate the *rounded* from the *flat* characters, you only need to ask which are fully developed. In *Hamlet*, for instance, you get to know Hamlet, Gertrude, and, of course, Claudius, the antagonist who opposes Hamlet. But you also gain some insight into the personalities and motivations of Horatio, Polonius, Laertes, even perhaps Ophelia. All of these characters are ones you'd probably put on your "rounded" list, though the degrees to which their characters are developed vary considerably.

Look at the cast on pages 1322–1323 and you'll find more flat characters than you might expect. Rosencrantz and Guildenstern are so close to being interchangeable that a contemporary play by Tom Stoppard that is a counterpoint to *Hamlet* does just that. And Osric is so insignificant (though funny) that he is often omitted from productions. You'll find that you have a hard time keeping the names straight among the courtiers, officers, and players, and that's because they are not only flat but static. They do not change.

The characters in a play that do change are *dynamic*. And usually the greatest change is that undergone by the *protagonist*. Oedipus, for instance, goes from ignorance to knowledge. Along the way he changes from being a proud man to a humble one, from someone who defies the gods to someone who recognizes their authority. And of course he goes from sight to blindness.

The opposite of a rounded, dynamic character is the stereotype or stock character. In *Hamlet,* for instance, Osric is the stereotypical fop, the courtier whose language is so flowery and flattery, so ingrained, that it obscures what he is trying to say. Or be on the lookout for the herdsman in *Oedipus the King*. You'll find him a stock character in that he is a tool of the plot, yet Sophocles's portrayal makes him more than a stick figure even though his character remains a flat one.

Whether rounded or flat, dynamic or static, characters in a play are involved in actions, events that have causes and effects. That chain of actions and their results provide the play with its plot and the conflict on which it turns. As in the short story, the plot is apt to include certain stages. *Exposition* provides necessary background; *complication* or *rising action* sets the plot in motion and leads to a *climax* or *crisis* that is the turning point of the play; what then follows is the *catastrophe*, the *falling action* that ends in *resolution*, the tying up of all the loose ends.

Thus as *Oedipus the King* opens, we hear the Chorus explain what is going on in Thebes, describing the plague that has devastated the city. In *Hamlet,* we are introduced to the turbulence in the state of Denmark and the ghost of the elder Hamlet. *The Glass Menagerie* opens with Tom Wingfield explaining his role as narrator. All these scenes are examples of *exposition*.

When the complication gets the plot rolling, we start to see the outlines of the conflict. Like conflict in the short story, conflict in drama can be internal or external, and it is often multi-layered. The conflict in *The Glass Menagerie*, for instance, can be seen within Tom as he tries to reconcile his ambitions with his responsibility toward his mother and sister. But once you start thinking about external conflicts, they seem everywhere: Tom vs. Amanda, the old world vs. the new, illusion vs. reality. And those are just a few possibilities.

The conflict is expressed through the language of the play, but it is important to remember that the concept of performance lends a broader meaning to the term. The language of drama includes not just what is said but also gesture, props, costume, and indeed silence. A pause at a tense moment in a play can be eloquent. As you read *Oedipus the King,* for example, think about how pacing can affect the scene between Oedipus and Tiresias. When their dialogue begins, if Oedipus pauses before he speaks, the hesitation would give the impression that he cannot believe what he hears from Tiresias. On the other hand, if he rushes into speech, he would impress you as too quick to anger.

But of course it is the words that carry the greatest part of a play's meaning, and your study of poetry can help you there. You will note that *Oedipus the King* and *Hamlet* are written in verse. In the original Greek, the prosody of *Oedipus the King* is quite complicated and employs meter that we rarely see in poetry written in English. For those reasons translators of the play usually change the original meter to blank verse, which gives a sense of the metrical form of the play without being distracting.

Even though the meter is changed, the other poetic elements that Sophocles draws upon remain the same—imagery, rhetorical devices, myth, symbolism, and irony. You'll see these elements at work as well in *Hamlet.* There you'll also hear the occasional use of rhyme and of prose, although blank verse predominates.

The Glass Menagerie doesn't use verse, but you'll certainly find that Tennessee Williams depends heavily on diction to convey symbolism. Myth also figures in the play, though in the sense of shared values rather than direct allusions to another culture's mythology.

Myth in *Oedipus the King* is obvious; it provides the plot. Its role in *Hamlet*, however, is far more subtle. Shakespeare gives us a world of ghosts and the traditional beliefs of his day, beliefs about personality types and good and bad revenge. Built into the fabric of the play is the idea of "right" kingship, that the king sets the moral tone for the country. It follows therefore that a "wrong" king, one who has murdered his way to a usurped throne, infects the kingdom. The something that is "rotten" in Denmark points to the nation's moral center.

Your earlier study of myth and symbolism introduced you to the idea of *archetype,* an image, plot pattern, or character type that recurs in the literature of many cultures. Both *Oedipus the King* and *Hamlet* present us with the archetype of the *tragic hero,* which you will read about below. Tom, in *The Glass Menagerie,* is a very different kind of hero, if he's a hero at all. Perhaps you can recognize in him a different archetype, that of the wanderer or of the poet.

The Nature of Drama

As the term suggests, the concept of the tragic hero is a figure associated with tragedy. You will be learning more about this archetype later, but for now, keep in mind that this archetype, the manner in which action is presented, and the possibility of staging distinguish drama from any other kind of literature.

Whether you are reading the play or seeing it on stage, you will find that Hamlet and Oedipus are very different from the archetype of hero that you read about in the short story. The old woman in Eudora Welty's "A Worn Path," pages 114–119, the boy in John Updike's "A & P," pages 363–367, the Indian in "Blue Winds Dancing," pages 313–317, are all heroes, but they are not tragic heroes.

Why not? All of them suffer, they tackle difficulties head on, and they have admirable qualities. Is the major difference one of form, that they are not in a play? And what about Icarus and Penelope? They certainly seem heroic and their lives were tragic. Where do the differences lie?

There is no easy answer, not even in the thousands of books that have addressed this question. But to put the difference as succinctly as possible, it's one of scale. What's important about Oedipus, about Hamlet, is that they take on forces far beyond their control. Both are called upon (in different ways) to cleanse their kingdoms. They succeed, but along the way they suffer and they learn and they are destroyed—the one literally, the other metaphorically. Yet their lives have made a difference: Thebes is raid of the plague, Denmark is restored to order.

The tragic hero does not need to be royal. T. S. Eliot wrote his verse tragedy *Murder in the Cathedral* about Thomas à Becket, the archbishop of Canterbury who chose God over his king and paid with his life. And a good case can be made for Willy Loman, the protagonist in Arthur Miller's *Death of a Salesman.* Nor need the tragic hero be male. Sophocles's Antigone and George Bernard Shaw's St. Joan in the plays that bear their names exhibit qualities associated with a tragic hero.

Your study of the protagonist in the short story will help you understand the nature of Hamlet and of Oedipus as well as the less tragic and less heroic Tom Wingfield in *The Glass Menagerie.* In a similar manner, your study of setting in the short story and in poetry will serve you well in your analysis of setting in drama.

But since most plays are meant to be staged, setting takes on a larger meaning. Setting for a play leads to staging, and staging not only includes the sets but the kind of stage that will be used, costumes, props, lighting, special effects, and actors' movements. Because staging is so important to drama, we will devote a complete lesson to it. For now, you only need to know what it involves.

If you decided to produce a play or even if you try to "see" it as you read it, you have to have a certain kind of stage in mind. A short story or poem will describe exactly what you are to see and will give you a perspective—a point of view—from which to see it, but that's not the case with drama. If you think about how you imagine a play, what you probably "see" is the old style proscenium or picture-frame stage, a platform that can be closed off from the audience by a curtain. Lesson 21 will show you other stage possibilities so that you can "see" a different kind of performance.

The idea of staging a play brings up another consideration that does not apply to the short story or poetry and that is *technology.* As a short story writer or poet, no matter whether you're dealing with pen and paper or computer and printer, your only limit is your imagination. You can invent scenes, worlds, galaxies. You don't have to build them.

But that's what the set designer does. The shape of the stage, the lighting available, the ways actors get on and off stage, the special effects possible are all technological matters. And they all affect the writing of a play and the audience's response to it.

How to Read a Play

Whether you read or see a play, you are involved in action as dialogue. You hear what is being said by the various characters, and you see, either in your imagination or on the stage, the action enacted before you. As reader or member of the audience, you are in a position quite unlike the reader of a short story or poem. In a sense, even when you read a play instead of seeing it the process is more participatory than the other two genres.

If that idea seems odd, think about the last film you saw where you stayed on in the theater to see the credits. Screen after screen rolls by with seemingly hundreds of names: actors, directors, producers, editors, assistants, photographers, stunt people, set designers, costumers, make-up people, grips, even something called Best Boy.

Now when you read a play, you are all of those people. You play all the parts, direct all the scenes, create all the sets—you do everything. The play on the written page invites you to participate; in fact, it demands that you do. It does not come to life until you see it and hear it, whether that is in your mind's eye and imagination or on the stage.

Perhaps the best way to read a play is to combine the ways you read short stories and poems—try to hear the lines and see the action. Play each part. For key scenes, read the parts aloud. Use the built-in pauses that come from the end of a scene or act to think about what you have read.

Those built-in breaks are also useful divisions for working out a guide to the play, a synopsis of the action. You'll find this kind of guide essential for a play like *Hamlet* that has many subplots, but it is also helpful for one with as straightforward a plot as *Oedipus the King*. Being able to note *what* happens *when* will reveal the play's structure and also serve as a good review of its various conflicts.

You may also find it fun and useful to take the part of director, casting the play you are reading and working out the actors' gestures, positions, entrances, and exits. You'll discover that analysis, interpretation, and understanding of the play are essential to directing its performance. Imagine Tom Cruise as Hamlet or Kathleen Turner as Gertrude. You'd have a very different *Hamlet*.

Summary

As you can see, drama has a long tradition that is both religious and secular. Rooted in ritual, it still speaks to our shared values in language honed by style. Its original religious focus has faded, but what remains is derived from tragedy and comedy, and the subjects are still universal—the individual, the family, human follies, absurd situations, loyalty, evil.

Drama—particularly drama in performance—moves us as perhaps no other genre can. We identify with the protagonist in a way that is far stronger than the link forged between the reader and the page and pronoun in a short story or poem. We become Oedipus or Hamlet or one of the Wingfields. This identification is stronger if we see the play performed, but it is there even on the page because as readers we are forced to play each role.

The three plays that are the focus of this section on drama are often produced on the stage, and many different versions of them have been made for television and film. If you find yourself at a video rental store, you might look to see if a video of one of the plays is available. Watching it after you have read the play will give your understanding a different dimension. You may find yourself arguing with the production or disagreeing with an interpretation, and you will be in a good position to do so.

VIEWING GUIDE

An important component of this lesson is the video. You will learn more effectively from it by thinking about the following questions and guidelines.

Before Viewing:

1. Review the chapter "The Dramatic Vision: An Overview," pages 1204–1318, and the introductory pages of "The Tragic Vision: Affirmation through Loss," pages 1265–1281. Pay particular attention to the following terms:

    Action
        conflict
        plot
        structure
            exposition
            complication or rising action
            crisis or climax
            catastrophe
            resolution
    Character
        protagonist and antagonist
        static and dynamic
        stereotype or stock
        tragic hero

    History
        commedia dell'arte
        comedy
        intermezzo
        miracle, mystery, and morality plays
        musical comedy
        Theater of Dionysus
        tragedy
        tragicomedy
    Staging

2. Review the scenes assigned by your instructor and those that will be shown on the video:

- *Oedipus the King,* Fagles: Lines 97–126 (Gould: Lines 57–64);
- *Hamlet,* Act I.ii.67–86;
- *The Glass Menagerie,* Scene 1, Speeches 1, 6–10, 28–38.

During Your Viewing:

1. Listen for key words in the history of the theater.
2. Look for clues to Oedipus's character.
3. Look for clues to the characters of Hamlet and Gertrude.
4. Listen for the major points the critics make about *The Glass Menagerie*.
5. Listen for what August Wilson says about how he writes plays.

After Viewing:

Give some thought to the following questions. You may want to write short answers in your journal or notebook.

1. Based on the scenes dramatized, what are your initial impressions of Oedipus, Hamlet, and Tom Wingfield?
2. To what extent do those impressions coincide with the ideas you had before watching the video?
3. What surprised you about the development of drama?
4. How does what August Wilson said relate to what the video had shown before the interview?
5. How would you define drama?

WRITING ACTIVITIES

After your study of this lesson, you should be able to recognize drama as a distinct form of literature. Your instructor will advise you which, if any, of the following writing activities you are to complete

244—*Literary Visions*

Formal Writing:

All of these activities call for a close reading of the scenes portrayed in the video. The purpose of each is to give you practice in analyzing a scene so that when you are asked to analyze a larger segment or whole play, you will know how to go about it. The first activity places you in the position of critic, analyzing the action; the second places you in the position of director, arguing for a different interpretation in the performance.

1. Choose one of the three plays and, first, write a synopsis of the action shown in the video. Using that synopsis, explain your interpretation of the action, covering what it reveals about characterization, structure, plot, conflict, and setting and staging.
2. Choose one of the three plays dramatized on the video and explain how and why you would have played the action differently.

Informal Writing:

Both of these activities emphasize differences. The first brings out the differences between the dialogue of everyday speech and the theater, and the second reveals in filmed drama how the camera functions as a form of narrator. Both of these assignments are time-consuming, but both will uncover differences more clearly and more tellingly than explaining them to you ever could.

1. Given the other person's permission, record an unstaged conversation of 5 to 10 minute duration. (Telephone talk lends itself well to this activity.) Next, transcribe what you recorded. Think about the differences between what you have as dialogue and the dialogue in the scenes from the video. Write a paragraph or two in which you discuss the differences.
2. Select a videotape made of a film that you are familiar with, and find a particularly important scene. Next write a synopsis of the scene, and then review your synopsis, noting the camera angles—what the camera shows you. In your journal or notebook, explain how the camera angles focus and reinforce the scene.

SELF-TEST

Match the items in column A with the definitions or identifications in B:

A	B
1. Tragic hero	a. Prop
2. Dionysus	b. An archetype
3. Modern musical comedy	c. Focuses on gesture, props, silence
4. Miracle play	d. Turning point
5. Morality play	e. Resolution
6. Language of drama	f. Stage
7. Commedia dell'arte	g. Greek god associated with drama
8. Melodrama	h. Deals with lives of the saints
9. Crisis	i. Focuses on improvisation
10. Proscenium	j. Deals with vice and virtue
	k. American contribution to theater
	l. Evolved from tragicomedy
	m. Greek contribution to drama

Answer the following multiple-choice items:

1. One distinguishing characteristic of drama is
    a. setting.
    b. characterization.
    c. symbol.
    d. dialogue.

2. Drama evolved from
    a. rituals.
    b. hymns.
    c. festivals.
    d. actions.

3. If you attended the spring religious festival in 5th century B.C. Athens, you would see
    a. sports competitions.
    b. two or three plays.
    c. only the plays by one dramatist.
    d. the best playwrights had to offer.

4. Television situation comedies are related to
   a. musical comedies.
   b. melodrama.
   c. comedy of manners.
   d. tragedy.
5. Drama in the Renaissance and 5th century B.C. Athens was similar in that it was
   a. secular.
   b. ceremonial.
   c. a golden age of tragedy.
   d. a golden age of satire.

In 100–250 words, answer the following short essay questions:

1. What is the context for the short speech in Act I.ii.244–246, and what does Hamlet risk?
2. Analyze Hamlet's speech in Act I.ii.76–86, from the perspective of poetry. What rhetorical devices does he use? What do they reveal about his character?
3. Reread Hamlet's speech in Act I.v.91–111, with your ear tuned for its tone. Write a paragraph or two explaining what you interpret as the tone of the speech.

ADDITIONAL READING ACTIVITIES

If you enjoyed listening to the interview in this lesson, you will probably want to read one of the plays August Wilson has written:

Wilson, August. *Fences.*
_____. *Joe Turner's Come and Gone.*
_____. *Ma Rainey's Black Bottom.*

LESSON 19

Playing the Part:
CHARACTER AND ACTION

ABOUT THE LESSON

When you studied the short story, you examined the idea of character from the perspective of point of view and setting, and some of what you learned there also applied to poetry. Although much of what you studied about character in the short story and poetry will apply to drama, there are several important differences.

First, the concept of point of view does not exist in drama in the same way it does in the short story. Unlike short stories, where the action is told to you, plays present the action through their characters. The action and plot in *Oedipus the King* and *Hamlet* begin and unfold through the dialogue of the characters. And although *The Glass Menagerie* opens with Tom Wingfield declaring that the "play is memory" and that he is both narrator and character, as soon as the characters appear on stage, the device of narrator recedes and only reappears fully at the very end of the play. Between those opening and closing scenes, the action and plot are carried by dialogue, and the narrator is present only as character.

The concept of setting also differs. Just as characters in a play present themselves directly, the setting is also a physical presence (that may be minimized). Even if you are reading a play instead of seeing it, the physical setting is often more backdrop than integral part. In fact, it's not unusual to see a play performed with so minimal a setting that the stage is called a "black box." In that case, dialogue carries the elements of setting crucial to character development and plot.

At the same time, there is much about character that carries over from the other genres to drama. As in short fiction, characters in drama are flat or rounded, static or dynamic, stereotypical and stock. And, of course, plays have their antagonists and protagonists. Protagonists who serve a higher order and pit themselves against forces far beyond their control are often heroic and tragic, hence the term *tragic hero*.

In this lesson, we will be concentrating on the characters in *Hamlet*. Not only does this complex and complicated play have a large enough cast to do justice to the full range of characterization, it also has a tragic hero. Studying the characters in *Hamlet* will help you later to more fully appreciate the play's plot and conflicts.

GOAL

This lesson will help you to recognize how drama presents character.

WHAT YOU WILL LEARN

When you complete this lesson you will be able to:

1. Explain how characterization is developed differently in drama than in other forms of literature.
2. Identify the standard characters in drama.
3. Describe various stock characters.
4. Recognize the qualities of the tragic hero.
5. Recognize character as a means of furthering exposition.
6. Discuss how a reader's response is affected by knowledge about the background and social and historical context of a drama and its author.

LESSON ASSIGNMENT

The following nine steps will help you master the objectives and achieve the goal for this lesson. The order differs from that in earlier lessons because of the complexity of the play.

Step 1: Read the OVERVIEW in this study guide, as well as the scenes and lines referred to in *Hamlet*.

Step 2: In your text, read "Renaissance Drama and Shakespeare's Theater" and "William Shakespeare, *Hamlet*," pages 1318–1322. The text will provide background for what you will read in the study guide and give you information about the play.

Step 3: This lesson, 19, deals primarily with *Hamlet*, so you should read the entire play, pages 1322–1421. The following scenes provide a context for the study guide discussion and video performances, and those marked with an asterisk (*) will be shown in the video.

- Act I.i
- Act I.ii
- Act I.vv
- Act II.ii.363–401*
- Act II.ii.446–519*
- Act II.ii.523–528*
- Act II.ii.540–549*
- Act II.ii.552–580*
- Act III.i
- Act III.ii
- Act III.iii
- Act III.i.56–69*
- Act V.ii

Step 4: Watch the VIDEO, following the steps in the VIEWING GUIDE in this study guide lesson.

Step 5: Reread the OVERVIEW to reinforce what you have learned in the text and the video and to help you complete the Writing Activities.

Step 6: Complete any WRITING ACTIVITIES assigned in this lesson.

Step 7: Do the SELF-TEST exercises in this study guide lesson.

Step 8: Read any of the ADDITIONAL READING ACTIVITIES assigned.

Step 9: Go back to the learning objectives in the WHAT YOU WILL LEARN section of this study guide lesson and be sure you can respond to each of them.

OVERVIEW

To analyze the characters in a drama, you should know something about the times in which the play was written, particularly if the play is not contemporary. Language and events can change rapidly. Often, knowing the social and historical background of a play provides a context that helps you to understand how the play was originally received as well as how to interpret it today.

For those reasons we will begin with a discussion of Shakespeare's times. Four hundred years have passed since then, so to convey the excitement and vitality of that age we'll start with a look at the broader context surrounding Shakespeare's life and then move on to the immediate historical and social context of *Hamlet*.

What were these Elizabethans like? What did they expect and believe that affected the way they understood a play like *Hamlet*? The question is a large one, so we'll only hit the most important points that relate to Elizabethan beliefs and drama. We will take a look at the wider context of *Hamlet* to see what it reveals about characterization—the concept of humors, the notion of the *Great Chain of Being*, the stage conventions, the style of acting, and the tradition of the *revenge play*.

From that point we will examine the characters in *Hamlet*, showing how they illustrate the range found in drama: those that are rounded or flat, static or dynamic; those that are stock; and finally the *tragic hero*.

Shakespeare's Times

Most of what we know about Shakespeare comes from records—documents recording property, theatrical performances, business letters, and legal transactions. Enough exists, however, to make some safe (although not iron-clad) assumptions. First, we can assume that Shakespeare was Shakespeare. Book after book has been written attempting to show that "Shakespeare" was any one of a number of people, most of them titled and well educated. Yet we know enough about Shakespeare to believe he wrote the plays attributed to him.

We know, for instance, that Shakespeare's life was bound up in the theater of the day. He was an actor (at one point playing the Ghost in *Hamlet*), a partner in a theatrical company, and, of course, a writer. Through this involvement, he must have known not only the plays written by his contemporaries but also the Greek and Latin models on which many of them were based. As a writer, he would also have known the works of a wide range of other writers—both contemporary and ancient. The histories of the ancient Greeks—as well as the philosophic works of contemporary French writers and earlier authors such as the Italians Dante and Boccaccio and the English Gower and Chaucer—made up his reading.

If you think about the age during which Shakespeare lived, you can understand how simply being alive and active in the London theater was an education. The year Shakespeare was born was the same year that Michelangelo and John Calvin died and that Galileo was born. A list of Shakespeare's contemporaries reads like a Who's Who of Western Literature: Ben Jonson, Cervantes, Roger Ascham, Sir Philip Sidney, Edmund Spenser, John Lyly, Thomas Kyd, Christopher Marlowe, Montaigne, Sir Francis Bacon, Thomas Campion, Thomas Middleton, Sir Walter Raleigh, Thomas Nashe, Lope de Vega, Beaumont and Fletcher—the list can go on and on.

Shakespeare's life saw the full impact of both the Renaissance and the Reformation. The excitement over discoveries in chemistry, biology, physiology, astronomy, geography, and mathematics paralleled that accompanying new directions in architecture, philosophy, religion, literature, and politics. The western world was seething with ideas, and in England this was the Age of Elizabeth, the beginning of overseas expansion that would eventually create the vast British Empire.

LESSON 19

Playing the Part:
CHARACTER AND ACTION

ABOUT THE LESSON

When you studied the short story, you examined the idea of character from the perspective of point of view and setting, and some of what you learned there also applied to poetry. Although much of what you studied about character in the short story and poetry will apply to drama, there are several important differences.

First, the concept of point of view does not exist in drama in the same way it does in the short story. Unlike short stories, where the action is told to you, plays present the action through their characters. The action and plot in *Oedipus the King* and *Hamlet* begin and unfold through the dialogue of the characters. And although *The Glass Menagerie* opens with Tom Wingfield declaring that the "play is memory" and that he is both narrator and character, as soon as the characters appear on stage, the device of narrator recedes and only reappears fully at the very end of the play. Between those opening and closing scenes, the action and plot are carried by dialogue, and the narrator is present only as character.

The concept of setting also differs. Just as characters in a play present themselves directly, the setting is also a physical presence (that may be minimized). Even if you are reading a play instead of seeing it, the physical setting is often more backdrop than integral part. In fact, it's not unusual to see a play performed with so minimal a setting that the stage is called a "black box." In that case, dialogue carries the elements of setting crucial to character development and plot.

At the same time, there is much about character that carries over from the other genres to drama. As in short fiction, characters in drama are flat or rounded, static or dynamic, stereotypical and stock. And, of course, plays have their antagonists and protagonists. Protagonists who serve a higher order and pit themselves against forces far beyond their control are often heroic and tragic, hence the term *tragic hero*.

In this lesson, we will be concentrating on the characters in *Hamlet*. Not only does this complex and complicated play have a large enough cast to do justice to

248—*Literary Visions*

the full range of characterization, it also has a tragic hero. Studying the characters in *Hamlet* will help you later to more fully appreciate the play's plot and conflicts.

GOAL

This lesson will help you to recognize how drama presents character.

WHAT YOU WILL LEARN

When you complete this lesson you will be able to:

1. Explain how characterization is developed differently in drama than in other forms of literature.
2. Identify the standard characters in drama.
3. Describe various stock characters.
4. Recognize the qualities of the tragic hero.
5. Recognize character as a means of furthering exposition.
6. Discuss how a reader's response is affected by knowledge about the background and social and historical context of a drama and its author.

LESSON ASSIGNMENT

The following nine steps will help you master the objectives and achieve the goal for this lesson. The order differs from that in earlier lessons because of the complexity of the play.

Step 1: Read the OVERVIEW in this study guide, as well as the scenes and lines referred to in *Hamlet*.

Step 2: In your text, read "Renaissance Drama and Shakespeare's Theater" and "William Shakespeare, *Hamlet*," pages 1318–1322. The text will provide background for what you will read in the study guide and give you information about the play.

Step 3: This lesson, 19, deals primarily with *Hamlet*, so you should read the entire play, pages 1322–1421. The following scenes provide a context for the study guide discussion and video performances, and those marked with an asterisk (*) will be shown in the video.

Elizabethan Beliefs

If you heard someone say "I'm in a bad humor," you'd not only know you should stay away, but you'd also be hearing humor used in its Elizabethan sense. By 1600—the time at which *Hamlet* was probably written—humor, meaning disposition or mood, was a way of classifying characters. In fact, the comedies of Ben Jonson, one of Shakespeare's contemporaries, are often classified *Comedy of Humors*.

Based upon the theories of the ancient physicians Hippocrates and Galen, the humors provided an explanation for human behavior. Elizabethans believed that the human body contained four liquids—blood, phlegm, yellow bile, and black bile—together called humors (spelled humours in British English). Each of these liquids was further associated with the elements. If one humor dominated the others, the result was disease; if the humors were balanced, the result was a perfect temperament. The concept of humors explained a person's moral, physical, and mental state.

To see how this idea might apply to characters in a play, let's see first how it looks reduced to essentials.

NAME	BLOOD	PHLEGM	YELLOW BILE	BLACK BILE
ELEMENTS	Air: hot moist	Water: cold moist	Fire: hot dry	Earth: cold dry
TRAITS	Sanguine: generous joyful amorous	Phlegmatic: dull pale cowardly	Choleric: angry stubborn impatient	Melancholic: thoughtful depressed indecisive

If you think about this chart from the perspective of an Elizabethan audience and with *Hamlet* in mind, you can see how tempting it might be to pigeonhole the characters. Just to use two examples, Hamlet would seem to be suffering from a melancholic humor and Claudius from a choleric one.

At the time, perhaps many readers and viewers saw the characters in *Hamlet* in terms of humors. To us, however, the limitations of the theory as applied to the play seem obvious. We now know much more about psychology and motivation, and we therefore see Hamlet as more than a melancholy type and Claudius as more than a choleric one.

Another belief that figures in the Elizabethan understanding of the play is the Christian idea of the Great Chain of Being. If you imagine a heavy chain of forged links that stands vertically, you will have grasped the central image. Now think of that top link as representing God, and then consider where on the chain you would put everything else. Odds are, you would place the angels next, then humans, then animals, and on down to plants and inanimate matter. Everything has its place linked together in a divine order.

The Elizabethan concept of the state also reflected this order. Just as God was at the head of the chain, so too the ruler of a country, king or queen, was at the head of the body politic. The ruler's right to govern stemmed from God, and as a result the king or queen was responsible to God, not the people.

Given the plot of *Hamlet,* you can apply this notion to Claudius's rule. Having murdered the rightful King, taken the throne, and married his brother's wife, he has sinned against the divine order. And his sin has direct consequences in that it infects his court and his kingdom. The picture you get of the court at Elsinore is one of espionage, lies, plots, and power-plays. As the guard Marcellus remarks, "Something is rotten in the state of Denmark."

Elizabethan Drama

As we are using the word here, *convention* has a special meaning far removed from the standard connotation of *a gathering of people.* In drama, as in poetry, the term refers to an unrealistic device that is readily accepted by the reader and audience. Among the conventions of the Elizabethan stage are three to note—the soliloquy, the aside, and the form of language.

If a character delivers a *soliloquy,* the convention is that the person is alone on stage and speaking directly from the heart. You will read more about Hamlet's soliloquies later in this study guide in the section on the tragic hero.

An *aside* differs from a soliloquy in that it is usually far shorter and spoken while other characters are on stage. The convention here is that only the audience—not the other characters—hear what is said. Like the soliloquy, the aside can be trusted. Again, the character is speaking from the heart. You will note, for instance, that the first words from Hamlet are an aside.

In Act I.ii.64–66, Claudius is holding forth as king, and having given Laertes permission to return to France, turns to Hamlet with "But now my cousin Hamlet, and my son / . . . How is it that the clouds still hang on you?" Between these two lines, Hamlet inserts an aside, "A little more than kin, and less than kind." Immediately we are alerted to his suspicion of Claudius, his emotional reaction to his new relationship—formerly as nephew, now as stepson—and his moral repugnance over his mother's remarriage.

This latter idea takes a bit of explaining. "Kind" in "less than kind" also encompasses the idea of "unnatural," and church law at the time held that is was incest to marry the wife of a brother, even a dead one. Thus Claudius's marriage to Gertrude affronted Hamlet not only on personal grounds but on religious ones as well.

Also, you will have noted that most of *Hamlet* is in verse, more precisely, unrhymed iambic pentameter or *blank verse.* Thus it was a convention to accept verse as normal speech, though we see prose in the play as well. True to the traditions of the time, prose is reserved for comic scenes (such as the dialogue between the grave diggers that opens Act V) or scenes in which a character is mentally distracted, as in Ophelia's mad scene.

You may also have noticed that a couplet often concludes a scene. The rhyme served two purposes. To the audience, it indicated the end of a scene or act; it also cued the actors scheduled to appear in the next scene. You'll also find the setting for the scenes is established by dialogue. The Elizabethan stage had no curtain, no sets or scenery, so the transition between scenes was swift.

Hamlet also gives us some idea of what was popular and the general style of acting in Shakespeare's time. The first glimpse we get is in II.ii.307–350, where Rosencrantz brings Hamlet up-to-date on the players who have come to Elsinore. According to Rosencrantz, the players are traveling because they no longer can command an audience in their resident theater, their popularity having been usurped by companies of child actors.

As your text explains, the reference here is a contemporary one. The "War of the Theaters," as it was known, took place in the year 1600, with adult actors and playwrights on one hand and child companies and their playwrights on the other. The battle was so heated that many were hesitant to attend the plays of the adult companies, "afraid of goose-quills," the pens of the satirists who wrote for the children.

When Guildenstern sums up the fight with "O there has been much throwing about of brains" and adds that the children have also overshadowed "Hercules and his load too," the reference is to Shakespeare's own company. Shakespeare is not above using his own goose-quill to poke his rivals. Hamlet, however, is more philosophic. He finds in the tale of the rival companies a parallel that points to the fickleness of popularity. While his father was king, people ridiculed Claudius; but now that Claudius is king, the same people pay high sums for his portrait in miniature.

The conversation that follows between Hamlet and the players also gives us information about Shakespeare's views on actors and acting. We discover, for instance, that the players are all male, for Hamlet teases one of the boys about having grown and hopes that his voice has not broken so that he can still play women's roles (lines 405–409).

Later, in lines 500–504, Hamlet directs Polonius to see that the players are well taken care of, "for they are the abstract / and brief chronicles of the time; after your death you were / better have a bad epitaph than their ill report while you / live." As you have just seen, contemporary events often found their way to the stage, and indeed actors, through the words of playwrights, did have the power to damage a reputation.

For a look at what Shakespeare considered good acting, turn to III.ii.1–40. Hamlet is coaching the player about the speech that he has written to be inserted into the scene the actors will perform for Claudius. His advice is not only sound, it attacks a style that must have been popular at the time, one summed up by our theatrical term "eating the scenery," or the more commonly used "hamming it up."

Some of the plays of the time may have invited overacting in much the same way as our melodramas. The revenge play, for instance, was a common genre, and it usually involved a ghost, a murder (usually quite grisly), a deranged revenger, and, of course, death. The audience that came to see *Hamlet* might well have expected a play that fit that genre, and they were probably familiar with the broad outlines of the play's plot.

After all, an earlier version of *Hamlet was* a revenge tragedy. Possibly written by Thomas Kyd, it appeared as early as 1589, some 11 years before the performance of Shakespeare's play, and a similar revenge story had turned up in Belleforest's *Histoires Tragiques,* published in 1576. All these versions were based on a much earlier Norse legend recorded around 1200 and printed in 1514 in the *Historica Danica* by the Dane Saxo Grammaticus.

In a sense then, the Elizabethan audience probably approached *Hamlet* in the same way an Athenian audience regarded *Oedipus the King*—both knew the general shape of the plot, and both were familiar with the genre of the play. But there the similarity ends, for *Hamlet* surpasses the limitations of the revenge tragedy and ends up sharing much in common with Greek tragedy—its scope, its scale, its conflicts, its sense of the heroic.

Types of Characters

Turn to the cast of characters on pages 1322–1323 in your text, so we can sort out the protagonist and antagonist, those that are flat or rounded, and those that are stock.

The first two are easy. The word *protagonist* means "chief contender" in the sense of main actor. Here that's obviously Hamlet. The character who opposes the protagonist is appropriately called the *antagonist,* meaning the actor who "contends against." Again, the identification is easy—Claudius.

Only Claudius? What about all those others who are after Hamlet? Because the antagonist is the primary source of opposition, and because Claudius sets all the other opposing characters in motion, Claudius is the antagonist.

Both Claudius and Hamlet are *rounded* characters in that they are fully developed. They are complex. Claudius, for instance, is not evil through and through but has a conscience, as you can see from his soliloquy in III.iii.36–72. And Hamlet is no saint; witness his harsh treatment of Ophelia.

Another quality of rounded characters is that they are *dynamic*; they change. We see Hamlet's mood swings and his slow movement toward final action. And we also see Claudius progress from a suspicious but generally well-intended stepfather to one set on murder.

Other rounded characters in the play, although some are more rounded than others, are Horatio, Polonius, Laertes, Fortinbras, Gertrude, and Ophelia. In fact, one distinct advantage of reading the play rather than seeing it is that you get a fuller picture of the characters. Modern productions, whether on stage, film, or videotape, are cut to allow for scenery and effects as well as the briefer attention span of the audience. As a result, characters such as Horatio, Laertes, and Fortinbras are often reduced to flatness.

For *flat* characters, you only need to look again at the cast: Valtemand, Cornelius, Rosencrantz, Guildenstern, Marcellus, Barnardo, Francisco, and Reynaldo—to say nothing of those who do not even have names. All are more or less one-dimensional. They are *static* in that they do not alter. Nor are they well developed. If you look carefully at the speeches of Rosencrantz and Guildenstern, for example, you'll find that they are almost interchangeable.

But being flat does not mean a character is unimportant. Take the opening scene of the play. Here is Barnardo standing guard, speaking the first line of the play to Francisco, who comes to relieve him. "Who's there?" asks Barnardo. The line is one of the central questions of the play. Who is the Ghost, an apparition sent from heaven or hell? Who is Hamlet, a madman or a crafty revenger?

Once Francisco is joined by Haratio and Marcellus, the dialogue and action that ensue bring the audience up-to-date on what is going on, providing necessary exposition. We learn that the Ghost walks in the guise of the elder Hamlet, the former king. And we also learn that Denmark is preparing for war.

Some time before, the elder Fortinbras, King of Norway, had gone to war against the elder Hamlet. Before the first battle, they had signed a pact: if Fortinbras lost, he would forfeit the lands he had taken; if Hamlet lost, he would give up an equal amount. In the battle that followed, Hamlet killed Fortinbras. Fortinbras's son, however, refused to abide by the pact his father had agreed to and, seeking revenge for his father's death, he now prepares to march on Denmark. This impending attack explains why sentries are posted and the nation is preparing for war. It may also explain why the Ghost appears, though Horatio suspects the Ghost signifies far more. When first he hears of the Ghost, he comments "This bodes some strange eruption to our state." Indeed it does. The questions of the Ghost's motives are essential to understanding of Hamlet's character.

If you step back and look at the scene in relation to the play as a whole, you will find that the characters—the flat Marcellus, Barnardo, and Francisco and the barely found Horatio—serve a number of purposes; they establish a martial framework for the play, set up an atmosphere of suspense, bring the audience up to date, and introduce at least three subjects that are important to the theme—identity, corruption, and revenge.

Less important is the *stock* or stereotypical character. Drawn from the earlier Italian *commedia dell'arte,* stock characters are still alive in slightly altered form in present day films and television shows where they turn up as the comic thug, the yokel, and the like. In *Hamlet* the best example of the stock character is Osric, the courtly fop who appears in V.ii. and is so ingratiating that Hamlet remarks that Osric as an infant probably asked permission to nurse: "A' did comply sir, with his dug before a' sucked it" (line 173).

It is Osric who informs Hamlet of Claudius's wager and proposal. Claudius has bet that with rapier and dagger Hamlet can outscore Laertes by at least three hits out of twelve. Hamlet accepts the challenge, thus acquiescing to the duel that brings about the carnage that we see later in the scene.

Osric provides some necessary comic relief. Just before his entrance, we have learned of Hamlet's reversal of Claudius's orders to Rosencrantz and Guildenstern that results in their deaths. And we also find Hamlet tallying up his grievances against Claudius. We know what will happen, but before it does we have some relief from tension and suspense thanks to this comic interlude with Osric.

Sometimes Polonius is played as though he were a stock character, and indeed the broad outline for his character can be found in the commedia dell'arte, where his prototype appears as the Dottore, the ancient and pompous doctor whose pretensions make him ridiculous. But Polonius is more than that. He is after all Claudius's chief minister, a sort of prime minister, and we know Claudius is no fool. Think too of Polonius's advice to Laertes:

> This above all, to thine own self be true
> And it must follow as the night the day,
> Thou canst not then be false to any man. — (I.iii.78–80)

If again you step back from these characters and look at them in relation to the play as a whole, you will find that they contribute more than you might first suspect. Osric reveals Hamlet's sense of humor as well as providing the reader or audience with emotional release from tension. And Polonius's advice to Laertes also states the position that Hamlet tries to achieve and shows what's awry with Claudius. "To thine own self be true" is an important motif in the play. Stock characters also often serve as confidantes or friends, as foils or contrasts, or as mirrors—all ways of establishing character.

The Tragic Hero

Lesson 18 pointed out that the concept of the tragic hero is complex. It involves a tragic world or cosmos, an individual in relation to that world, and also the society in which that person lives. The list of additional reading for this lesson mentions several books that explore the idea of the tragic hero, but here we will only give the essential details.

The tragic world or cosmos of *Hamlet* is a Christian one. As you can assume from the earlier discussion of the Great Chain of Being, a divine order controlled all things. But that order is neither easily understandable nor even at times recognizable. Divine order simply exists. And evil also exists. The tragic cosmos focuses on the interplay of coexisting good and evil.

Now think about Hamlet. In I.v. he is charged by the Ghost to avenge the elder Hamlet's "most foul, strange and unnatural" murder, but there are crucial conditions:

> But howsoever thou pursues this act,
> Taint not thy mind, nor let thy soul contrive

Against thy mother aught; leave her to heaven,
And to those thorns that in her bosom lodge
To prick and sting her — (lines 84–88).

But who is this Ghost? Is it really the elder Hamlet or does it assume that shape? The identity of the Ghost is important because it could represent heaven or hell. If from hell, the Ghost is there to tempt Hamlet into destroying himself; if from heaven, the Ghost charges Hamlet with divine retribution.

Yet Hamlet is only mortal. He had suspected Claudius had murdered his father. When the Ghost states outright that "The serpent that did sting thy father's life / Now wears his crown" (line 39), Hamlet responds with "O my prophetic soul!" His suspicions are confirmed. Yet as much as he wants to believe, he must test the identity of the Ghost. Then if the Ghost is indeed from heaven, Hamlet must cleanse himself of all personal motive so that he can act with justice. And then there's the matter of his mother. Gertrude loves Claudius. How then can he reawaken her conscience so that he can kill Claudius without hurting her?

Hamlet decides to feign madness, a ploy that allows him greater liberty than he might ordinarily have. And it also allows him to push aside Ophelia so that he is not encumbered by her as he pursues his goal. Then too there's the likelihood that Hamlet overheard Polonius's plan to "loose my daughter to him." The basis for this idea is a bit complicated, but bear with it. It's one way to explain Hamlet's later treatment of Ophelia.

In conversation with Claudius and Gertrude (II.ii.85–167), Polonius had explained his theory that Ophelia's rejection of Hamlet (which Polonius had forced) was the cause of Hamlet's madness. When Claudius wisely asks "How may we try [this theory] further?" Polonius states that Hamlet often "walks four hours together / Here in the lobby" and proposes that at that time he "loose my daughter to him." He and Claudius will watch what happens from behind a tapestry.

Given the Elizabethan theater, there's a good chance that Polonius's comment about Hamlet's habits was a stage direction, cuing the actor playing Hamlet to walk across a space above the stage, a sort of balcony referred to in Shakespearean plays as "above" or "aloft." He would then reappear on stage, a few lines later, with the cue, "But look where sadly the poor wretch comes reading."

If Hamlet indeed overheard Polonius, he would not only know that Claudius and Polonius were set to spy on him but also that Ophelia was an accomplice in that she agreed to be part of it. His knowledge would also explain his later reference to Polonius as a fishmonger (II.ii.174), which at the time meant a pimp, and as Jephthah (II.ii.385), the biblical figure forced to sacrifice his only daughter. Jephthah had made a hasty promise that resulted in the sacrifice; Polonius had made a hasty assumption that was to cause the death of Ophelia, who was his only daughter.

Up to this point in the play, the forces of evil seem to have the day. Claudius, "that incestuous, that adulterate beast" (I.v.42), has murdered the King, usurped the throne, and infected the kingdom. He suspects Hamlet and has set Rosencrantz and Guildenstern to spy upon him.

But Hamlet has set his own espionage plot in motion. He has asked the players to enact a scene that duplicates the Ghost's description of the murder of the elder Hamlet and, not trusting his own eyes, he has also asked Horatio to watch Claudius during the performance. It is against this background that Hamlet delivers the "To be, or not to be" soliloquy that reveals some of the characteristics of the tragic hero (III.i.56–89).

Hamlet at this point does not know for sure that the Ghost represents divine justice, but he deeply suspects that is so—in which case he must act as its instrument and rid the kingdom of infection so that order can be restored. He is neither entirely free nor entirely bound. He could choose to ignore the Ghost's charge and return to his studies in Germany; he could choose to act immediately; he could choose to check the truth of the Ghost's tale and if it rings true, act as charged. It is this last course of action that he has decided to follow.

But the decision is not easy. In this soliloquy, Hamlet thinks about suicide, finding death "a consummation / Devoutly to be wished." Yet, he reasons, if death were an easy alternative, who then would put up with the trials of life. He speculates

> ... that the dread of something after death,
> The undiscovered country, from whose bourn
> No traveller returns, puzzles the will,
> And makes us rather bear those ills we have,
> Than fly to others that we know not of. — (lines 78–82)

He concludes that "conscience does make cowards of us all," holding us back from action.

There's an echo here of Hamlet's first soliloquy (I.ii.129–159), for there he wished "that the Everlasting had not fixed / his canon gainst self-slaughter." As we see him in that first speech, he is tortured by the difference between his father and Claudius—as "Hyperion to a satyr"—and by his mother's hasty marriage, which he refers to as "incestuous sheets." What stands out from this speech is his suffering, and that emotion also characterizes "To be, or not to be."

Suffering is one of the main qualities of the tragic hero. In fact, Aeschylus, the ancient Greek tragedian, stated that "wisdom comes alone through suffering." Caught in a tragic cosmos, the tragic hero elects to contend with evil, suffers, learns, and dies.

In this soliloquy which occurs at the beginning of the third act, Hamlet sees the evil surrounding him, has pledged to set it right, and suffers. Once he is sure the Ghost's word is true, he can move to more direct action, action that in the end affects the society he lives in.

There's a hitch, of course. To carry out the Ghost's command, to act as the arm of divine justice, is also to commit murder, a sin. Within the tradition of revenge tragedy, revenge always brings death to the avenger. And so it does to

Hamlet. By then, of course, Claudius is responsible for not only the death of Hamlet's father but for Hamlet's as well, and indirectly the deaths of Ophelia, Rosencrantz and Guildenstern, Laertes, and Gertrude. Quite a list.

But Hamlet is not guilt free. Even if you could justify his killing of Claudius, Hamlet has Polonius to answer for, and his treatment of Ophelia certainly contributed to her suicide just as his taunting of Laertes spurred Laertes to deeds he would not normally have considered.

Another characteristic helps distinguish the tragic hero from other protagonists, and that is what's often referred to as the *tragic flaw*. The Greek word for this is *hamartia*—meaning error, shortcoming, or weakness. Sometimes this flaw is seen as pride or arrogance—known in Greek as *hubris*. What's important here is that the flaw is double-edged. If, for instance, you find that Hamlet has a tragic flaw in that he thinks too much—to the point where his intellect paralyzes his actions—you would also have to admit that this same characteristic makes him a superb plotter, as his plan for the play within the play and his escape from Rosencrantz and Guildenstern show.

And there we have the tragic hero, neither guilty nor guiltless, torn between good and evil, suffering, dying, but in doing so, restoring order in society. Ultimately the tragic hero reaffirms the greatness of the individual.

Summary

In the accompanying video, you see Hamlet addressing the Players, but in a larger and more metaphorical sense Hamlet is the director of the play's action. He rids himself of Ophelia, sets "The Mousetrap," rekindles his mother's sleeping conscience, arranges the deaths of Rosencrantz and Guildenstern, and rids the kingdom of corruption and evil.

The supporting cast is a large one, but the scope of the play is vast. We see rounded characters and flat ones, dynamic and static ones, stock or stereotypical ones. *Hamlet* is a play that surpasses convention. Hamlet transcends the role of protagonist and becomes a tragic hero, and even relatively minor characters such as Polonius, though grounded in comic prototypes, go beyond their expected limits.

The play itself transcended any that had come before it. No mere revenge tragedy, *Hamlet* has a richness and complexity of language, plot, and characterization that exceeds even the best of the ancient Greek tragedies. Written in the year 1600, it is the first of Shakespeare's great tragedies and is followed within the short span of five years by *Othello, King Lear,* and *Macbeth.*

Shakespeare's tragedies were enjoyed by the same audiences that watched comedies and histories—an audience that ranged from royalty to commoner. It was not until after his death that his plays were generally available in printed form. In 1623, two of Shakespeare's fellow actors collaborated with printers and publishers to bring out a collected edition of Shakespeare's plays, thirty-six of them. That edition is dedicated to the acting company's patrons but it is also dedicated to "To The Great Variety of Readers." Those readers encompassed a range from "the most able, to him that can but spell," evidence of a popularity then that remains true today.

VIEWING GUIDE

An important component of this lesson is the video. You will learn more effectively from it by thinking about the following questions and guidelines.

Before Viewing:

1. Review "Renaissance Drama and Shakespeare's Theater," pages 1399–1404, and "William Shakespeare's, *Hamlet*," in the text, pages 1404–1502.
2. Review *Hamlet*, paying particular attention to the scenes that your instructor emphasizes. Try to hear the dialogue in each of the following scenes:

   - Act II. ii. 363–401
   - Act II. ii. 446–519
   - Act II. ii. 523–528
   - Act II. ii. 540–549
   - Act II. ii. 552–580
   - Act III. i. 56˘

During Your Viewing:

1. Note the costumes and scenery.
2. Watch for gestures and movements by the actors.
3. Listen for verbal clues to the characters played by the actors.
4. Listen for what the critics say about Polonius and about Hamlet's inaction.
5. Listen for the major points John Vickery makes about Shakespeare's language.

After Viewing:

Give some thought to the following questions. You may want to write short answers in your journal or notebook.

1. How did the acted versions of the scenes differ from what you imagined when you read them?
2. Did you disagree with any points made by the critics?

3. Which of the critics' ideas would you like to know more about and why?
4. What interested you most about the interview with John Vickery and why?
5. If you had to play a part in *Hamlet*, which would it be and why?

WRITING ACTIVITIES

After your study of this lesson, you should be able to recognize how drama presents character. Your instructor will advise you which, if any, of the following writing activities you are to complete.

Formal Writing:

All of these activities allow a good deal of choice and call upon what you have learned from previous lessons as well as this one. The first, for example, draws upon the close reading skills you developed in your study of poetry. And the next two activities call upon your study of characterization in the short story as well as the discussion of rounded and stock characters in this study guide. Activity 4 calls your attention to differences in interpretation.

1. Select one of Hamlet's other soliloquies and analyze what it reveals about his state of mind at that time. You will find those soliloquies in I.ii.129–159; I.v.92–132; II.ii.525–580; III.ii.365–376; and IV.iv.32–66.
2. Choose one of the scenes with stock characters (other than Osric) and analyze what the scene contributes to characterization in the play.
3. Between Hamlet and Claudius on the one hand and all the interchangeable, stock, and flat characters on the other, there are a number of characters that can be called rounded but who vary in degrees of roundedness. Select one of those characters to argue that he or she is indeed rounded.
4. Compare and contrast the actors' interpretations of Hamlet's "To be or not to be" speech. Which do you prefer and why?

Informal Writing:

While both of the assignments that follow call for theatrical or production-oriented approaches to the play, they will also lead to a greater understanding of character. In Activity 1, you will be analyzing the relationship between actor and character, and in Activity 2, you will examine the relationship between character and theme. Both activities also call for you to make links between your own world and that of the play.

1. Choose from among the celebrities you are familiar with or from people you know to cast one of the roles in *Hamlet*. The next step is to write a short essay explaining your casting and how that person would play the part.
2. If you prefer, play director by choosing one of *Hamlet*'s themes to emphasize, then reshape the time of the play to underscore that theme. You might, for instance, take the same kind of approach that *West Side Story* book to *Romeo and Juliet* and reset *Hamlet* into a world of gang wars instead of kingdoms. The written part of this assignment consists of your explaining what era you would move the play to, why, and how it might work.

SELF-TEST

Match the items in column A with the definitions or identifications in B:

A	B
1. Flat characters	a. Speech revealing thoughts not heard by others on stage
2. Stereotyped characters	b. Physically and intellectually active character
3. Humors	
4. Soliloquy	c. Undergo change
5. Rounded characters	d. Primary character opposed to main character
6. Protagonist	
7. Tragic hero	e. Concept explaining human behavior
8. Antagonist	f. One-dimensional characters
9. Commedia dell'arte	g. Main character
10. Dynamic characters	h. Multi-dimensional characters
	i. Stock characters
	j. Contends with cosmos, suffers
	k. Speech revealing thoughts and spoken alone on stage
	l. Source of many stock characters
	m. Concept explaining ethics

Answer the following multiple-choice items:

1. Characterization in drama differs from characterization in other genres because it is presented through

a. narration.
   b. dialogue.
   c. conflict.
   d. action.

2. Which is NOT typical of the tragic hero?
   a. Suffering
   b. Guilt and guiltlessness
   c. Conflict with the cosmos
   d. Pure representation of good

3. Which of the following is NOT a modern stock character?
   a. The pathetic drunk
   b. The dumb athlete
   c. The bimbo with a heart of gold
   d. The absent-minded professor

4. The concept of humors does NOT explain
   a. disease.
   b. behavior.
   c. morality.
   d. destiny.

5. An Elizabethan audience seeing *Hamlet* would expect a(n)
   a. revenge tragedy.
   b. original play.
   c. cast of men, women, and children.
   d. play written for the educated.

In 100–350 words, answer the following short essay questions:

1. The first time you see Claudius is in I.ii.1–39. What does his opening speech reveal about his character?
2. Analyze what Claudius's soliloquy in III.iii.36–72 reveals about his state of mind and character.
3. Fortinbras might be considered a mere tool of the plot, a character that appears directly and indirectly but always as a way to keep the plot rolling. Write a short essay explaining what else Fortinbras contributes to the play.

ADDITIONAL READING AND VIEWING ACTIVITIES

If you enjoyed reading the play and listening to the interview in this lesson, you may want to read more about *Hamlet*. Here is a list of suggested readings:

Bradbrook, Muriel C. *The Living Monument: Shakespeare and the Theatre of His Time.*
Bradley, A. C. *Shakespearean Tragedy: Lectures on "Hamlet," "Othello," "King Lear," "Macbeth."*
Schoenbaum, Samuel. *Shakespeare: The Globe and the World.*
Sewall, Richard B. *The Vision of Tragedy.*
Wilson, J. Dover. *What Happens in Hamlet.*

And if you would like to see the play performed, the following productions are often available in public libraries and videotape rental stores:

Film (1948), starring Laurence Olivier.
Film (1969), starring Nicol Williamson.
Videotape (1970), starring Richard Chamberlain.
Videotape (1979), starring Derek Jacobi.
Videotape (1991), starring Mel Gibson.

LESSON 20

Patterns of Action:
PLOT AND CONFLICT IN DRAMA

ABOUT THE LESSON

You first encountered the literary meanings of *action* and *plot* back in Lesson 5, when you studied the short story. At that time, we worked from a simple notion of structure—that of beginning, middle, end—to the more complex arrangement of *exposition, complication, crisis, climax,* and *resolution.* That five-part structure is one you saw in the short story, but it is even more pronounced in drama.

Oedipus the King and *Hamlet* are good examples to illustrate the workings of action and plot in drama because their structure is so different. *Oedipus the King,* typical of ancient Greek tragedies, has one plot and moves swiftly through the five stages mentioned above. Thus the action and plot have unity. You can also see that the action is confined by tight limits of space and time. Everything on stage takes place in one spot and within 24 hours—in fact, within the span of an afternoon.

In contrast, *Hamlet* seems to sprawl. The action on stage covers a number of days—even months—and the scenes take place in a variety of locations. The plot is supplemented by subplots so numerous that at times it's hard to keep track of who is plotting against whom.

But whether a plot is simple or complex, it is carried along by character and its presentation through dialogue. In fact, because the ties between character and plot are very strong, the lesson on character preceded this one on action and plot.

In this lesson, you will use what you learned about character in drama to explore structure and plot. And you will take a close look at *conflict*—the element that is the essential component of plot and action. Here again you can draw on your earlier study of the short story, for conflict in drama also has its internal and external dimensions. And perhaps in no place in drama are those dimensions more clearly and eloquently drawn than in the two plays we will examine.

GOAL

This lessons will help you to understand the functions of action, plot, and conflict in drama.

WHAT YOU WILL LEARN

When you complete this lesson you will be able to:

1. Discriminate among action, plot, and conflict.
2. Identify exposition, complication, crisis, climax, and resolution.
3. Discuss the applicability of the unities of time, place, and action to drama.
4. Differentiate among levels of conflict within drama.

LESSON ASSIGNMENT

Working through the following nine steps will help you master the objectives and achieve the goal for this lesson:

Step 1: In your text, review pages 1204-1221 in "The Dramatic Vision: An Overview" and pages 1265–1281 in "The Tragic Vision: Affirmation through Loss." The text will provide background for what you will read in the study guide, explain the key terms, and give you some information about the plays you have been reading.

Step 2: This lesson, 20, will deal primarily with *Oedipus the King* but will also focus on *Hamlet*. The following scenes provide a context for the study guide discussion and video performances, and those marked with an asterisk (*) will be shown in the video.

- *Oedipus the King*, Fagles: Lines 1–244 (Gould: Lines 1–210)
- *Oedipus the King*, Fagles: Lines 338–401 (Gould: Lines 302–358)*
- *Oedipus the King*, Fagles: Lines 1010–1178 (Gould: Lines 929–1077)*
- *Oedipus the King*, Fagles: Lines 1215–1310 (Gould: Lines 1115–1190)*
- Oedipus the King, Fagles: Lines 1351–1684 (Gould: Lines 1233–1540)
- *Hamlet*, Act II.ii
- *Hamlet*, Act V.ii

Step 3: Read the OVERVIEW in this study guide lesson.

Step 4: Watch the VIDEO, following the steps in the VIEWING GUIDE in this study guide lesson.

Step 5: Reread the OVERVIEW to reinforce what you have learned in the text and the video and to help you complete the Writing Activities.

Step 6: Complete any WRITING ACTIVITIES assigned in this lesson.

Step 7: Do the SELF-TEST exercises in this study guide lesson.

Step 8: Read any of the ADDITIONAL READING ACTIVITIES assigned.

Step 9: Go back to the learning objectives in the WHAT YOU WILL LEARN section of this study guide lesson and be sure you can respond to each of them.

OVERVIEW

In this lesson, we will start with structure. You will learn first about the various kinds of formal structures unique to drama and how they developed.

We will then move to action and plot to review the terms *exposition, complication, crisis, climax,* and *resolution* that you studied in relation to short fiction. Next, we will analyze these elements in drama with examples from *Oedipus the King* and *Hamlet* and explore the interweaving of character and plot so that the relationship between the two is clear.

Finally, we will discuss conflict, concentrating on the various kinds of conflict found in the two plays under discussion and again relating them to character.

As in the short story and poetry, character, plot, and conflict are only means to an end, and that end is *theme*. A full discussion of theme will come later in this study guide, but keep in mind that everything you read about drama leads to theme. The discussion of conflict in this lesson will give you a number of ideas that will serve as the bases for possible themes.

Structure

Structure refers to the way the action and plot are put together. In your study of poetry, you saw that a poem was composed of a number of formal elements, lines, and stanzas. The comparable elements in drama are scenes and acts. These breaks in the work—whether poetry or drama—are intentional. A poet stops one line and begins another for reasons of rhythm and sound as well as sense; a dramatist ends one scene and begins another to underscore the action and plot. And just as the poet groups lines into larger units of sound and sense called stanzas, the dramatist groups scenes into larger units called acts.

When you were introduced to drama, you read that one way to keep track of the action was to write out a synopsis of the scenes. If you have not done that for *Oedipus the King*, now is a good time to do so. *Oedipus the King*, you will note, is not divided into acts; yet by looking at its formal structure, you can see how acts and scenes evolved.

Looking only at the divisions in the play, you find that *Oedipus the King* is framed by a *prologue* with *parados* and a concluding *exodos*. The prologue consists of a dialogue between Oedipus and the Priest and then Oedipus and Creon, followed by the parados or entrance of the Chorus and the first choral ode. The exodos, at the end of the play, ends with another choral ode and the departure of the actors and Chorus.

Within the framework set by the prologue and parados at the beginning of the play and the exodos at the end, the action is carried by a series of four episodes interspersed with *stasimons* or choral odes. The only other formal element of the play's structure is the *kommos* or dirge—a lament sung by the Chorus with one or both of the principal actors.

From the episodes in Greek tragedy, we get the division into acts that we see in *Hamlet* as well as many contemporary plays. Produced as written, *Hamlet* is a long play that has enough action to justify its division into five acts, each with a number of scenes—as few as two but also as many as seven. Today most plays are a good deal shorter than *Hamlet,* and their action is reduced accordingly, usually resulting in three acts, each with one to three scenes.

Action and the Elements of Plot

In drama, action refers to just that, an event or series of events or deeds performed by the characters. The idea of *plot* arises when actions are linked by causes or relationships. If you were to say "I ate an apple, and I got sick," you would be describing two separate and not necessarily related actions. Change that to "I ate an apple that made me sick," and then you introduce the principle of causation. Carry the idea one step further to "I ate an apple that made me sick because my brother poisoned it so that he could be sole heir" and you have a plot—actions that not only involve causation but also motive, a crucial element of plot.

Whether a play is in episodes or acts, three acts or five, its action can be analyzed by using the elements of structure you studied in the short story: *exposition, complication, crisis, climax,* and *resolution.* As you probably remember, these five components are often visually represented by a triangle that indicates emotional intensity.

Exposition can occur throughout a play, but the greatest part usually occurs at the beginning and brings the reader up-to-date about actions that have occurred before the time of the play. It also introduces the characters, sets the tone, and presents the problem. In *Oedipus the King,* for instance, the prologue and parados provide the exposition. The Chorus describes the plague upon the city; Creon reports what the gods say must be done to end it; Oedipus elects to carry out the gods' commands; and the Priest asks for the blessing of the god Phoebus Apollo upon Oedipus.

In *Hamlet,* you find that what had been separated as introductory matter in Greek tragedies has been incorporated into Act I. But again, the initial scene introduces the characters, sets the tone, and presents the problem. The problem as we first see it, however, is mysterious. The first scene simply indicates that the Ghost has appeared because of some disturbance within the state; it's not until Scene v that we find out the full nature of the problem and what Hamlet must do to solve it.

Once we know of the problem and its potential solution, what follows is *complication,* also known as *rising action.* In *Oedipus the King,* two questions occupy the action: "Who killed Laius?" and "Who is Oedipus?" The two come together with the same answer as Oedipus pursues truth and finds it. That moment of revelation is the play's *crisis* or turning point, and it may also correspond with the play's *climax* or emotional peak.

Some scholars differentiate between crisis and climax by associating crisis with plot—the points at which the main character's fate alters irrevocably—and climax with emotional intensity, the point at which the audience is most moved. Often these points occur simultaneously, hence the blurring of the terms.

In *Oedipus the King,* it is hard to distinguish between climax and crisis. Both appear to occur at the end of Episode 4 when Oedipus realizes the truth. His acknowledgement of the truth is the point on which the plot turns:

> O god —
> all come true, all burst to light!
> O light — now let me look my last on you!
> I stand revealed at last —
> cursed in my birth, cursed in marriage
> cursed in the lives I cut down with these hands!
> —(Fagles — lines 1306–1310; Gould — lines 1187–1190)

From this point on, what follows is *catastrophe* or *falling action;* Jocasta commits suicide, and Oedipus blinds himself with the broche from her dress. Finally, we have the *resolution,* the tying up of the loose ends of the plot: Oedipus takes on the punishment he has decreed for the murderer of Laius—exile—and the chorus reminds us that no life can be considered happy until it has run its full course.

There's an implication in this last ode that the gods are jealous of mortal happiness and therefore apt to send down punishment. Oedipus, once favored by the gods, has lost his crown, his queen, his children, and his country. At first he saw what was around him but was blind to the truth; now that he can see the truth, he blinds himself. He cannot look upon what he has done.

Plot and Subplot

The plot of *Oedipus the King* moves forward along a single line to solve the problem of who killed Laius. Every move Oedipus makes toward a solution implicates him further, to the point where his identity merges with that of the killer. Yet in *Hamlet,* every move by Hamlet seems to complicate matters and lead to subplots.

Is the Ghost an emissary from heaven or hell? Hamlet sets in motion the play within the play to test the Ghost's version of Claudius as murderer. Not trusting his own eyes to interpret Claudius's response, he asks Horatio to watch as well.

Is Hamlet insane? Claudius sets Rosencrantz and Guildenstern to spy upon Hamlet and find out. Then Polonius uses Ophelia as bait and, with Claudius, watches the result. Later Polonius spies again, figuring Hamlet will be honest with his mother.

Will Hamlet live to take his revenge? Claudius sends him to England, where he is to be put to death. Hamlet escapes, and then Claudius plots with Laertes to kill him. Claudius proposes that Laertes use a poisoned weapon to kill Hamlet in a duel. Laertes has just the right poison; even so, Claudius backs up the plan with another. Should Laertes fail to wound Hamlet, Claudius will arrange for Hamlet's drink to be poisoned.

What will happen to young Fortinbras? Having first raised an army to march on Denmark, Fortinbras shifts his aim to Poland after his uncle, still King of Norway, rules out war on Denmark. Returning from Poland by way of Denmark, Fortinbras arrives to see the royal court littered with the bodies of Hamlet, Laertes, Claudius, and Gertrude. He then assumes the Danish crown.

Why all these subplots? That's the question that takes us to motive and to conflict.

Conflict

Think back to the discussion of the tragic hero in the last lesson and you'll remember the idea of the tragic cosmos—a higher world that encompasses the immediate one. For Oedipus, it is the world of the Greek gods; for Hamlet, the divine order of things. The problem that each hero confronts results from a *conflict* or discontinuity between the higher order and the lower one. In Thebes, the plague will continue until the murderer of Laius is punished; in Denmark, the corruption in court will fester until the murder of the elder Hamlet is avenged. Both Oedipus and Hamlet contend with unpunished evil and set out to right the wrongs infecting their countries.

Let's examine how Oedipus goes about it. Once he hears from Creon that the plague will be lifted when the killer of Laius is banished, he sends for Tiresias, the ancient holy man who can see the future. But Tiresias is reluctant; Oedipus has had to send for him twice. When Tiresias does appear, he is testy, demanding to be allowed to go home. Oedipus pleads with him, but Tiresias turns petulant: "None of you knows — / and I will never reveal my dreadful secrets, / not to say your own" (Fagles—lines 373–375; Gould—lines 333–334). From petulance he moves to disobedience: "You'll get nothing from me" (Fagles—line 380; Gould—line 338).

That's just the kind of statement that is guaranteed to offend, enrage, and challenge Oedipus, who responds by losing his temper. In his rage, he accuses Tiresias of having planned Laius's murder, and Tiresias, also enraged, goads Oedipus with the truth stated plain, "*You* are the curse, the corruption of the land" (Fagles—line 401; Gould—line 358).

Now if you follow the dialogue carefully, you'll see that in this exchange Tiresias tells Oedipus the truth not once but six times. Yet the truth is blunted by Oedipus's anger, even when Tiresias spells out Oedipus's fate in detail, as he does in fully developed form in lines 469–486 (Fagles; Gould—lines 457–467). From this point in the play, Oedipus hunts himself.

Thus we see that what had started as conflict between Oedipus and an external evil has now turned inward—in two senses. Not only is Oedipus hunting the killer who is himself—a matter of plot—he is also in conflict with his own pride and temper—a matter of character.

You know from your study of Hamlet that the tragic hero is neither all good nor all evil. Yes, Oedipus loses his temper and in so doing blasphemes, and yes, it was this same temper that led him to kill Laius; but this is the same Oedipus who, fearing his fate, fled what he believed to be his home, who saved the city of Thebes from the Sphinx, who relentlessly pursues the truth even when he suspects where it is leading. Oedipus's desire to know and not to know are almost equal, yet he presses on.

You can state the major conflict in *Oedipus the King* in a number of ways, but let's take one: Oedipus versus evil. As he endeavors to rid the city of the plague by finding the killer of Laius, he encounters other conflicts, all minor and all of his own making. He charges Tiresias with the murder, accuses Creon of treason, and attacks Jocasta's honor, falsely saying she is ashamed of his presumed low birth.

The play's conflicts—major and minor—raise the problem of Oedipus's responsibility for his fate. Whose fault is it? Is he fated to carry out these acts? And if so, how then can he be held accountable for them? Or do his temper, impetuousness, and pride bring about his own downfall? Is there some middle ground between these two views?

You may remember that the tragic hero is neither completely guiltless nor guilty, and Oedipus exemplifies this dilemma. Think about the qualities of the tragic hero. Faced with the challenge of ridding the city of evil, Oedipus accepts it and thereby pits himself against a powerful force. And even when he knows where his hunt is leading him, he continues. His suspicions torture him, and when they are confirmed, he accepts responsibility for his actions and learns from them, asking at the end of the play to be exiled to the mountains, to Cithaeron, where he can live out his life as he began, subject to fate—fate foreseen but not determined by the gods.

Yet the tragic hero's suffering must be redeeming. At the end of *Oedipus the King*, for instance, we find that Oedipus's struggle has three results: he learns much about himself, the plague is lifted from the city, and the cosmic order is restored.

The primary conflict in Hamlet has similar results. Hamlet also learns about himself, that which was "rotten" in Denmark is purged, and the divine order is restored. Unlike Oedipus, however, Hamlet dies. Even so, tragedy is ultimately uplifting, for it reaffirms and validates the greatness humanity can achieve.

A major difference between *Oedipus the King* and *Hamlet* is the complexity of the plot, for Hamlet has all sorts of subplots, each of which involves a conflict. By the end of the play, the external conflicts are resolved: Hamlet's double check of the Ghost's story reveals that the Ghost has told the truth; Fortinbras is slated to be King of Denmark by peaceable means; and Hamlet, directly or indirectly, causes the deaths of all those who had plotted against him—Polonius, Rosencrantz and Guildenstern, Laertes, and Claudius.

The internal conflicts are more complicated. Claudius has revealed that he has a conscience, but because he cannot give up what he has killed for, his conflict is resolved only by his death. Gertrude, on the other hand, married Claudius without knowing of his crime. When, during the scene in her closet, Hamlet confronts her with the truth, she seems to suffer genuine remorse. Whether she can follow Hamlet's advice and avoid a physical relationship with Claudius, we never find out. She dies, ironically and inadvertently, by her husband's hand.

Then there are those who are touched by madness. Ophelia—torn between her love for Hamlet and her duty to her father—chooses her father and, as a result, is rejected by Hamlet. The conflict is too much for her, and she goes mad. Madness for Hamlet, however, is more illusion than reality.

Some critics take a Freudian approach to the play and maintain that Hamlet's internal conflict is caused by his love for his mother. They see Hamlet so obsessed by his mother's remarriage that he feels betrayed by her and is unable to act. Other critics, who apply what we now know about depression—that it is an abnormal condition—see Hamlet as paralyzed by his psychological state, unable to act. And then there are those who find Hamlet too intellectual to move toward action or too sensitive to carry out bloody deeds. Many of these critics maintain that his internal conflict, whatever its cause, brings with it some degree of madness.

To support that view, let's look at a key speech that Hamlet makes to Horatio, his loyal friend and supporter.

> . . . in my heart there was a kind of fighting
> That would not let me sleep; methought I lay
> Worse than the mutines in the bilboes. Rashly—
> And praised be rashness for it: let us know,
> Our indiscretion sometimes serves us well
> When our deep plots do pall, and that should learn us
> There's a divinity that shapes our ends,
> Rough-hew them how we will —(V.ii.4–11).

Hamlet goes on to describe his discovery of Claudius's plot to have him murdered and his rewriting of the orders so that the sentence will fall upon Rosencrantz and Guildenstern instead—another example of how "divinity shapes our ends."

So what do we learn here? Hamlet admits an intense internal conflict that some would call madness. He calls it "a kind of fighting / That would not let me sleep" and compares his suffering to that of mutineers chained to an iron bar.

At the time the play was written, "mutiny" referred to any act of rebellion against authority—a meaning that helps us understand Hamlet's metaphor. If you view Hamlet as intellectual, scholarly, more inclined to thought than action, you can interpret the metaphor as his view of his inner conflict. He has rebelled against his own nature and is chained to the Ghost's commands, reduced to thinking like a criminal—plotting and scheming.

The conflict between Hamlet's nature and his charge leads to his committing rash acts that nonetheless serve his goal when his more carefully laid plans go awry. Hamlet therefore concludes "there's a divinity that shapes our ends" no matter what we do.

When you think about what "rash" acts Hamlet has committed, you may come up with a list that includes his rejection of Ophelia, his inadvertent killing of Polonius, and his leaving with Rosencrantz and Guildenstern for England. Yet all worked to further his goal. His rejection of Ophelia leaves him unencumbered to pursue his revenge, though it also contributes to her madness and suicide. And Polonius's death reveals at least two things—that Polonius is a spy and that Hamlet is capable of action. After all, Hamlet thought that he was stabbing Claudius. As for Hamlet's leaving for England, he is ordered to do so by the King and so may not have had much choice. Yet his trip reveals the depth of Claudius's evil and adds to Hamlet's grievances against him. Thus all of these "rash" acts served Hamlet's purposes.

Hamlet's reference to the "divinity that shapes our ends" reinforces the moral center of the play. Hamlet has been charged by the Ghost to avenge his father's murder and restore order to the state. Hamlet accepts his role as the arm of divine justice, but being only mortal he cannot control all events. Yet, because his cause is just, even his impulsive acts work to good ends. The subplots and their conflicts—both internal and external—are resolved.

Summary

The differences between structure, action, plot, and conflict in *Oedipus the King* and *Hamlet* represent a difference in emphasis between ancient drama and that of the Elizabethan age and beyond. From the time of the tragedies of ancient Greece to the 16th and 17th centuries and up to the present, we see a growing interest in character.

The tragedies of the ancient Greeks stressed plot over character. Although few of the hundreds of Greek tragedies have survived the centuries intact, we know a fair amount about them from the philosopher Aristotle, who lived from 384–322 B.C. In his treatise *The Poetics,* Aristotle sets out both a description and aesthetic theory and states that plot is the "soul of tragedy."

Thus in *Oedipus the King* we see one plot carried by the actions of the tragic hero. The conflict is simple and stems from the question, "Who killed Laius?" Although that question shades into "Who is Oedipus?" both come together as Oedipus discovers his parentage and his deeds. The single-minded unity of the plot combines with the compressed unities of time and place to give the play a relentless quality further emphasized by irony. The effect on the reader or audience is powerful.

The end of *Hamlet* may be equally moving, but the means to that end differ. Written during an era of intense interest in the individual, *Hamlet* stresses character over plot. Thus we see all the complexities of Hamlet's character and those of Claudius as well. And we are given a realistic period of time and variety of place in which to observe them. Gone are the unities of plot, place, and time.

To understand clearly this shift from plot to character, consider the role played by the Chorus in *Oedipus the King*. Grouped as Thebean elders, the Chorus comments on the action from some middle perspective between character and audience. The Chorus certainly knows more than the audience, yet it is somewhat removed from the action, commenting rather than participating. By the time of *Hamlet,* however, it's as though the Chorus has split apart into a number of characters all of whom are directly involved in the action.

Horatio, for instance, advises Hamlet and comments in much the same way that the Chorus responds in *Oedipus the King*. But Horatio is an individual, and so are Barnardo and Marcellus and Osric and so on. They may be flat, but they are individual.

This emphasis on the individual is one we see carried into the 19th century. You will find it in Europe in the plays of Henrik Ibsen and August Strindberg and in Russia in those by Anton Chekov. By the turn of the century, the Irish playwright George Bernard Shaw had popularized the drama of ideas that provided an intellectual background for the later plays of Germany's Bertolt Brecht. On the American stage, characterization and ideas blend in modern classics such as Tennessee Williams's *The Glass Menagerie* and *Streetcar Named Desire* or Arthur Miller's *Death of a Salesman* and *The Crucible*. Yet driving all characterization is the idea of conflict, the key element of plot.

VIEWING GUIDE

An important component of this lesson is the video. You will learn more effectively from it by thinking about the following questions and guidelines.

Before Viewing:

1. Review pages 1204–1224 in "The Dramatic Vision: An Overview" and pages 1265–1281 in "The Tragic Vision: Affirmation through Loss."
2. Review *Oedipus the King* and *Hamlet,* paying particular attention to the scenes that your instructor emphasizes. Try to hear the dialogue in each scene.

During Your Viewing:

1. Within the dramatizations, listen for verbal clues that relate to action, plot, and conflict.
2. Note the different kinds of conflict presented in the dramatizations.
3. Listen for the major points made by the critics.
4. Listen for the major points made by A. R. Gurney.

After Viewing:

Give some thought to the following questions. You may want to write short answers in your journal or notebook.

1. How did the acted versions of the scenes differ from what you imagined when you read them?
2. Select two of the acted scenes and explain why they might have been chosen.
3. Which comment by one of the critics interested you most and why?
4. Given the interview with A. R. Gurney, explain why you would or would not want to read one of his plays.
5. Which point in *Oedipus the King* do you find the most moving and why?

WRITING ACTIVITIES

After your study of this lesson, you should be able to understand the functions of action, plot, and conflict in drama. Your instructor will advise you which, if any, of the following writing activities you are to complete.

Formal Writing:

The first activity asks you to evaluate the effect of the primary internal and external conflicts in *Oedipus the King*. You will find that thinking about the various conflicts and choosing which is the more dramatic will clarify your understanding of the concept of conflict. The second activity is similar to the first in that it asks you to do some preliminary work and to write about the conclusions you draw, but Activity 2 emphasizes dramatic sequencing, particularly how Sophocles uses a familiar plot yet builds suspense. Activity 3 asks you to wrestle with one of the play's central questions, but you'll find that limiting the problem to one scene makes it easier to deal with. Of course, if your instructor suggests it, you can expand Activity 3 to the play as a whole.

1. Identify what you find to be the major internal and external conflicts in *Oedipus the King*. Which do you find the most dramatic and powerful and why?
2. Compare the actual sequence of events to the sequence presented in the play. Write an essay in which you explain the reasons you find for Sophocles's rearrangement of the order.
3. Select a scene in which Oedipus reveals an aspect of his character and use it to argue for your view of his relative guilt or guiltlessness.

Informal Writing:

Both activities call for argumentative essays. The first will lead you to think about the fate of Oedipus and the role of irony in the play. The second relates to plot indirectly by asking you to examine the different ways violence can be handled and then to argue for its direct or indirect inclusion in the plot.

1. Consider whether *Oedipus the King* would have been a more powerful play if it had ended with Oedipus's death instead of his exile. Think through the life he faces blind, the reasons he gouges out his eyes, why he asks for exile, and where he will be exiled. Consider too how a scene with Oedipus dead might parallel the closing of *Hamlet*. Write an essay arguing which is the more just punishment, exile or death.
2. You may have noticed that all of the violence in *Oedipus the King* takes place off stage. Today, however, it's rare not to see it close up, not matter what the medium—stage, television, or film. Think about one or two examples of contemporary plays, films, videos, or television shows that present violence graphically. Then write an essay in which you evaluate the effect of that presentation and argue whether violence is best described (as in *Oedipus the King*) or depicted. Which has the greater impact on the audience? Which has the greater impact on the plot?

SELF-TEST

Match the items in column A with the definitions or identifications in B:

A	B
1. Early version of Act	a. Exposition
2. Turning point of plot	b. External conflict
3. Explanation and introduction	c. Crisis
4. Oedipus vs. Tiresias	d. Resolution

5. Rising action
6. Incidents linked by causation and motive
7. Peak of emotional intensity
8. Winding up of conflict
9. Event or deed
10. Falling action

e. Plot
f. Internal conflict
g. Complication
h. Episode
i. Kommos
j. Action
k. Catastrophe
l. Prologue
m. Climax

Answer the following multiple-choice items:

1. Which of the following units of structure sometimes occur simultaneously?
   a. Exposition and resolution
   b. Climax and crisis
   c. Complication and climax
   d. Crisis and resolution

2. Which is NOT true of Elizabethan tragedy?
   a. Observes unities of time, place, and plot
   b. Emphasizes character
   c. Contains subplots
   d. Involves multiple conflicts

3. Which statement about plot is NOT true: In tragedy, plot
   a. links actions.
   b. provides motive, cause.
   c. involves conflict.
   d. ends in death.

4. Which of the following is the most important difference between Greek and Elizabethan tragedy?
   a. Development of episodes into acts
   b. Shift from plot to character
   c. Increase in number and type of characters
   d. Violation of unities of time, place, and plot

5. A scene is to an act as a(n)
   a. aside is to a soliloquy.
   b. episode is to an act.
   c. kommos is to an episode.
   d. line is to a stanza.

In 100–300 words, answer the following short essay questions:

1. Oedipus becomes King of Thebes because he solves the riddle of the Sphinx. What was that riddle and how does it parallel the action in *Oedipus the King*?
2. The discussion of conflict in this study guide maintains that the primary conflict in *Oedipus the King* can be stated in a number of ways and then identifies one, Oedipus versus evil. How else might the major conflict be stated and why?
3. In what way or ways does Jocasta further the plot in *Oedipus the King*?

ADDITIONAL READING ACTIVITIES

If you enjoyed listening to the interview in this lesson, you will probably want to read one of the plays A. R. Gurney has written. They are available in the following edition:

Gurney, A. R. *Four Plays.* (Includes *Scenes from an American Life, Children, The Middle Ages,* and *The Dining Room*)

LESSON 21

Perspectives on Illusion:
SETTING AND STAGING IN DRAMA

ABOUT THE LESSON

If you have ever seen a play performed on the stage and then seen the same play adapted for film or video, you were probably struck by a difference that was hard to identify but was certainly there. Put *The Sound of Music* on stage, and without even realizing it, we find ourselves accepting the conventions of musical comedy—actors bursting into song, dances occurring in the middle of a scene, and the like. But if you see *The Sound of Music* on film, these same conventions are apt to bother you because we bring to film certain expectations that we don't bring to the theater. The major one is realism.

You can test out this idea by comparing what it's like to see a scary film in a movie theater and then on video. Film is much more realistic. And the difference between the effect of film and that of video is caused by more than the size of the screen. It's also tied to the environment. You watch a video at home in familiar, comfortable surroundings; you watch a film in a dark theater filled with strangers.

Whether you are in the theater for a film or a play, when the lights go down, you are willing—even eager—to enter another world. But film can take you places that a stage cannot, and film can splice time in ways plays cannot. These differences in physical and temporal surroundings are crucial and make the language of a play more important than its visual aspects.

You may come away from a film dissatisfied with its plot and characterization but so overwhelmed by its beauty or special effects that you'd recommend the film to a friend. That's not apt to happen in serious drama, however, for it relies on character, plot, staging, and language for its effect. And of those elements, staging is the least important, which is why you can read a play and get so much pleasure from it. But to say staging is the least important aspect of drama is not to say it doesn't matter. In fact, setting and staging contribute to character, tone, plot, and theme.

In this lesson, we'll be looking at the role that setting and staging play in *Oedipus the King*, *Hamlet*, and particularly *The Glass Menagerie*. By setting, we mean the physical and temporal aspects of the play—where and when it takes place. By *staging,* we mean how that setting is presented on stage—the type of stage used and the props and technology available at the time. We'll also be discussing the idea of realism in drama. With that in mind, you will find it useful to think of realism not as a fixed term but as various points on a continuum ranging from most to least realistic, from, say, a grisly version of the last scene in *Hamlet* to a highly stylized, virtually bloodless interpretation.

GOAL

This lesson will help you to recognize how setting and staging form the world of the play.

WHAT YOU WILL LEARN

When you complete this lesson you will be able to:

1. Differentiate between setting and staging.
2. Describe how staging evolved.
3. Recognize different types of stages.
4. Differentiate realistic from non-representational drama.
5. Discuss how production of a play would differ in thrust, proscenium, and arena settings.

LESSON ASSIGNMENT

Working through the following nine steps will help you master the objectives and achieve the goal for this lesson:

Step 1: In your text, review the section "Performance: The Unique Aspect of Drama," pages 1211–1214 in Chapter 23, "The Dramatic Vision: An Overview." Also read Chapter 26, "Visions of Dramatic Reality and Nonreality: Varying the Idea of Drama as Imitation," pages 1614–1619. The text will provide background for what you will read in the study guide, explain the key terms, and give you some information about the plays you will be reading.

Step 2: This lesson will deal primarily with *The Glass Menagerie*, pages 1643–1692, but will also mention *Oedipus the King*, pages 1281–1318, and *Hamlet*, pages 1322–1421. In addition to reading *The Glass Menagerie*, you may want to review the following scenes that provide a context for the study guide discussion and video performances. Those marked with an asterisk (*) will be shown in the video.

- *Oedipus,* Episode 3, Exodos
- *Hamlet,* I.iv
- *Hamlet,* I.v
- *Hamlet,* III.iv
- *The Glass Menagerie,* Scenes 1 & 7
- *The Glass Menagerie,* Scene 1, Speech 1*

Step 3: Read the OVERVIEW in this study guide lesson.

Step 4: Watch the VIDEO, following the steps in the VIEWING GUIDE in this study guide lesson.

Step 5: Reread the OVERVIEW to reinforce what you have learned in the text and the video and to help you complete the writing activities.

Step 6: Complete any WRITING ACTIVITIES assigned in this lesson.

Step 7: Do the SELF-TEST exercises in this study guide lesson.

Step 8: Read any of the ADDITIONAL READING ACTIVITIES assigned.

Step 9: Go back to the learning objectives in the WHAT YOU WILL LEARN section of this study guide lesson and be sure you can respond to each of them.

OVERVIEW

The interview you will see in the video for this lesson is with Chris Barecca, a set designer and instructor in theatrical design at Columbia University. He points out the degree to which anyone involved in production must first be an interpreter of the play—an expert reader. As Barecca implies, a valid interpretation must be grounded in the text.

Throughout the discussion that follows, we will emphasize the plays as literature—as works with settings established by the playwrights that enhance character, plot, atmosphere, and theme. We will also be talking about staging but in general terms dealing with the different types of stages that can be used for productions: *proscenium, thrust,* and *arena.* Because this course focuses on plays as literature and not as theater, we will not discuss the more technical aspects of production, such as blocking out the movements of the actors and working out the lighting.

To illustrate how setting and staging evolved, we will examine *Oedipus the King, Hamlet,* and *The Glass Menagerie* as representative of their times, paying particular attention to *The Glass Menagerie.* We will then turn to other kinds of staging so that you can better understand how different directors can interpret a play in a variety of ways.

Setting and Staging in the Theater of Ancient Greece

As you may recall from the lesson that introduced you to drama, the theater of the ancient Greeks resembled two circles—an inner circle that is the orchestra and an outer one, the entire structure. Imagine the face of a clock. The seating area or *theatron*—from which we get our word *theater*—would take up the space from about two o'clock to ten o'clock, leaving the rest open for playing areas.

To the left and right of the playing area—at say, two o'clock and ten o'clock—are aisles or *parados* that run from the orchestra or inner circle to the outside. These are the passages that the chorus uses for entrances and exits. They would be easily visible if you were watching a play.

If you were a member of the audience, you would be one person out of about 14,000 to 20,000 seated in a tier in the outer circle, looking down on the orchestra, where the chorus sings and dances and where part of the dramatic action takes place. You would have a good view of the altar to Dionysus that stands in the center of the orchestra as a constant reminder of the religious context of all the performances.

At the far side of the orchestra is the playing area that research suggests was a somewhat elevated platform or *proskenion*. It is here that most of the action of the play takes place. In back of the proskenion is the *skene* or wooden scene-building that serves a number of purposes. Its interior is used as a dressing-room and place for the actors to gain access to the playing area, and its exterior provides a background for the action of the play, hence our term *scene*. The facade of the skene is painted to look like the front of a palace.

Some evidence suggests that Sophocles—in addition to being the leading playwright of the time—invented scene-painting, which perhaps was a painted cloth or screen placed in front of the skene. We do know that if an indoor scene was called for, a platform was rolled out of the skene. Plays that called for the descent of a god or disappearance of a character employed a crane-like structure that could be used to raise or lower an actor.

Even if you were sitting in the row furthest from the playing areas, you would probably be able to follow the words and action clearly. The layout of the theater took advantage of the natural acoustics of the hillside, and the thicksoled boots and masks worn by the actors improved seeing as well as hearing. Lighting was never a problem because all plays were performed by daylight.

To sum up the staging of Greek plays, it was minimal. And considering the emphasis Greek tragedies placed on the unity of plot, there was no need for elaborate sets or changes of costume. You can see, for instance, that the stage directions in *Oedipus the King* are very simple; in fact, they were added much later.

Yet if you step back from the performance of the play and consider its meaning, you will find that two settings—although never seen—figure significantly in the plot, Phocis and Cithaeron. It was at Phocis, "the place where three roads meet" (line 735), that Oedipus killed Laius. Jocasta's mention of that place is Oedipus's first clue that he may indeed be the murderer of Laius.

In fact, the place is so vivid to him that when Jocasta mentions it, he ignores the substance of the prophecy she has just related (which, of course, is the same one he has heard) and concentrates instead on the location of the murder: "Where is the place where this was done to him?" (line 737). When Jocasta identifies it more precisely, Oedipus cries, "Oh, Zeus, what have you willed to do to me?" (line 743).

At this point in the play, Oedipus suspects the truth, but both he and Jocasta take refuge in the report that Laius was killed by several men, not just one. The audience, knowing the story, knows that is a false hope and is moved by the irony—Oedipus thinks he cannot have killed Laius, but that is not so.

Irony also surrounds the role played by Cithaeron, the mountain on which Oedipus was found. When that becomes known at the end of Episode 3, the Chorus sings of Cithaeron as "countryman / of Oedipus, his nurse and mother" (lines 1096–1097). The Chorus celebrates Cithaeron as Oedipus's birthplace and speculates upon the gods and goddesses that may be his parents. The truth, as we know, is quite different, and it is to Cithaeron that Oedipus asks to return at the end of the play: "Then let my fate continue where it will!" (line 1468).

Setting and Staging in Elizabethan Times

Like *Oedipus the King*, the actual time of *Hamlet* is a vague "some time ago." More than likely, when the two plays were originally produced, the actors wore the clothes of their own times. Place, however, was thematically important.

In *Hamlet*, the most striking thing about the court at Elsinore is the imagery associated with it—images of disease, corruption, and putrefaction. When Marcellus remarks, "Something is rotten in the state of Denmark" (I.iv.90), he sounds a keynote for the play.

Now think for a minute about the Great Chain of Being that you learned about in the discussion of Elizabethan beliefs in Lesson 19. Just as God was at the head of the chain, so too the ruler of a country was head of the state—responsible only to God. In Denmark, however, the divine order has been shattered by Claudius's murder of the elder Hamlet. With a king who is not only a murderer but an incestuous one as well, it follows that the state is corrupt, diseased.

The atmosphere of the court is so riddled with suspicion that espionage is the order of the day. No one feels the weight of this atmosphere more than Hamlet who states that even the heavens "appeareth nothing to me but a foul and pestilent congregation of vapours" (II.ii.295–296).

Claudius also is weighed down by the effects of his sin. As you remember, he does have something of a conscience. He knows his guilt and declares, "O my offence is rank, it smells to heaven" (III.iii.36). Yet he is unrepentant.

Claudius's murderous and incestuous acts breed corruption, and Hamlet berates his mother with that fact:

> ... Nay but to live
> In the rank sweat of an enseamed bed,
> Stewed in corruption, honeying, and making love
> Over the nasty sty. — (III.iv.92–95)

By the end of the play, Denmark seems awash with plots, counterplots, and blood. In reporting to Fortinbras, Horatio sums them up,

> ... so shall you hear
> Of carnal, bloody and unnatural acts,
> Of accidental judgments, casual slaughters,
> Of deaths put on by cunning and forced cause,
> And in this upshot, purposes mistook,
> Fall'n on th' inventors' heads... — (V.ii.363–368)

Yet at the end of the play, these deaths—particularly that of Claudius—are signs that order has been restored. Fortinbras will assume the crown rightfully; the links are restored to the chain. The play ends with the stage direction "Exeunt marching: after the which a peal of ordnance are shot off" (page 1421).

That stage direction is more necessary than you might think. Put *Hamlet* on a contemporary stage, and after the bearing away of the bodies and the sound of the shots, the curtain would fall. But the Elizabethan stage had no curtain. With that last stage direction, two ends are accomplished—the carrying off of the bodies clears the stage, and the shots signal the end of the play.

As was the case with *Oedipus the King*, the stage directions for *Hamlet* were added some time well after the initial performances of the play. But before we analyze Elizabethan stage directions and how they were carried out, let's take a look at the theaters of the time so we can better understand how plays were staged and what the audience saw.

In 1509, just shy of a hundred years before *Hamlet*, London had a little over 50,000 inhabitants and no public playhouses. Yet by the time *Hamlet* was first produced, London's population had boomed to some 200,000, and there were around eight public theaters.

Facts about Elizabethan productions are hard to come by because the theaters were built with wooden frames, and often the roofs were thatch. What with the occasional storm, flying spark, or misaimed fireworks, theaters burned down with some regularity. In fact, Shakespeare's Globe Theater burned down in 1613 because a small cannon used for a performance of *Henry VIII* ignited some paper that then swept up through the open courtyard and caught in the thatch of the roof. The design varied from one theater to another, but enough evidence has been amassed to detail the characteristics of the Elizabethan stage.

Judging from the records and accounts of the time, we can get a fairly accurate idea of the typical Elizabethan theater. Imagine a three story round or polygonal building with a hollow core or courtyard that is open to the air, and you have a good idea of the Elizabethan playhouse. Like the Greek theater, it had tiered seats, but they were arranged much more steeply, rising vertically in three stories covered by a roof rather than spreading out horizontally toward the rear in the open air. Looking down from a tier, you would see what in the Greek theater had been the orchestra, a playing area, has become the "pit," reserved for the audience. Like the plays in ancient Greece, those in Elizabethan times were performed by day and used no artificial light.

If you were to attend an Elizabethan play, you would have a choice first of sitting or standing. For a penny, you could stand in the pit, the paved courtyard that was pen to the air and, of course, the light. For an additional penny, you could have a seat in one of the covered galleries that made up the three stories that looked down upon the pit. For yet another penny, you could have a cushioned seat, and for an additional sixpence—about equal to the daily wage of a worker— you could be seated in one of the Lords' rooms. These most expensive seats were partitioned from the galleries and could be used as boxes for seating or as additional space for the play's action. No matter whether you sat or stood, you would never be more than some 70 feet from the performance.

Let's say you bought a seat on the front tier of the second story. You would find yourself looking out onto the open-air pit that contains a wide raised platform stage. Directly behind the platform stands the superstructure for the stage, three stories' worth, with a wooden canopy extending from the top story over the platform below. As the audience crowds in, the seats about you are taken and the space around the platform below becomes crowded with standing one-penny "groundlings."

Most of the play's action takes place on the platform jutting out into the pit, what we would now call a thrust stage. Raised about five feet above the ground, the platform measures some 43 feet across and 28 feet deep. The area beneath this platform is hollow, where the actors can move about. You find this is what's happening in *Hamlet* when the Ghost's voice repeats "Swear" (I.v.149). The platform also contains a trap door, which in *Hamlet* serves as Ophelia's grave.

As previously mentioned, at the rear of the platform stands the superstructure for the stage, an integral part of the building, rising three stories. The first floor of the superstructure is the "tiring house," short for "attiring house," where actors change costume much as they did in the Greek skene. And like the skene, the tiring house has doors that open onto the platform. These are double doors and quite large, large enough so that when they are fully opened a scene can be played in the space they reveal.

In *Hamlet*, this is the space that Polonius uses to overhear the conversation between Hamlet and his mother. As the language of the play indicates, the area was hung with a curtain or *arras*. Perhaps, too, this is the space used to enact "The Murder of Gonzago," the play within the play Hamlet uses to confirm the Ghost's story.

The second floor of the superstructure could be used as additional playing area or seating space. Often this story is where balcony scenes were played (as in *Romeo and Juliet*), but it could also serve as a gallery or as expensive seating. You probably find it used in *Hamlet* as the area where Hamlet walks, reading a book and overhearing Polonius's plot to "loose" Ophelia to him and spy on what results.

On the highest level are the musicians and the stage hands who take care of special effects, such as the firing of cannon that ends *Hamlet*. Reaching out from this level is the projecting roof or canopy that covers most of the platform below and is supported by pillars that could be incorporated into the action. As for the roof over the stage, it is indicated in stage directions as "above" or "aloft." When Hamlet calls attention to "this most excellent canopy the air, look you, this brave o'erhanging firmament, this majestical roof fretted with golden fire" (II.ii.292–295), more than likely he would have gestured toward the ceiling overhanging the stage.

If you were sitting in that seat in the second story, odds are that you could not see the turret that is perched at the back of this roof, topping the third story. Yet you would know it is there because from this turret, performances are announced with a flag and trumpet call, leading one preacher to bemoan the attendance at Paul's Cross with the remark, "Will not a filthy play, with the blast of a trumpet, sooner call thither a thousand than an hour's tolling of a bell bring to the sermon a hundred?"

He probably was not exaggerating. A typical Elizabethan playhouse may have held as many as 3,000 people. Given good weather and a popular play, a theater would fill with an audience that came both to see and be seen. Lords and laborers, men, women, and children, watched and listened, occasionally flagging down a hawker of food or drink for some refreshment. What with the noise of the crowd, the hustle of the vendors, the action on stage, and the sound effects, attendance at the theater had far more in common with a contemporary American afternoon baseball game than a formal evening at a Broadway play. After all, the Elizabethan theater offered two or three hours of solid entertainment for only a penny—a price well within reason for most.

Two or three hours? You may well be wondering how a play like *Hamlet* was performed in that short a time. Just reading the play, we are struck by its scope, to say nothing of its 20 scenes. How then could it be performed in the space of some two to three hours?

Remembering the final action in *Hamlet* and the carrying off of the bodies, you have one answer—no time was taken for a curtain rising and dropping because there was no curtain. Nor was there any scenery. Flip through the pages of *Hamlet*, and you'll discover that the stage directions for the settings are minimal—"Another room at the castle," "Another part of the platform," and the like. Remember too that these stage directions were added later.

Anything the Elizabethan audience needed to know about the physical setting was built into the language of the play. Thus in *Hamlet* as Act I.iv opens, instead of seeing what we might today—a dimly lit stage against a backdrop of battlements rimed with frost—we have Hamlet saying, "The air bites shrewdly, it is very cold," and asking, "What hour now?" When Marcellus says that midnight has already sounded, Horatio responds, "I heard it not: it then draws near the season / Wherein the spirit held his wont to walk." With this reference, the setting is indicated as the battlements where the Ghost was seen before.

You will find also that entrances and exits are indicated by lines within the play. In the same scene as above, Horatio's comment "Look my lord it comes" cues the actor playing the Ghost. You will also note that any time the language of the play is blank verse, the end of scenes and acts is preceded by a couplet. The rhyme not only has the effect of rounding off the action but is also an auditory cue for audience, actors, and musicians.

Remove the curtain, drop all set changes, let each scene follow right on the heels of the other, and you have a fast-moving production. Watching a performance in Elizabethan times was not the all-day theatrical marathon that it was for the Greeks. If you came to see *Hamlet*, you entered the theater around two o'clock, watched scene build on scene, listened to the musicians during the short breaks between acts, and left the theater around five o'clock. What you saw was the world of a play built almost entirely on language; it not only carried the action, plot, and characterization but also created the atmosphere, painted the scenery, set the time, and cued the actors.

Setting and Staging in Modern Times

If you were to see *Oedipus the King* or *Hamlet* staged today, you would probably be seeing the play produced with the same techniques that were available for the original production of *The Glass Menagerie*—lighting, sets, special effects, the works. But there's an important difference. In *The Glass Menagerie*, you have the author's elaborate stage directions that not only describe the set and atmosphere but flesh out the characters as well.

As your text points out, *The Glass Menagerie* is an interesting mixture of the realistic and nonrealistic, with the language in the former category and the narrator, lighting, music, and screen projections in the latter. Up to the 19th century, realism was not technically possible, even if it were desired. After all, how could you produce a night scene if the play had to be put on in broad daylight?

To state the history of drama very simply, prior to the 19th century, drama in England and Europe tended to fall in one of two categories. There were serious plays—many of which were written in verse—that dealt with extraordinary situations, kings and princes, heroic deeds, and death. And then there were nonserious plays that dealt with extraordinary situations, court figures and exaggerated characters, predictable or absurd deeds, and happy endings.

In reaction to this second type of drama, playwrights in the late 19th century began to write serious plays that dealt with realistic characters who faced realistic problems. Henrik Ibsen, for instance, writing in Norway in the last half of the 19th century, focused on issues of feminism and idealism. And in England, George Bernard Shaw, the Irish playwright, virtually chased melodramas off the Victorian stage with his dramas of ideas.

The staging of these realistic plays was also realistic. Gone were the fantastic sets of the melodramas, and in their place were more lifelike depictions of everyday households. With the advent of gas lighting for the stage around 1820, it was also possible to produce realistic changes to reflect sunlight, moonlight, and other effects.

Most of the staging at this time consisted of a proscenium arch, named after the Greek *proskenion*—the playing area in front of the skene—behind which was a picture-frame stage. Today we use the term *proscenium* to describe this kind of stage. The proscenium theater is one you are probably familiar with. Imagine a building essentially consisting of two very large rooms—one for the audience and the other for the players. Dividing the two is the proscenium arch, which often contains a curtain. Behind the arch or frame is the playing area enclosed by three walls. The audience sits in front and looks through the invisible fourth wall.

Above, behind, and to the left and right of the playing area are the actors' dressing rooms, the storage areas for sets and props, the controls for the curtain, special effects, lighting, and the like. The basic design for theaters such as this was developed as early as the 17th century in Italy, and variations on it can be found in descriptions of 18th century productions in England, where an apron or platform extended beyond the arch as a diminished version of the Elizabethan platform. By the 19th century, however, this apron had been cut back to just a few feet, which is the style for the proscenium theaters we have today.

When *The Glass Menagerie* opened, it opened in just such a theater. If you read the stage directions at the beginning of the play carefully, you can see how the stage was set. Within the proscenium arch was a scrim or gauzy curtain painted to resemble a tenement wall. Lit from the front, the scrim seems solid, but once the area behind it is illuminated, the scrim is transparent.

As the play opens, the scrim is in place, and Tom's first speech takes place before it, giving the audience the illusion of looking at the Wingfield's exterior tenement wall. When Tom says, "I think the rest of the play will explain itself," the lights go on behind the scrim to reveal the interior scene as though the audience is looking through the wall of the tenement. Then once the dining room scene is underway, the scrim rises and does not fall again until Tom's last speech.

If you were to compare the stage directions for *The Glass Menagerie* with those for *Oedipus the King* and *Hamlet*, you would be struck by several contrasts. Probably the first thing to catch your eye would be that the stage directions for The Glass Menagerie are extensive. They cover not just entrances and exits but characterization, atmosphere, staging, props, lighting, and a philosophy of the theater. What's more, they are written by the playwright for the published version of the script. Williams himself tells you straight out that

> The scene is memory and is therefore nonrealistic. Memory takes a lot of poetic license. It omits some details; others are exaggerated, according to the emotional value of the articles it touches, for memory is seated predominantly in the heart. The interior is therefore rather dim and poetic.—(page 1647).

If you were a member of the audience, the staging of the opening scene—Tom's speech and the dining room dialogue—would prepare you for a play that mixed realistic and nonrealistic elements. As this point, the proscenium stage and interior set are realistic; the backdrop for Tom and his opening speech are not.

Yet if you read the play instead of seeing it, the preliminary stage directions and production notes prepare you for a far more unrealistic play than the one that follows. Once you get beyond the first scene, the characters and their dialogue probably strike you as quite realistic. Their actions, motives, conflicts, and language are not very far removed from those of people we know.

But let's first look at the elements of the play that Williams relates to "a conception of a new, plastic theatre which must take the place of the exhausted theatre of realistic conventions if the theatre is to resume vitality as a part of our culture" (page 1645). These elements include Tom's multiple role as narrator, stage manager, and character, and the play's lighting, music, and screen devices. All of these elements call attention to the play as a play, as a dramatic fiction. The effect is to break down the first convention of realism—that what is being portrayed mimics reality.

Williams apparently worried about the episodic structure of the play. With the action spread over seven scenes, he thought "the basic structure or narrative line may be obscured from the audience; the effect may seem fragmentary rather than architectural" (page 1646). To avoid that impression, he employs music and lighting. The music provides "emotional emphasis to suitable passages," and a "free, imaginative use of light can be of enormous value in giving a mobile, plastic quality to plays of a more or less static nature" (page 1647).

Originally Williams had planned to use a screen on the set. At key points, various images and titles would be projected onto the screen to "give accent to certain values in each scene" (page 1646). Thus the screen would serve a structural function by highlighting certain motifs or ideas that then would link the scenes together. Williams also thought that the screen device would have a "definite emotional appeal" and saw in it many "possibilities." Yet the device was neither used in the first production of the play, nor is it usually used in subsequent productions.

Williams's original concern about the episodic nature of the play was directed at the audience's possible "lack of attention," not the play's structure. When the play was in rehearsal, Williams found that the character of Amanda—as performed by Laurette Taylor—was strong enough to impress the audience with the play's unity, so he dropped the idea of the screen. That was in 1945.

Since that time, audiences have developed a high tolerance for what may initially appear unrelated or interrupted action. As television viewers, for instance, we readily string out our attention over commercial interruptions and with serial programs even carry our interest from one week to another. For the contemporary audience, Williams's screen images and titles would serve little function and might indeed seem overkill, which would explain why they are rarely used in contemporary productions.

Whether we read the play or see it, what shatters any realistic expectation we may have is Tom's role. His opening speech is addressed directly to the audience, and is first line reveals him to be the controller of the action. Then he states the purpose of the play: "I give you truth in the pleasant disguise of illusion" (page 1648). He makes us conscious of the play as a play, a work of the imagination, of illusion, but emphasizes that its meaning is concerned with reality, "truth."

Tom goes on to set the time of the play—the thirties—and the social context—the depression and the Spanish Civil War. He then briefly describes his role as narrator and character and informs us who the other characters are, noting that Laura's gentleman caller is an "emissary from a world of reality that we *the other characters* were somehow set apart from" and symbolizes "the long-delayed but always expected something that we live for" (page 1648). Tom also calls our attention to his father—who only appears in a large photograph on the wall—and then, at his mother's call, takes up his role as character in the play.

Yet Tom is also upon occasion the stage director. In the first scene, no sooner do we get used to him as a character than his role changes again; he reads as though from a script when his mother tells her tale of gentlemen callers, and then he signals cues for lighting and music.

One reason Williams may have set the staging of the play somewhere between the realistic and nonrealistic is that the idea of reality and illusion is central to its meaning. When you think about it, you realize that Tom is right—that Jim is the only representative of reality in the play. Amanda, Laura, and even Tom live in worlds of their own making that bear little resemblance to the real world.

The real world that surrounds the Wingfields is harsh, ugly, beaten down, poor. Tom's job does not bring in much money, and Amanda's sales of magazine subscriptions over the telephone are more attempts and failures than successes. As for Laura, she cannot face the outside world long enough to prepare for a job much less hold one.

The Wingfields—like so many families during the Depression—are barely surviving. We know that Amanda wars her long-vanished husband's bathrobe, and that Laura's overcoat has been revamped from one of Amanda's. Their poverty makes Amanda's preparations for Laura's gentleman caller all the more pathetic, and it's interesting to note that those preparations also include a rose-colored lamp shade. The light that it imparts is both soft and illusionary, as in the cliché about seeing life through rose-colored glasses.

The soft light given off by the lamp is soon interrupted by darkness—an indication that Tom did not pay the electric bill. Even that harsh reality is blunted when light returns in the form of candles. They give off a warm, muted glow that also blurs rough edges.

And then there's the glass menagerie, the fragile world of glass that seems to be the only world Laura can relate to. It is also a part of the setting. She notes that, "My glass collection takes up a good deal of time" (page 1683), and she is particularly proud of her unicorn, "one of the oldest. It's nearly thirteen" (page

1684). The way she says that makes you think she marks the birthday of each animal.

The similarities between Laura and the unicorn are obvious, and we shall explore them later in the lesson on symbolism. For now, it's enough to note some parallels between the setting and the action. Amanda has protected Laura just as Laura protects her menagerie. After Laura shares her glass world with Jim, he inadvertently breaks off the unicorn's horn. He has literally shattered her fantasy world of glass as later his announcement of his engagement will shatter her fantasy world of expectations. Her gift to him of the broken unicorn signals the end of her hopes.

So too at the end of the play, Amanda seems to recognize reality and the end of hope. Earlier, in Scene 2, she had told Laura "Why, you're not crippled, you just have a little defect—hardly noticeable, even!" (page 1654). But later toward the end of Scene 7, Amanda refers to Laura as "crippled," her recognition of a bleak reality. As for Tom, he thought running away could save him from his family but at the end, he realizes it cannot: "Oh, Laura, Laura, I tried to leave you behind me, but I am more faithful than I intended to be!" (page 1691).

These last lines of Tom's are spoken in his role as narrator. As he speaks, the action continues behind him but in silence. He concludes his speech by again playing stage manager, saying to the unhearing Laura, "Blow out your candles, Laura—and so goodbye . . ." (page 1691). The play ends with the action of Laura blowing the candles out. Tom's memory, however, lives on. As the ellipses at the end of his speech indicate, something has been omitted or suppressed.

Variations in Setting and Staging

One of the main effects of introducing nonrealistic elements into a play is to distance the audience. In *The Glass Menagerie*, Tom's presence as narrator is a constant reminder that even though the dialogue, action, and plot are realistic, the play is indeed a play. The device of a narrator is particularly effective when used in a proscenium theater. In that kind of theater, the audience is so used to the proscenium arch that they easily adopt the convention that what happens on stage is real, just as in Shakespeare's time they accepted the convention of the soliloquy.

Other playwrights use unrealistic sets, dialogue, characterization, or plot to distance the audience. Instead of asking "What will happen next?" audiences watching a highly nonrealistic play are apt to ask, "What is happening?" Plays such as those by Bertolt Brecht, Eugene Ionesco, and Samuel Becket employ stylized sets, flat characters, seemingly nonsensical dialogue, meaningless gestures, or unmotivated actions to focus the audience's attention on the ideas presented in their plays.

Modern and contemporary plays are also often staged in ways that affect the distance between the action and the audience. For instance, *arena* staging, also known as *theater-in-the-round*, places the actors in the center of the audience, drawing them into the action. Plays produced in this manner call for little in the way of sets, for there are no walls.

Even though arena staging solves some problems, it presents others. The actors must play to four sides, not just the one or three, for what member of an audience wants to see the backs of the actors' heads. Think, for instance, of how an actor should deliver a soliloquy; to be seen by everyone, the actor may have to move more than the language of the soliloquy supports.

Noting that even with arena staging the audience is separated from the action, some playwrights and directors have tried to break down the separation by making the audience part of the play. In productions such as these, you might find that the person sitting next to you is really a character in the play or that the action is broken up into several physical locations that you are invited to visit in whatever order you wish.

Productions such as these are apt to say as much about the nature of drama, reality, or life as they are about the play. And soon, of course, what was once a novelty becomes a *convention*—an unrealistic device or technique that the audience readily accepts. The auditorium lights go down, the stage lights go up, and we enter the world of the drama.

Summary

Setting and staging are both intrinsic and extrinsic elements of a play. They are intrinsic because they are part of the action. *The Glass Menagerie*, for example, is clearly set in the thirties, and its characters are clearly American. They speak, act, and dress like Americans of the 1930s.

At the same time, the play's setting and staging can be manipulated externally. Depending on whether *The Glass Menagerie* is produced for a thrust, proscenium, or arena stage, the play will have a different relationship with its audience. And often a play's theme will speak to a situation far different from the setting of the play. During World War II, for instance, *Julius Caesar* was frequently produced in Nazi-occupied France. The fact that the play was by Shakespeare made it all right with the Germans; that it was about the murder of a dictator cheered the French.

The immediate context of the audience obviously affects the reception and interpretation of a play. Produce *Hamlet* in a Marxist country, and you will probably find a Marxist Hamlet, supported by the citizenry and fighting the old guard forces of corruption.

So when you read or see a play, you need to keep in mind three different concepts of setting and staging—the historical perspective of the audience, the physical and temporal aspects of the play, and the manner in which the setting is presented. If you keep these three views in mind, you'll have a good grasp of how setting and staging function in drama.

VIEWING GUIDE

An important component of this lesson is the video. You will learn more effectively from it by thinking about the following questions and guidelines.

Before Viewing:

1. Review the section "Performance: The Unique Aspect of Drama," pages 1211–1214 in Chapter 23, "The Dramatic Vision: An Overview." Also review Chapter 26, "Visions of Dramatic Reality and Nonreality: Varying the Idea of Drama as Imitation," pages 1614–1619.
2. Review the works assigned, paying particular attention to the ones your instructor emphasizes. Try to hear the dialogue in the scene or scenes.

During Your Viewing:

1. Watch for the elements of nonrealistic setting.
2. Watch for the elements of realistic setting.
3. Look for links between setting, character, and conflict.
4. Listen for what the critics say about setting.
5. Listen for the major points Chris Barecca makes about the sources and techniques he uses to stage a play.

After Viewing:

Give some thought to the following questions. You may want to write short answers in your journal or notebook.

1. Did anything about Williams's reading surprise you? Why or why not?
2. What evidence do you find in the video that—as Williams says—the "scene is memory and is therefore nonrealistic"?
3. What point made by the critics interested you most and why?
4. What point made by Barecca interested you most and why?

WRITING ACTIVITIES

After your study of this lesson, you should be able to recognize how setting and staging form the world of the play. Your instructor will advise you which, if any, of the following writing activities you are to complete.

Formal Writing:

Of these three activities, the first is the easiest because it has the narrowest focus. At the same time, it will concentrate your attention on how setting supports other elements in the play. The second activity calls attention to what is easy to miss in a reading of the play. By noting where and why music is introduced, you will be able to understand the overall pattern Williams is after. Because the third activity asks for an overall assessment of the realistic and nonrealistic parts of the play, it is more difficult. Not only do you have to work with the play as a whole, but evaluation is a higher order of thinking than analysis. Assessment is also the point of Activity 4, where you are asked to evaluate a presentation in the video.

1. Choose any scene except the first from *The Glass Menagerie* and analyze how its setting (including props) relates to character and conflict.
2. Review your outline of *The Glass Menagerie* to see where music is indicated. Write an essay that examines the role of music in the play and evaluates its effectiveness.
3. To what extent does the mixture of the realistic and nonrealistic add to or detract from *The Glass Menagerie*? Write a short essay that explains and backs up your opinion.
4. How effectively does the video present Williams' reading of Tom's speech? Analyze how well the model and images support the speech.

Informal Writing:

Both activities focus on setting, one on the smaller details and the other on the larger issues. Both also call for updating the play to the present. That process will first put you in the position of a reader analyzing the existing setting. Then you will shift to the perspective of a playwright working out a new setting.

1. You know that *The Glass Menagerie* is set in the 1930s in a poor section of St. Louis. Imagine that you want to update the play to the present. In your journal or notebook, list all the important components of the play's setting as it was written. Select several and note their contemporary counterparts. Write a page or two explaining your choice or choices.
2. If you prefer, consider the larger questions of the play's setting. If you were going to shift the action to the present, what city and neighborhood would you select? What would be the Wingfields' race? What might be the counterpart to the gentlemen callers? Write an essay that explains your answer to one of these questions or a similar one that you devise.

SELF-TEST

Match the items in column A with the definitions or identifications in B:

A	B
1. Proscenium stage	a. Physical and temporal aspects of the play
2. Realistic drama	b. Stage opon on three sides
3. Setting	c. Calls attention to the plays as play
4. Staging	d. Scene building
5. Thrust stage	e. Platform extending beyond proscenium arch
6. Skene	f. Area next to platform
7. Nonrealistic drama	g. Area behind proscenium arch
8. Arena stage	h. Stage open on four sides
9. Pit	i. Painted curtain
10. Apron	j. Means by which play is presented
	k. Platform behind proscenium arch
	l. Mimics reality
	m. Stage open on one side

Answer the following multiple-choice items:

1. Performances of Greek tragedy involved
    a. realism.
    b. song, dance, and dialogue.
    c. arena staging.
    d. varied sets.

2. Elizabethan theater used a(n)
    a. thrust stage.
    b. arena stage.
    c. proscenium stage.
    d. theater-in-the-round.

3. Which was NOT used in theatrical performances prior to the 19th century?
    a. Special effects
    b. Artificial light
    c. Music
    d. Stage machinery

4. Which is characteristic of nonrealistic drama?
    a. Everyday speech
    b. Rounded characters
    c. Minimal or stylized sets
    d. Clear motivation

5. *The Glass Menagerie* employs
    a. music, dance, and dialogue.
    b. multiple sets.
    c. five acts.
    d. nonrealistic devices.

In 100–275 words, answer the following short essay questions:

1. The action of *The Glass Menagerie* takes place essentially in one setting, the interior of the Wingfields' apartment. What does the play gain by having the action confined to such a limited space?
2. Select one of the play's lighting directions and discuss what it contributes to the particular action it applies to.
3. Choose one item from the set and write an essay that explores its significance to the play as a whole.

ADDITIONAL READING ACTIVITIES

If you enjoyed reading about staging and listening to the interview in this lesson, you may want to read more works on the subject.

Cole, Edward C. and Harold Burris-Meyer. *Scenery for the Theatre.*
Gurr, Andrew. *The Shakespearean Stage 1524–1642.*
Langley, Stephen (ed.). *Producers on Producing.*
Nicoll, Allerdyce. *The Theatre and Dramatic Theory.*

LESSON 22

Speech and Silence:
THE LANGUAGE OF DRAMA

ABOUT THE LESSON

It may seem odd to talk about the language of costume, gesture, and movement, to say nothing of the language of silence, but when you think of theater, all of these non-verbal things have something to "say." And when you think about everyday life, you can find this kind of non-verbal language as well. The punk look, the urban cowboy, the preppie look all in a way are costumes that say something about the wearer. In fact, you could think of the fashion and cosmetics industries as founded on the idea that clothes and make-up "speak."

As for gesture, you need only to look as far as the nearest irate driver. Think too of how much can be packed into a shrug or a wave of the hand or a shake of the head. And facial expressions are so eloquent that they often have their own overused vocabulary. Popular romance novels are full of passionate glances and romantic looks, and mediocre mysteries tend toward sinister smiles and deadly stares. Fiction that relies on descriptions such as these is also apt to characterize the way a person moves. A character in a romance may sweep, flounce, or stride manfully; one in a mystery may skulk, sneak, or creep.

Silence and pauses have meanings too. A sob story to the officer who is writing you a ticket may be met with silence that can mean "I can't believe this person is telling me this" or with a simple sarcastic "Sure." Pauses, on the other hand, can indicate a fumbling for words in a difficult situation or a reluctance to deliver unpleasant news. And sometimes they can be an unconscious linguistic habit, a non-verbal version of the "y'know" that so often fills out conversation.

In this lesson, you'll be learning how all these means of expression operate in drama. And, of course, you'll also learn about the more standard meaning of dramatic language—verbal expression. Spoken language in the form of dialogue not only reveals character but also ties in to a play's theme. Your study of setting and staging has already emphasized how Cithaeron is associated with Oedipus's fate and how Hamlet's Denmark has become a diseased kingdom. In both cases, the association was made through language in the form of imagery. And in both cases, the imagery directly related to the plays' themes.

298—*Literary Visions*

You have already studied the conventions of the soliloquy and the aside—two Elizabethan forms of dramatic language. In addition, your reading of *The Glass Menagerie* acquainted you with realistic and nonrealistic elements of drama—elements that also show up in the play's language. This lesson will build on what you have already learned to further your understanding of verbal as well as nonverbal language in drama.

GOAL

This lesson will help you to recognize how the various forms of dramatic language relate to action, character, and theme.

WHAT YOU WILL LEARN

When you complete this lesson you will be able to:

1. Describe the language of costume.
2. Give examples of the language of gesture, movement, and expression.
3. Interpret the language of silence.
4. Give examples of dramatic irony.
5. Relate dramatic language to character, action, and theme.

LESSON ASSIGNMENT

Working through the following nine steps will help you master the objectives and achieve the goal for this lesson:

Step 1: In your text, review the sections on "Language, Imagery, and Style Bring the Play to Life"(page 1205) and "Tone or Atmosphere Creates Mood and Attitude" (page 1210) in the chapter "The Dramatic Vision: An Overview" (pages 1204–1264) The text will provide background for what you will read in the study guide, explain the key terms, and give you some information about the plays you will be reading.

Step 2: Read the specific scenes your instructor assigns. This lesson, 22, will deal primarily with *The Glass Menagerie*. The following scenes provide a context for the video performances, and those marked with an asterisk (*) will be shown in the video.

- *Oedipus the King,* Episodes 1, 2, and 4.
- *Hamlet,* Act I.ii
- *Hamlet,* Act III.ii
- *Hamlet,* Act III.i.56–65*
- *Hamlet,* Act III.i.89–92*
- *Hamlet,* Act III.i.114–137*
- *The Glass Menagerie,* Scene 1
- *The Glass Menagerie,* Scene 7, Speeches 67–126, 263–267*

Step 3: Read the OVERVIEW in this study guide lesson.

Step 4: Watch the VIDEO, following the steps in the VIEWING GUIDE in this study guide lesson.

Step 5: Reread the OVERVIEW to reinforce what you have learned in the text and the video and to help you complete the Writing Activities.

Step 6: Complete any WRITING ACTIVITIES assigned in this lesson.

Step 7: Do the SELF-TEST exercises in this study guide lesson.

Step 8: Read any of the ADDITIONAL READING ACTIVITIES assigned.

Step 9: Go back to the learning objectives in the WHAT YOU WILL LEARN section of this study guide lesson and be sure you can respond to each of them.

OVERVIEW

As is the case with your own writing, a playwright's *diction*—the choice of words—must be appropriate. When you studied diction, connotation, and denotation in the short story and in poetry, you learned about the range of diction from the most informal to the most formal. And you studied what diction contributed to the overall work. In poetry, for instance, the words associated with Miniver Cheevy, pages 876–877, created an image of him as a royal kind of person.

The same tie between diction and character is at work in drama. But because drama comes to you directly from the characters and what they say, diction is crucial to drama. The language must fit the character.

But that "fit" can involve unrealistic as well as realistic speech. You may recall that the previous lesson stated that realism in drama was a concern of the 19th century, implying that up until that time, plays tended to be unrealistic. Thus in those earlier plays, we have conventions such as the aside and the soliloquy; in addition, many plays were written in verse—hardly the medium of realistic speech.

In judging whether language fits the character, you must consider the conventions of the time. But once you accept them, the language must suit. We accept blank verse for Hamlet, for example, but we would not accept his use of the simple, straightforward blank verse of a Robert Frost poem. Hamlet's language must reflect the richness and complexity of his character.

In this lesson, we will examine the relationship among language, action, and character. First we'll look at the language of speech and of silence, and then we'll explore the language of gesture, movement, and expression. Although we will focus primarily on *The Glass Menagerie*, we will also use *Oedipus* and *Hamlet* to illustrate the points under discussion.

Speech and Silence

To gain a solid understanding of the relationship between character and speech in drama, you need to do the same kind of careful analysis that you would do with a poem. In *Oedipus the King*, for example, a close study of his opening speech reveals a great deal about the character of Oedipus. The first note he strikes is one of concern, such concern that—as he says—he decided to listen and speak directly to the group of Tehban supplicants instead of sending someone in his place. "I . . . have come out myself," he says, "I, Oedipus, a name that all men know" (lines 7–8).

With that one line, Oedipus sounds the note of irony that rings so heavily throughout the play. The irony is at least two-fold—his name literally means "swollen-foot," a reminder of the manner in which as an infant he was left to die. Also his name will be infamous, for he will be known throughout the country as the murderer of his father, the husband of his mother, and defiler of the land. Sophocles employs irony to affect the audience, and the effect is horror and apprehension, for the audience, of course, already knows these things. The irony lies in the discrepancy between the audience's knowledge and Oedipus's ignorance.

Thus this short opening speech works on two levels. It reveals some of Oedipus's character, and on a larger scale it sets the ironic tone of the play. Jocasta's first appearance functions in a similar manner. Just before she appears, Oedipus has lost his temper with Creon, and the two end up trading insults. Oedipus accuses Creon of being a traitor, and Creon—stung to anger—accuses Oedipus of being a tyrant. Enter Jocasta:

> Wretched men! What has provoked this ill-advised dispute? Have you no sense of shame, with Thebes so sick, to stir up private troubles? Now go inside! And Creon, you go home! Don't make a general anguish out of nothing!—(lines 639–643)

Because of this speech, the audience immediately sees Jocasta in a motherly role, as though she is breaking up a quarrel between two naughty boys. She separates them, ordering them away in the manner of a referee breaking up a fight and sending the combatants to separate corners. But the speech also works on a larger level by deepening the irony; the audience knows that Jocasta is in reality Oedipus's mother.

Silence has a more subtle role to play, for rarely will you have a playwright indicate in stage directions "Silence here." But if you play a scene in your mind, you will realize where dramatic pauses are appropriate. Think, for example, of the beginning of Episode 4 and Oedipus's exchange with the Herdsman. The pace is swift as line by line Oedipus presses the Herdsman for the truth. The dialogue snaps back and forth in one-line exchanges, leading up to the Herdsman saying, "I have come to the dreaded thing, and I shall say it," to which Oedipus responds, "And I to hearing it, but hear I must" (lines 1174–1175).

At this point, imagine the action slowing with a pause before the Herdsman's response, "He was reported to have been—his son. / Your lady in the house could tell you best." And then imagine another pause before Oedipus asks, "Because she gave him to you?" Pause again for the Herdsman to say, "Yes, my lord." From this point on it's as though the truth must be dragged out, with both Oedipus and the Herdsman reluctant to hear it, and the hesitations leading up to Oedipus's anguished outburst:

> Ah! All of it was destined to be true! Oh light, now may I look my last upon you, shown monstrous in my birth, in marriage monstrous, a murderer monstrous in those I killed.—(lines 1187–1190).

Speech and silence, pauses and outbursts give dialogue a varied pace and a dramatic tension. Consider, for example, the dumb show in *Hamlet*. In terms of the play's action, it pantomimes the action that the players will perform in what Hamlet has chosen to call "The Mouse-trap." At the same time, the show mimics the crime Claudius has committed. On a larger scale, the dumb show is Hamlet's plot to test the Ghost's word.

And if you step back from the action and consider the play as a whole, you'll find that the dumb show also has thematic implications. It's as though the court is so diseased that words can no longer be trusted. Only actions can reveal truth. Yet Hamlet is more a man of words than actions.

When Hamlet is finally moved to action, his speech is short and his actions direct. Having heard from Laertes that the foil was poisoned as was the cup of wine that Gertrude drank in Hamlet's honor, Hamlet first stabs Claudius and then, as though that death were not good enough, pours what remains in the poisoned cup down Claudius's throat.

When Hamlet, dying, asks Horatio "to tell my story" (V.ii.332), it's as though words have regained their value. Claudius's sins—his murder of the elder Hamlet, incestuous marriage, and usurping of the crown—had poisoned words, devalued them. Thus we find the play riddled with discrepancies between words and actions. For example, Hamlet comments, "That one may smile, and smile, and be a villain" (I.v.108); Polonius advises Reynaldo, "By indirections find directions out" (II.i.63); Claudius comments, "My words fly up, my thoughts remain below, / Words without thoughts never to heaven go" (III.iii.97–98).

The difficulty of matching words to actions comes through strongly in *The Glass Menagerie* with a major difference—realistic speech. There you do not find the lofty verse of *Oedipus the King* or the intense poetic grandeur of *Hamlet* but rather ordinary prose more akin to the kind of speech you might hear every day.

But to say that is not to say that language in *The Glass Menagerie* is ordinary. If you take a hard look at Scene 7 and the dialogue between Laura and Jim, you can see how carefully the pauses and the speech are orchestrated. First, consider the setting and characters.

Here is Jim, who Tom as narrator has already declared the "most realistic character in the play, being an emissary from a world of reality that we were somehow set apart from. But . . . I am using this character also as a symbol; he is the long-delayed but always-expected something that we live for" (page 1648). And here is Laura, whose childhood illness has left her with a slight limp and a brace strapped to the shorter of her legs. Williams tells us in his stage directions that because of the "defect," "Laura's separation increases till she is like a piece of her own glass collection, too exquisitely fragile to move from the shelf" (page 1645).

These two unlikely souls—one living in fantasy, the other in reality—are brought together by the maneuverings of Amanda, who casts each of them in an ill-fitting role: Jim as a "gentleman caller" and Laura as the once youthful Amanda—beautiful and much sought-after. The irony is that the gentlemen callers and the young Amanda are probably Amanda's fantasies, so in this scene we find illusion built upon illusion.

The setting too is illusionary. Instead of the harsh light of day or even the artificial illumination of light bulbs, the scene is played by candlelight. Yet irony enters again, for the candlelight is more necessity than romance. Tom did not pay the light bill. Amanda glosses over that fact in much the same way she glosses over the ugly side of all reality—by romanticizing. As she gets ready to hustle Tom and herself off to the kitchen so that Laura and Jim will be alone, she tells Jim, "I'll give you this lovely old candelabrum that used to be on the altar at the Church of the Heavenly Rest" (page 1678). Leave it to Amanda to give the candle holder the proper singular Latin form and an exotic history as well.

As the scene between Jim and Laura starts, Williams tells us that Laura "can hardly speak from the almost intolerable strain of being alone with a stranger" (page 1678). As their dialogue unfolds, Laura's responses are limited to just a few words and dotted with pauses in the form of dashes. When Jim comments that she said she has hard him sing, Laura replies haltingly, "Oh, yes! Yes, very often . . . I—don't suppose—you remember me—at all?" (page 1680). The ellipses, the dashes, the question all imply a shyness and insecurity bordering on the pathological.

As the scene progresses, Laura's speech smooths out, but when she speaks of herself, the old insecurity and hesitation return: "I—I—never had much luck at—making friends" (page 1681). When Laura asks Jim about his old girlfriend and inquires if he's "still—going with her," Jim responds negatively. To him, the girlfriend is ancient history; he dismisses it easily. To Laura, however, his response is cause for hope—her hope. She falls into silence, fingering a piece from her glass menagerie.

Laura's silence continues, and Jim must ask her twice about what she has been doing since high school. Coming where it does, Laura's silence implies that her hope revolves around taking the place of Jim's old girlfriend, of being part of someone, of being loved, of breaking out of her isolation.

The conversation turns to Laura's glass collection and to the unicorn in particular, her "favorite," she says, who "must feel sort of lonesome" (page 1684). When the music from the dance hall across the street wafts into the room, Jim asks Amanda to dance, deflecting her "inferiority stuff" with "I'm not made out of glass" (page 1685). They dance, they bump the table, the unicorn falls, its horn breaks. Laura remarks, "Now it is just like all the other horses" (page 1686).

This moment marks Laura's breakthrough into the real world. Like the unicorn, she has been fragile, protected, unique, isolated. Now, thanks to Jim, she has come out of her protected fantasy world and is no longer alone. She has also become vulnerable. Jim tells her she is pretty and—carried away by his own pep talk—he kisses her. Her response is again fantasy. Williams describes her as having a "bright, dazed look." As she looks down into her hand, she has a "tender, bewildered expression" and "looks up, smiling, not hearing *Jim's* question." He asks another, but, Williams tells us, "she doesn't seem to hear him but her look grows brighter even" (page 1687).

As Jim blunders into an apology, retraction, and explanation, his speech takes on the same qualities hers had possessed earlier—pauses, hesitations, tentativeness as indicated by dashes, ellipses, question marks. In response, Laura retreats. As Jim crashes on to describe his feelings for his fiancée, Laura sways, stricken. Williams tells us "Laura struggles visibly with her storm. But Jim is oblivious; she is a long way off" (page 1688). She finally breaks her silence to give him the glass ornament and remarks, "A—souvenir" (page 1688). She only speaks again once. When Amanda learns the truth about Jim and he is about to leave, Amanda says "I wish you luck—and happiness—and success! All three of them, and so does Laura! Don't you, Laura?" Laura responds as if on cue, "Yes!" (page 1690).

Laura does not speak again, and the audience is left with the impression that having once become vulnerable—only to have her hopes crushed—she will never chance it again. Like the unicorn, for a while she was like the others—the people in the real world—but now that feeling too is only a "souvenir." She retreats into her fantasy world, which is also a world of silence.

This interpretation is only one of many. It is somewhat traditional in that the approach to the play is formal, aesthetic, confined largely to understanding the work on its own terms as a work of art and a work of literature. As such, the interpretation does not rely on externals, apply, for instance, a certain stance or theory and reading the work from that perspective. Yet such readings can be very rewarding.

Critics who take a biographical approach to literary works make much of Tennessee Williams's early years, when he lived with his sister and mother in a run-down neighborhood in St. Louis. They also find many parallels between Tom and Laura and Williams and his sister, who lived a withdrawn life at home, then later was diagnosed as a schizophrenic and placed in an institution.

Other critics who take a psychological approach to literature see in Laura a case history of withdrawal. They find the scene with Jim a study of Freudian sexual repression and denial. But no matter what approach you take to the play, what counts most is the text. The play as a whole and this last scene in particular are masterpieces of character portrayal through language—of speech and of silence.

Costume, Gesture, and Movement

Like the language of silence, the language of costume, gesture, and movement calls upon your imagination when you read a play. Sometimes, as is the case with more modern plays, the playwright will describe the costumes and indicate the gestures and movements that the actors should make. You have seen Tennessee Williams do just that with *The Glass Menagerie*. But more often, particularly with older plays, these directions are left blank. The reader fills them in with the imagination; the audience sees them interpreted by the director.

What has come down to us as the script for *Oedipus the King*, for example, contains little in the way of stage directions. Yet by piecing together information from Sophocles's contemporaries, we know that in the original performance the actors wore the clothing of the day. The only unrealistic elements of their costumes were masks and boots with built-up soles, the better to be heard and seen by the throng of people attending the play. The actors' movements on stage must have been somewhat restricted by their platform boots, and the masks took away any need for facial expressions, but these devices also made it easier for the audience to see and follow the action.

The size of the theater also suggests that the acting style was broad and somewhat stylized. After all, small gestures would be lost in a theater that holds 16,000 to 20,000 people. At the same time, the masks, boots, and stylized acting focused the audience's attention on the play's language and action. That action would include seeing Oedipus limp every time he moved—thus reinforcing dramatic irony by reminding the audience of his name and origin.

By Elizabethan times, costumes had become elaborate. Although the actors still appeared in the garb of the day, the clothing was often quite splendid. It was not unusual for the lords and knights of the times to bequeath their finer garments to their servants, who then sold them to acting companies. In addition, actors supplemented their costumes with objects related to their roles, thus making it easy to identify the characters. In the coronation scene from Shakespeare's *Henry VIII*, for instance, the Lord Chancellor comes on stage "with purse and mace before him," and the Queen appears under a canopy "in her robe . . . her hair, richly adorned with pearl, crowned" (IV.i).

Occasionally you will find that the language of the play indicates a costume. The first time Hamlet appears on stage, for instance, Gertrude implores him to "cast thy nighted colour off" (I.ii.68). Thus we know that he is dressed in black, the color of mourning. We also know the depth of his grief for his dead father, for he tells us that "I have that within which passes show, / These but the trappings and the suits of woe" (I.ii.85–86).

What little we know about the acting style of those times indicates that gestures were still somewhat broad and stylized, with actors striking a pose and then delivering their speeches. Yet we also know from *Hamlet* that overacting was not the ideal. You may recall that in Act III.ii Hamlet advises the players on how to deliver a speech. Warning them first of overacting, he goes on to describe an exemplary style—"suit the action to the word, the word to the action" (lines 16–17).

We can assume that this style was the goal of Shakespeare's players. That being the case, we can imagine how the role of Hamlet would be played. If we think of Hamlet as an intellectual who is more inclined to thought than action, then on stage his movements would be deliberate. But then there's the mad Hamlet. If you think of him as not only feigning madness but at times genuinely mad, then you can imagine a Hamlet whose movements wing between the sluggishness of depression and the frenzy of mania.

Much less is left to the imagination in modern plays in which the playwright has provided extensive descriptions and stage directions. As *The Glass Menagerie* opens, for example, Williams tells us that Tom enters "dressed as a merchant sailor." And as the first scene unfolds, every movement is accounted for in the stage directions. Similarly as Scene 2 begins, we are told exactly what Amanda is wearing, what it signifies, and the expression on her face.

As we read the play, we can imagine the smaller movements that characterize the various roles: Amanda's nervousness, Laura's withdrawn droop and slight limp. Tom's pacing as though he were caged, Jim's larger-than-life gestures and clumsiness. All of these smaller movements add to characterization and to theme, for they suggest the claustrophic, illusionary world that the Wingfields live in.

These smaller details of costume, gesture, and movement are in part made possible by the technology of the times. The possibilities of lighting, for instance, are almost limitless. A spotlight can focus an audience's attention on an individual actor in a way impossible for performances that must take place during daylight. And, of course, variations in lighting can emphasize an action or part of a set.

Also consider acoustics. With modern electronics it's possible to sit in the furthermost row and still hear a whisper on stage. Then too today's theaters take sight-lines into consideration in a way that the theaters of ancient Greece and Shakespeare's times could not. Today it's hard to find a bad seat in a theater. In part, that's because today's playhouses are smaller than those available to Shakespeare or Sophocles. A large Broadway theater holds around 1,500 people, compared to twice that number for Shakespeare and ten times for Sophocles.

All these changes affect what an audience can see and therefore how a part can be played. As a result, acting today is often subtle, and characterization is built around small details of costume, gesture, movement, and expression. This focus coincides with today's intense interest in the individual, motivation, and psychology. Except for melodrama and certain forms of comedy, gone is the broad style of acting common to earlier centuries.

Summary

You may have seen a production in which costume, gesture, and movement overshadowed the play. Beyond the category of serious drama, musicals and comedies often depend on non-verbal effects for their success. Slapstick comedy relies upon movement, gesture, and expression for its laughs, and musicals can sometimes count on spectacular costumes, special lighting, and sets for their entertainment value. But serious drama depends upon language.

When you see a serious drama performed, you are presented with all the aspects of language—verbal and non-verbal—as interpreted by the director. What the actors wear, what they say or don't say, how they say it, their expressions, gestures, and movements all contribute to the play's meaning. By fleshing out characterization, emphasizing action, and reinforcing theme, the language of drama is what determines a play's success or failure.

You now know that the language of theater is more than words. It is also made up of pauses, costumes, gestures, expressions, and movements. When you read a play, you need to keep these various forms in mind, often without the aid of fully developed notes by the playwright. In a way, then, reading drama requires more imagination on your part than reading other genres of literature. You have more parts to play, more gaps to fill to make the voices on the page come alive. But once you can do that—once you are a skilled reader of plays—you will find that you are also a much more informed viewer and therefore a far better critic—even of productions such as films and television shows.

VIEWING GUIDE

An important component of this lesson is the video. You will learn more effectively from it by thinking about the following questions and guidelines.

Before Viewing:

1. Review the sections on "Language, Imagery, and Style Bring the Play to Life"(page 1205) and "Tone or Atmosphere Creates Mood and Attitude" (page 1210) in the chapter "The Dramatic Vision: An Overview."
2. Review the works assigned, paying particular attention to the ones your instructor emphasizes. Try to hear the dialogue, particularly the pauses, in each scene, and try to work out possible gestures, expressions, and movements.

During Your Viewing:

1. Listen for pauses and silences.

2. Note the costumes.
3. Look for gestures, expressions, and movements.
4. Listen for what the critics say about Williams's use of verbal and non-verbal language.
5. Listen for what Michael Kahn and Emily Mann say about a play's text.

After Viewing:

Give some thought to the following questions. You may want to write short answers in your journal or notebook.

1. What did you learn about the language of silence?
2. Of the non-verbal forms of dramatic language, which struck you as the most important and why?
3. Which was the least important and why?
4. What points do both the critics and the director agree upon?
5. In one sentence, describe the job of a director.

WRITING ACTIVITIES

After your study of this lesson, you should be able to recognize how the various forms of dramatic language relate to action, character, and theme. Your instructor will advise you which, if any, of the following writing activities you are to complete.

Formal Writing:

All three activities deal with different aspects of dramatic language. If you liked to analyze character in the short story, and if you liked to analyze poetry, you will also enjoy the first two activities. Activity 1 examines the relationship between language and character, and the second activity focuses on the relationship between language and setting. Both are traditional in that they concentrate on spoken language. If your interests lie more on the side of performance, you will find the next activity rewarding. It examines the relationship between character and costume by placing you in the position of director. Note that for Activity 3, unless you elect do to *Hamlet* in modern dress, you may have to do some research. Costumes are also the focus of Activity 4, where you are asked to evaluate their effectiveness in the video presentation of scenes from *The Glass Menagerie*.

1. Take any speech from *Oedipus the King* and analyze what it reveals about the character.

2. Analyze the language of *The Glass Menagerie*'s dialogue for clues about its time and place. Write an essay explaining what you found and what conclusion your evidence leads you to.
3. Choose any character other than Hamlet, select a scene from the play that features that character, and describe in detail what the person is wearing and why.
4. Analyze the significance of the costumes used in the video dramatization of Williams's Scene 7. Explain what the costumes add to your interpretation of the play and evaluate their appropriateness.

Informal Writing:

Activity 1 deals with *The Glass Menagerie* and emphasizes the relationship among action, character, and expression, but it can relate to theme as well. The second activity asks you to apply what you have learned about the language of the theater to another medium. Both put you in the position of director.

1. Select any exchange of dialogue from *The Glass Menagerie*. Focus on one of the characters, and think about what might be that person's facial expressions. In your journal or notebook, key those expressions to the lines and describe them, explaining your decisions.
2. Select a short poem or a song that you like and think about how it might be presented on television. Copy the text you've selected and insert your stage directions. If you want a model for this activity, take one of the scenes from *The Glass Menagerie* and use its stage directions as your guide.

SELF-TEST

Match the items in column A with the definitions or identifications in B:

A	B
1. Language of costume	a. Blank verse
2. Aside	b. Greek dress
3. Masks	c. Laura's slight limp
4. Language of gesture	d. Unrealistic use of language
5. Realistic language	e. Worn for Greek tragedy
6. Language of silence	f. Jim's grasping of the "dance card"
7. Language of movement	g. Laura's response to Jim's kiss
8. Unrealistic language	h. Dashes and ellipses

9. Language of expression
10. Contemporary dress

i. Worn for Elizabethan plays
j. Tom's stance
k. Prose
l. Laura's response to Jim breaking the unicorn
m. Amanda's old hat

Answer the following multiple-choice items:

1. Which statement is NOT true? Stage directions are
   a. minimal in ancient Greek plays.
   b. built into the language in Elizabethan plays.
   c. often provided by modern playwrights.
   d. spoken by the actors in Greek plays.

2. Which statement is NOT true? Dramatic language in a play
   a. reveals character.
   b. is autobiographical.
   c. relates to action.
   d. reinforces theme.

3. Most contemporary theaters are
   a. larger than Elizabethan theaters.
   b. larger than ancient Greek theaters.
   c. the same size as Elizabethan theaters.
   d. smaller than Elizabethan theaters.

4. Acting in serious drama today tends to be
   a. subtle.
   b. stylized.
   c. broad.
   d. restrained.

5. Which is an example of dramatic irony?
   a. Hamlet's costume
   b. Amanda's costume
   c. Laura's limp
   d. Oedipus's limp

In 100–250 words, answer the following short essay questions:

1. In *The Glass Menagerie*, Tom's last speech takes place as the action continues silently behind him. Review Williams's description of that action and analyze its meaning.
2. Choose any short exchange of dialogue from *The Glass Menagerie* that strikes you as realistic and explain why you find it so.
3. Analyze how speech reveals character and supports the action in any short exchange of dialogue from *Hamlet*.

ADDITIONAL READING ACTIVITIES

If you enjoyed reading the play and listening to the interview in this lesson, you may want to read more works that deal with interpreting the language of the theater from the perspective of literature and performance. Here are some suggested readings:

Baker, George P. *Dramatic Technique.* (Classic on just what the title says)

Clurman, Harold. *On Directing.* (Fun to read and informative)

Cole, Toby and Helen K. Chinoy (eds.), *Actors on Acting.* (Good collection of wide-ranging information and experiences)

Egri, Lajos. *The Art of Dramatic Writing.* (Written in the 1940s but still used in many college courses)

LESSON 23

The Vision Question:
MYTH AND SYMBOLISM IN DRAMA

ABOUT THE LESSON

The lesson you just finished discussed costume as a form of dramatic expression, and if you put yourself in the position of the director of a play, you can easily link costume to symbolism. Claudius, in Elizabethan productions of `Hamlet`, carried a scepter and wore a crown, both symbols of kingship. And when Hamlet first comes on stage, he is wearing black, the color that in our culture symbolizes death, as a sign or symbol of mourning.

Costume is only one possible connection to symbolism, for, as you may remember from earlier lessons, a *symbol* is anything—object, person, place, idea, or situation—that stands for itself and also suggests a larger meaning. And you may also recall that symbols can be classified according to the context of the meaning they suggest.

It may help to think of a literary text at the center of three widening concentric circles. The circle nearest the work would be that of the *private symbol,* one that only takes on significance within the context of the short story, poem, or play. Laura's glass collection in *The Glass Menagerie* is a good example. If you did not know the play, the objects would have no symbolic value.

The next circle would be that of the *cultural symbol*—one that draws its meaning from a particular culture. Thus when Hamlet appears dressed in black, we automatically associate the color with death and mourning. Yet other cultures would not make that connection. Someone who had grown up with certain Oriental traditions would associate white with death, and a member of the Zuni tribe of Native Americans would connect black with the fertile earth.

The widest circle is that of the *universal symbol*—one that spans many different cultures. Light and dark, the seasons, water, earth, and so on appear as symbols with similar meanings in many cultures. And if you think about universal symbols in human form, you will quickly find a link between symbol and myth—the *archetype*. The archetype, you may recall, is the original pattern or model on which all others are based. Various myths, for example, may present us with different characters who perform heroic deeds, but what all those myths have in common is the archetype of the hero. The hero, the temptress, the devil,

312—*Literary Visions*

and the like are all archetypes in that they are figures that represent the essence of a number of myths.

Within Western culture, many of those myths have their origins in ancient Greek legends. Sophocles gives us one version of the myth of Oedipus, and his play presents us with an archetype of the hero. But you will recall that *myth* has several meanings. In addition to referring to legends that account for natural and supernatural phenomena, myth can also refer to a recurring idea or character type that represents a culture's ideals, shared beliefs, or strong emotions. Arthur Miller built his play *Death of a Salesman* on one version of the American Dream—the idea that success is all-important.

In this lesson you will be drawing upon what you have already learned about the different kinds of myths and symbols and applying that to drama. We will start with a brief mention of where *allegory* fits into drama and then move on to concentrate on symbol and myth.

All three plays that you have studied deal with different kinds of myths and symbols. Seeing how they function in drama will lead you to find parallels in different media. You may find that slasher and horror movies draw upon myths that embody our deepest fears, and you may link the classic archetypes with their somewhat debased versions, the stereotypes. The fall guy, the trickster, the snake-oil hustler are all comic counterparts to familiar archetypes.

GOAL

This lesson will help you understand the function of myth and symbol in drama.

WHAT YOU WILL LEARN

When you complete this lesson you will be able to:

1. Recognize the importance of myth in drama.
2. Distinguish between myth and allegory.
3. Identify the function of symbols.
4. Identify and analyze recurring myths within our culture.
5. Distinguish among categories of symbol.

LESSON ASSIGNMENT

Working through the following nine steps will help you master the objectives and achieve the goal for this lesson:

Step 1: In your text, review "Symbolism and Allegory" in the chapter "The Dramatic Vision: An Overview," pages 1210–1211, and "Aristotle's Concept of Catharsis," pages 1271–1272, in the Chapter "The Tragic Vision: Affirmation Through Loss." The text will provide background for what you will read in the study guide, explain the key terms, and give you some information about the plays you will be reading.

Step 2: Read the specific scenes your instructor assigns. This lesson will deal primarily with *Oedipus the King* but will also bring in relevant portions of *Hamlet* and *The Glass Menagerie*. The following scenes provide a context for the video performances, and those marked with an asterisk (*) will be shown in the video.

- *Oedipus the King*, Fagles: Lines 1–52 (Gould: 1–57)*
- *Oedipus the King*, Fagles: Lines 168–276 (Gould: 151–248)*
- *Oedipus the King*, Fagles: Lines 1612–1684 (Gould: 1481–1540)*
- *Hamlet*, II.ii
- *Hamlet*, V.ii
- *The Glass Menagerie*, Scenes 1 and 7

Step 3: Read the OVERVIEW in this study guide lesson.

Step 4: Watch the VIDEO, following the steps in the VIEWING GUIDE in this study guide lesson.

Step 5: Reread the OVERVIEW to reinforce what you have learned in the text and the video and to help you complete the Writing Activities.

Step 6: Complete any WRITING ACTIVITIES assigned in this lesson.

Step 7: Do the SELF-TEST exercises in this study guide lesson.

Step 8: Read any of the ADDITIONAL READING ACTIVITIES assigned.

Step 9: Go back to the learning objectives in the WHAT YOU WILL LEARN section of this study guide lesson and be sure you can respond to each of them.

OVERVIEW

Myth and *symbol* figure significantly in the history of serious drama and in contemporary works, so that is what this lesson will concentrate upon. You have already studied the concepts of myth, allegory, symbol, and allusion in connection with the short story and poetry. For the short story—myth, allegory, and symbol are the most important concepts; for poetry—myth and allusion are key terms; and for drama—myth and symbol are crucial. Yet at one point in the history of drama, allegory was also important.

So that you can have a fuller understanding of the place of allegory in drama and be able to identify some of its characteristics in the plays, films, and television dramas you may see, we start our discussion with allegory.

Allegory

When you studied the short story, you learned about *allegory*, where every significant event and character functions on both a literal and a symbolic level as part of an overall pattern. *Pattern* is the key word. Hawthorne's story "Young Goodman Brown," page 385, for instance, can be read as an allegory that illustrates the dangers of the Puritan concern with original sin. From that perspective, the characters represent abstract qualities: faith, doubt, good, evil. Everything fits into a pattern—a one-to-one relationship—to support the story's central idea.

Allegory in drama turns up in the appropriately named morality play. You may recall from the introductory drama lesson that during the Middle Ages mystery and miracle plays evolved from Christian religious ceremonies. Mystery plays illustrated the path to salvation, and miracle plays focused on the lives of the saints. By the late Middle Ages—probably around the late 14th century—these forms of drama gave rise to the morality play. If you read *Everyman* in school, then you are familiar with this kind of dramatic allegory. Typically concerned with the conflict between good and evil or the way in which a Christian faces death, the characters in these dramas were named for what they represented—Greed, Good Deeds, Vice, and soon. All the characters fit a scheme, a pattern, to support an overarching and obvious moral—hence the name for this type of drama.

Morality plays were popular up to the mid-16th century but gave way to the tragedies, comedies, and history plays that characterize the range of Shakespeare's works. Occasionally you will find a remnant of the morality play in contemporary drama or film. If you see the Seven Deadly Sins personified in a film or television show, with, say, one of Hollywood's current sex queens playing the part of Lust, you'll recognize an element from the morality play.

Occasionally you may also see a contemporary work that lacks the kind of characterization and action you would normally associate with drama, in which case you might consider allegory to see if the play makes more sense on that level. If the characters represent ideas and the action is stylized, you may be watching a contemporary secular allegory. But for the most part that kind of play is the exception, and the old-time morality play remains closely associated with religious drama and rarely appears on the secular stage.

Myth

The most basic definition of myth is one given in the *Princeton Encyclopedia of Poetry and Poetics*, that myth expresses and therefore symbolizes "certain deep-lying aspects of human and transhuman existence." Often myth takes the form of ancient legend, and that is what Sophocles's *Oedipus the King* is built upon. The outline of that myth is simple, but the details get complicated. By piecing together a number of accounts from various Greek and Latin sources, however, it's possible to reconstruct the details of the myth that provides the basis for Sophocles's play. The version that follows is based on Robert Graves's study of the sources that he reports in his book *The Greek Myths*.

Laius—King of Thebes and husband of Jocasta—consulted the Delphic Oracle and learned that any child he had would be his murderer. To avoid this fate, he turned his back on Jocasta but did not explain why. Not knowing the reason for his rejection, Jocasta got him drunk and seduced him. When she gave birth to a male child nine months later, Laius seized the infant, pierced his feet with a nail, binding them together, and abandoned him on Mt. Cithaeron. It was there that the infant was found by a Corinthian shepherd, who named him Oedipus because of his deformed feet and took him to the Corinthian court of Polybus.

Polybus raised Oedipus as his own child, but after being criticized for not resembling his parents, Oedipus consulted the Delphic Oracle only to be told that he would kill his father and marry his mother. Oedipus decided to avoid that fate by not returning to Corinth, but as he walked into a narrow place in the road, he mete Laius, who was on his way to Delphi to ask the Oracle how to rid Thebes of the Sphinx. Laius, in his chariot, ordered Oedipus aside, and Oedipus retorted that he acknowledged only the gods and his own parents as "his betters." Enraged, Laius ordered his charioteer to drive on, and one of the wheels struck Oedipus's foot. Oedipus then killed the charioteer, and when Laius became tangled in the reins, Oedipus lashed the horses so that they dragged Laius to his death.

Oedipus continued on his journey, entered Thebes, and solved the riddle of the Sphinx. The Thebans hailed Oedipus as king, which he became by marrying Jocasta. Thebes was next ravaged by a plague that the Dephic Oracle said would only stop if the murderer of Laius was expelled. Tiresias then appeared at court and told Jocasta that the murderer was Oedipus, who had killed his father and married his mother.

Tiresias's word was first doubted, but it was confirmed by Periboea, the wife of Polybus, who wrote to tell of the death of Polybus in Corinth and to reveal that Oedipus was not their child but had been found on Mt. Cithaeron. The truth verified, Jocasta committed suicide. As for what happened to Oedipus, two different accounts survive. One—followed by Sophocles—has Oedipus put out his eyes, obey his own command to banish the murderer of Laius, and die in exile. The other—followed by Homer—has Oedipus dying heroically in battle.

Like all legends, the myth of Oedipus probably contains some historical fact. Robert Graves speculates that the myth probably arose out of a dispute over the right to kingship. Theban custom held that kingship was determined through the matriarchal line; as you can see in *Oedipus the King*, Oedipus gains the crown by marrying Jocasta. Corinthian custom, however, held that kingship was determined by the patriarchal line. Quite possibly the historical Oedipus conquered Thebes, married Jocasta, and overturned the Theban matriarchal tradition, substituting the patriarchal one of Corinth. To protest, Jocasta committed suicide, and the citizens of Thebes rose up against Oedipus, banishing him.

Whatever the origin of the Oedipus myth, Sigmund Freud found in it an expression of what he believed is every son's unconscious wish, hence the term *Oedipus complex*. From a psychological perspective, the myth also embodies the age-old conflict of father and son and the child's desire to replace the father. Viewed from the perspective of these unconscious conflicts, the story of Oedipus, historical or not, becomes myth because it expresses those "certain deep-lying aspects of human and transhuman existence" that myth speaks to.

Sophocles must have also seen in it the opportunity to explore every facet of cosmic irony as well as the complex nature of the tragic hero. He was not alone. We know that at least 13 Greek dramatists took up the myth of Oedipus in their plays. But what is particularly interesting about Sophocles's account is his treatment of Oedipus and the tragic cosmos. Oedipus is neither completely guilty nor completely innocent; the gods foretold but did not determine his fate.

In the original myth of Oedipus, the focus is on Oedipus's search for his identity; in Sophocles's version, that focus is overshadowed by Oedipus's search for the killer of Laius. The irony lies in the two being the same. Yet we see Oedipus as someone who has tried to "do the right thing." When the Oracle at Delphi told him he would murder his father and marry his mother, he vowed not to return to Corinth. When he killed Laius, it was not without cause. When Thebes was plagued with the Sphinx, he solved the riddle and saved the city. When he swore to find Laius's murderer, he kept to his word.

At the same time, what made Oedipus great—his belief in himself—was also his downfall. Carried to extreme and coupled with power, that confidence can become the arrogance of a tyrant, which is just what Creon accuses Oedipus of having become. And given Oedipus's treatment of Creon and Tiresias and also Jocasta, we probably agree.

The play therefore uses the myth to explore the many-layered horrors of existence. We see Oedipus contend with his identity, his guilt, and finally his knowledge that he has killed his father, married his mother, and cursed his children with the heritage of incest. The play not only explores fears, doubts, and dreads, it also shows us what can happen when a person exceeds mortal reach an challenges powers far beyond personal control. The true horror here is that from the beginning of the play the audience knows what will happen.

Oedipus defeats himself and destiny wins, but the conflict affects all concerned and for the better, though the price is acute pain and suffering. Oedipus ends up a wiser man, physically and materially diminished but spiritually enlightened; Thebes is rid of the plague; and the audience or reader has been able to identify with the action and tragic hero so that the effect of the play is ennobling. Aristotle, in his *Poetics*, calls his latter effect *catharsis* and describes tragedy as "arousing pity and fear in such a way as to accomplish a purgation of such emotions." We read or watch, we identify, we are horrified, we learn, and we become emotionally aroused and then cleansed.

In these respects the ending of *Hamlet* is quite similar; we identify with Hamlet, and that identification excites our emotions, which are brought into balance by the end of the play. And like *Oedipus the King, Hamlet* is based upon ancient legend. In Norse mythology, the name Hamlet appears as Amlothi, meaning desperate in battle. The legend is reported in full in Saxo Grammaticus's *Historica Danica*, which was written around 1200 and printed in 1514. Possibly working from an account of the Hamlet legend in the Frenchman Belleforest's *Histoires Tragiques* and a Hamlet play, now lost, that had appeared some eleven years earlier, Shakespeare adapted the legend to his own times and their beliefs.

We have already seen how *Hamlet* deals with the Elizabethan myth or belief in the Great Chain of Being (Lesson 19), so here we'll deal with a different belief dealing with the idea of chance. If you examine the last act of *Hamlet* carefully, you will find that it reinforces a generally held belief that chance was divinely ordained. This idea is a variation of the Christian mythos that what may appear to humans as accident or chance is nonetheless part of a divine plan and not chance at all.

You can find this idea stated most clearly in Hamlet's words, "There's a divinity that shapes our ends, / Rough-hew them how we will" (V.ii.10–11). You hear it again when Horatio tries to get Hamlet to avoid the duel, to which Hamlet replies "there is special providence in the fall of a sparrow" (V.ii.202–203). Thus all the turns of the plot, all the delays, all the acts of Hamlet's "antic disposition," work their way toward justice. In the last scene, Laertes and Claudius are killed by their own poison just as Rosencrantz and Guildenstern meet the end they had planned for Hamlet. As for Polonius, Ophelia, and Gertrude, their deaths, though seeming "accidents," make sense in the grand scale of things, one only fully known to Providence. And Hamlet has killed, so he too must die, even though his revenge was in service of restoring divine order. Thus at the end of the play we see this order restored, and the tragic cosmos continues.

The Glass Menagerie may or may not be a tragedy—and it certainly does not use myth in the same way as *Oedipus the King* or *Hamlet*—yet if you read the play carefully, you can see another kind of myth at work. The kind of myth you find in *The Glass Menagerie* also expresses and therefore symbolizes "certain deep-lying aspects of human and transhuman existence," but the aspects it expresses are bound to a particular culture, in this case an archetype of American culture. If you think about Amanda from the perspective of the archetypal representative of a myth, you may well find yourself staring at a latter-day version of the Southern belle.

According to the myth, the Southern belle is not supposed to show intelligence but to exude charm. On the surface she is social, well-mannered, full of wit and charm, pretty, and always correctly dressed. Beneath that surface she is scheming, cunning, ambitious, and hard-hearted—hence the term "Steel Magnolia." If you have seen *Gone with the Wind*, then you also know that Scarlett O'Hara is one of the best examples of this archetype.

Now apply that pattern to Amanda. We know that her youthful days—real or imagined—when she was receiving gentlemen callers back in Blue Mountain, were Amanda's moments of glory. Her description of the one Sunday when she received 17 gentlemen callers, "planters and sons of planters" (page 1649), echoes Scarlett O'Hara's entertainments at Tara. And like Scarlett, Amanda is very concerned with appearances. The decorations for Jim's visit and her attempts to always appear "properly" dressed reflect that, just as her attempts to charm Jim reveal her arsenal of social niceties.

But we suspect that, underneath all that, Amanda is a survivor. The unkindest view of her would find her using Tom to support the family and caring only to have Laura married off. But what makes Amanda an example of an archetype instead of a stereotype is that she is complex. She genuinely loves Tom, just as she genuinely loves Laura. Her problem is being able to accept and love them for what they are instead of what she wishes they were.

Symbol

If we look closely at Amanda's gentlemen callers, we will be able to see how they can be viewed as *private, cultural,* and *universal* symbols. It all depends on your perspective. From the perspective of the youthful Amanda, the gentlemen callers she received at Blue Mountain functioned as a *private symbol* representing not just her own popularity but also a romantic, carefree way of life and an infinite number of opportunities for a life in which she would live happily ever after. Yet from Amanda's present vantage point, they represent missed opportunity, a life she might have led.

But if you step out of Amanda's shoes and think of the play as a whole, the gentlemen callers become part of the myth of the Southern belle and therefore these men are a *cultural symbol* representing the plantation way of life that existed before the Civil War. Within the myth, young men and always handsome, romantic, charming, adventurous, rich, honorable, and courtly.

Sound familiar? If so, you are on your way to the next step, in which the gentlemen callers are a *universal symbol*. Add together all those qualities mentioned earlier, and you have the old standby—the knight in shining armor. To make the connection between the gentlemen callers and the archetype of the romantic hero, you need to change your perspective so that you see the play as part of a literary tradition that embraces many different ages, cultures, and literary forms. From that point of view, the gentlemen callers fit a whole tradition of romantic rescuers, and that of course is just what Amanda wants for Laura. Once again, however, Amanda mistakes what she gets for what she wants and is crushed when Jim turns out not to fit the role.

Usually, however, a symbol will function on just one level in addition to the literal one. In *Hamlet*, for instance, you already recognize the connection between Hamlet's black clothing and a cultural symbol of mourning. And the idea of Hamlet as an example of the avenger allows you to interpret his character as a universal symbol. But private symbols are also at work in the play.

Think, for example, of the scene toward the end of Act II.ii in which Hamlet asks the Player to deliver the speech concerning the murder of Priam, King of Troy. The Player does so in words that describe Priam's murder at the hands of Pyrrhus and the reaction of Hecuba, wife of Priam. As the actor delivers the lines describing Hecuba, Polonius notes that the actor is crying and calls for an end to the speech. When shortly thereafter Polonius and the players exit, Hamlet, in a soliloquy, berates himself.

Hamlet finds the Player an ironic symbol of his own inaction. Here is an actor working himself up into a outburst of emotion over nothing, "What's Hecuba to him, or he to Hecuba, / That he should weep for her?" (lines 532–534). Had he Hamlet's motivation, the actor would "Make mad the guilty and appal the free, / Confound the ignorant, and amaze indeed / The very faculties of eyes and ears" (lines 538–540). Hamlet chastises himself as a "John-a-dreams" who "can say nothing" (lines 542–543). Realizing the irony of that statement, he goes on to berate himself for giving speeches instead of taking action and then reveals his plan for the play within the play "Wherein I'll catch the conscience of the king" (line 580). Hamlet treats the actor and his speech as symbolic comments on his own situation.

Private symbols also occur in *Oedipus the King*. Among the most memorable are Jocasta's pins or brooches, with which Oedipus blinds himself. Oedipus, maddened with the truth of his identity, bursts into Jocasta's room and finds that she has hanged herself. He cuts her down, rips the brooches from her dress, and drives their pins into his eyes. On a symbolic level, Oedipus has ironically given literal meaning to his earlier blindness to truth. With this act, he has also bound himself to Jocasta for life; the connection between Jocasta and his blindness will always be with him. It becomes a permanent reminder of his fate, which he could not escape and was too blind to see. Yet outside the play, the brooches and his use of them have no meaning, which is why the symbol is private.

As for a cultural symbol, think of the manner in which Oedipus's feet were bound. Within early Greek culture, exposing a child to the elements was not considered murder because fate could always intervene. In Oedipus's case, fate may have been worse than death, which is yet another irony in the play. The nail that pierced Oedipus's feet, however, signified that the child was unwanted and given over to the gods. Indeed.

Once again, however, if you step back from the particular way in which the child was abandoned and if you consider only the child, you will see that Oedipus's origins suggest the universal archetype of the foundling. Within the Judeo-Christian tradition, the foundling appears as Moses, and here lies another irony, for traditionally the foundling goes on to greatness and good fortune. You see this idea at work in modern romance novels in which the foundling scullery maid turns out to be the heiress or the foundling stable boy is eventually revealed to be the lord of the manor. But then there's Oedipus. In his case, his story is not only an ironic version of the archetype but a lesson in all the complexity and horrors of existence.

Summary

Within drama, the tragic hero is an archetype, and within *Oedipus the King* and *Hamlet*, this archetype is at work. Both Oedipus and Hamlet symbolize what is noble about human beings. They encounter forces larger than themselves; they contend with those forces; they suffer; they are literally or figuratively destroyed; yet they have also triumphed. Oedipus's suffering has saved Thebes; Hamlet's actions have restored order in Denmark. And ultimately, they have had an effect on the reader or audience. The myth of the hero has been re-enacted and played out to its conclusion; the audience realizes what is important is not that Oedipus and Hamlet were destroyed but that they lived.

The Glass Menagerie has no tragic hero, and you can make a case that it has no hero at all, merely an antagonist and a protagonist. But the play uses cultural myth and symbolism to show how illusion and reality interweave and how expectations can be crushed by both illusion and reality. And you can make a case for the play having the myth of the hero by drawing upon a universal archetype that occurs in many myths.

If, for instance, we define Tom Wingfield as the traveler or wanderer, always in search of something intangible and probably unattainable, then we can regard him as a universal symbol. He fits within the same tradition as the Flying Dutchman, the Ancient Mariner, and the Wandering Jew, all of whom committed a sin and were condemned never to rest.

Myths in all their guises use symbols to convey meaning. But not all symbols are related to myths. Private symbols achieve meaning only within their immediate contexts. But cultural and universal symbols can usually be traced to cultural or universal myths.

VIEWING GUIDE

An important component of this lesson is the video. You will learn more effectively from it by thinking about the following questions and guidelines.

Before Viewing:

1. Review "Symbolism and Allegory" in the chapter "The Dramatic Vision: An Overview," in the text, pages 1210–1211, and "Aristotle's Concept of Catharsis," pages 1271–1272.
2. Review the works assigned, paying particular attention to the ones your instructor emphasizes. Try to hear the dialogue in each scene as it might relate to myth and symbolism.

During Your Viewing:

1. Watch the sets, costumes, and props for possible symbolic meaning.
2. To find clues and symbols, listen to the language and how it is delivered.
3. Consider each character or group of characters as possible archetypes.
4. Listen for the critics' explanations of why Greek audiences enjoyed familiar plots.
5. Listen for what Carol Gelderman says about the Oedipus myth.
6. Listen for David Hunsaker's ideas about myth.

After Viewing:

Give some thought to the following questions. You may want to write short answers in your journal or notebook.

1. What characters struck you as possible archetypes and why?
2. What sets, costumes, or props seemed to carry symbolic value and why?
3. What elements of myths did you find emphasized?
4. Given what the critics and Hunsaker have to say, what makes some myths universal?
5. Why is Hunsaker attracted to the Alaskan myths?

WRITING ACTIVITIES

After your study of this lesson, you should be able to understand the function of myth and symbol in drama. Your instructor will advise you which, if any, of the following writing activities to complete.

Formal Writing:

The first of these activities places you in the position of the audience watching *Oedipus the King* and asks you to consider one of the features of the production—the wearing of masks. The purpose is to draw your attention to the symbolic value of one of the conventions of Greek tragedy and thereby provide a greater understanding of the impact of the play at the time it was written. The next two activities are rather standard, and both ask you to step back from *Oedipus the King* and consider characters other than the tragic hero as symbols. Activity 4 calls upon what you learned about the language of drama and uses it to analyze the elements of myth apparent in the video presentation of the parados.

1. The ancient Greeks used masks for practical purposes so that the actors could be better seen and heard. At the same time, the masks had symbolic value. Write a short essay exploring what that value might be.
2. Discuss the symbolic value of the Chorus in *Oedipus the King*.
3. Discuss the symbolic value of Tiresias in *Oedipus the King*.
4. Analyze the video presentation of the parados, pointing out the elements of myth that it emphasizes and how it does so.

Informal Writing:

Both activities ask you to take what you have learned about symbol and myth in drama and apply it to a work in another medium. The point is to make you more aware of symbolism and myth in the popular media and, by analysis and contrast, bring about a fuller understanding of their possible functions.

1. Flip through the pages of a popular magazine looking for full-page ads that you find effective. When you have noted several, go through them again looking for symbols and archetypes. For example, many cosmetic ads are new versions of the old archetype of the Temptress. Once you have chosen an advertisement that suggests an archetype or several related symbols, include the ad in your journal or notebook along with your analysis of its mythic or symbolic qualities.
2. If you would prefer, select a video production of a song and explore it for mythic or symbolic qualities. Write your analysis so that you also describe the video, perhaps including the lyrics, and then analyze it in terms of myth and symbolism.

SELF-TEST

Match the items in columns A with the definitions or identifications in B:

A	B
1. Private symbol	a. Model on which all others are based
2. Symbol	b. Belief held by members of a particular group
3. Allegory	c. Stock character
4. Morality play	d. Pattern of symbols that support theme
5. Cultural symbol	e. Belief held by a family
6. Cultural myth	f. Conveys meaning to a certain group of people
7. Universal symbol	g. Anything that stands for itself and has a larger meaning
8. Tragic hero	h. Pattern of symbols supporting character
9. Archetype	i. Archetype within drama
10. Stereotype	j. Drama illustrating how to live a Christian life
	k. Conveys meaning that spans different cultures
	l. Drama illustrating life of saint
	m. Receives meaning from immediate context

Answer the following multiple-choice items:

1. Which characteristic does NOT fit the archetype of the tragic hero?
   a. Suffering
   b. Death or destruction
   c. Conflict with larger forces
   d. Guilt

2. Cutting a wedding cake is primarily a
   a. private symbol.
   b. cultural symbol.
   c. universal symbol.
   d. myth.

3. A particular archetype would
   a. be found in only one culture.
   b. be recognized only by the originator.
   c. embody one or two characteristics.
   d. embody a number of characteristics.

4. Myth is most useful in drama because it
   a. enlarges meaning.
   b. creates parallels.
   c. builds on the familiar.
   d. is easily recognized.

5. Which statement about symbol is NOT true: Symbols
   a. are widely used in literature.
   b. appear in popular media.
   c. have restricted meanings.
   d. function on the literal level.

In 100–250 words, answer the following short essay questions:

1. As you have read, the myth of Oedipus has two different endings. What makes the one Sophocles chose the better for drama?
2. In the scene between Jim and Laura in Scene 7 of *The Glass Menagerie*, what symbolic significance can be attached to the phrase "Blue Roses"?
3. Select a speech from *Hamlet* in which one of the characters uses language in a symbolic manner and analyze it. You might, for instance, consider one of Hamlet's "antic" speeches.

ADDITIONAL READING ACTIVITIES

If you enjoyed reading the plays and listening to the interview in this lesson, you may want to read more about the subjects under discussion. Here are some suggestions:

Esslin, Martin. *The Field of Drama: How the Signs of Drama Create Meaning on Stage and Screen.*
Schechner, Richard. *Between Theater and Anthropology.*
Turner, Victor. *From Ritual to Theatre: The Human Seriousness of Play.*

LESSON 24

A Frame for Meaning:
THEME IN DRAMA

ABOUT THE LESSON

A play's theme is to its elements almost as a hub is to a wheel. Character, action, plot, conflict, language, setting, staging, symbol, and myth are all bound to the theme. But a theme is not a hub in the sense of a hub of a wheel because the elements of a drama are not all equal. Some plays may stress language over action or plot over character and so on.

If you think of a hub in its more modern sense as the center of an airline's operations, then you will have a better image of how a theme functions. Theme is at the center of a play, and all the elements take off from there, although some may have short routes and others more developed ones in that a playwright may not give equal weight to the elements of drama. And just as large airlines may have a number of hub airports, plays may (and usually do) support a number of themes.

You have already studied how a short story or a poem can support several themes, so in a way this lesson will be a review. Again, you will find it helpful to distinguish among several related terms: *interpretation, subject, theme,* and *meaning*. An *interpretation* is a person's explanation of a work's subject—what it is about—and what it says about that subject. Identifying the *subject* of a work is relatively easy, but usually each work will suggest several subjects. More often than not, the subject can be stated in one or two words. Duty, family, revenge, identity, illusion, fate, justice are all one-word subjects for the plays you have read, and still the list does not cover all the possibilities.

Once you have chosen the subject(s) and are starting to consider what the play has to say about it, you are exploring the *meaning* of the work and are on your way to a possible *theme*. One way to discover the theme is to work from your notes. You might start with what you have identified as the subject and place that word in the middle of a blank sheet of paper. Then as you think of ideas that relate to that word, write them down in another space, draw a circle around them, and then connect the circles to your subject with straight lines. As you think of more ideas, you may find they relate more to a subpoint than to the subject, so

326—*Literary Visions*

you would connect them with the subpoint. By the time you have filled up much of the sheet, you should be able to extract a theme from what you have on the paper. Ask yourself what the playwright is saying about the subject; examine the evidence you have accumulated. Then make a one-sentence assertion that is broad enough to cover most of your main points. The result will be a theme.

If you were to work up an assertion for each of the subjects you had found in a work, you would have a fuller idea of its *meaning*. But meaning goes beyond theme and also includes the means by which the themes are conveyed and the overall effect on the reader. Meaning, then, is an all-inclusive term. In this lesson we will be most concerned with subject and theme, major components of meaning.

Your study of theme in the short story and poetry will help you in your analysis of theme in drama, but the scale here is quite different. The plays covered in this course are all full-length dramas, roughly equivalent to novels or epics as opposed to their more compact cousins, short stories and poems. For that reason, we will focus upon one play—*Hamlet*—instead of giving equal treatment to *Oedipus the King* and *The Glass Menagerie* as well.

GOAL

This lesson will help you to appreciate how the various elements of drama combine to present the meaning of drama.

WHAT YOU WILL LEARN

When you complete this lesson you will be able to:

1. Explore the relationship of subject to theme.
2. Differentiate between subject and theme in drama.
3. Determine the theme(s) of a play.
4. Give examples of common subjects found in drama.
5. Recognize that there may be more than one theme in a drama.

LESSON ASSIGNMENT

Working through the following nine steps will help you master the objectives and achieve the goal for this lesson.

Step 1: In your text, review "The Dramatic Vision: An Overview," pages 1204–1225, and in "The Tragic Vision: Affirmation Through Loss," pages 1265–1281, "Seriousness, Completeness, and Artistic Balance," page 1273, and "William Shakespeare,

Hamlet," pages 1322–1421. The text will provide background for what you will read in the study guide, explain the key terms, and give you some information about the plays you have read. If you want to learn more about the variety of ways to interpret texts, read Chapter 29 "Critical Approaches Important in the Study of Literature," pages 1854–1875.

Step 2: Read the specific plays your instructor assigns. This lesson, 24, will deal primarily with *Hamlet*. Act III.iv.1–179 will be shown in the video.

Step 3: Read the OVERVIEW in this study guide lesson.

Step 4: Watch the VIDEO, following the steps in the VIEWING GUIDE in this study guide lesson.

Step 5: Reread the OVERVIEW to reinforce what you have learned in the text and the video and to help you complete the Writing Activities.

Step 6: Complete any WRITING ACTIVITIES assigned in this lesson.

Step 7: Do the SELF-TEST exercises in this study guide lesson.

Step 8: Read any of the ADDITIONAL READING ACTIVITIES assigned.

Step 9: Go back to the learning objectives in the WHAT YOU WILL LEARN section of this study guide lesson and be sure you can respond to each of them.

OVERVIEW

Although this lesson concentrates on *Hamlet*, we will also use *Oedipus the King* and *The Glass Menagerie* to illustrate various points and to help clarify the role of theme. But *Hamlet* will take center stage, so to speak, and for two reasons. First, it is a very complex play and therefore a good choice to show how the elements of drama relate to and support theme. Second, *Hamlet*'s complexity and scale make it a difficult play to interpret, so further discussion seems in order.

For the sake of clarity and focus, we will take one interpretation of *Hamlet* and show how various elements of the play support it. But try to remember that other interpretations are equally valid, and as you read this discussion, look for points to argue with. You will find other interpretations outlined in the Summary section, and putting them up against the discussion and your own views, you should be able to work out your own analysis. For a concise summary of various critical approaches, see Chapter 33 in your textbook. There, Roberts takes "Young Goodman Brown" and interprets it from a variety of different critical perspectives, all of which can also be applied to *Hamlet*. The result is a wealth of themes.

The sections that follow will deal first with finding a play's subject and will proceed to working out its theme. We will be discussing theme in relation to setting and staging, characterization and conflict, and finally language, symbol, and myth. Each section begins with a general statement that you can apply to any play and goes on to examine how the element under discussion relates to a theme in *Hamlet*. As you read each section, you will see how it overlaps with the others. All the elements are related and are parts of the whole.

Subject and Theme

When it comes to interpretation, literature—unlike most mathematics—has no one right answer but many. Therefore what you look for in interpretation is not whether an analysis is right but whether it is valid. What is and is not valid? A valid interpretation is one that achieves a reasonable fit between the facts of the work and the particular approach you take to it. If, for instance, you were to interpret *Hamlet* from the perspective of a Freudian critic, then the facts of the play should mesh with the major beliefs of Freudian psychology.

But let's ignore psychology for a bit, stand back from a play, and see where its subject may take you. Identification of subject is often a good first step toward determining a play's theme. For *Oedipus the King* you may record a list of possibilities: destiny, pride, kingship, identity, justice, guilt, family, to name a few.

Let's say you choose family and come up with the hypothesis that Oedipus's crime is essentially one against family. He murders his father and marries his mother, is therefore guilty of patricide and incest, and pays the price. But this interpretation ignores at last one crucial fact—at the time, Oedipus did not know Jocasta was his mother. The interpretation fails to take into account the relevant facts and is therefore not valid.

Usually you can head off this kind of error by choosing the subject carefully. Look for one on your list that is large enough to include several of the others, for generalization is an important step towards finding a theme. In the list for *Oedipus the King*, for example, pride can also cover destiny, identity, and justice. If you select pride as your subject and consider all the relevant facts, you will be on your way to a valid interpretation of theme.

But what of *The Glass Menagerie*, to say nothing of *Hamlet*? Where should you start? Again, try making a list of possible subjects. For *The Glass Menagerie* you may come up with family, duty, illusion, expectations, and even justice. For *Hamlet* you would probably start with revenge, but you would also include several other possibilities: identity, duty, evil, justice, and guilt are just a few.

Choosing justice from among those possibilities, we find that it is related to several others—duty, revenge, guilt. In thinking about all those related ideas, we can revise the subject a bit and narrow it to divine justice. Having identified that, we can take the next step and set out an idea for a theme—divine justice demands self-sacrifice. This is the theme we shall explore in the discussion that follows.

Setting, Staging, and Theme

In thinking about the setting and staging of a play, it's best at first to consider setting in the same way you thought about it in the short story and poetry: as it applies to the physical and temporal aspects of the work, where and when it takes place. Then you can think about the larger meanings associated with time and place.

In *Hamlet*, the setting is Elsinore, where "Something is rotten in the state of Denmark" (I.iv.90). As the nation arms for war with Norway, the Ghost makes its appearance, which, as Horatio suggests, portends "some strange eruption to our state" (I.i.69). When the Ghost speaks to Hamlet and reveals the manner of its death, we understand what is "rotten." Claudius has murdered his brother, committed incest by marrying his sister-in-law, and usurped the crown. While the first two acts are clearly sins, Claudius has also sinned by becoming king, for a ruler is also the spiritual leader of the country and its citizens. Claudius corrupts that balance, and it therefore follows that he infects his court and country. Elsinore, the physical setting where most of the action takes place, is diseased.

The Ghost sets out the clear solution to the problem by charging Hamlet with revenge tempered by justice, thereby purifying the state and restoring divine order. Justice is the key word here, for Hamlet must carry out this act without rancor or hate; the Ghost decrees "Taint not they mind, nor let thy soul contrive / Against thy mother aught" (I.v.86–86).

This burden weighs heavily on Hamlet, who regards Denmark as a "prison" (II.ii.24). That impression is reflected in the clothes he wears, black for mourning but also black for his mood. Overall, the setting gives rise to an atmosphere of gloom charged with tension. The tension comes from Hamlet's impending revenge, his "antic disposition," and all the espionage that takes place.

As for staging, the Elizabethan theater had no sets or scenery or lighting to speak of, so that the language of the play has to indicate what is what. In I.i., for example, Horatio indicates that the sun is coming up with "But look, the morn in russet mantle clad / Walks o'er the dew of yon high eastward hill" (lines 166–167). Cues for entrances are also built into the language of the play, as in Horatio's comment (I.iv.38) that cues the actor who plays the Ghost, "Look my lord, it comes."

This information is important to the reader or director of the play, for it explains Hamlet's harsh treatment of Ophelia. If Hamlet knows that Claudius and Polonius are spying on him and that Ophelia is a willing accomplice, then his treatment of her, though harsh, can be justified. It would be justice in the Old Testament sense of an eye for an eye, and that is the kind of justice the Ghost wants.

The staging conventions of the time allow Hamlet to find out about this plot in two ways. If you take Polonius's line "You know sometimes he walks four hours together / Here in the lobby" (II.ii.160–161) as a cue for the actor playing Hamlet to walk across the balcony above the stage, then Hamlet overhears the whole scheme. But even if he did not hear the conversation between Claudius and Polonius, it's possible that when the play was produced, Claudius and Polonius gave themselves away as they spied on Hamlet and Ophelia. Hamlet has just finished his soliloquy and seeing "The fair Ophelia" coming, murmurs to himself the wish that she remember him in her prayers: "Nymph, in thy orisons / Be all my sins remembered" (III.i.88–89).

Claudius and Polonius are listening as dialogue begins. Ophelia returns the presents Hamlet had given her, concluding with "There my lord." Now you can imagine Claudius or Polonius (probably Polonius) peering out from behind the arras to see what is going on, for Hamlet then turns on Ophelia with "Ha, ha, are you honest?" And so begins his verbal destruction of Ophelia.

At the end of the play, Elsinore is cleansed. Hamlet's revenge is complete, and justice has ruled: Rosencrantz and Guildenstern, Laertes, and Claudius are dead, fallen victim to their own schemes, which is certainly justice; Gertrude, who was not guilty of the elder Hamlet's death but was guilty (according to the Ghost) of adultery and incest, is dead as well, murdered inadvertently by her lover; Polonius and Ophelia die by accident, but both had been infected by the diseased court; and finally Hamlet is dead as well, but then he has to die, for he has committed murder. Murder even in a just cause is murder; the revenger must die. Yet Hamlet is the hero and gets a hero's honor. The stage is cleared as his body is borne away. Justice is served all around.

Character, Conflict, and Theme

Your knowledge of the elements of literature will also help you locate a theme. For instance, you can recall that your earlier study of conflict revealed how it can exist on many levels as well as internally and externally. Considering *Hamlet* through the lens of this one element, you can find almost every conceivable type of conflict.

Dealing with external conflict and working from the most abstract to the most concrete, you would start with good versus evil. Good is portrayed by the Ghost—a divine stand-in calling for retribution—and by Hamlet, who is charged with carrying out that retribution. Evil is Claudius, who has sinned against God, family, and the state.

Moving to a less abstract level, we find Hamlet versus Claudius and all those who Claudius has set in motion—Rosencrantz and Guildenstern, Laertes, even Polonius. Hamlet's one ally and the only person he trusts absolutely is Horatio, so we would place Horatio on Hamlet's side of the conflict. Ophelia and Gertrude are trickier. Ophelia did indeed love Hamlet, yet when she had to choose between Hamlet and her father, she chose her father. Move Ophelia over to Claudius's side.

Gertrude loves Hamlet also, yet his predictable displeasure at her marrying Claudius did not affect her. If we can trust the Ghost's word (and we know there is no reason not to), we know that although Gertrude knew nothing of Claudius's killing of the elder Hamlet, she is only "seeming-virtuous" and had been seduced by Claudius before her husband's death (I.v.41–57). Yet she is not beyond redemption. The Ghost also tells Hamlet to "leave her to heaven, / And to those thorns that in her bosom lodge, / To prick and sting her" (I.v.86–88).

In the conflict between Hamlet and Claudius, Gertrude is caught in the middle. When Hamlet reveals the truth to her, she cries "Thou turn'st my eyes into my very soul, / And there I see such black and grained spots / As will not leave their tinct" (III.iv.89–91). He has indeed pricked and stung her conscience. But we never find out if her conscience can rule her will, for we do not discover if she has followed Hamlet's plea for abstinence. Hamlet has "cleft" her "hart in twain" (line 156), leaving her torn between son and husband.

Gertrude's response reveals her internal conflict, and given her past performance, you suspect that her conscience is no match for what the Ghost labels "lust." Her protests to Hamlet echo those of Claudius, who desires pardon but wants to keep everything he killed for, "My crown, mine own ambition, and my queen" (III.iii.55). Claudius's struggle with his internal conflict is one he resolves by stifling his conscience.

The greatest degree of internal turmoil is obviously that of Hamlet. Torn between trust and doubt, action and inaction, boiling revenge and not "tainting" his mind, his love for his mother and his disgust at her remarriage, his concentration on his mission and the distraction of his love for Ophelia, his sanity and his "madness," Hamlet practically personifies internal conflict.

Perhaps the best assessment of Hamlet is that by Ophelia, who sees him as royal and intellectual, a person of "noble mind ... The courtier's, soldier's, scholar's, eye, tongue, sword, / The expectancy and rose of the fair state, / The glass of fashion, and the mould of form, / Th'observed of all observers ..." (III.i.150–154). Being courtier, soldier, scholar, and his father's son, Hamlet's first response to the Ghost's tale is rage and instant agreement, "It is an honest ghost" (I.v.138). To carry out its command, Hamlet decides to adopt an "antic disposition."

Yet Hamlet lives in a world of doubt and distrust, and the intellectual in him makes him think of what was commonly believed about ghosts, that this apparition could be an emissary of heaven or of hell. Hamlet therefore prepares the play within the play to test the Ghost's word. Given the beliefs of the times, we cannot fault him for this, and indeed the test seems more a sign of prudence and wisdom than procrastination.

At the same time, on the chance that the Ghost is indeed telling the truth, Hamlet must not be idle but must ready himself for revenge. His motive for his treatment of Ophelia is therefore two-fold: he knows that she has sided with Polonius and Claudius, and he knows that he must act alone, unencumbered by emotional ties, by love. He casts her aside, wounding her with his words. Then he springs "The Mouse-trap" and is convinced of the truth of the Ghost's words.

But Claudius has a mouse-trap of his own and orders Hamlet to England with Rosencrantz and Guildenstern, who are to spring it. Before Hamlet leaves, he finds Claudius praying and draws his sword to kill him. Once again, prudence, wisdom, and this time justice prevent him. After all, Hamlet reasons, his father was killed without having a chance to confess; if Claudius dies in prayer, his soul will go to heaven. Justice will only be served if Claudius is killed when engaged in "some act / That has no relish of salvation in't" (III.iii.91–92). In fact, this is just what Hamlet thinks he has done when he spears what turns out to be Polonius, hiding behind the arras and spying on Hamlet's conversation with Gertrude. Had it been Claudius, Hamlet would have killed him justly.

There's a double irony here. First, as we know but Hamlet doesn't, Claudius was not able to pray. Hamlet could have killed him and settled the whole matter of revenge. Second, as we know but Hamlet doesn't, it is Polonius not Claudius who is hiding behind Gertrude's arras. Hamlet's leap to action results in his killing the wrong person.

At this point—Act IV—Claudius dispatches Hamlet to England with Rosencrantz and Guildenstern; Laertes returns to Denmark to find his father slain and his sister mad; and Horatio receives a letter from Hamlet explaining his escape. Claudius, his plot to have Hamlet killed having failed, plans anew with Laertes as an ally. Note that the first plot—the duel with Laertes's poisoned weapon—has a back-up in the form of the poisoned cup and that Claudius has goaded Laertes to the boiling point of revenge—a nice counterpoint to Hamlet and his mission.

Act V opens with the Clown's talk of death, and death becomes the motif for the act, first in the form of Ophelia's burial and then in the form of all the deaths at the end of the play. In the final scene, Hamlet speaks to Horatio of "a kind of fighting / That would not let me sleep" and notes that

> Our indiscretion sometimes serves us well
> When our deep plots do pall, and that should learn us
> There's a divinity that shapes our ends,
> Rough-hew them how we will.—(V.ii.8–11)

The immediate context for this remark is Hamlet's escape from the ship that is carrying him to England, but the statement has wider implications as well. Think of Hamlet's failure to kill the kneeling Claudius and his killing of Polonius, whom he mistook for the king. And, of course, there's Hamlet's fortuitous escape from Rosencrantz and Guildenstern. Hamlet has tried to carry out the Ghost's command, but his attempts have been foiled. In the first instance, the king was praying; in the second, he killed Polonius, not the king. Yet the fact that Claudius was spared turns out to supply Hamlet with more evidence of Claudius's sins. En route to England, Hamlet reads Claudius's message that arranged for the death of Hamlet. Thus Claudius further damns himself. At this point, Hamlet sums up the charges against Claudius:

> He that hath killed my king, and whored my mother,
> Popped in between th'election and my hopes,
> Thrown out his angle for my proper life,
> And with such cozenage—is't not perfect conscience
> To quit him with this aim? And is't not to be damned,
> To let this canker of our nature come
> In further evil?—(V.ii.64–70)

To this, Horatio adds that Claudius will soon know that Hamlet turned the plot intended for him against Rosencrantz and Guildenstern. That practical point aside, Hamlet has now satisfied his conscience that letting Claudius live is a greater sin than killing him. But before that can happen, there is the duel. Gertrude drinks to Hamlet's good fortune, not knowing that Claudius has prepared the poisoned cup for Hamlet; Laertes wounds Hamlet with the tainted rapier; the two grapple and, in the scuffling, exchange weapons; Hamlet wounds Laertes; Gertrude collapses saying she's poisoned, Laertes confesses and blames the king. Hamlet responds by stabbing Claudius with the poisoned rapier, then holds him and pours the poisoned drink down his throat. Claudius is doubly dead. And he dies in sin. He had even tried to blame Gertrude's collapse on the fact that she sees Hamlet wounded. He dies as he has lived, as Hamlet sums him up, an "incestuous, murderous, damned dane" (line 308).

But justice must come full circle, Hamlet too must die, for he has killed. He dies, however, without the guilt of Laertes's or Polonius's deaths, for Laertes offers an exchange of "forgiveness": "Mine and my father's death come not upon thee, / Nor thine on me" (lines 313–314). Hamlet dies with only the guilt of Claudius's murder, a murder demanded by the Ghost, who represents divine providence. Hamlet has had to sacrifice himself for the Ghost's cause, which is harsh justice indeed.

To explore the relationships among a subject, its setting and staging, and characterization and conflict in any play, you can use the same process described here in relation to *Hamlet*. First, select a general subject that the play examines, and then ask yourself about the nature of conflict. The idea of conflict will automatically take you into characterization. Armed with a subject, conflict, and characterization, you can move easily to an analysis of language, symbol, and myth.

Language, Symbol, Myth, and Theme

Up to this point in the lesson, we have been dealing with broad issues, first identifying a subject, examining the context for that subject—the setting and staging—and then laying out in broad strokes the characterization and conflict. Now our focus gets narrower and the analysis deeper.

To explore how the language of a play relates to its theme, it's usually best to start by identifying key speeches or dialogue, for it's there too that you will discover possible symbols and references to myths. Such an analysis will also take you into characterization. In addition, you need to remember that in drama, language becomes not just the written or spoken word but also gesture, movement, expression, costume, and even silence.

In *Hamlet*, the key speeches are easy to identify, for they are the soliloquies. In these speeches, Hamlet revels what is in his mind, and the convention of the soliloquy is that we can believe him. All told, Hamlet delivers six soliloquies, seven if you count what he says when Claudius is trying to pray. (It seems legitimate to count it because although Claudius is on stage, he does not hear anything that Hamlet says.) On the assumption that analytical thinking is a sound path to greater knowledge, it follows that an analysis of these speeches will lead to a better understanding of Hamlet's character, the archetype of the tragic hero, and the theme of the play. So let's start by listing the soliloquies and their immediate contexts.

TEXT	CONTEXT	SPEECH
I.ii.129–159	After first court scene with Gertrude	O that this too too sullied flesh ...
I.v.92–112	After hearing news from the Ghost	O all you host of heaven! ...
II.ii.524–580	After setting up the play within the play	O what a rogue and peasant slave ...
III.i.56–88	After Claudius and Polonius agree to set Ophelia on Hamlet	To be, or not to be ...
III.ii.365–376	After Claudius has given himself away, as have Rosencrantz and Guildenstern; before confronting Gertrude	'Tis now the very witching time of night ...
III.iii.73–96	While Claudius prays	Now I might do it pat ...
IV.iv.32–66	After seeing Fortinbras's army	How all occasions do inform against me ...

While each of these speeches reveals a great deal about Hamlet, his role as tragic hero, and the theme of the play, we will concentrate on the last one, for in it Hamlet resolves once and for all on revenge. But first we need to set a context by tracing the relationship of the other soliloquies to this one.

We first find Hamlet in the throes of his grief over his father's death, his mother's remarriage, and his stepfather/uncle's base character. Next we see him enraged and taking the Ghost's word on face value. His temper still inflamed, he turns it on himself in his next speech and moves to action, the play within the play that will test the Ghost's veracity. Even though his plan is set, he continues to berate himself and in "To be or not to be" he speculates on his inaction. The fifth soliloquy takes place after Claudius has reacted guiltily to the play within the play. Here, Hamlet prepares himself to confront his mother with the truth, thereby carrying out one of the Ghost's commands. On his way to her, Hamlet finds Claudius praying, prepares to kill him, but realizes justice would not be done because Claudius's soul would go to heaven.

Hamlet delivers his last soliloquy as he is headed to England in the so-called care of Rosencrantz and Guildenstern. On the way to the ship, they pass Fortinbras and his army marching toward Poland and what appears to be a senseless battle over a "little patch of ground" (IV.iv.18). Hamlet finds in this impending battle a symbol or example similar to the one he found earlier ("O what a rogue . . ."), when he compared his motives to that of the Player weeping.

Hamlet questions why he has not carried out the Ghost's charge, why "yet I live to say, 'This thing's to do' " (line 44), asking himself if his delay has been caused by forgetfulness or being to scrupulous, "thinking too precisely on th'event" (line 41). He totes up his record so far, finding that he has "cause, and will, and strength, and means" (line 45) to carry out revenge and that examples all about "exhort" him, examples such as this army that marches to battle over nothing. The example "shames" him, for he has a "father killed, a mother stained," which act as incentives to his intellect ("reason") and his emotions ("blood"). That being the case, he concludes by resolving "from this time forth, / My thoughts be bloody, or be nothing worth" (lines 65–66).

This soliloquy gives us a good idea of what Hamlet thinks of his progress toward carrying out the Ghost's command, but can we trust his opinion? And why is he resolving this when he's on his way to England? If we view Hamlet as the kind of person who is led first by his heart, and therefore rushes to judgment, but then double-checks what his heart tells him with his head, and therefore reconsiders his judgment, then we can make more sense out of this soliloquy.

Hamlet's heart has told him the Ghost is right, as his first soliloquy indicates, but then he reconsiders and figures out a way to double-check the Ghost's word—the play within the play. Objectively viewed, that decision is sensible, not procrastinating. Hamlet's mouse-trap works, and Claudius reveals his guilt. Almost immediately thereafter, Hamlet has the chance to kill him but does not, lest Claudius's soul go to heaven. Again, his decision is wise. If this missed opportunity is what Hamlet refers to as a cowardly "scruple / Of thinking too precisely" about the outcome of his actions, he's wrong. To have killed Claudius while he was praying would not have been justice, for Claudius killed the elder Hamlet without allowing time for prayer or final sacrament. The irony, of course, is that Claudius cannot pray; Hamlet could have justly killed him.

In fact, Hamlet's only other opportunity was the one he took advantage of, only to discover it was Polonius, not Claudius, he had killed. As though it were not bad enough to kill the wrong person, after Hamlet has confronted his mother with the truth, the Ghost appears again "to whet thy almost blunted purpose" (III.iv.111). But the Ghost's statement is ambiguous. Does it call Hamlet to task in a general way or quite specifically? If it's general, then we can make little sense of it, for Hamlet chose not to kill the praying Claudius for good reason and did kill Polonius thinking he was Claudius. Let's try the specific.

Just before the Ghost reappears, Hamlet has been brutalizing his mother over her "lust." She has acknowledged her guilt ("Thou turn'st my eyes into my very soul"), but he continues, working himself into a frenzy over images of "the rank sweat of an enseamed bed, / Stewed in corruption, honeying, and making love / Over the nasty sty" (lines 92–94). She again asks him to stop, his words having achieved their purpose, "These words like daggers enter in mine ears" (line 95), but on he goes to tear apart Claudius (lines 97–101). Gertrude pleads again, "No more," but Hamlet merely picks up his pace, "A king of shreds and patches—" And then the Ghost appears.

Given this context, the Ghost's prodding seems a specific one, as if to say, "You've done enough here, now get on with the main event." The Ghost then immediately calls Hamlet's attention to Gertrude's distress and tells him to "step between her and her fighting soul." It's as though Hamlet has overstepped his obligation in regard to his mother and must be reined in.

But circumstances prevent Hamlet's taking any further action toward vengeance at this point. He must leave for England, for so the king has ordered. And he cannot disobey the king. Seeing his opportunity slip away, he vents his desperation in this soliloquy and vows, no matter what, he will seek vengeance. perhaps it is this very desperation that enables him later to make his miraculous escape from the ship and to return to Denmark.

If this interpretation were carried into production, the Hamlet we would see delivering this soliloquy would be impassioned and desperate, frustrated but not mad. The anger here is a cold anger, an intellectual rage, not an uncontrolled outburst of emotion.

But in general Hamlet does think "too precisely," as this soliloquy illustrates, for he is flogging himself unnecessarily. Yet when you think about it and consider the characteristics of the tragic hero, this kind of self-recrimination makes sense. Hamlet is caught between the command for just revenge ("Taint not thy mind," says the Ghost) and his personal revenge, getting even with Claudius for his acts of murder and incest. And he is caught in the paradox of the Ghost's charge—he must be a righteous avenger by being a killer. We see him balance this paradox later in Act V when he poses two rhetorical questions: Given Claudius's past and present acts, is it not "perfect conscience" to kill him? And it is not "to be damned" to let him live? (V.ii.67–70).

Yet there's no getting around the fact that murder is murder. Hamlet is both guilty and guiltless. That paradox combines with all of his inner conflicts to bring about suffering in the highest degree. At the same time, his fate is the one he chooses. Hamlet could have ignored the Ghost by writing it off as a devil or a sign of the general preparation for war. True, it would be disquieting to have the Ghost keep on stalking the battlements, and the evil that Claudius exudes would spread ever wider, so that was not really a path Hamlet could have chosen.

But there's another possibility. He could have believed the Ghost but dodged its charge. To do that, he would have had to behave himself sufficiently at court to gain Claudius's trust and therefore be granted what he had first, before the Ghost, desired—permission to return to his studies in Germany at Wittenburg. But to follow that path, Hamlet would have to be a hypocrite and coward, and he is neither.

Instead, Hamlet chooses the path of the tragic hero, the only path his integrity allows him—he gives his word that he will carry out the Ghost's commands. By committing himself to the Ghost's charge, "let not the royal bed of Denmark be / A couch for luxury and damned incest" (I.v.82–83), he aligns himself with a higher order, a tragic cosmos, far beyond his control. Here he is a mortal who must carry out divine justice. He rises to the challenge; he chooses his moment; he completes his mission, and he dies, as he must. Such exact justice would be cruel if it did not serve a higher order. Hamlet dies, but the state is purged of evil, and a rightful ruler will assume the crown.

Hamlet, as interpreted in this discussion, is an archetype of the tragic hero. He rises to the challenge of a force beyond his control and does so for the greater good. But he also has his personal motives to contend with, and the result is internal conflict. He suffers; he learns to master his emotions; he learns the continued evil that Claudius is capable of; he acts, and he dies, having sacrificed himself for a higher order, for justice. As he enacts all this, he becomes a symbol for all of us, representing the highest plane of nobility humans can reach and reaffirming the greatness of the individual. Hamlet also becomes a symbol for the self-sacrifice that divine justice demands, thereby linking character and symbol to theme.

Summary

The interpretation that served as the basis for the discussion above is one of many possible ones. Many critics see Hamlet quite differently, as a procrastinator who has to be pushed into action; others see him as genuinely mad at times; and still others find him overly attached to his mother. And you can see how these three views can blend into one: Hamlet, unnaturally attached to his mother, regards Gertrude's marriage to Claudius as betrayal and therefore sinks into depression; and because that depression borders on and occasionally dips into madness, it explains Hamlet's inaction.

All of these possible interpretations are based on our own cultural, educational, and personal experiences. If you lived in a matriarchy or knew nothing of psychology or suffered through the death a parent followed swiftly by the survivor's remarriage, you would read the play very differently. Chapter 29 in your textbook reveals the range of interpretations made possible by various critical approaches to literature.

And given a different view of Hamlet, you will probably come up with a different theme for the play, for, as you have seen, character and theme are closely connected. And you have also seen how the other elements of the play relate to theme. As you interpret a play or film or television drama, you can follow the same process outlined in this discussion: considering possible subjects, selecting one that seems promising, working up a draft statement of theme, and then thinking through how the various pieces—character, conflict, symbol, language, myth—fit into that whole.

As you think through your initial interpretation of theme, you will find yourself revising it, sharpening it to fit the evidence you have gathered. In fact, some writers prefer to start with a fairly clear idea of the subject and then consider the elements of the work, deducing the theme from the information they have gathered. No matter what way you prefer to work, you will find that the more time you spend thinking and writing about your interpretation of theme, the clearer it will become.

VIEWING GUIDE

An important component of this lesson is the video. You will learn more effectively from it by using the following questions and guidelines.

Before Viewing:

1. Review "The Dramatic Vision: An Overview," pages 1204–1225, "The Tragic Vision: Affirmation Through Loss," pages 1265–1281, "Seriousness, Completeness, and Artistic Balance," page 1273, and "William Shakespeare, *Hamlet*," pages 1322–1421 in the text.
2. Review the works assigned, paying particular attention to the ones your instructor emphasizes. Think of one or two themes, in addition to the one discussed in the study guide, that would work for *Hamlet*.

During Your Viewing:

1. Listen for links between the themes you have identified and the characters.
2. Listen to the characters' language for support for those themes.
3. Look for props, gestures, movements, and expressions that support those themes.
4. Listen for the distinction between primary artists and interpretive artists.
5. Listen for comments emphasizing the importance of the playwright and the text of the play.
6. Listen for what David Hwang says about the universality of themes.

After Viewing:

Give some thought to the following questions. You may want to write short answers in your journal or notebook.

1. What element provides the strongest support for your interpretation of theme and why?
2. What specific language in the play best supports your interpretation?
3. What advice that the critics gave about theme did you find most helpful?
4. What did you find most interesting about David Hwang's comments and why?
5. In what ways has this video portion changed the way you go about finding the theme of a play?

Amy

A Frame for Meaning—339

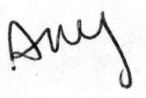

WRITING ACTIVITIES

After your study of this lesson, you should be able to appreciate how the various elements of drama combine to present meaning. Your instructor will advise you which, if any, of the following writing activities you are to complete.

Formal Writing:

The first activity will clarify what may be a confusing use of terms and generate ideas about the themes in *Hamlet*. The other activities are all straightforward and rather traditional, and all three call for your own interpretation of a play's theme, but the activities differ greatly in scale. The second is the narrowest, but that's not to say that it doesn't demand the same attention and length of analysis as the others, just that the view is deeper. The third may be more difficult in that you have not heard or read much about theme in *The Glass Menagerie*. For that reason, the activity is focused on only one element. The fourth is probably the most difficult in that it calls for an original perspective on what is by now very familiar material. But all of these activities will provide you with a focus that will help you clarify your concept of theme.

Oedipus's responsibility is his own

1. Mary Poovey uses "theme" almost synonymously with subject. List her ideas as subjects and for each, work up a fully developed statement of theme.
2. Write an essay in which you analyze one of Hamlet's soliloquies to support your interpretation of the play's theme.
3. Select one of the elements of drama and write an essay that uses it as the key to your view of theme in *The Glass Menagerie*.
4. Assuming your interpretation of theme in *Hamlet* differs from the one outlined in this lesson, present your case for your view.

Informal Writing:

For the benefit of visually and graphically oriented students, the first activity asks you to express your understanding of theme through the image of a metaphor. Thinking through the detail of the metaphor will help you understand how theme relates to the other elements of drama and will also serve as a quick review of metaphor, a figure of speech essential to poetry. The second activity explores the role of theme in *The Glass Menagerie* by placing you in the position of tutor. The assumption behind this activity is that teaching is one of the best ways of learning.

1. This lesson in the study guide has used two metaphors for the concept of theme—as the hub of a wheel and as the hub of a major airline. Think of one

of your own and then in your journal or notebook describe the metaphor and explain how it works as a definition.
2. Imagine you have a friend taking this course who can't grasp the idea of theme in *The Glass Menagerie* and has come to you for help. In your journal or notebook, write down, as specifically as possible, what you would do to help your friend interpret the theme of the play. You might start, for instance, by working from the familiar to the unfamiliar.

SELF-TEST

Match the items in columns A with the definitions or identifications in B:

A

1. Meaning
2. Hamlet and Tom Wingfield
3. Interpretation of drama
4. Amanda and Claudius
5. Subject
6. Symbols of disruption
7. Theme
8. Possible subject for *The Glass Menagerie*
9. Oedipus and Hamlet
10. The Tragic Cosmos

B

a. Force beyond human control
b. Revenge and justice
c. Flat characters
d. Fire escape and dining room
e. Thebes and Elsinore
f. Theme, presentation, and effect
g. What the work is about
h. Protagonists
i. Antagonists
j. Tragic heroes
k. Reality and illusion
l. Explanation of subject and theme
m. What a work asserts about its subject

Answer the following multiple-choice items:

1. *Oedipus the King*, *Hamlet*, and *The Glass Menagerie*
    a. All of the following are correct.
    b. deal with similar subjects.
    c. present universal themes.
    d. represent their times.
2. A valid interpretation
    a. includes symbolism.
    b. covers several themes.
    c. takes account of opposing views.
    d. takes account of relevant facts.

3. Archetype is to myth as
   a. legislature is to government.
   b. eagle is to a hawk.
   c. justice is to crime.
   d. saint is to religion.
4. A theme is a(n)
   a. fact.
   b. assertion.
   c. subject.
   d. description.
5. The tragic hero is
   a. a dramatic archetype.
   b. a universal archetype.
   c. only found in Greek drama.
   d. only found in Renaissance drama.

In 100–250 words, answer the following short essay questions:

1. Consider what you know about *The Glass Menagerie* and write a short essay identifying the possible subjects you find in the play, selecting one of them, and then explaining why you find it the most interesting.
2. Consider several possible subjects for *The Glass Menagerie*. Choose one, and in a short explanatory essay develop it into a theme by using an analysis of one character to support it.
3. How you interpret *Oedipus the King* depends on your view of how the play treats fate—of whether the gods simply knew the future or controlled Oedipus's destiny. What is your interpretation?

ADDITIONAL READING ACTIVITIES

If you enjoyed reading the play and listening to the interview in this lesson, you may want to read some of David Hwang's works, as listed below:

Hwang, David. *M. Butterfly*. (A full-length play that won a Tony award)

MODULE V

Conclusion

LESSON 25

Casting Long Shadows:
THE POWER OF LITERATURE

ABOUT THE LESSON

Way back at the beginning of this course, we staked out a map of literacy. On that map the widest circle is composed of those of us who, unless physically impaired in some way, are the orally literate. Within that large circle is a smaller one, made up of people who can read and write—those who are print literate.

Yet there's a big difference between someone who can read signs and address bills and someone whose life is fully engaged in reading and writing. So within the circle of print literacy is an even smaller one we can call critical literacy. These are people who interact with what they read and write, active readers who interpret texts in relation to the culture and world the reader inhabits and the larger culture and world shared with others. Knowledge of that larger culture and world is sometimes called *cultural literacy*.

This course has been an introduction to literature and also an introduction to critical literacy. Having studied the short story, poetry, and drama and having written essays, you are now a far more critical reader and writer than you were when you began this course. This lesson will bring together some of the concepts you have studied so you can explore how these various genres fit into the broader pattern we call literature.

And so you can see where you fit in that pattern, we'll take another look at the interrelation of writer, text, reader, and the different worlds they inhabit. This reexamination is a summary, but it is also more than that. Just as any given work is more than the sum of its elements, so too the act of interpretation is more than the sum of its parts. By now you have realized that interpreting a work of literature is itself a creative act.

GOAL

This lesson will help you to recognize the relationships among the various genres of literature.

WHAT YOU WILL LEARN

When you complete this lesson you will be able to:

1. Describe how literature provides access to cultures, times, and places.
2. Discuss how literature is shaped by the reader and how the reader is shaped by literature.
3. Give examples of how different genres shape meaning differently.
4. Recognize the relationships of various genres to the contemporary media of film and television.

LESSON ASSIGNMENT

Working through the following eight steps will help you complete the objectives and achieve the goal for this lesson.

Step 1: Read the OVERVIEW in this study guide lesson.

Step 2: Reread the specific works your instructor assigns. All of the following will be the focus of this lesson and will be cited in the video.

Poems:

- "Death of the Ball Turret Gunner," pages 639–640.
- "Dover Beach," pages 694–695.
- "My Last Duchess," pages 697–698.
- "Preludes," pages 735–736.

- "Metaphors," page 1099.
- "Dulce et Decorum Est," pages 802–803.
- "Theme for English B," pages 1083–1084.
- "Nikki-Rosa," pages 920–921.
- "The Ballad of Birmingham," page 927.
- "Patterns," pages 1149–1152.
- "Auto Wreck," pages 1175–1176.
- "Not Waving but Drowning," page 1177.
- "Revolutionary Petunias," pages 1186–1187.

Stories:

- "Everyday Use," pages 108–114.
- "First Confession," pages 357–359.
- "I Stand Here Ironing," pages 586–590.
- "The Bear and the Colt," Appendix A in this study guide, pages 385–388.

Plays:

- *Hamlet*, pages 1322–1421.

Essays:

- "A Love that Transcends Sadness," Appendix A in this study guide, pages 365–367.

Step 3: Watch the VIDEO, following the steps in the VIEWING GUIDE in this study guide lesson.

Step 4: Reread the OVERVIEW to reinforce what you have learned and to help you complete the Writing Activities.

Step 5: Complete any WRITING ACTIVITIES assigned in this lesson.

Step 6: Do the SELF-TEST exercises in this study guide lesson.

Step 7: Read any of the ADDITIONAL READING ACTIVITIES assigned.

Step 8: Go back to the learning objectives in the WHAT YOU WILL LEARN section of this study guide lesson and be sure you can respond to each of them.

OVERVIEW

You've spent several weeks studying each of three genres of literature—short fiction, poetry, and drama. And during that time you have been writing about what you have read. Some of those papers explained your interpretation and were analytical; other assignments may have described your responses and were personal; still others may have explored various fictional or poetic techniques and were literary.

Writing about what you have read requires a different kind of thinking than just talking about it. By writing, you have had to think through many of the same questions that professional writers face: Where do I begin? What do I want to say? How shall I organize my ideas? What tone is appropriate? What style should I use?

We will start this lesson with a discussion of the differences between visual and print presentations and then move to the similarities and differences among the three genres you have been studying. From that starting point, we will compare the kind of writing you have been doing with the short fiction, poetry, and drama you have read and take a closer look at what they have in common: a text, a writer, a reader, and the worlds in which each of them lives. Keep in mind as you read those sections that no one part—text, writer, reader, worlds—stands alone. All interact. Both writing and reading are dynamic, creative acts.

Literature

Short fiction, poetry, and drama are alive and well in the United States in various visual and written forms. Much of the short fiction and drama that surrounds us comes to us over the medium of television. There, sitcoms, soap operas, adaptations of short stories, novels, or plays, and written-for-television dramatic specials occupy a large percentage of television's programming hours.

And if you think of films you have seen recently, you find a whole world of fiction that comes to us in a movie theater or on video cassette. Sometimes these films are adaptations of short stories or novels; sometimes they represent original screenplays.

To find the poetry that surrounds us, you only need go to your radio dial, tape, or compact disc player. Song lyrics and lyric poetry have much in common, and rap music can be seen as a kind of poetry. Poetry also shares some characteristics with unlikely forms such as greeting cards, bumper stickers, graffiti, and advertisements. Rhyme and rhythm can sell a product, make a comment, or express an emotion.

The hour-long drama written for television, the film, and the song lyric share a number of characteristics with short fiction, poetry, and drama. Like the works you have been reading, these others are complete in themselves and have an identifiable structure. And they often provide insight into people, worlds, and situations very different from our own. If they are done well, they stir our minds and our emotions.

How then do they differ from what we have been calling literature? How do we distinguish between these kinds of popular works and the serious fiction and poetry we may find in the pages of magazines such as *The New Yorker* and *Harper's* or the plays we see performed on and off Broadway, as well as in local playhouses and on college campuses?

The line between popular culture and literature is hard to draw, but we do it all the time. Think of the word you associate with a particularly memorable film—Hitchcock's *Psycho* or John Ford's *Stagecoach*—and odds are the term is not "literature" but "classic." These movies and others like them are outstanding examples within the genre of film—"classics" in that sense. "Literature" is a word we associate with texts we read, with print, even though the original form of a work may have been oral, such as the *Iliad* or many ballads.

The printed form allows us to analyze language with a concentration and precision not yet possible with spoken or visual texts. We can start and stop at will, move back and forth in the work, and examine one part in relation to another even when many pages separate the passages in question.

This kind of active reading is necessary with literature, for the reader is the interpreter. Scripts for film and television are interpreted for you by any number of people before you see the final version. The director and actors, the people behind the cameras, and the editors all play significant roles in making (interpreting) a script into what you see. The same holds for music. What you hear is a singer's interpretation of a lyric.

The importance of interpretation also reveals why plays are included in both theater and literature courses. If the focus is on production (the interpretation by the director, actors, set designers, and the like), the course will be found in a drama department; if the focus is on the text (the interpretation by the reader), the course will be in an English department.

Whether play or poem or short story, the written text demands interpretation. And that interpretation is rewarding. Reading "First Confession," pages 354–359, you may find yourself reliving your own struggles with religion, or reading "My Last Duchess," pages 697–698, you may be reminded of someone you know who also collects people along with art or who has an obsessive need to control.

Literature allows you to see through another's eyes, feel what someone else feels even though you may have little in common with that person. To identify with Nikki-Rosa or the mother in "Everyday Use," pages 108–114, you need not have grown up black and poor. Nor do you have to be English and have fought in World War I to be moved by "Dulce et Decorum Est," pages 802–803. Literature allows you to bridge cultures and times and participate in the richness and complexity of human existence.

How literature does this depends upon the genre. Let's take one idea and see how the different genres present it. Love, death, family, and coming of age are all topics commonly dealt with in literature, but let's take the notion of "identity."

The three plays presented in this course explore the idea in the greatest depth. "Who am I?" is central to Oedipus and to Hamlet, and in a different way to Tom Wingfield (who perhaps never finds out). A far less full inquiry is found in all initiation stories—think of "First Confession," pages 354–359, "Barn Burning," pages 333–343, "The Bear and the Colt," pages 385–388 in the study guide—as well as others such as "I Stand Here Ironing," pages 586–590, and "Everyday Use," pages 108–114. As for poetry, you get quick insightful answers in "Theme for English B," pages 1083–1084, "Dulce et Decorum Est," pages 802–803; "Nikki-Rosa," pages 920–921; and "Metaphors," page 1099.

The different effects of these genres can be understood by examining some generalizations about the characteristics that make them distinct. Short fiction depends upon narrative to tell a story that centers on conflict, either internal or external or both. Although some kinds of poetry, such as the epic, also include conflict, much of poetry relies upon economy, imagery, and sound to convey ideas and emotions. Drama also involves ideas and emotions but focuses on action and its consequences. Unlike short fiction, drama presents action directly, as dialogue printed on the page or spoken on the stage.

Although these genres differ in form and effect, they also have much in common. *Hamlet*, for instance, is written in verse, and the image of the mother ironing is as powerful as many found in poetry. And as you have come to know, the various elements of literature serve as useful terms for interpreting all three genres.

The Text and Its World

Whether analyzing a work you have read or reworking a draft you have written, you start with the text. But that text has a life of its own. If you have ever found your own old letters, a poem or story that you wrote, or a journal or diary you kept some years ago, you know how true that statement is. Often you feel distanced from your text to the point of wondering "Did I really write *that*?"

Literary texts also have their own worlds. In *Hamlet*, the soliloquy and the aside are conventions of the Elizabethan stage, and we must accept them as such. To protest that the soliloquy is unrealistic is to deny the larger context of Elizabethan drama. Conventions in poetry are also important. Knowing the characteristics of the ballad, for instance, sets up certain expectations for "The Ballad of Birmingham." We not only expect a certain form but also that the poem will focus on a dramatic event.

On another level, there is the world depicted in the text. As readers we must accept the text's initial premise, but having done that, everything else must make sense. In "The Lottery," pages 140–146, for an extreme example, we must grant that such a world can exist. After that step, we need to examine the fictional world. Amy Lowell's "Patterns," pages 1149–1152, for instance, shows us a much earlier time, a time of powdered hair and whalebone corsets. If we do not recognize that world for what it is, we have a hard time making sense of the poem.

We must also know who is telling the story. The narrator in "Patterns" is also the main character in the poem, as reflected in the first person "I." Had the poet chosen third person, the distance between the reader and the character would be greater. The choice of point of view is a fact of the text, but the effect of point of view is a matter of interpretation, the role of the reader. Concentrating on the world of the text means knowing its conventions and bare bones—the facts that can be determined about the text.

The Writer and the Writer's World

The words writers use and the way they use them are determined by the times they live in. If you had been writing an essay 20 years ago, you would have used the pronoun "he" to mean all humans, and you wouldn't have thought twice about it. But now we live in different times. The women's movement has sensitized us to language in a way that now makes it difficult to use "he" without implying that it excludes "she." As a result, the editorial policy in almost all newspapers, magazines, and publishing houses rules out the old use of the pronoun. Writers avoid the problem in a number of ways such as switching to the plural "they" or recasting the sentence to get around having to use any pronoun.

What has shifted in the example of *he* is not the word's denotation—its dictionary meaning—but its connotation, its emotional, psychological, or social implications. You can see the same idea at work in Langston Hughes's "Theme for English B." The poem was published in 1959, a time in the United States when segregated schools were still much in evidence and the civil rights movement was only just gathering momentum. That time explains why Hughes might have had the narrator refer to himself as "colored." Today that word has been displaced by "black," "Afro-American," or "African-American."

The way words are constructed into sentences also changes over time, as almost any Shakespearean sonnet will reveal. Pronunciation can also change over the years. In Shakespeare's times, a poet might choose two words as an exact rhyme; now, some four hundred years later, that exact rhyme may strike the modern reader as an eye rhyme. In reading poetry written more than a hundred years ago, therefore, it's important to know how words were pronounced at that time or else we might miss a rhyme or mistake the meter.

To interpret a text, then, we need to consider the world in which the writer lives or lived and how language was used at that time. You have no doubt noted that the editor of your textbook has provided footnotes to help you understand any major changes in language.

The Reader and the Reader's World

Just as the times writers live in influence their works, so too our times determine how we read. War poems, such as "The Death of the Ball Turret Gunner," pages 639–640, and "Dulce et Decorum Est," pages 802–803, take on different meaning if you read them when your country is at war. The horrors that might have seemed distant—the hosing out of a body and the choking effects of gas—become immediate, real, powerful.

It's also important to recognize how your personal world affects your reading. A story such as "I Stand Here Ironing," pages 586–590, will have different meanings to readers who see it from different perspectives. A mother may condemn the mother in the story; a feminist may see her as a victim of a male-dominated society; a Marxist may see the story as portraying the evils of a capitalist system; a Freudian may see it as portraying the predictable effects of neglect. And because of the story's richness, all of these views can be supported.

On the other hand, interpretations that are sure to fail will ignore the world of the text and the writer and will interpret the work *only* from a personal view. In the case of "I Stand Here Ironing," someone who as a child had spent several years in a convalescent home similar to the hostile environment of the one in the story might have difficulty focusing on the text. The result might be an interpretation that sees Emily as wholly unsuccessful and doomed, the mother as a monster. Such a reading would ignore Emily's talents as a comedian and her mother's lack of alternatives.

Summary

Literature has intellectual, emotional, cultural, and aesthetic dimensions that make it more demanding than the kinds of texts we're faced with every day—newspapers and magazines, letters, memos, or reports. These demands make the act of reading a fluid, dynamic, create one. As we read an essay, poem, play, or short story, we suspend our impulse to build meaning as one might build a house, placing one brick upon another. Instead we enter a world in which we build meaning by walking around, getting a feel for the place, and then examining everything that lives there, considering relationships and emotional responses.

As readers, we are drawn into a literary text that is in part the expression of the writer's times. The text itself gives us a self-contained, ordered world where we can recognize characters and situations and see and feel events and times through others' eyes. We look for correspondences between our own lives and culture and those that we find on the pages before us. The connections we find there bring us pleasure and insight.

VIEWING GUIDE

An important component of this lesson is the video. You will learn more effectively from it by thinking about the following questions and guidelines.

Before Viewing:

1. Reread the OVERVIEW in this study guide paying particular attention to the term *literature* and to the distinctions between print and other kinds of literacy.
2. Review the work assigned, paying particular attention to the ones your instructor emphasizes.

350—Literary Visions

During Your Viewing:

1. Listen for the ways in which literature differs from ordinary life.
2. Listen for how characterization draws in the reader.
3. Note how literature reveals other worlds.
4. Listen for the differences in the critics' interpretations.
5. Listen for the different effects of the different genres.

After Viewing:

Give some thought to the following questions. You may want to write short answers in your journal or notebook.

1. List the characteristics the video associates with literature.
2. Which of the dramatic excerpts had the greatest emotional effect on you? What was that effect, and why did the dramatization evoke it?
3. Which of the two views of Hamlet's character do you find more compatible with your own? How do you see Hamlet?
4. Which of the two views of the conflict in *Hamlet* do you find more compatible with your own and why?
5. What character in the dramatizations do you identify with the most and why?

WRITING ACTIVITIES

After your study of this lesson, you should be able to recognize the relationships among the various genres of literature. Your instructor will advise you which, if any, of the following writing activities you are to complete.

Formal Writing:

Because this lesson comes at the end of the course, almost all of the activities are approximately the same level of difficulty. The first one, however, is the easiest because it comes with a ready-made thesis, one borrowed from the video. Activities 2 through 4 call for analytical essays, but each draws upon a different kind of thinking. The second, for instance, calls for definition, while the third depends upon process analysis. Causal analysis and comparison and contrast are elements of the fourth activity.

1. Select one of the excerpts from the video and write an essay that more fully explains the link between the full text of the work and the host's point about it.
2. Write an essay in which you fully define one of the genres of literature, drawing from appropriate works to illustrate your points.

3. Think of how you read a work of literature and how you "read" a television show. Select an example from each medium—print and television—and write an essay comparing and contrasting the process you go through.
4. Select two works from different genres that share a common theme. Write an essay in which you discuss how the genre affects the presentation of the theme.

Informal Writing:

Both of the activities develop the idea of the emotional connection between the work and the reader by asking you to examine your response to a particular work or character of your choosing. The result will be a personal essay in which you compare, directly or indirectly, your world to that of the writer and the text.

1. Select one of the works you have read that has had the greatest emotional effect on you. Consider works that have affected you positively or negatively, ones that you enjoyed or disliked. After you have picked a work, jot down in one column the events in the story and in an opposite column, your response to them. Think through the lists and write an informal essay that explains your reaction to the work.
2. Many of the works you have read presented worlds perhaps not so far removed from your own, while others presented characters or situations or times quite removed. Think back on the works that interested you the most. If you could be any of the characters you have read about, who would you be and why?

352—*Literary Visions*

SELF-TEST

Match the items in column A with the definitions or identifications in B:

A

1. "My Last Duchess"
2. Conflict and characterization
3. Critical literacy
4. Dialogue
5. "froth-corrupted lungs"
6. Imagery and compactness
7. Print literacy
8. "A melon strolling on two tendrils"
9. An iron

B

a. Characteristic of poetry
b. The ability to read and write
c. Insight into how it feels to be pregnant
d. Characteristic of essays
e. Symbol of pre-WPA world of the Depression
f. The world of 16th century Italy
g. Characteristic of drama
h. The ability to read analytically
i. Characteristic of short fiction
j. Insight into war
k. The world of 19th century England
l. Insight into setting

Answer the following multiple-choice items:

1. Which of the following is NOT usually considered literature?
   a. Short story
   b. Essay
   c. Editorial
   d. Drama

2. Which statement most accurately describes the reader of literature? The reader must
   a. interpret.
   b. be culturally literate.
   c. have prior knowledge about the author.
   d. have prior knowledge about the period.

3. The writer, text, reader, and the worlds they inhabit are
   a. interdependent.
   b. personal.
   c. separate.
   d. exclusive.

4. Which of the following is NOT related to literature?
   a. A film based on an original screenplay
   b. A documentary for television
   c. A newscast
   d. A situation comedy

5. The world of a text comes most to life when the
   a. writer is creating it.
   b. world it depicts reflects the writer's.
   c. text is hard to understand.
   d. reader responds to it.

In 100–250 words, answer the following short essay questions:

1. Think about the host of *Literary Visions* as though she were a character in a play. How would you characterize her?
2. Think about the writing you have done in this course and about yourself in it as narrator. How would you characterize yourself?
3. Choose one of the excerpts used in the video, including ones only presented visually. What reasons can you find for choosing *that* particular excerpt from the work?

ADDITIONAL READING ACTIVITIES

If you enjoyed reading the short stories, poems, and plays covered in this lesson, you may want to own any of several available and relatively inexpensive anthologies:

Guernsey, Otis L. and Jeffery Sweet. *Best Plays*. (An anthology that comes out annually)
Mathiessen, F. O. (ed.). *Oxford Book of American Verse*.
Pritchept, V. S. (ed.). *Oxford Book of Short Stories*.
Ulanov, Barry (ed.). *Makers of the Modern Theater*.
Woods, Fredrick (ed.). *Oxford Book of English Traditional Verse*.

LESSON 26

Continuing Visions:
THE USES OF LITERATURE

ABOUT THE LESSON

Lesson 25 reviewed what you have learned about literature and summarized the dynamic relationships among writer, text, reader, and the worlds they inhabit. This lesson steps back a bit to consider how not just literature but language itself shapes our lives and our view of the lives of others.

Literature is the highest form of language, and as such it is not usually our daily fare. The kind of language that we live with day to day is more of the meat, bread, and potatoes or rice and beans variety—advertisements, television shows, newspapers, and the like. Often we simply accept what we see and hear on face value, but if we are critical readers, we can read, listen, and look more deeply. When we do, we see that language is not only informing and ennobling but that it can also be deceptive and confusing.

To make you more aware of the power of language—for good and for ill—this lesson examines the impact of literature and of the more everyday use of words. In doing that, we'll be discussing some of the works you have read, some of the well known "classics" of American culture, and some of the more common kinds of jargon and advertisements.

GOAL

This lesson will help you to appreciate the power, practicality, and impact of language in contemporary literature and media.

WHAT YOU WILL LEARN

When you complete this lesson you will be able to:

1. Discuss how language shapes meaning in contemporary literature and media.

2. Give examples from contemporary literature and media of how language can deceive, confuse, and mislead.
3. Describe how literature conveys and questions the values in our culture.

LESSON ASSIGNMENT

Working through the following eight steps will help you complete the objectives and achieve the goal for this lesson:

Step 1: Read the OVERVIEW in this study guide lesson.

Step 2: Read or review any specific works your instructor assigns. The following will be referred to in this lesson:

<u>Cited in the video but not previously assigned (and not in the text):</u>

- *Uncle Tom's Cabin*, Harriet Beecher Stowe.
- *The Jungle*, Upton Sinclair.
- *Roots*, Alex Haley.
- *The Grapes of Wrath*, John Steinbeck.

<u>Cited in the video and dramatized or discussed in earlier video:</u>

- "Everyday Use," Alice Walker, pages 108–114.
- "A Worn Path," Eudora Welty, pages 114–119.
- "Barn Burning," William Faulkner, pages 333–343.
- "A Jury of Her Peers," Susan Glaspell, pages 189–202.
- "The Horse Dealer's Daughter," D.H. Lawrence, pages 471–482.
- "I Stand Here Ironing," Tillie Olsen, pages 586–590.
- "Death of the Ball Turret Gunner," Randall Jarrell, pages 639–640.
- "Dover Beach," Matthew Arnold, pages 694–695.
- "Dulce et Decorum Est," Wilfred Owen, pages 802–803.
- "Nikki-Rosa," Nikki Giovanni, pages 920–921.
- "Do Not Go Gentle Into That Good Night," Dylan Thomas, page 930.
- "Snapshot of Hue," Daniel Halpern, page 1132.
- "Patterns," Amy Lowell, pages 1149–1152.
- *Oedipus*, Sophocles, pages 1281–1318.
- *Hamlet*, William Shakespeare, pages 1322–1421.
- *The Glass Menagerie*, Tennessee Williams, pages 1643–1692.

- "A Love That Transcends Sadness," Willie Morris, Appendix A in this study guide, pages 365–367.
- "The Bear and the Colt," N. Scott Momaday, Appendix A in this study guide, pages 385–388.

Step 3: Watch the VIDEO, following the steps in the VIEWING GUIDE in this study guide lesson.

Step 4: Reread the OVERVIEW to reinforce what you have learned in the text and the video and to help you complete the Writing Activities.

Step 5: Complete any WRITING ACTIVITIES assigned from this lesson.

Step 6: Do the SELF-TEST exercises in this study guide lesson.

Step 7: Read any of the ADDITIONAL READING ACTIVITIES assigned.

Step 8: Go back to the learning objectives in the WHAT YOU WILL LEARN section of this study guide lesson and be sure you can respond to each of them.

OVERVIEW

If you were to spend a day followed at every step by an invisible note-taker who recorded every instance you used language—spoken or written, as well as created, listened to, or read—you would be amazed at the result. Language and our use of it is something we are apt to take for granted. But we shouldn't.

In this series, you have studied the literary uses of language, which also means that you have seen the ways it can show us perspectives we might not otherwise have. And you have read and heard language at its best in the form of carefully crafted prose, poems, and plays. This lesson will briefly review the uses of literature and then examine how language affects us day to day.

We shall begin with a quick look at how language shapes meaning in literature and the media, move to how language can also confuse and deceive, and end with how literature conveys and questions our culture's values.

The Positive Use of Language

William Faulkner, in his Nobel Prize speech that you hear at the end of the video for this lesson, speaks of the writer focusing on the "problems of the human heart," on "universal truths"—and that focus is certainly evident in the works you have read. You cannot read stories such as "A Worn Path," pages 114–119, "A Jury of Her Peers," pages 189–202, or Faulkner's own "Barn Burning," pages 333–343, and not be moved by the courage of the protagonists. Nor can you read and hear poems such as "Dulce et Decorum Est," pages 802–803, "Do Not Go Gentle Into That Good Night," page 930, or "The Death of the Ball Turret Gunner," pages 639–640, without confronting your own ideas of death. And the plays *Oedipus the King*, *Hamlet*, and *The Glass Menagerie*, show us the complexities of various kinds of responsibilities—political, familial, personal.

The power of fictional worlds can also be seen in the way they have affected our everyday speech. We may say, for instance, that a particular Southern type is a "real Scarlett O'Hara" or that an oily minor bureaucrat is a "Uriah Heep." Both Margaret Mitchell and Charles Dickens would be pleased. So would any number of writers whose characters have become bywords even though their works are seen rather than read. Television and film, for instance, have contributed J. R., Mr. Spock, and Miss Piggy.

Star Wars, after all, was the name of a movie before it became the phrase adopted first by the media and then by the military to refer to sophisticated weaponry. And for many of us, the title of Joseph Heller's novel *Catch 22* has become synonymous with a no-win situation, just as Aldous Huxley's title *Brave New World* (a phrase borrowed from Shakespeare's *The Tempest*) raises images of a totalitarian state.

Sometimes the worlds of literature, popular culture, and reality become so close that the borders between them blur. Tom Wolfe's novel *Bonfire of the Vanities* was published shortly before the public revelations about insider stock trading and religious corruption. In many ways, then, literature and popular culture act both as mirror and crystal ball.

The Negative Use of Language

But the power of the word has its negative side as well. George Orwell's perceptive essay, "Politics and the English Language," points out how language can be used to mislead, confuse, and deceive. In fact in one of his novels, *1984*, Orwell coined the word *doublespeak* for just this use of language.

When you studied poetry, you analyzed the importance of connotation—the emotional quality of words. "Home," "house," "domicile" can all have the same denotation but very different connotations, and which word you choose depends on the context in which you use it. But there's a difference between shades of meaning, meaning intended to put a positive value on what is essentially negative, and meaning intended to deceive. If we substitute *cemetery* for *graveyard*, for instance, we are simply making death a bit less direct; if we go a step further and call a graveyard a *memorial garden*, we are hiding reality. *Cemetery* is an example of *euphemism*; *memorial garden*, an example of doublespeak.

Next time you go to the grocery store, look at the labels given to toothpaste or laundry soap sizes. You may well find that what you think of as "small," "medium," "large" are actually labeled "large," "giant," "jumbo." That's doublespeak. Or when you go to a restaurant, examine the prose of the menu, and you may find only "juicy, thick" steaks no matter what you see on your plate.

You also can see doublespeak clearly at work in advertising—often in the subtle form of innuendo. Some ads work on the suggestion that if you buy "Brand X" aftershave, make of car, kind of lipstick, you will be sexy and attractive. And these days, we not only have celebrities from sports or the silver screen selling a product, sometimes it's their own products. Buy a movie star's perfume, the advertisement suggest, and some of the glamour will come with it.

We are conditioned to see a certain amount of exaggeration in advertising, and we are used to a degree of euphemism and doublespeak in everyday matters. We can get dulled to language. "Have a nice day" has become an empty phrase, though it does no harm. What *does* do harm is the doublespeak that blunts reality and makes the bad neutral or even acceptable. Euphemism changes "wife beater" into "wife abuser"; doublespeak renames the "War Department" the "Department of Defense." "Lies" are sometimes glided over as "miscommunications."

The term that sprang into popular use during World War II that is associated with this kind of misuse of language is "propaganda," the spreading of facts, ideas, or rumors deliberately presented in such a way that they further or damage a cause or subject. Propaganda can agitate for change or appeal to keeping the status quo; it can paint beautiful pictures or false ones.

Political flyers, speeches, even college catalogues often paint a more positive picture than the truth can support. At its worst, propaganda appears in the form known as "hate literature," pamphlets and the like aimed at building up a certain group or belief by viciously attacking others—and with no regard for the truth.

In a country where freedom of the press is guaranteed by a constitution, such obvious lies and deceptions can be spotted—some easily, others if we look hard enough. We know, for instance, that we cannot believe everything we read or hear or we will be at the mercy of deceptive advertisers, hucksters, and politicians. Being critically literate can protect us.

Literature and Culture

Often the underside of language and the life it represents is revealed through literature. The real horrors of a police state, for instance, have been exposed in the novels of the Russian writer Alexander Solzhenitsyn that depict Stalin's "work camps." Other novelists have imagined a totalitarian future in works such as Orwell's *1984*. There he creates a world ruled by "Big Brother," a familiar term that has entered the language to mean a faceless, repressive government.

Being available in print and therefore available to be read and reread, analyzed, and reinterpreted, literature mirrors a culture's values in a deeper way than works presented orally or visually. A television documentary may shock us and draw attention to a problem we know little about, but a work of literature on the same subject will do that and more, for it will draw us into a world we can identify with emotionally. When *Uncle Tom's Cabin* was published, for example, it brought the evils of slavery into homes that had had virtually no contact with it, and it did so by making slavery into something that has a direct effect on people whose hearts we can identify with.

Now, well over a hundred years after the Civil War, the novel still affects us. We can still be moved to horror at the system of slavery the novel portrays, yet most of us are familiar with it in another way. To call an African-American an "Uncle Tom" is no compliment. Behavior that was perceived as acceptable in the 1800s is no longer so.

By using plot, character, setting, symbolism, tone, and style, writers of short stories, poetry, and drama invite us into a fictional world that often gives us the best and the worst of our culture. We can see that worst in "Barn Burning," pages 333–343, where we not only meet the twisted Snopes but the world of the sharecropper that helped produce him. We don't need to be female or pregnant to feel what pregnancy's like when we read Sylvia Plath's "Metaphors," page 1099.

Literature can also question a culture's values. Wilfred Owen's "Dulce et Decorum Est," pages 802–803, criticizes unthinking, blind patriotism that glorifies war. *The Glass Menagerie* asks us to reexamine family loyalty and responsibilities and to question the fantasies that drive us. Susan Glaspell's "A Jury of Her Peers" shows us how preconceptions about gender can blind us to the truth.

So literature not only mirrors a culture's values but often does so in the same way that Hamlet forces Gertrude to see herself. Just as Gertrude's mirror reveals her faults and flaws, literature—by revealing what we are—can reveal what we can and should be.

Summary

The critics you see in the video that accompanies this lesson speak of why they value literature and how it enriches their lives. Benjamin DeMott says that the "training you get as a reader is the training that, ultimately, makes you more capable as a human being of dealing with situations and people different from yourself." Being an active, critical reader allows you to distance yourself enough in unfamiliar situations so that you can reflect upon them instead of being sucked in or overwhelmed by them.

What you gain, as Marjorie Perloff says, isn't something that you "convert into dollars and cents . . . but an inner value . . . a whole way of seeing things." You recognize commonalities among disparate peoples and circumstances because your imagination has been stretched. As a result, as Mary Helen Washington emphasizes, you are not satisfied with "superficial answers and superficial questions." And your life is richer for it.

These critics are writers as well as readers. Together with the authors you have seen and heard in this series, they believe in the joy and pain and power of creating a text. Those are the same emotions you see at work when anyone who writes—professional writer, critic, student, citizen—has examined a subject to make it his or her own through the written word.

Literature, as Faulkner says in his Nobel speech, shows us "the problems of the human heart in conflict with itself . . . love and honor and pity and pride and compassion and sacrifice." Faulkner spoke particularly to "the young man or woman writing today" in hopes of reminding them and all of us that "the poet's voice need not merely be the record of man, it can be one of the props, the pillars to help him endure and prevail." Through literature we hear the poet's voice, and we "prevail."

VIEWING GUIDE

An important component of this lesson is the video. You will learn more effectively from it by thinking about the following questions and guidelines.

Before Viewing:

1. Reread the OVERVIEW in this study guide, paying particular attention to the positive and negative uses of language and the ways in which literature relates to culture.
2. Review any works assigned, paying particular attention to the ones your instructor emphasizes. Try to hear the dialogue in each scene.

During Your Viewing:

1. Listen for the ways books have changed society.
2. Listen to what the critics say about how literature has changed the ways they view the world.
3. Note the kinds of activities going on in the elementary and high school classrooms.
4. Listen to what the prisoners say about their writing.
5. Listen to what the homeless women say about their writing.

After Viewing:

Give some thought to the following questions. You may want to write short answers in your journal or notebook.

1. How would you summarize what the critics say about the importance of reading?
2. How would you summarize what the various groups shown throughout the video say about the importance of writing?
3. How would you summarize how reading and writing affect you?
4. How do the quotations shown on the screen relate to what the critics say?
5. How do the shots from the various works relate to Faulkner's speech?

WRITING ACTIVITIES

After your study of this lesson, you should be able to appreciate the power, practicality, and impact of language in contemporary literature and media. Your instructor will advise you which, if any, of the following writing activities you are to complete.

Formal Writing:

The activities that follow all have the same level of difficulty and call for analysis of a particular work of your own (or your instructor's) choosing. What you may find, however, is that writing about one genre is easier for you than the others. Some students, for example, find the compact form of the poem easier to work with than short fiction or drama, yet others find that prosody calls for a kind of analysis that they have difficulty with. It's probably best to let your taste be your guide and to choose the work that had the most impact on you, no matter what the genre.

1. Some works draw their power from questioning one of society's values and others from creating a distinct picture of a time or person. Choose a work assigned previously and analyze how it achieves one of these purposes.
2. According to the Host, "literature at its best creates an awareness of the essential worth of an individual." Select one of the works you have read for this course and explain how it deals with that "essential worth."
3. Literature, according to Faulkner, deals with "the old verities and truths of the heart." Using one of the works you have read for this course, analyze the "old verities and truths" it exemplifies.
4. Select any of the critics on this show whose views you most agree or disagree with and write an essay explaining why. Make sure you illustrate your points with support from a particular work you have read for the course.

Informal Writing:

Both of these assignments call for you to analyze your connection with language. The first uses your own experience to explore the power of words, and the second draws upon your reading and writing for the course and its effect on you.

1. Recall the times when you felt the power of words, either ones you read or ones you wrote, either negatively or positively. Perhaps a note in school got you in trouble, a comment on something you had written or a letter shattered or delighted you, or an advertisement or contract tricked you. In your journal or notebook, re-create that time so that it has a similar impact on an imagined or real reader. If some of the facts are dimmed by time, don't worry

about it and just create plausible ones instead. What's important is the truth of the event and the emotion—not the accuracy of minor details.
2. Think through the works you have read for this course and select the one that had the greatest impact upon you. In your journal or notebook, explain your connection to the text and why it had the impact it did.

SELF-TEST

Match the items in column A with the definitions or identifications in B:

A

1. *The Jungle*
2. *Oedipus the King, Hamlet, The Glass Menagerie*
3. "Barn Burning"
4. Funeral director
5. Propaganda
6. Intentionally deceptive use of
7. *Uncle Tom's Cabin*
8. *Grapes of Wrath*
9. "I Stand Here Ironing"
10. "Ducle et Decorum Est"

B

a. Doublespeak
b. Positive or negative coloring
c. Attacks discrimination
d. Influenced Pure Food and Drug Act
e. Pun
f. Depicts life of sharecropper family
g. Portrays plight of migrant workers
h. Attacks romanticizing of war
i. Aided cause of abolitionists
j. Reflects effects of depression
k. Plays depicting "human heart in conflict with itself"
l. Euphemism
m. Advertising

Answer the following multiple-choice items:

1. Being critically literate enables you to
    a. do all of the following.
    b. spot doublespeak
    c. interpret texts.
    d. relate fictional experiences to your own.

2. Literature differs from works presented visually or orally in that literature
    a. makes fewer demands on the reader.
    b. is easier to relate to.
    c. is more difficult to understand.
    d. engages the reader more deeply.

3. Literature can do all of the following except
   a. determine a culture's values.
   b. reflect a culture's values.
   c. change a culture's values.
   d. predict a culture's values.

4. Which of the following is the greatest abuse of language?
   a. Propaganda
   b. Euphemism
   c. Doublespeak
   d. Exaggeration

5. Which of the following statements is NOT true?
   a. Euphemism is common to language.
   b. Doublespeak is confined to Orwell's *1984*.
   c. Connotation deals with a word's emotional effect.
   d. Exaggeration is frequently used in advertisements.

In 100–250 words, answer the following short essay questions:

1. Think about the video component of *Literary Visions* as a whole and as a genre. What similarities and differences do you note between it and the genres you have studied?
2. Take another look at the title of the series and the titles of the individual lessons. (See the Table of Contents for this study guide.) In what way or ways are they appropriate or inappropriate?
3. One advantage that a course taught in a classroom can have over one that takes place over television is interaction. If the classroom is run as a discussion, there is opportunity for questions and answers—interactive dialogue. What ways do you find that this telecourse tries to compensate for that lack? To what extent did you find those ways effective?

ADDITIONAL READING ACTIVITIES

If you enjoyed reading about the material in this lesson, you may want to read some of the works listed below:

Buhle, Paul (ed.). *Popular Culture in America.*
Eco, Umberto. *Travels in Hyper-Reality.* (American culture viewed through the elements of literature)

Fell, John L. *Film and the Narrative.*
Gitlin, Todd (ed.). *Watching Television.*
Wheeler, David (ed.). *No, But I Saw the Movie.* (Short stories made into movies)

APPENDIX A

Additional Reading

A Love That Transcends Sadness

By Willie Morris

Not too long ago, in a small Southern town where I live, I was invited by friends to go with them and their children to the cemetery to help choose their burial plot. My friends are in the heartiest prime of life and do not appreciate departing the Lord's earth immediately, and hence, far from being funereal, our search had an adventurous mood to it, like picking out a Christmas tree. It was that hour before twilight, and the marvelous old graveyard with its cedars and magnolias and flowering glades sang with the Mississippi springtime. The honeysuckled air was an affirmation of the tugs and tremors of living. My companions had spent all their lives in the town, and the names on even the oldest stones were as familiar to them as the people they saw everyday. "Location," the man of the family said laughing. "As the real estate magnates say, we want *location*."

At last they found a plot in the most venerable section which was to their liking, having spurned a shady spot which I had recommended under a giant oak. I know the caretaker would soon have to come to this place of their choice with a long, thin steel rod, shoving it into the ground every few inches to see if it struck forgotten coffins. If not, this plot was theirs. Our quest had been a tentative success, and we retired elsewhere to celebrate.

Their humor coincided with mine, for I am no stranger to graveyards. With rare exceptions, ever since my childhood, they have suffused me not with foreboding but with a sense of belonging and, as I grow older, with a curious, ineffable tenderness. My dog Pete and I go out into the cemeteries, not only to escape the telephone, and those living beings who place more demands on us than the dead ever would, but to feel a continuity with the flow of the generations. "Living," William Faulkner wrote, "is a process of getting ready to be dead for a long time."

I have never been lonely in a cemetery. They are perfect places to observe the slow changing of the seasons, and to absorb human history—the tragedies and anguishes, the violences and treacheries, and always the guilts and sorrows of vanished people. In a preternatural quiet, one can almost hear the palpable, long-ago voices.

I like especially the small-town cemeteries of America where the children come for picnics and games, as we did when I was growing up—wandering among the stones on our own, with no adults about, to regard the mystery and inevitability of death, on its terms and ours. I remember we would watch the funerals from afar in a hushed awe, and I believe that was when I became obsessed not with death itself but with the singular community of death and life together—and life's secrets, life's fears, life's surprises. Later, in high school, as I waited on a hill to play the echo to taps on my trumpet for the Korean War dead, the tableau below with its shining black hearse and the coffin enshrouded with the flag and the gathering mourners was like a folk drama, with the earth as its stage.

The great urban cemeteries of New York City always filled me with horror, the mile after mile of crowded tombstones which no one ever seems to visit, as if one could *find* anyone in there even if the wished to. Likewise, the suburban cemeteries of this generation with their carefully manicured lawns and bronze plaques embedded in the ground, all imbued with affluence and artifice, are much too remote for me. My favorites have always been the old, established places where people honor the long dead and the new graves are in proximity with the most ancient. The churchyard cemeteries of England haunted me with the eternal rhythms of time. In one of these, years ago as a student at Oxford, I found this inscription:

> Here lies Johnny Kongapod
> Have mercy on him, gracious God,
> As he would on You if he was God,
> And You were Johnny Kongapod

Equally magnetic were the graveyards of eastern Long Island, with their patina of the past touched ever so mellowly with the present. The cemetery of Wainscott, Long Island, only a few hundred yards from the Atlantic Ocean, surrounded the schoolhouse. I would watch the children playing at recess among the graves. Later I discovered a man and his wife juxtaposed under identical stones. On the wife's tomb was "Rest in Peace." On the man's at the same level, was "No Comment." I admired the audacity of that.

But it is the graveyards of Mississippi which are the most moving for me, having to do, I believe, with my belonging here. They spring from the earth itself, and beckon me time and again. The crumbling stones of my people evoke in me the terrible enigmas of living. In a small Civil War cemetery which I came across recently, the markers stretching away in a misty haze, it occurred to me that most of these boys had never even had a girl friend. I have found a remote graveyard in the hills with photographs on many of the stones, some nearly one hundred years old, the women in bonnets and Sunday dresses, the men in overalls—"the short and simpler annals of the poor." I am drawn here to the tiny grave of a little girl. Her name was Fairy Jumper, and she lived from April 14, 1914 to Jan. 16, 1919. There is a miniature lamb at the top of the stone, and the words: "A fairer bud of promise never bloomed." There are no other Jumpers around her, and there she is, my Fairy, in a far corner of that country burial ground, so forlorn and alone that it is difficult to bear. It was in this cemetery on a bleak February noon that I caught sight of four men digging a grave in the hard, unyielding soil. After a time they gave up. After they left, a man drove toward me in a battered truck. He wanted to know if some fellows had been working on the grave. Yes, I said, but they went away. "Well, I can't finish all by myself." Wordlessly, I helped him dig.

One lonesome, windswept afternoon my dog and I were sitting at the crest of a hill in the town cemetery. Down below us, the acres of empty land were covered with wildflowers. A new road was going in down there, the caretaker had told me; the areas was large enough to accommodate the next three generations. "With the economy so bad," I had asked him, "how can you be *expanding*?" He had replied: "It comes in spurts. Not a one last week. Five put down the week before. It's a pretty steady business.

Sitting there now in the dappled sunshine, a middle-aged man and his middle-aged dog, gazing across at the untenanted terrain awaiting its dead, I thought of how each generation lives with its own exclusive solicitudes—the passions, the defeats, the victories, the sacrifices, the name and dates and the faces belong to each generation in its own passing, for much of everything except the most unforgettable is soon forgotten. And yet, though much is taken, much abides. I thought then of human beings, on this cinder of a planet out at the edge of the universe, not knowing where we came from, why we are here, or where we might go after death—and yet we still laugh, and cry, and feel, and love.

"All that we know about those we have loved and lost," Thornton Wilder wrote, "is that they would wish us to remember them with a more intensified realization of their reality. What is essential does not die but clarifies. The highest tribute to the dead is not grief but gratitude."

An excerpt from the novel

Tripmaster Monkey: His Fake Book

by Maxine Hong Kingston

Somewhere between Fairfield and Vacaville, theirs was the only vehicle on the road. Wittman turned the car radio—shit-kicking caballero music—off. He pulled the Porsche to the roadside and killed the engine. A turn of the ignition key switched off the world's noise. They twisted out their cigarettes in the ashtray. It's against the law to toss them because peat smolders. At night, you sometimes see parts of an underground fire, and a smell like bread baking. A stream of white butterflies frittered by, on and on. A flock of small black birds came next; the ones at the top were high in the sky, the ones at the bottom flew through the yellowing grass, and they were the same continuous flock. At last the birds tailed away. Next, yellow moths blew about; they will alight in another season, and become the mustard flowers of January. They hear a car at a distance, and then it arrived, and passed them. It had gathered eventfulness, passed, and pulled it away at seventy miles an hour. The silence reclosed. A soul extends in nature, then you are aware of having one. Buildings, jackhammers, etc., chop it up, and you took drugs to feel it. The extent of the soul is from oneself to wherever living beings are.

Too low in the sky came a black warplane. Its two winglights glared in the bright day. Its flat belly had hatchdoors—for bombs to drop out. The plane was the shape of a winged bomb. The humming and roar must have been underlying everything from some time. It had no insignia, no colors, no markings, no numbers. It hung heavy in the air. It passed overhead and off to the right. Wittman started the car, and drove fast to get out of there. But the plane came back around, skulking around and around. The sky seemed not to have enough room for it. Like a shark of the ocean inside a tank. How is it that I co-exist with that dead impersonal thing which moves, and is more real than the fields and more real than this unprotectable girl? Its noise replaced thought and om. Evil is not an idea. It is that. Sharks swim in schools. This thing was unpaired, singular in the isolation of the sky. Somebody ought to report it to Berkeley. And call Travis Air Force Base; one of their experiments is loose, blindly circling where Primary State 12 intersects I-80. But people who've seen the evil plane and heard it forget to do anything about it when they get back. Its dull blackness and noise are somehow subliminal, and cause helplessness and despair. They just want to hurry and get to their people. Good thing Wittman will be with his mother right away.

Ruby Ah Sing lived in sight of the capitol. A fence went around her property, a flower garden and a house with a porch and a porch swing. The years she had lived in trailer parks and her roomette on the train, she had had a dreamhouse. She'd settled down in old Sac for her boy, to give him a home, which he drove past. Take the long way. He had liked better living on the train, reading funny books in his fold-down bunk, everything you own at your toes. Sometimes the window had seemed to be a long television screen scrolling sideways, and sometimes another room, and sometimes a dream. In pajamas, he lay against the window, moving through a city street. Underneath him, hobos and Mexicanos were riding next to the wheels; they fell off in their sleep. Once a circus traveled with them, or they traveled with a circus. The aerialists spoke European, but the clowns were friendly with everyone. He wore his monkey outfit for them. They warned him of the circus tradition of tossing enemies and wise asses off the train. Boys and girls in Europe were riding in cattle cars, and were trampled. That was why he had had to give an anti-jap speech from the caboose. The men around the potbelly stove gave him a yellow flag. A steward let him serve lunch. Never work as an animal trainer; if an elephant shits in the ring, you have to shove the broom up there where the sun don't shine. Going through a black tunnel, a conductor said, "They say a thousand chinamen used a thousand tons of dynamite to make this cut. I don't know the truth of that." The engine puffed out worlds—"Elephant. Elephant."—through the semiconscious nights. Trestles, trigonometrical puzzles worked out by ancestors, carried him across canyons. His father waited at stations, where he'd be waving hello or goodbye. The train whistled woo woo. Ruby and Zeppelin had a joke about wooing each other.

"Sutter's Fort is that way," said Wittman. "Sac High. I graduated from Sac High. That's the Greyhound Station. Crocker, who invested in the railroad, built that museum. That's the old Old Eagle Theatre. The first theater was the Chinese puppet theater on I Street. That's the Governor's Mansion. That's the hotel where congressmen go to wheel and deal." He drove around the capitol. "Los Immigrantes go in that door to become citizens. There's the peanut man. I used to buy peanuts from him to feed the squirrels." It was an easy town to learn. A Street, B Street, C Street, and so on, and the number streets gridding the other way.

"The Land Hotel," said Taña. "There's a Land Hotel, isn't there?"

"Yes. Near the Senator. It's a fleabag."

"That's where we used to stay summers when I was a little girl. During the war. I didn't know it was a fleabag."

"Well, maybe it wasn't a fleabag back then."

Suddenly Wittman was coughing hard. His lungs were not made for an open-air car.

"Are you all right?" asked Taña, patting his shoulder.

"I'm okay. I always cough when I get near home."

"That's interesting. Whenever I've ridden the bus and heard somebody coughing, and I turn around, most of the time they're Chinese."

"Yeah, they're on their way home."

"It gets me in the stomach," said Taña. "Half a bottle of Kaopectate, and I'm ready to see my mother. I'm on my way out the door, and she says right in front of my date, and our double-dates, 'Are you wearing your bra? Get upstairs, young lady, and put on a brassiere. You're too big to be going out all over town without a brassiere.' Does your mother do that? It probably was a fleabag. I remember I always wanted to stay at the other one."

"The Senator."

"Yeah. One night, really hot, we had to keep the window open. I heard someone singing down the street. In the morning, I look out the window, and there was a sailor asleep in a phone booth. What's the main street? Is it Main Street?"

"K Street."

"On K Street, there was a captured Japanese plane, tan with big red circles on the wings. An open cockpit, and a ladder. My father made me sit in the cockpit, and I was crying because I thought it was going to fly away with me. My mother got really mad at my father. I sat in it for about five seconds. Don't laugh," she said, laughing.

"I'm not," said Wittman, coughing.

"Later I saw home movies of myself in that Zero, me in my pinafore and white stockings and real long hair, trying to climb out of the cockpit. Alice in Wonderland bombs Pear Harbor."

The folks are going to love her, thought Wittman. Ruby and Zeppelin are really going to love her. I love her myself. No brassiere, wow! I have to buy her a leopard-skin bathing suit so we can play Sheena, Queen of the Jungle. Me Chimp.

Ruby Ah Sing, Wittman's mother, had a maple tree, the crown-leaves gold and red now. The crowns of many kings on a hat rack. The pear tree had some pears, and green leaves, and dead black leaves on long offshoots, and flowers. Wild in the time machine.

Through the screen door—the crack clack crash of mah-jongg. Oh, no, mah-jongg day. That's why, all those Coupe de Viles to have squeezed a parking space among. The son of the house would have turned about but for the girl he was with. Always do the harder thing. He opened the door, went ahead, held it for Taña.

Ruby screamed. "Eeek!" Stood up and screamed again, pointing. And Auntie Sadie screamed, and Auntie Marleese ran to him. His mother eeked him again. "Eeek!" What's wrong? The white girl? A hobo bumbled after them inside? "What have you done to yourself?" She put her hands to her cheeks.

"You used to be such a beautiful boy!" shouted Aunt Marleese, looking up at him.

"Too much hair," said Aunt Sadie. "Much too hairy."

"You go shave," said Mother. "Shave it off! Shave it off! Oh, hock geen nay say!" That is, "Scares you to death!" "Gik say nay!" That is, "Irks you to death!" "Galls you to death!" Clack! Clack!

"No act, Ma!" he said.

"Don't say hello to your mother," she said.

"Never you mind sticks and stones, honey boy," said Auntie Bessie. "Have a heart, Ruby."

A dog jumped on him. "Down, Queenie. Behave," said Auntie Jadine, its owner. "Where you manners, Queenie?" Those who usually spoke Chinese talked to the yapperdog in English. "Down, Queenie. Come heah." They spoke English to him and to the dog. American animals.

"GOOD dog," said Wittman. It mind-fucks dogs to be called good when they're trying to be fierce.

"Wit Man has come to see his momma," explained the aunties, one to another. "Good boy. Big boy now." Clack clack clack. A racket of clack clack clack. "All grow up. College grad, haw, Wit Man?" Nobody asked if he were a doctor or an engineer yet. How tactful. Not asking about work at all. "Sit. Sit. Here's an empty chair by me, dearie. Come meet me." Taña got a side chair at one of the dining tables.

"Oh, I be so sorry I didn't recognize you, Wit Man," said Auntie Sadie. "You so changed."

"That's okay, Auntie Sadie."

"Come talk to your Aunt Lilah."

"Hello, Aunt Lilah. Hello, Auntie Dolly," said Wittman. "Hello, Aunt Peggy." He went to each auntie, shaking hands with some, kneeling beside this one and that one for her to take a better look at him. "He was a cute biby." "Why you not visit Auntie more often?" "Me too, honey boy. Visit you Aunt Sondra too." The ladies called themselves "ahnt," and Wittman called them "ant." "Hair, Big City style, isn't it, dear?" said Auntie Dolly of San Francisco, ruffing his hair. "Beard in high style, Ruby. Wit Man Big City guy now."

The ladies at his mother's table were comforting her. "Hairy face, fashion on a plate," said Auntie Sophie. "You the one sent him to college, Ruby." Clack. Clack.

"Where I go wrong, I ask you," said Wittman's mother. "He was clean cut. He used to be soo mun." That is, "He used to be soigné." "He doesn't get his grooming from me. Kay ho soo kay ge ba, neh. Gum soo. Soo doc jai." That is, "He takes too much after his father, neh. So like. Too alike." "Moong cha cha. Both of the, father and son, moong cha cha."

"In Hong Kong now, they say m.c.c.," said Auntie Peggy, who was up on the latest.

"M.c.c." "M.c.c." The aunties tried the new Hong Kong slang. "Moong cha cha" means "spacy," spaced out and having to grope like a blindman.

Meanwhile, at Taña's table, Aunt Dolly, who was sophisticated, was saying, "What's your name, honey? Tan-ah. What a pretty name. Russian? Do you play, Tan-ah? I'll show you how to play. This is a very famous Chinese game. Mah-jongg. Can you say 'mah-jongg'?" Auntie Dolly had been a showgirl in New York, and knew how to endear herself to foreigners. She did introductions. Good. Wittman did not want to announce Taña to the room, and he was not about to tablehop with her like a wedding couple. "That's Madame S. Y. Chin. This is Madame Gordon Fong." Et cetera. "Hello," said Taña. Well, you can't expect her to say, "How do you do, Madame." And if she said "How do you do, Mrs.," the lady would feel demoted. Meet Madame Wadsworth Woo. How do you do, Woo? "Madame" to you. Madame. Shit. Madame Chiang Kai Shek. Madame Sun Yat Sen. Mesdames Charles Jones Soong and T. V. Soong. Madame Nhu. All the cookbook ladies are madames too. And all the restaurant guys are generals. Generalissimo. "Let me show you how to play, honey." Don't trust anybody who calls you "honey," Taña. It's a verbal tic.

"My name is Maydene Lam," said Auntie Maydene. "Call me Maydene, dear."

"How do you do, Maydene."

"I've always liked your name," said Auntie Lily Rose. "Such a pretty stage name. Maydene Lam"

"Isn't it delicious? There are four little girls named after me in the Valley." Clickity Clackity.

"What beautiful hair you have, Tan-ah. She's gorgeous, Wit Man!" yelled Aunt Dolly. "You are so fair. Isn't she fair?!"

"Thank you," said Taña, who hadn't yet learned that compliments need to be denied and returned.

Every auntie had jet-black dyed hair. Why do women as they get older have to have fixed hair? Because of beauty fixed at 1945. These were the glamour girls of World War II. Taking after the Soong sisters and Anna Chennault, who married guys in uniform. Whenever the aunties' pictures appeared in the papers—Chinese or English—they were identified as "the lovely Madame Houston W. P. Fong," "the beauteous Madame Johnny Tom." They were professional beauties. To this day the old fut judges vote for the Miss Chinatown U.S.A. who most reminds them of these ladies. Quite a few of them had been Wongettes—"Ladies and gentlemen, Mr. Eddie Pond proudly welcomes to the Kubla Khan the beautiful Wongettes, Chinese Blondes in a Blue Mood." "Myself, I am a blonde at heart," said Auntie Dolly. Don't you look askance at her, Taña, with your sanpaku eyes, or else I'm getting a divorce.

"Ciao!" "Poong!" "Kong!" Action. "Eight ten thousands!" "Mah-jongg!" Clack! Clack! "Mah-jongg!"

"Wit Man, over here," said Ruby.

"Coming, Mother," said Wittman. He stood behind her to look at her winning hand.

"Talk to See Nigh here," said the mother.

"You enjoying the game, See Nigh?" he said to the lady whom he had never met before.

"Oh, how well behaved," said the See Nigh, the Lady. "So dock-yee. And such good manners. Most boys with beards are bum-how. He doesn't have to call me See Nigh. You call me Auntie, Wit Man."

His mother spoke sotto voce, in Chinese, "Who's the girl?"

"My friend. A good friend," he said in English. One shouldn't speak a foreign language in front of people who don't understand it, especially when talking about them. Don't add to the paranoia level of the universe.

"Serious?"

"Sure."

"How serious?"

"Serious, okay?"

Gary Snyder had gone to Japan to meditate for years, and could not spend five minutes in the same room with his mother. Beat his record.

"So you walk with her," said Auntie Marleese. "Old enough to mix the girls." Go after girls with an eggbeater.

"She's so rude, she's not talking to me," said Mom. "She's hurt my feelings, Wit Man."

"Introduce you gal to you mama, young man," said Auntie Sophie. Clack!

"Hey, Taña," he called over to her table. "Meet my mother, Ruby Ah Sing. Ma, meet my pahng yow, Tan-ah." "Pahng yow" means "friend"; maybe Taña would think it meant "wife."

"Hi." Taña waved. Click.

"You aren't growing up to be a heartbreakin' man, are you, honey boy?" said Aunt Lilah.

"Speak for your own self," said back-talking Wittman. She was a glamour girl still raising hell at seventy-five. She gets you alone for a moment, she'll confide her romance. "Honey, this entre news is on the Q.T., and must not go further than this very room. My beloved is a sai yun. He's fifty-five years old, and so distinguished. All his clothes are Brooks Brothers. My sai yun lover is offering to divorce his wife for me, but I don't want to be married. Monday, Wednesday, and Friday are enough." A "sai yun" is a "western man," which isn't correct; we're westerners, too.

"U.C., state-run public school, does not teach them to present themselves socially," Auntie Jean was explaining. She was an authority on higher education, a son at Harvard, a daughter at Wellesley, where the Soong sister who married Sun Yet Sen went, another son at Princeton, the baby daughter at Sarah Lawrence. "As I said to Mayling Soong, I-vee Leak be A-number-one all-around. They learn how to make money, and they learn to go around in society. Very complete." The cruel thing to say back to her is: "What eating club does Ranceford belong to?" But you don't want to be mean to her. They will graduate, and never come back.

"At U.C., this one learned: grow hair long," Mom agreed. "Grow rat beard. And go out with bok gwai noi." As if dating las gringas wasn't his idea, he had to be taught. "You ought to see them there at Berkeley. Doi doi jek. Yut doi, yow yut doi." Pair after pair (of mixed couples). Jek," an article used with livestock.

"Doi," an article used with poultry. "You meet my Wit Man too late, See Nigh. You missed out on one good-looking boy."

"You still got one matinée idol under the hair, Ruby," said Aunt Marleese. "Cut it for your poor mother, Wit Man. I remember when you were yay high. I used to change his diapers. You were deh, Wit Man. He was so deh." Click click. She gave them an example of deh, her head to one side, a finger to her dimple, coy lady pose. The aunties smiled at him like he was going to act deh any moment for his mother at least, do babytalk, act babyish, and bring out motherly love.

"Cut it off, Wit Man," said his mother. "Cut it off. I'll pay you." Clack!

"Just—. Just—," said Wittman. "Just —." Just lay off me. Cut me some slack. Let me be. And let me live.

All this time at four tables, outspread fingers with red nails and rings of gold and jade pushed and turned the tiles with wheels of bones and plastic, clockwise and counterclockwise. The sound of fortune is clack clack clack. They built little Great Walls, and tore them down. Crash! "You in luck today, Maydene." "Not luck like you, Dolly." "Poong!" "I've got a hot one," said Mom, fanning a tile like she was putting out a match. "Dangerous. Dangerous." She's got a red dragon. "Aiya." "The wind shifts to the west." "Here comes the green dragon." "The white dragon." "A hot one." "Four circles. Kong!" "Ciao!" shouted Wittmans' mother, pouncing on the tile that the See Nigh had discarded. "One, two / three bamboo!" "Mah Jeuk birds all in a row." (Is "mah-jongg" a white word, then, like "chop suey," a white food?) "Your mama, one cutthroat," said Auntie Sophie. "You working hard, Wit Man?"

"I've been fired." Let 'em have it.

"Fired!" His mother screamed. "Fired! Fired!"

"It's okay, Ma. I didn't like the job anyway."

"Four years college." Mom put down her tiles. She shut her eyes, a mother defeated. She's an actress. She's acting. You can't trust actors, feel one thing and act another. She put her hand on her brow. Chewed the scenery. "What are we to do?"

The chorus gals snowed her with more comfort. "He'll get a job again, Ruby." "Nowadays they try out jobs, then settle down." "Wit Man be smart. He'll be rich one of these days."

"He read books when he was three years old. Now look at him. A bum-how."

"Don't you worry. He's one good boy." "He be nice and tall." "He always has beautiful gallo friends." "He'll turn out for the better."

He should shut them up with Rilke: *It would be difficult to persuade me that the story of the Prodigal Son is not the legend of him who did not want to be loved. When he was a child, everybody in the house loved him. He grew up knowing nothing else and came to feel at home in their softness of heart, when he was a child.*

But as a boy he sought to lay aside such habits. He could not have put it into words, but when he wandered about outside all day and did not even want to have the dogs along, it was because they too loved him; because in their glances there was observation and sympathy, expectancy and solicitude; because in their presence one could do nothing without gladdening or giving pain. . . . But then comes the worst. They take him by the hands, they draw him toward the table, and all of them, as many as are present, stretch inquisitively into the lamplight. They have the best of it; they keep in the shadow, while on him alone falls, with the light, all the shame of having a face.

... No, he will go away. For example, while they are all busy setting out on his birthday table those badly conceived gifts meant, once again, to compensate for everything. Go away for ever.

O King of Monkeys, help me in this Land of Women.

"And so-o-o much talent, too-o much talent." "He got upbringing, Ruby; you gave him upbringing he cannot lose." "He got foundation." "You one good mother." "He's clean, too. Most beardies are dirty." Clackety clack clack. "And such good grades. Remember his report cards?" "He was so cute. Do you still have dock-yee knees, honey boy? You have got to tapdance for your Aunt Lilah again."

Mom's best friends were cheering her up, letting her brag out her happy, proud memories. "I remember, three years old, he made five dollars reading. His father bet a bok gwai lawyer that our biby could read anything. They took the biggest book down from the shelf. He read perfect. 'He's been coached on that book,' said the lawyer, and sent his secretary out to buy a brand-new *Wall Street Journal*. Our Wit Man read the editorial. He won five dollars. We let him keep it. Does he eat regular?" she asked Taña.

"Sure. He eats." Clack!

Does a mother, even an artiste mother who led a free youth, and chose her own husband, does such a mother want her son to have a free artistic life? No. Rimbaud wanted his kids to be engineers.

"You need a job?" asked Auntie Mabel. "I got one gig for you, dear. You come to Florida with me, and do my revue."

"You still doing your revue, Auntie May-bo?"

"Yeah, I do revue. You come, eh, Wit Man. We need a fella in the act."

"In Florida, you dance? You sing?"

"No-o-o. I stand-up comedy. My gals dance and sing. I train them. Miss Chinatown 1959, 1962, and 1963—all in my act." She liked breasts and balls jokes. The punchline: "One hung low. Ha ha." Miss Mabel Foo Yee, the Kookie Fortune Cookie. You had to hand it to her, though. Women aren't funny, and she's still cooking. Cook dinnah, Auntie May-bo. She herself had won beauty contests umpteen years ago. And went on to fan-dance, almost top billing with Miss Toyette Mar, the Chinese Sophie Tucker, and Mr. Stanley Toy, the Fred Astaire of Chinatown, Miss Body Wing as Ginger, and Prince Gum Low, and Mr. Kwan Tak Hong, the Chinese Will Rogers, who also danced flamenco. Wittman had seen Auntie May-bo topless at Andy Wong's Skyroom. The first tits he'd ever seen, scared the daylights out of him. A blare of brass and a red spotlight—Aunt Mabel had slinked about the Skyroom, snaking her arms and legs like Greta Garbo and Anna May Wong, legs tangoing out of her slip dress. The light shrank to head-size, and the spot held her face. Chopsticks in her hair. False eyelashes blinked hard, and the light went out. She ran about with incense sticks, writing red script in the dark. Red lights flashed on. The front of her dress broke away. Gong. Gong. Lights out. Gong. Lights on. Auntie Mabel stood with arms and naked tits raised at the ceiling. You looked hard for two seconds, the lights went out. Gong. Lights on—she was kneeling with wrists together, tits at ease, eyelashes downcast. Lights out, climactic band music, The End.

She was saying, "My gals, queen of the prom. Court princess, at least. I teach them. Mothers of junior-high gals say to me, 'Start her on her make-up, May-bo.' I teach them hair and dress. They do not go out in blue jeans or with no gloves." Wittman had met some of these trained gals. They looked like young Aunt Mabels. They wore their hair in beehives with a sausage curl or two that hung down over the shoulder. Today Aunt Mabel had on one of her specially ordered Hong Kong dresses. The mandarin collar was frogged tight, but thee was a diamond-shaped opening that showed her lace underwear and her old cleavage. Her old thigh flirted through a side slit. There was a lot of perfume in the room, My Sin, Chanel No. 5, Arpège, most of it coming from her. To their credit, no girl of Wittman's college generation would be caught dead in Chinese drag.

"Good you get fired from demeaning employment. You get back into show biz, honey. For you, Aunt Carmen has special ten percent," said Aunt Carmen, a theatrical agent. She sometimes charged twenty percent, twice as much as the regular (white) agents. Her clients, Chinese and Japanese types, who'd gotten SAG cards from *Flower Drum Song* and SEG cards from *Duel in the Sun*, and hopeful ever since, were hard to place. The go-between (white) agent had to make his ten percent too. The actors didn't ask how come these double agents weren't getting 5%–5%. She was up from L.A. to touch base with the talent in the Bay Area and Seattle, and the home folks in the Valley. She had a corner on the West Coast talent. (Auntie Goldie Joy of Manhattan handled the East Coast. The two of them had helped book S. I. Hsiung and his all-Caucasian Chinese opera, starring Harpo Marx and Alexander Woollcott, into theaters in San Francisco and London and New York.)

"You a good type, Wit Man," said Auntie Carmen. "Your gal a good type too. You an actress, darling? Lose ten pounds, you be one actress."

"No, I'm not," said Taña. "I'm an assistant claims adjuster." Why won't she tell them she's a painter?

"We need a man in the act, Wit Man," said Auntie Mabel. "You be interested, huh." Because local boys don't wear tights, Wittman had been the boy brought in from out of town to play the prince. "You were a natural, such good ideas. Tan-ah, you should have seen him, wearing his underpants outside his regular pants, like comic-book superheroes, he said. You got personality, Wit Man." There was a song that went, "Walk personality, talk personality." "Come on. Sometimes we play Reno. North Shore Lake Tahoe."

"Auntie Mabel, I like do Shakespeare."

"You snob, Wit Man. You will be hurt and jobless. We have one elegant act. High-class educated gals." Yeah, like Patty (Schoolteacher) White, the stripper in—and out of—cap and gown and eyeglasses. She was showing that you make more money working North Beach than the School District, and you get more appreciation too.

"You join Auntie May-bo's revue," said Mom, "you meet prettier gals," Clack! Putting the girlfriend in her place.

"I know a girl who would like your boy," said the See Nigh, who didn't speak English. "She came from Hong Kong only a month ago, and already has a job. Her sponsor pulls influence, and her papers are legal. She's a very good old-fashioned, traditional girl. Not in this country long enough to be spoiled. She'll make a good wife."

"Listen to See Nigh, Wit Man," said Mother. "A Chinese girl like that doesn't like beards. You be one Beatnik, you scare her away. You be clean-cut All-American Ivy-Leak boy, okay?"

"I've got a daughter I hope she don't marry somebody second-rate," said Auntie Marleese. "Gail is so smart, professors gave her a personal invitation to attend Stanford University, and pay her to go there. You know S.A.T.? Best S.A.T. in California. Ten thousand points. Pre-med. Her teachers tell me that they never taught a more intelligent girl."

"You still not get Gail married yet?" said Auntie Doll. Clack! The showgirls had been young when it was smart to be catty.

"My Betty," said Auntie Lily Rose, "made valedictorian again. *And* she is popular. *And* she is the first Chinese girl president of her parachute club. She never told me she jumps out of airplanes till after her one hundredth jump. She had to tell me, she landed on her face. Still pretty but. Only chipped one tooth. She said, 'I saved the altimeter.' Any of you know of a good boy, help settle her down?"

Wittman ought to say, "Bring me your daughters. I'll talk to them with my hom sup mouth and touch them with my hom sup hands. Hom sup sup." A hom sup is a salty drippy pervert.

"Come on, honey boy," called Auntie Bessie. "Tapdance for us. You the cutest most dock-yee fatcheeks. Tan-ah, did you tell him he's one great soft shoe? Come on, Wit Man, do some soft shoe, huh?" They remember, he had taken classes in Good Manner and Tap Dance at Charlie Low's school. Eddie Pond of the Kubla Khan had also sponsored schools, and given to the community his expertise in engineering, insurance, real estate, and law. The showmen completed to be most socially responsible.

"No, thanks, Auntie Bessie."

Auntie Bessie sang, "'I won't dance. Don't ask me. I won't dance. Don't ask me. I won't dance, monsieur, with yo-o-ou.' No even for your favorite aunt, honey boy?"

"Hey, Auntie Bessie, do you still say Yow!?" She had played Laurie in the Chinese Optimist Club production of *Oklahoma*. And sang and danced in all the best Big City clubs—Eddie Pond's Kubla Khan, Charlie Low's Forbidden City, Fong Wan the Herbalist's, Andy Wong's Chinese Skyroom. Benny Goodman and Duke Ellington had swung in those clubs too. "'Okla—, "kla—, Okla—,'" sang Wittman to start her off.

"'And when we sa-a-ay Yow!" Auntie Bessie was on her feet. "'Yow! A yip I yo I yay! we're only sayin' you're doin' fine, Oklaho-ma, okay.'" She had worn a white lace Laurie dress with a half-dozen petticoats, and wigged out her hair with black ringlets. She held her hand over her heart, and sang some more,

> *"Don't sigh and gaze at me.*
> *Your sighs are so like mine.*
> *Your eyes mustn't glow like mine.*
> *People will say we're in love.*
> *Don't throw bo-kays at me.*
> *Don't please my folks too much.*
> *Don't laugh at my jokes too much."*

"'Who laughs at *yer* jokes?'" said Wittman as Curly.
"'People will say we're in love.'" He had fallen in love with her himself. She'd kept her stage make-up on for the cast party. He had stood beside her at the community sing around the piano, and saw her powdery wrinkles. Off stage, she sang and smoked at once. "Don't daa de dada daah? Line? Line?"

Taña sang her the line in the sweetest voice, "'Don't dance all night with me.'"

"Oh, Tan-ah can sing." said the aunties. "Good, help out."

Taña and Bessie sang together.

> *"Till the stars fade from above.*
> *They'll see it's all right with me."*

And all the showgirls chimed in, "'People will say we're in love.'"

"Good, Bessie!" "Ho, la!" "Bessie just as good as ever." "Good, Tan-ah!" "Wit Man, you never said she's show business."

"She's not. She's an assistant claims adjuster."

"Thank you, Tan-ah," said Aunt Bessie.

"Thank *you*, Auntie Bessie," said Taña. "You have a beautiful voice."

"Tan-ah, I tell you," said Aunt Dolly, "that voice of Bessie's bought an airplane for World War II."

"And the rest of us, too," said Aunt Sophie, "we were stars. We put on so many shows, and so many people paid to watch us dance and sing, we raised enough money to buy an airplane."

"We toured nationwide," said Aunt Lily Rose. "We had the most active chapter of the Association of Vaudeville Artists."

"Remember? Remember we were dancers in the Dance of the nations," said Auntie Mable. "We each did a solo to honor our brave allies. I was Miss France."

"I was Miss Great Britain," said Ruby Long Legs.

"I was Miss Belgium," said Aunt Sondra.

"I was Miss Russia," said Aunt Lilah.

"I was Miss China," said Aunt Bessie.

"I was Miss Finlandia," said Aunt Maydene.

"I was Miss U.S.A.," said Aunt Sadie, who had been with another Jadine, Jadine Wong and her Wongettes, those dancing Chinese cuties.

"Money was not all that we raised," said Aunt Lilah, winking at Wittman. She had danced with petite Noel Toy and the Toyettes.

"We had a painting party," said Aunt Carmen, "and painted our airplane—a Chinese Flag and an American Flag—red, white, and blue."

"We painted across our airplane in Chinese and English: California Society to Rescue China," said Auntie Marleese, swooping her hand like a rainbow. "And we did, too—rescued China and won World War II."

"Auntie Bessie's brother flew it to China and became a Flying Tiger," said Auntie Jean. "And is now a pilot for China Airlines."

"Hungry, Ma," said Wittman. "What's there to eat?"

"Go eat," said Mother. "So help yourself. Sow mahng mahng." "Mahng mahng" is the sound of being skinny. "Fai dut dut" and "fai doot doot" are the sounds of being fat. "Eat. Eat. Don't wait for us."

"Wittman grabbed Taña's hand, and beat it to the kitchen.

There were cartons and covered dishes on every surface, more warming in the oven, and more cooling in the refrigerator. The cartons came from the restaurants which some aunties owned and some hosted, queens of nightlife. When you're out on the town, your rep for setting it on fire depends on them treating you and your gal right. Also, when an actor loses his will to audition, they give him a meal on the house. The food in cartons was courtesy of the chefs, letting themselves go, back-home cooking that they don't do for the customers.

"You must be very hungry," said Taña, watching Wittman load his plate. "It was getting really interesting in there. I want to tell them about *my* airplane."

"World War II was where I came in. I've heard their war stories so many times. How Mom and the aunties used their beauty to get this country to go to war, to rescue ladies-in-distress, who looked, for example, like themselves. The next thing, they'll tell about their parades that stretched from one end of the country to the other and stopped the U.S. selling scrap iron to Japan. And Auntie Doll will do her speech about buying war bonds instead of opium. Taña, you'll never meet people who love working unless they're in show business. They used to have work that they loved. Now they're housewives who have nothing better to do than sit around all day playing mah-jongg until they die. It's tragic."

Taña was looking at him out of sanpaku eyes. He'd been aware all along that she was gwutting his family with that scrutiny from another world. Judy Garland had sanpaku eyes, too much eyewhite under the irises, and John Lennon does too. Elvis and Brando act like their eyes are sanpaku by looking out from lowered heads. Over her chow mein, Taña was feyly giving him lots of eyewhite. If she says "dragon ladies," definitely divorce.

"What's so tragic about mah-jongg?" she asked. "It keeps them home. They're not out escalating our involvement in Southeast Asia." Taña's E.S.P. almost let her foresee that Auntie May-bo, Miss Australia Down Under, would take her troupe to Vietnam.

"You don't have to be so understanding. The highpoint of a life shouldn't be a war. At the war rallies, they performed their last, then the theater died. I have to make a theater for them without a war."

"They would love to perform again, I know it. Your mother and Lily Rose and Peggy and Aunt Bessie—they're still pretty, and want to show it off. I'm sorry; I'm not going to say 'still pretty' about old people anymore. That's like 'She's pretty—for an old lady.' 'He's hard-working—for a Negro.' Some women *get* pretty in old age. I plan to be that way."

"Did you recognize any of them? You can see them on the late show. Peggy played Anna May Wong's maid, when Anna May Wong wasn't playing the maid herself. Come here. I want you to meet a respectable member of my family. I have a granny. She hates mah-jongg. She's not invited to the front room. Why don't we bring her some food?"

They carried plates and bowls to the back of the house, where he called at a door, "PoPo, tadaima-a-a," Japanese. No little-old-lady voice answered, "Okaerinasai." She had taught him more phrases than that, but when he tried them out on Japanese speakers, they didn't seem to mean anything. She spoke a language of her own, or she was holding on to a language that was once spoken somewhere, or she was more senile than she appeared. Wittman opened the door, but no little old pipe-smoking lady there. They put the dishes on her coffee table, and sat on her settee and her footstool. The room was webbed with lace that she had tatted from thread. The light made shadow webs, everything woofing and wefting in circles and spirals, daisies, snowflakes, the father eyes of white peacocks. Well, if you're going to be a string-saver, you can do better than roll it up into a ball. He opened the windows and started the room buoying and drifting.

GrandMaMa owned a phonograph but mostly Cantonese opera and "Let's Learn English" records. There were pictures of little Wittman in his disguises—sumo wrestler, Injun with fringe, the Invisible Man (which he had worn only once because everybody felt bad for "the poor burned boy"), opera monkey. "Are you supposed to be a monkey?" asked Taña. "Not 'supposed to be.' I *am*," said Wittman. "That's true," laughed Taña. Pictures of aunties shaking hands with F.D.R. and Truman. A girl—Jade Snow Wong?—christening a liberty ship at the Marin Shipyards. The thermos of hot water sat next to tea glasses, which were jelly glasses caked with what looked like dry dirt. "Want some tea?" Wittman offered. "It's supposed to look like that. You're supposed to let the tea residue keep accumulating." Against the day when you can't afford tea leaves? So when you drink water, it Zenly reminds you of tea? "Like a wooden salad bowl," he explained.

"No, thanks anyway," she said, which was all right. He didn't want a girl who would gulp it right down saying, "How interesting. How Zen. Say something Chinese."

They sat quiet. He did not turn on the t.v. to watch some Sunday sport. Taña was probably picturing his grandmother as an old bride—? Miss Havisham—or a spider woman. They lit up smokes. He hadn't smoked in front of Mom, who would've said, "Quit, you. You quit."

"Your grandmother's in show business too." Taña was looking at the memory village on the dresser. It did look like a stage designer's model for a set. There were rows of houses with common walls, like railroad flats of New York, like shotgun apartments of the Southwest, except no doors from home to home. The rows were separated by alleys, which were labeled with street names. Two of the houses had thatch roofs that opened up; ladders led to lofts. The rungs were numbered; the adobe steps with only two-risers were also numbered, one, two. One of the houses had a brick stove; the next-door had two stoves. Toy pigs, numbered, lived inside the houses and walked in the alleys. The rich man's house had a larger courtyard and more wings than the others, plus flowered tiles, and parades or boatloads of people and animals atop the horn-curved eaves. In the plaza was a well, and beside the well (where PoPo had fetched water) was the temple (where the men whistled at her and made remarks, and she dropped and broke her water jar, and the men laughed). Away from the houses was the largest building, the music building for the storage and playing of drums and horns. There were numbers on the lanes and paths out to the fields. It was autumn; the fields were shades of gold. One of the fields was edged with thirty-three lichee trees. "Twenty of those trees belonged to my great-great-uncle," said Wittman, "and three of them belonged to my great-grandfather. He didn't plant them or ever see them. He sent the money to grow them; some autumns his family thought of him, and mailed him dried lichee. Near harvest time, the boys, my cousins far removed, stayed awake nights guarding the trees with a loaded gun." A bridge went over a stream. Above the rice fields was a pumpkin patch and a graveyard. "People from this village don't like Hallowe'en or pumpkin pie. They've eaten too much of it. Pumpkins were the only crop that hardly ever failed. Like your Irish potatoes. People's skin turned orange from eating nothing but pumpkins. Slanty-eyed jack-o'-lanterns. I used to run Crackerjack cars on the paths, and boats on the rivers. Should the I.N.S.—Immigration—raid this room, looking for illegals, they can take this model as evidence, and deport our asses. Everybody who claimed to have come from here studied this model, and described it to Immigration. It is not a model of anything, do you understand? It's a memory village." He slid the model onto his open hand and held it like a birthday cake. "This is it. My land. I am a genie who's escaped from the bottle city of Kandor. I have told you immigration secrets. You can blackmail me. And make me small again, and stopper me up. But if I don't have a friend to tell them to, where am I?"

"Thank you, Wittman. I won't tell."

"Thank you. I'm trusting you with my life, Taña, and my grandma's life." But he was holding out on her the documentation. In PoPo's Gold Mountain trunk was the cheat sheet, a scroll like a roll of toilet paper with questions and answers about the people and the people who live in those houses. Nobody had destroyed the scroll or the memory village. Wonder why.

"This room smells like a grandma's room," said Taña. "I have two grandmas, and their houses smell like this. Tell me when I get the old-lady smell, Wittman. Or do they get it from using a powder that's out of fashion? Orrisroot, lavender."

"Salonpas. The old lady who lives here may not be my grandmother. She showed up one day, and we took her in. I've tested her for her background: I watched for her to hurt herself, and heard what she said for 'Ouch!' She said, 'Bachigataru.' Japanese. At New Year's, she doesn't go to the post office to have her green card renewed, so either she's an illegal alien or she's a regular citizen. The night she showed up she brought news about relatives that we shouldn't have lost touch with. My parents acted like they understood her, 'Yes, the cousins.' 'Of course, the village.' 'Yes, three ferries west of the city, there live cousins and village cousins. Anybody knows that.' They didn't let on that they'd lost their Chinese. You want to know another secret? She may be my father's other wife, and they're putting one over on my mom. Not to get it on sexually, she's old, but so that my mom will take care of her." The strange old lady pulled her apron to her back, a cape, and hung a twenty-four-carat gold medallion to her front, a breastplate, and belted herself with a twenty-four-carat gold buckle shield. Waving fans of dollar bills, she danced whirlygiggly the way they danced where she came from. They couldn't very well turn her away.

He wandered in back of her shoji screens, opened her closet, walked into her bathroom. No gramdma dead or alive. Her long pipe was gone; her shoes were nowhere to be found. In the medicine cabinet was his grandfather's safety razor. He wet his moustache and beard, soaped up, and shaved his face clean. "That ought to freak my mother out," he said. "How do I look?"

"You look better," said Taña. So why is she looking at herself in the mirror instead? She ought to be touching and kissing his nude face. *In any case I felt a certain shyness ... such as one feels before a mirror in front of which someone is standing.*

"My mother hasn't seen my face for a while. I'm going to give her a break. She's my mother, after all, and has a right to see her son's face."

"Wittman, answer me something," said Taña. "Honestly. Promise?"

"Yes. What?"

"What does 'pahng yow' mean? You called me that to your mother."

Uh-oh, thought Wittman.

"It doesn't mean 'wife,' does it?"

"No, it means 'friend.' Let's go. I'm ready to smoothface my mother."

Holding hands with his wife and friend, he led her back to the mah-jongg games. He did not let go of her hand.

"Ma, what do you think?" he asked, poking his clean-shaven face in front of her mah-jongg tiles.

"What do I think about what?" said Ruby. "You eat enough, Wit Man? You looking skinny."

He straightened up, tucking is wife's hand under his arm. "Ma, where's PoPo?"

"Out."

"Whereabouts?"

"To the Joang Wah to see a movie."

"I'll go pick her up, give her a car ride back." Leave home, come back visit, give the old folks a ride.

"No need. She'll get a car ride."

"I'll pick her up anyway."

"She may not be there. She does errands."

"She's not in an old-age home, is she, Ma? You didn't dump her? She's not dead?" Said in front of the aunties, who were all ears.

"She's alive. Strike you dead for saying such a thing."

"She isn't really at the movies. Where is she?"

"Wit Man, I have taken good care of her for twenty years." Arranging her tiles. Gin.

"Ruby took in a poor stranger lady, and gave her food and a home," said Aunt Lilah.

"The money you spent on her," said Aunt Jadine, "you sacrificed your own pleasures." Her commadres were helping Mom out giving her back-up. Certain aunties who were present needed to loudly let everyone know that they were against bringing a grandma over from China to be a charwoman. They hadn't talked *their* old lady into signing her Hong Kong building over to them, then selling it to pay for her expenses in America.

"And I taught her a skill," said Ma. "She can run wardrobe anywhere." Grandma had earned her keep, mending costumes, ironing, sleeping in dressing rooms as dark-night security watchwoman.

"Oh, you're too kind, Ruby." "Ruby has a big heart. Big-hearted Ruby—what they call you behind your back."

"Okay, Ma," said Wittman. "Where is she?"

"Your father has her."

"He took her camping?"

"He has to take care of her too. He has to take responsibility. She's from his side."

He walked to the door, pulling his lady with him. "I'm going to find her."

"I took responsibility long enough," shouted Ruby. "You find her, you the one responsible. You never took too much responsibility before. What for you care about the old lady all of a sudden?"

"I want to announce something to her. We gotta go. Bye, everybody."

"Tan-ah, go so soon?" "Say, Wit Man." "Don't go already." "You going?" "Stay eat with us." "Kiss auntie goodbye." "What you announcing?" "Where you going so fast, young man?"

"Going on our honeymoon. Bye."

Out to the porch and gate and street, chasing the bride and groom, came the voices and the clacking. "Your what?" "Eeek!" "What did he say?" "They married." "Who?" "Congratulations, honey boy." "Happy long life, Tan-ah!"

"Married!" shouted Wittman. "Goodbye, Mrs. Ah Sing!" called Taña. "Thank you for the delicious luncheon."

Taña got in on the driver's side, her turn at the wheel. "Steve McQueen taught me how to drive," she said, and peeled away from the curb. She took her passenger's cigarette, and sucked hard on it. "Let's go to Grandma's rescue." She sped out of town. Her pointy nose cut into the wind, born for a convertible. He directed her to the American River. At the turn-off, she did a double-clutch downshift from the highway to the frontage road. Her hair was blowing back, a giant brush of a mane painting the hills its own color.

The Bear and the Colt

By N. Scott Momaday

He was a young man, and he rode out on the buckskin colt to the north and west, leading the hunting horse, across the river and beyond the white cliffs and the plain, beyond the hills and the mesas, the canyons and the caves. And once, where the horses could not go because the face of the rock was almost vertical and unbroken and the ancient handholds were worn away to shadows in the centuries of wind and rain, he climbed among the walls and pinnacles of rock, adhering like a vine to the face of the rock, pressing with no force at all his whole mind and weight upon the sheer ascent, running the roots of his weight into invisible hollows and cracks, and he heard the whistle and moan of the wind among the crags, like ancient voices, and saw the horses far below in the sunlit gorge. And there were the caves. He came suddenly upon a narrow ledge and stood before the mouth of a cave. It was sealed with silver webs, and he brushed them away. He bent to enter and knelt down on the floor. It was dark and cool and close inside, and smelled of damp earth and dead and ancient fires, as if centuries ago the air had entered and stood still behind the web. The dead embers and ashes lay still in a mound upon the floor, and the floor was deep and packed with clay and glazed with the blood of animals. The chiseled dome was low and encrusted with smoke, and the one round wall was a perfect radius of rock and plaster. Here and there were earthen bowls, one very large, chipped and broken only at the mouth, deep and fired within. It was beautiful and thin-shelled and fragile-looking, but he struck the nails of his hand against it, and it rang like metal. There was a back metate[1] by the door, the coarse, igneous[2] grain of the shallow bowl forever bleached with meal, and in the ashes of the fire were several ears and cobs of corn, each no bigger than his thumb, charred and brittle, but whole and hard as well. And there among the things of the dead he listened in the stillness all around and heard only the lowing of the wind . . . and then the plummet and rush of a great swooping bird—out of the corner of his eye he saw the awful shadow which hurtled across the light—and the clatter of wings on the cliff, and the small, thin cry of a rodent. And in the same instant the huge wings heaved with calm, gathering up the dead weight, and rose away.

All afternoon he rode on toward the summit of the blue mountain, and at last he was high among the falls and the steep timbered slopes. The sun fell behind

---

[1]METATE: stone used for grinding corn and other grains.
[2]IGNEOUS: formed from previously molten rock.

the land above him and the dusk grew up among the trees, and still he went on in the dying light, climbing up to the top of the land. And all afternoon he had seen the tracks of wild animals and heard the motion of the dead leaves and the breaking of branches on either side. Twice he had seen deer, motionless, watching, standing away in easy range, blended with light and shadow, fading away into the leaves and the land. He let them be, but remembered where they were and how they stood, reckoning well and instinctively their notion of fear and flight, their age and weight.

    He had seen the tracks of wolves and mountain lions and the deep prints of a half-grown bear, and in the last light he drew up in a small clearing and made his camp. It was a good place, and he was lucky to have come upon it while he still could see. A dead tree had fallen upon a bed of rock; it was clear of the damp earth and the leaves, and the wood made an almost smokeless fire. The timber all around was thick, and it held the light and the sound of the fire within the clearing. He tethered the horses there in the open, as close to the fire as he could, and opened the blanket roll and ate. He slept setting against the saddle, and kept the fire going and the rifle cocked across his waist.

    He awoke startled to the stiffening of the horses. They stood quivering and taut with their heads high and turned around upon the dark and nearest wall of trees. He could see the whites of their eyes and the ears laid back upon the bristling manes and the almost imperceptible shiver and bunch of their haunches to the spine. And at the same time he saw the dark shape sauntering among the trees, and then the others, sitting all around, motionless, the short pointed ears and the soft shining eyes, almost kindly and discreet, the gaze of the gray heads bidding only welcome and wild goodwill. And he was young and it was the first time he had come among them and he brought the rifle up and made no sound. He swung the sights slowly around from one to another of the still shadowy shapes, but they made no sign except to cock their heads a notch, sitting still and away in the darkness like a litter of pups, full of shyness and wonder and delight. He was hard on the track of the bear; it was somewhere close by in the night, and he knew of him, had been ahead of him for hours in the afternoon and evening, holding the same methodical pace, unhurried, certain of where it was and where he was and of every step of the way between, keeping always and barely out of sight, almost out of hearing. And it was there now, off in the blackness, standing still and invisible, waiting. And he did not want to break the stillness of the night, for it was holy and profound; it was rest and restoration, the hunter's offering of death and the sad watch of the hunted, waiting somewhere away in the cold darkness and breathing easily of its life, brooding around at last to forgiveness and consent; the silence was essential to them both, and it lay out like a bond between them, ancient and inviolable. He could neither take nor give any advantage of cowardice where no cowardice was, and he laid the rifle down. He spoke low to the horses and soothed them. He drew fresh wood upon the fire and the gray shapes crept away to the edge of the light, and in the morning they were gone.

It was gray before the dawn and there was a thin frost on the leaves, and he saddled up and started out again, slowly, after the track and into the wind. At sunrise he came upon the ridge of the mountain. For hours he followed the ridge, and he could see for miles across the land. It was late in the autumn and clear, and the great shining slopes, green and blue, rose out of the shadows on either side, and the sunlit groves of aspen shone bright with clusters of yellow leaves and thin white lines of bark, and far below in the deep fonds of land he could see the tops of the black pines swaying. At midmorning he was low in the saddle of the ridge, and he came upon a huge outcrop of rock, and the track was lost. An ancient watercourse fell away like a flight of stairs to the left, the falls broad and shallow at first, but ever more narrow and deep farther down. He tied the horses and started down the rock on foot, using the rifle to balance himself. He went slowly, quietly down until he came to a deep open funnel in the rock. The ground on either side sloped sharply down to a broad ravine and the edge of the timber beyond, and he saw the scored earth where the bear had left the rock and gone sliding down, and the swatch in the brush of the ravine. He thought of going the same way; it would be quick and easy, and he was close to the kill, closing in and growing restless. But he must make no sound of hurry. The walls of the funnel were deep and smooth, and they converged at the bank of the ravine some twenty feet below, and the ravine was filled with sweet clover and paintbrush[3] and sage. He held the rifle out as far as he could reach and let it go; it fell upon a stand of tall, sweet clover with scarcely any sound, and the dull stock shone and the long barrel glinted among the curving green and yellow stalks. He let himself down into the funnel, little by little, supported only by the tension of his strength against the walls. The going was hard and slow, and near the end his arms and legs began to shake, but he was young and strong, and he dropped from the point of the rock to the sand below and took up the rifle and went on, not hurrying but going only as fast as the bear had gone, going even in the bear's tracks, across the ravine and up the embankment and through the trees, unwary now, sensible only of closing in, going on and looking down at the tracks.

And when at last he looked up, the timber stood around a pool of light, and the bear was standing still and small at the far side of the brake, careless, unheeding. He brought the rifle up, and the bear raised and turned its head and made no sign of fear. It was small and black in the deep shade and dappled with light, its body turned three-quarters away and sanding perfectly still, and the flat head and the small, black eyes that were fixed upon him hung around upon the shoul-

---

[3]PAINTBRUSH: plant with colorful, tufted flowers.

der and under the hump of the spine. The bear was young and heavy with tallow, and the underside of the body and the backs of its short, thick legs were tufted with winter hair, longer and lighter than the rest, and dull as dust. His hand tightened on the sock and the rifle bucked and the sharp report rang upon the walls and carried out upon the slopes, and he heard the sudden scattering of birds overhead and saw the darting shadows all around. The bullet slammed into the flesh and jarred the whole back body once, but the head remained motionless and the eyes level upon him. Then, for one instant only, there was a sad and meaningless haste. The bear turned away and lumbered, though not with fear, not with any hurt, but haste, slightly reflexive, a single step, or two, or three, and it was overcome. It shuddered and looked around again and fell.

The hunt was over, and only then could he hurry; it was over and well done. The wound was small and clean, behind the foreleg and low on the body, where the fur and flesh were thin, and there was no blood at the mouth. He took out his pouch of pollen and made yellow streaks above the bear's eyes. It was almost noon, and he hurried. He disemboweled the bear and laid the flesh open with splints so that the blood should not run into the fur and stain the hide. He ate quickly of the bear's liver,[4] taking it with him, thinking what he must do, remembering now his descent upon the rock and the whole lay of the land, all the angles of his vision from the ridge. He went quickly, a quarter of a mile or more down the ravine, until he came to a place where the horses could keep their footing on the near side of the ridge. The blood of the bear was on him, and the bear's liver was warm and wet in his hand. He came upon the ridge, and the colt grew wild in its eyes and blew, pulled away, and its hoofs clattered on the rock and the skin crawled at the roots of its mane. He approached it slowly, talking to it, and took hold of the reins. The hunting horse watched, full of age and indifference, switching its tail. There was no time to lose. He held hard to the reins, turning down the bit in the colt's mouth, and his voice rose a little and was edged. Slowly he brought the bear's flesh up to the flaring nostrils of the colt and smeared the muzzle with it.

And he rode the colt back down the mountain, leading the hunting horse with the bear on its back, and like the old hunting horse and the young black bear, he and the colt had come of age and were hunters, too. He made camp that night far down in the peneplain[5] and saw the stars and heard the coyotes away by the river. And in the early morning he rode into the town. He was a man then, smeared with the blood of a bear. He shouted, and the men came out to meet him. They came with rifles, and he gave them strips of the bear's flesh, which they wrapped around the barrels of their guns. And soon the women came with switches, and they spoke to the bear and laid the switches on its hide. The men and women were jubilant and all around, and he rode stone-faced in their midst, looking straight ahead.

---

[4]ATE . . . LIVER: that is, to acquire the animal's strength.
[5]PENEPLAIN: nearly flat land surface in an advanced stage of erosion.

APPENDIX B

Answer Key

Answer Key for the Self-Test

Lesson 1—First Sight: An Introduction to Literature

Matching exercises:

1. h (Study Guide)
2. d (Study Guide)
3. a (Study Guide)
4. g (Study Guide)
5. e (Study Guide)

Multiple choice:

1. c (Study Guide)
2. a (Study Guide)
3. d (Study Guide)
4. a (Study Guide)
5. d (Study Guide)

Short essay sample answers:

1. "Literary Visions" and "First Sight" play upon the act of seeing. I expect to see in several ways: seeing the videos, seeing the texts themselves, and seeing my way to understanding what I read. "Visions," a plural form, not only suggests that there's more than one way of "seeing" a work but that "seeing"

All page references are to *Literature: An Introduction to Reading and Writing*. Sixth Edition, by Roberts and Jacobs it may take some imagination. The word also conjures up the idea of writer as visionary, inspired, someone ahead of the times. The "visions" I expect to see are the texts discussed in the course and their visual presentations. That the first lesson is called "First Sight" makes good sense; it gives me a glimpse of what is coming—a first look at literature as a whole.

2. When I see the news on television, it's often oversimplified, cut to fit the allotted time, and soon over. Ask me what the lead stories were, and I might remember, but then I might not. Ask me a day later and it's probably going to be lost. I have a difficult time retrieving it. The newspaper can be very different. The stories are presented in greater detail, and I can go back to them, study them if I wish. If I need to track down a lead story two days later, I can usually dig out the paper or if necessary find it in the public library. There's a permanent record that can be retrieved, reexmined, reevaluated, questioned, judged. Print is permanent; electronic media is, for the most part, temporary unless someone has videotaped the program.

3. The "Summary" contains a quotation from Solzhenitsyn's Nobel Prize speech in which he emphasizes the importance of literature. As an allusion, the quotation serves several purposes. It supports the lesson's idea that literature affects our lives and that it speaks beyond the boundaries of a particular time, place, or culture. The content of the quotation fits the lesson, and perhaps the speaker is equally important. Solzhenitsyn is not your standard English teacher but a winner of the Nobel Prize for Literature. He's even alive. And he's not a pampered literary pet but a Russian novelist who struggled to write, to be published, and to be read. The person behind the words lends the quotation an authenticity that's impressive.

Lesson 2—Ways of Seeing: Responding to Literature

Matching exercises:

1. i (Study Guide)
2. e (Study Guide)
3. b (Study Guide)
4. f (pp. 38–41; Study Guide)
5. a (Study Guide)
6. h (Study Guide)
7. j (Study Guide)
8. d (Study Guide)
9. g (Study Guide)
10. c (Study Guide)

Multiple choice:

1. c (Study Guide)
2. d (Study Guide)
3. b (Study Guide)
4. d (Study Guide)
5. d (Study Guide)

Short essay sample answers:

1. For popular shows, I looked at the weekly listing of Nielsen ratings and discovered that popular only means most watched. "60 Minutes," for instance, is listed even though it raises complex issues. To make the distinction work with television, I have to take the idea of complexity and apply it to individual shows. Using that standard, situation comedies, game shows, and soap operas obviously fall into the category of popular television. But a documentary series or a good made-for-television film crosses the line into serious television, for both deal with complex issues and do not understate their complexity. This last idea makes me rethink "60 Minutes," which now I would put into the popular category. It raises issues, but sometimes it treats them superficially. Serious shows should not only raise complex issues, but also explore them in some depth.

2. The word *literacy* raises images of afternoon tea, bearded poets, English accents, and little old ladies in white gloves. What comes to mind is my idea of a literary salon. Everybody there is genteel, well read (or able to fake it), and white. That image falls apart when I see Earnest Gaines, Sandra Cisneros, David Hwang. The writers in the video are real, young and old, of varied ethnic backgrounds, and intense. Hardly the stiff upper lip, ice water in the veins type, they care about what they do and care intensely. They want what they write to make a difference, to have an impact. And that's the idea the discussion conveys about literature—that it's something alive, vital, that it makes a difference in how we feel, think, and see things. That idea is far removed from the droning, bloodless voices in my hypothetical literary salon.

3. The novels of John LeCarre strike me as good examples of works that straddle the line between popular and serious fiction. They are popular in that they fit the general category of the spy novel—action packed, a plot full of twists and turns, and a good look at modern day espionage. Yet what raises them above the ordinary or generic spy story are those same characteristics that make a novel serious literature: *conflict, characterization, atmosphere,* and perhaps most of all, *style*. These are well written, carefully crafted books. *The Little Drummer Girl*, for instance, conveys what it feels like to be a hostage and explores the true terror of terrorism. The plot is complex, but that is true of most spy novels; what makes this one different is that the characters, conflicts, and atmosphere are also complex. Whether anyone will still be reading LeCarre fifty years from now is another question. For the present, he's a writer who goes far beyond the limits of his genre and produces thought-provoking fiction that bears rereading.

Lesson 3—A Personal View: The Art of the Essay

Matching exercises:

1. f (Study Guide)
2. k (Study Guide)
3. d (pp. 3–4; Study Guide)

Multiple choice:

1. a (Study Guide)
2. d (Study Guide)
3. b (Study Guide)

Matching exercises:

4. b (Study Guide)
5. j (Study Guide)
6. h (Study Guide)
7. a (Study Guide)
8. m (Study Guide)
9. e (Study Guide)
10. i (p. 5)

Multiple choice:

4. c (Study Guide)
5. a (Study Guide)

Short essay sample answers:

1. "A Love That Transcends Sadness" is the title of Morris's essay, and it works on several levels. First of all, it invites the reader who responds with an automatic but almost unconscious, "What is it?" Once into the essay, the reader realizes that Morris's subject is cemeteries but meets the subject positively, for the title has already set up a positive expectation. After all, what could be negative about a love that transcends sadness? And finally, when the reader has finished the essay, the title helps steer the way to a thesis. If the title is combined with the subject, Morris's information about the subject, his tone, and his persona, it's possible to state the thesis very simply: A proper cemetery expresses a "love that transcends sadness."

2. The basic structure is chronological, with Morris starting at a point "not too long ago," shifting back to his early childhood then forward to high school, then moving forward again to some indefinite time that is less recent, and ending up with "now." Plotting that structure rules out any neat straight arrow or even a circle or a series of building blocks. Those are structures easily associated with the formal essay. Instead, Morris's structure resembles a spiral. The line representing the essay's structure would start at NT (for "not too long ago"), drop down to early childhood and then start spiralling back to the present, ending at point N (for "now"), which would be above the starting NT. The result is a loose, seemingly rambling organization more characteristic of the informal essay.

3. Rereading the essay and hunting for allusions, I found a number of place names that seemed to serve more as necessary details than as allusions, so I had to firm up my definition of the term. An *allusion*, as I am defining it, is a reference that has meaning in its own right, in that someone who did not know the allusion would still be able to understand the point of the sentence, but the allusion goes beyond that meaning to bring in additional ones. By that standard, some of the place names are allusions, some are not. I am ruling out *Southern, America,* and *England* because they seem more general locators, facts, rather than allusions. I'm also ruling out *Wainscott, Long Island* because it is so specific that few readers would have any associations with it. That leaves me with *Mississippi, New York,* and *Oxford*, all of which evoke emotional responses.

So place names is one category, a geographical one. In addition, Morris uses one allusion drawn from the world of business, two from American history, and three from literature. The geographical allusions (New York, Oxford, and Mississippi) not only nail down the locations of his examples but add to his points. Mississippi is so mysterious to me that I'm even willing to admit the people there shop for cemeteries the way they shop for Christmas trees. To the general reader, I expect Mississippi raises images of the Old South—slavery, plantations, and a genteel tradition. But Morris's Oxford is not the Oxford of Mississippi but of England, an ancient seat of study and scholarship that makes the inscription he found there all the more amusing. As for New York, many people find it as overwhelming and faceless as Morris found its cemeteries, a place where people are numbers, not humans.

Morris's historical allusions (Korean War, Civil War) anchor the times he speaks of, and the mention of the Korean War helps establish his age. He uses the Civil War cemetery to make a point about lives being cut short, wasted, which then leads naturally into the grave of Fairy Jumper.

As for the literary allusions, they place Morris's ideas in a long tradition of literary wisdom, from the humorously profound (Faulkner) to the seriously profound (Wilder), with a stop-off at Thomas Gray's churchyard to build in a bit of poignancy as well. Morris's allusions fit. Some help create a sense of real detail; others invoke atmosphere and contribute to his tone, and a few provide genuine humor. The first allusion in the essay is a humorous one that compares selecting a burial plot to prizing "location," the first rule of real estate.

Lesson 4—Reflected Worlds: The Elements of Short Fiction

Matching exercises:

1. j (Study Guide)
2. e (Study Guide)
3. l (Study Guide)
4. f (Study Guide)
5. a (pp. 363–366; Study Guide)
6. d (Study Guide)
7. b (Study Guide)
8. c (Study Guide)
9. i (pp/ 363–366; Study Guide)
10. g (Study Guide)

Multiple choice:

1. b (pp. 365–367; Study Guide)
2. b (pp. 357–359)
3. d (pp. 354–359, 363–366; Study Guide)
4. c (Study Guide)

Short essay sample answers:

1. The most striking difference between the three girls and the A & P's regular patrons is that the girls are wearing bathing suits and walking barefoot in the store—something the regulars find shocking. In addition, the girls are not really shopping. They're just picking up one item—and an exotic one at that. Their dress (or undress) implies that perhaps they do not care what the others think of them or that the idea of "proper dress" applies to other people. The girls also spend time on the beach, unlike the A & P regulars who rarely have the leisure time or inclination to go there. These details indicate that the girls are from a different economic background than the locals.

2. At the beginning of the story, Jackie is terrified of his feelings toward his sister and grandmother because he thinks what he feels is "sinful." While his sister's taunts intensify his feelings, his catechism teacher simply reinforces his guilt by horrifying him about the consequences of sin. All this changes, however, when Jackie confesses to the priest. The priest finds Jackie's feelings quite normal and sympathizes with Jackie's view of Nora (the priest has seen her strike Jackie). Relieved of his "sins," forgiven, and having done penance (though a mild one), Jackie is freed of guilt and heads toward home a happy boy, not even bothered by his sister's comments. He has discovered that his "sins" were not so dreadful after all.

Lesson 5—The Story's Blueprint: Plot and Structure in Short Fiction

Matching exercises:
1. f (Study Guide)
2. i (Study Guide)
3. l (p. 276)
4. d (video)
5. a (video)
6. e (pp. 275–276)
7. g (p. 276; Study Guide)
8. h (pp. 313–315; Study Guide)
9. j (Study Guide)
10. b (Study Guide)

Multiple choice:
1. b (video)
2. d (pp. 275–276; Study Guide)
3. a (pp. 276–278; Study Guide)
4. b-e-f-a (pp. 275–276; Study Guide)

Short essay sample answers:
1. While some of the incidents that might indicate Phoenix's mind is slipping can be put down to her failing eyesight and fatigue, two stand out and suggest that that she is getting senile. The first occurs after she has been walking for quite sometime and has crossed the log over the creek. Resting after this "trial," she thinks she sees a boy offering her a slice of cake. When she reaches for it, nothing is there. The second takes place in the clinic, after she announces, "Here I be." She appears to go into a trance and doesn't hear or see anything around her. When she comes out of it, she admits "my memory had left me." Her memory had indeed failed her, and at the end of the story the reader is left doubting her claim, "I not going to forget him again."

2. The story's exposition, paragraphs 1–11, spells out the difference in values. To be Indian means "peace." It means to be at one with nature, to live in calmness, to share, to sing, to create beautiful things. To be white means to be "always dissatisfied." It means to rush, to worry, to be anxious about "one's place in the thing they call Society," to live indoors, to listen to the singing of others, "to do everything you don't want to, never doing anything you want to." The difference is summed up by one's attitude toward legend, the "old woman under the ice." Whites believe in fact, Indians in mystery.

Lesson 6—Telling Their Tales: Character in Short Fiction

Matching exercises:

1. c (p. 127; Study Guide)
2. k (pp. 586–590; Study Guide)
3. j (Study Guide)
4. d (Study Guide)
5. a (Study Guide)

Multiple-choice:

1. a (video)
2. d (pp. 177–178)
3. d (pp. 127–129)
4. c (pp. 173–180; Study Guide)
5. c (pp. 173–180)

Matching exercises:

6. f (Study Guide)
7. e (p. 140; Study Guide)
8. l (p. 590)
9. g (pp. 177–178)
10. i (pp. 177–178)

Short essay sample answers:

1. As the story opens, we see Sarty hungry, wearing old, patched, ill-fitting clothes, his hair uncombed, his feet bare. A wagon and two "gaunt" mules are his family's only transportation, and what belongings have survived their "dozen and more movings" are battered and broken. The family's life is hard. They own little, and their only potential for income comes from their labor—their sweat, their mules, and their tools. No amount of hard work seems to help much. Sarty is a hard worker, a trait Faulkner tells us he inherited from his mother, but even so, the family never seems to benefit. The Snopes's life is one of hardship.

2. The setting for "The Lottery" is quite realist—a small farming town where the talk is of "planting and rain, tractors and taxes." The time is late June, and the local people are gathering at the town square where the postmaster is about to conduct the annual lottery. Some of the characters are stock ones: an old man lamenting the loss of traditions, housewives exchanging pleasantries. And the family that "wins" the lottery has plausible reactions, ranging from relief at not being the individual chosen to crying that "it wasn't fair." The setting, the stock characters, and the believable reactions give the story a sense of verisimilitude.

3. Even though we get to know Emily indirectly, her character is rounded. As the story opens, we learn that she "needs help." Her mother's interior monologue shows us why that may be so. Although Emily was a beautiful baby, her early years were not happy. Deserted by her father when she was

Appendix B—397

8 months old, she was left with a neighbor while her mother worked to support them. Later Emily is farmed out to her grandparents, then reunited with her mother. Still needing to work, the mother places Emily, age 2, in a poorly run nursery school and then still later, when Emily is 7, in a convalescent home. The result is that Emily is in conflict with her younger sister, whom she envies, and that Emily feels unloved, particularly by her mother. We see a shy, hesitant, insecure girl whose only release comes when she takes on the part of another, ironically a comedian. We see Emily change, and we understand how complex she is.

Lesson 7—In That Time and Place: Setting and Character in Short Fiction

Matching exercises:

1. g (p. 513)
2. j (p. 200)
3. i (Study Guide)
4. a (video)
5. k (p. 188)
6. d (pp. 511–512)
7. e (p. 513)
8. b (pp. 261–262)

Multiple choice:

1. b (video)
2. c (entire lesson)
3. d (pp. 226–228)
4. c (pp. 224–225)
   d (Study Guide)

Short essay sample answers:

1. Minnie Wright is in the middle of cleaning up in the kitchen—perhaps listening to her canary sing—when her husband grabs the bird cage, rips one of the door hinges, seizes the bird and wrings its neck. She stops cleaning. He probably storms upstairs. Alone, she takes up her sewing basket, finds some silk to wrap the dead bird in, and places it in a box. She tries to quilt but is too upset to sew anything but ragged stitches. Later, after her husband falls asleep, she goes to the barn, finds some rope, ties a noose, goes upstairs, slips the rope over her husband's neck and strangles him. In shock, she returns downstairs, puts the canary's box in her basket, puts away her quilting, and hides the bird cage.

    It is Mrs. Hale who notices the half-full bag of sugar, and she wonders what might have interrupted Minnie. Then Mrs. Hale sees the "shabbiness" of Minnie's clothes, concluding that Wright was "close." A dish towel flung in the middle of her half clean, half dirty kitchen table also catches Mrs. Hale's eye, as does the broken stove and the ragged quilting. Mrs. Peters then finds

the bird-cage, and together they note its wrenched hinge. The body of the bird and manner of its death provide the final clues. Knowing the kind of person Minnie used to be and how her husband stifled her, they solve the murder and judge the murderer.
2. The key word here is "illimitable" for it implies that the power of the Red Death is infinite. The contrast here is effective. The Red Death's power is limitless; Prospero's was limited. Note also that paragraph 2 describes Prospero's attempt to limit the disease by walling himself in with his courtiers. Instead of keeping off the Red Death, however, Prospero has walled him in. Death provides the setting and subject that frame the short story. Poe begins and ends with the disease and its effects. Through these ironies and contrasts Poe suggests that no one is all-powerful, that no one—no matter how rich, how powerful, how imaginative—can escape death.

Lesson 8—The Author's Voice: Tone and Style in Short Fiction

Matching exercises:

1. b (Study Guide)
2. h (Study Guide)
3. d (video)
4. c (pp. 328–329)
5. a (Study Guide)
6. i (Study Guide)
7. k (Study Guide)

Multiple choice:

1. d (video)
2. c (Study Guide)
3. d (entire lesson)
4. b (entire lesson)
5. a (entire lesson)

Lesson 9—Suggested Meanings: Symbolism and Allegory in Short Fiction

Matching exercises:

1. j (p. 385)
2. c (Study Guide)
3. f (p. 376; Study Guide)
4. g (pp. 471–472)
5. d (Study Guide)
6. e (pp. 412–413)

Multiple-choice:

1. c (video)
2. d (Study Guide)
3. c (Study Guide)
4. a (p. 377; Study Guide)
5. c (pp. 376–377; Study Guide)

7. a (Study Guide)
8. l (pp. 376–377; Study Guide)
9. k (p. 479)
10. h (pp. 376–377)

Short essay sample answers:

1. Before his night in the forest, Brown appeared to be a typical Salem Puritan. He had been taught his catechism and was sure in his faith, as indicated by his questioning Faith about whether she doubts him. During the journey, however, it becomes apparent that he has agreed to meet the "stranger," has too much pride to be seen by his fellow villagers, and freely makes his way to the communion place. After witnessing the evil he sees there, he returns a broken man who sees evil and hypocrisy in every face he meets. The journey, therefore, becomes a metaphor for his spiritual passage from faith to doubt.

2. The tinker's appearance and actions suggest he is an archetype for the wanderer. He seems to appear out of nowhere. As Elisa is gardening, she hears the squeak of the wagon and sound of hooves, looks up and sees the tinker. The wagon is the kind used to settle the West, but the time of the story is the 1930s. Then too, the tinker has an odd assortment of animals—a horse teamed up with a burro to pull the wagon and a lean mongrel dog pacing under it. It's almost as though they are witch's familiars. The tinker himself is described as a large, powerful, sexual man with eyes like those of teamsters and sailors—other travelers. He seems to think his unlikely team can pull anything and points that out to Elisa, perhaps as an indication of supernatural powers. And, of course, he is full of guile, managing to talk Elisa into letting him do some work and giving him some of the flowers. When he leaves, Elisa notes he goes in a "bright direction. There's a glowing there." He represents the mythic wanderer who may change lives but moves on.

3. Perhaps Lawrence is suggesting that the only thing more terrifying than being loved is not being loved. Certainly the Mabel we see at the beginning of the story is alienated from what remains of her family. Lawrence notes, for instance, that her brothers, "had talked at her and round her for so many years, that she hardly heard them at all" (page 473). We also know that she refuses to move in with her sister and has nowhere else to go. Her only consolation is tending the grave of her mother. Alone, poor but full of the "curious sullen, animal pride that dominated each member of her family" (page 475), she chooses death over life. Yet the life and passion the doctor awakens within her is almost as terrifying as a life alone, for it represents an elemental, sexual, mysterious, overwhelming force that binds the two of them together.

Lesson 10—The Sum of Its Parts: Theme in Short Fiction

Matching exercises:

1. e (pp. 354–359, 262–265)
2. h (Study Guide)
3. g (Study Guide)
4. j (pp. 140–146, 108–114)
5. a (Study Guide)
6. m (pp. 510–514; Study Guide)
7. i (pp. 586–590)
8. b (Study Guide)
9. k (Study Guide)

Multiple choice:

1. c
2. b (Study Guide)
3. c (Study Guide)
4. b (does not deal with family or heritage)
5. d (Study Guide)

Short essay sample answers:

1. The story is written from the perspective of an adult reliving an experience in his youth, an event that saw him change from the innocence of childhood to the experience of adulthood. In that sense, "Araby" is a story about coming of age. Just as the young boy's romantic expectations of the bazaar are shattered by the reality of it, so too his romantic notions of Mangan's sister are destroyed by the idle chatter and flirting of the young woman tending the booth. He realizes that Mangan's sister is as out of reach as the porcelain vases at the booth. And perhaps he also realizes that Mangan's sister has more in common with the young woman selling porcelain than with his fantasies of her. The result is shame and bitter disappointment.

2. One of the subjects dealt with in "Araby" is the loss of innocence and resulting disillusionment. The first two paragraphs not only describe the story's setting but also relate to its subject by foreshadowing the theme—that coming of age involves being able to separate illusion from reality, and the price one pays is emotional, "anguish and anger." As the story opens, Joyce equates school to jail by pointing out that when classes are over, the "School set the boys free." But their freedom is limited by their immediate neighborhood. The neighborhood is characterized by a "blind" street, an "uninhabited" house, and other buildings with "brown imperturbable faces." The houses are muted, staid, as if "conscious of decent lives within them." On a symbolic level, the main character is not only a prisoner in school but in his own fantasies; his fantasies about Mangan's daughter and the exotic, romantic bazaar "Araby" are his own and, as he comes to know, have no basis in reality. The reality, however, is like his neighborhood—closed-in, dull, constrained. His life is as blind as his street, which is why at the end of the story he is angry and pained.

3. The images associated with Mangan's sister are religious ones that reinforce the story's narrative of a small boy's loss of innocence. To arrive at that interpretation, think of Mangan's sister as a Madonna figure. Light is an icon for holy figures, and Joyce describes her as though she were illuminated by holy light: "her figure defined by light," he says. Later in the story, light again illuminates her in a doorway. The main character tells us "her name was like a summons to all my foolish blood," and "her image accompanied me even in places the most hostile to romance." His love for her is a "chalice," and he tells us that "her name sprang to my lips at moments in strange prayers and praises which I myself did not understand." The language associated with her is the language of religion. Joyce speaks of "confused adoration." Alone in the room where a priest had died, the boy assumes the position of prayer and murmurs "O love! O love! many times." He pledges to bring her a present from the bazaar but finds that he cannot afford one. At the bazaar, he also observes a young woman flirting with two men, and then the call comes that "the light was out." The bazaar was almost deserted and its wares beyond his means; Mangan's sister was no Madonna, and indeed his life had no light. He wakes from his romantic and religiously-tinged fantasies to find a world dulled by the ordinary. The story depicts the disillusionment and pain incurred by the loss of childhood innocence.

Lesson 11—The Sacred Words: The Elements of Poetry

Matching exercises:

1. f (Study Guide)
2. j (Study Guide)
3. m (Study Guide)
4. l (Study Guide)
5. a (Study Guide)
6. i (pp. 631–633; Study Guide)
7. d (Study Guide)
8. g (Study Guide)
9. e (pp. 628–629; Study Guide)
10. b (Study Guide)

Multiple-choice:

1. a (Study Guide)
2. c (Study Guide)
3. b (Study Guide)
4. d (Study Guide)
5. d (pp. 628–631; Study Guide)

Short essay sample answers:

1. The first 13 lines of the poem are in quotation marks, indicating that they are spoken by someone. The words themselves, however, seem more of a jumble of snatches from patriotic songs than a straightforward coherent narrative. "Land of the pilgrims," "dawn's early," "my / country 'tis of," all come from popular patriotic songs, including "The National Anthem." Within this context, the speaker praises "these heroic happy dead" who died in war—"the roaring slaughter." The occasion therefore appears to be a Fourth of July ceremony during which we remember those who died to defend "the voice of liberty." The last line—a comment by the poet—on the surface may indicate the speaker's stage fright, dryness, or emptiness. Deeper than that, the meaningless stringing together of catch phrases, the irony of the "happy dead," and the flat tone of the last line suggest that the poet is satirizing the emptiness of most patriotic celebrations. The last line perhaps describes not so much the speaker's nervousness as his hollowness. He is simply going through the motions.

2. The poem is based on the idea that night is death and light is life, and Thomas uses this idea to urge his father (and by implication all who are nearing the end of their lives) to fight against death. The imagery of light is woven through the poem, starting with the direct reference in line 3, then building in each stanza with "lightning," "bright," "sun," up to stanza 5, where the poet uses both "blinding" and "blaze." The next stanza ends the poem with the word "light." Throughout, light is equated with life (line 3), power (line 5), and honor (line 7). The "men who caught and sang the sun in flight" are those, like the poet, who celebrated life. The climax of the poem occurs in the fifth stanza, in which Thomas implies that those who are blind nonetheless "see with blinding sight"—that blindness need not mean despair. For that reason, Thomas urges his father to "Rage, rage against the dying of the light," which at this point in the poem is both blindness and the fading away of life.

Lesson 12—A Sense of Place: Setting and Character in Poetry

Matching exercises:

1. i (p. 707)
2. b (Study Guide)
3. c (Study Guide)

Multiple choice:

1. d (Study Guide)
2. c (Study Guide)
3. a (p. 686; Study Guide)

Matching exercises:

4. b (Study Guide)
5. f (Study Guide)
6. n (pp. 694–695; Study Guide)
7. l (Study Guide)
8. h (Study Guide)
9. g (pp. 697–698)
10. d (Study Guide)

Multiple choice:

4. c (pp. 686–687; Study Guide)

Short essay sample answers

1. As the title states, the speaker is a "conjurer." Whether the speaker is a man or a woman is not clear; nor is there any direct evidence of the speaker's age. The vocabulary, however, is that of an adult who uses words such as "periodically," "stamen," "nonchalant," and "stalactites." At the same time, the speaker's lack of feelings and general cruelty are those of a very mean child or a psychopath. Having cast a spell over a group of people, two of whom are lovers, the conjurer has miniaturized them and then created an environment for them in a mayonnaise jar, much in the same way a child might keep fireflies or ants. The people have disappointed the conjurer by not being entertaining; quite the contrary, they complain and are ungrateful.

    The conjurer may have some unconscious glimmer of remorse in that he or she dreams the lovers have crawled inside his or her ear "with candles / trying to find my brain in a fog." Perhaps the candles imply the speaker feels some pain because of the lovers, but no matter. The conjurer awakes dimly remembering a "trick." It's as though the speaker has thought, "Oh yes, now I remember what I was going to do with them." What that may be is not spelled out, but it is awful. One imagines a slow, painful death. After all, the conjurer did not rescue the man who was attacked by the ant (lines 11–15).

2. The Nymph appears to be not only a realist but ironic, polite, and slightly flirtatious. The first stanza makes it clear that the Nymph is onto the shepherd, for she begins with a conditional "If the world and love were young / And truth in every shepherd's tongue." Such, she implies, is not so. The next three stanzas spell out what is so: the weather changes for the worse, the nightingale stops singing, flowers fade, winter comes, love does not necessarily last, and nature's adornments fall away, "In folly ripe, in reason rotten." That being the case, the shepherd's enticements cannot persuade her "To come to thee and be thy love." The last stanza lets him down politely, in that she states another conditional: "could youth last . . . Had joys no date nor age no need," then she might agree to "live with thee and be thy love."

3. The literal situation is clear. Standing in front of a window, the speaker is in Dover, England, looking out into the night across the English Channel and off to the French coast, where a light "gleams and is gone." Initially, the scene

seems "calm," "tranquil," but underneath its peacefulness lies "the grating roar / Of pebbles" that "bring / The eternal note of sadness in." This contrast between illusion and reality then becomes the controlling image in the poem.

The same "note of sadness" existed for Sophocles, and it reminds the speaker of the loss of "The Sea of Faith." Now in the mid-19th century, all that was once certain has vanished, leaving "neither joy, nor love, nor light, / Nor certitude, nor peace, nor help for pain." All one has left is the person one loves, as in "Ah, love, let us be true / To one another!" As for the rest, it is "Swept with confused alarms of struggle and flight, / Where ignorant armies clash by night." What seems beautiful is in reality "a darkling plain."

Lesson 13—Tools of the Trade: Words and Images in Poetry

Matching exercises:

1. e (p. 730; Study Guide)
2. j (pp. 653–654; Study Guide)
3. a (pp. 653–655; Study Guide)
4. d (p. 729; Study Guide)
5. f (pp. 654–655)
6. b (p. 727; Study Guide)
7. g (p. 659; Study Guide)
8. i (p. 653–661; Study Guide)
9. k (p. 730; Study Guide)
10. c (p. 658; Study Guide)

Multiple choice:

1. a (Study Guide)
2. d (pp. 726–727)
3. d (pp. 726–733)
4. d (Study Guide)
5. b (pp. 656–658)

Short essay sample answers:

1. The contrast in diction parallels the obvious contrast in "Snow" between the interior and exterior scenes. Inside, MacNeice depicts a room with a huge bay window where the speaker sits comfortably, warmed by a fire, peeling and eating a tangerine, and contemplating a vase of pink roses, the snow outside, and the variety of this world. Outside, the scene is white and cold with snow. The contrast between the white snow and the pink roses—which are separated by transparent glass—reminds the speaker of all things that exist in parallel ("collateral") yet conflicting ("incompatible") relationships. He draws the conclusion that the "World is crazier and more of it than we think, / Incorrigibly plural." He remarks, "There is more than glass between the snow and the huge roses." What that may be he leaves unspecified, implying that it is a mystery. The contrasts, the variety we find around us, he implies, assault our senses—"On the tongue on the eyes on the ears in the

palms of one's hands"—and is wonderful though not always kind, "More spiteful and gay than one supposes." Again, contrasts control the poem.

Lesson 14—Seeing Anew: Rhetorical Figures in Poetry

Matching exercises:

1. d (pp. 760–761; Study Guide)
2. i (p. 767; Study Guide)
3. g (p. 766; Study Guide)
4. k (p. 765; Study Guide)
5. a (p. 766; Study Guide)
6. e (pp. 760–761; Study Guide)
7. m (p. 760; Study Guide)
8. l (Study Guide)
9. f (p. 766; Study Guide)
10. b (pp. 804–805)

Multiple choice:

1. c (pp. 760–761; Study Guide)
2. d (p. 800; Study Guide)
3. c (pp. 760–761; Study Guide)
4. c (p. 766; Study Guide)
5. d (p. 767; Study Guide)

Short essay sample answers:

1. The three images in line 4 relate to the three metaphors that preceded it. An elephant is known for its ivory, a ponderous house for "fine timbers," and a melon for its "red fruit." In all three cases, what is mentioned in line 4 is what is most precious about the elephant, house, and melon. So, too, the unborn child the speaker is carrying is precious, emphatically so, which explains the exclamation point. The next five lines convey several ideas—that the fetus is developing, that the mother is a means to an end, a "cow in calf," bloated, and unable to turn back. What is important, however, is the value of the life inside her, which is what makes line 4 the key line in the poem.
2. *Conjoin* means "to join together; unite; combine" (Webster's *New World Dictionary*), but the poem gives the word added meaning by placing it within the context of marriage and using the metaphor of the "monster" onion. The first stanza simply describes the onion—a double "joined under one transparent skin"—the kind most readers have seen. Stanza 2 compares the onion to "freaks," a two-headed calf and Siamese twins, stressing the two halves' mutual dependence.

    The onion is transformed into a metaphor in stanza 3, where it becomes a symbol of the speaker's marriage. The man and woman are "conjoined" in marriage in much the same way that the onion, two-headed calf, and Siamese twins are conjoined: "To sever the muscle could free one, / but might kill the other." The poem then sounds a note of irony, for the onion as metaphor is something seen only by the woman because "men / don't slice onions in the kitchen, seldom see / what is invisible."

What is invisible is the "transparent skin" joining the double onion and the equally invisible bonds of marriage. The woman concludes "We cannot escape each other," but the reader is left wondering if the man holds the same belief. Presumably not, since the bond is invisible. The reader is left with the idea that only women appreciate what *conjoined* by marriage means—mutually dependent for existence—and the suggestion that women are far more aware of invisible ties than men.

3. The tone in the poem is mixed, as indeed one's feelings might well be toward a father who inspires both love and fear. The speaker in the poem is the adult who was the small boy waltzed about by his drunken father. The setting is the house where the family lives. The narrative is simple—the father comes home drunk, sweeps up the boy, waltzes him around, and takes him off to bed. The boy's mother does not approve, and the dance itself is wild enough to rattle pans off their shelves.

The father apparently works with his hands, for one knuckle is "battered" and his palm is "caked hard by dirt." Or perhaps he has been in a fight. His roughness is evident in that when he misses a step, his belt buckle scrapes the boy's ear. Also he "beat time" on the boy's head. In spite of these seemingly negative facts, the tone is mixed, part elation, part anxiety.

The hyperbole in line 3, where the speaker describes himself as the boy who "hung on like death," the word *romped* in line 5, and the image of "clinging" in the last line suggest that the boy is exhilarated. Yet the understatement in line 4 ("Such waltzing was not easy"), the scraped ear, the beating of time on the boy's head suggest that the boy was fearful, anxious. The speaker's "Papa's waltz" was loving and frightening, caring and out of control, joyful and insensitive.

Lesson 15—An Echo to the Sense: Prosody and Form in Poetry

Matching exercises:

1. i (p. 900; Study Guide)
2. h (pp. 845–846; Study Guide)
3. k (Study Guide)
4. d (pp. 851–852: Study Guide)
5. c (p. 852; Study Guide)
6. g (p. 847; Study Guide)
7. m (pp. 902–903; Study Guide)
8. b (pp. 855–856; Study Guide)

Multiple choice:

1. d (pp. 845–846)
2. a (p. 850; Study Guide)
3. d (pp. 841–843, 845–846; Study Guide)
4. d (entire lesson)
5. c (Study Guide)

9. j (p. 852; Study Guide)
10. e (p. 855; Study Guide)

Short essay sample answers:

1. The overall meter is iambic tetrameter, but there are some variations. Line 1 is regular, but then the two that follow both begin with a trochee that emphasizes the position of the eagle. Given that variation and emphasis, it seems legitimate to read the last foot of the first stanza as a spondee ("he stands"), again for emphasis. The image depicted is of the eagle as master of what he surveys.

    The second stanza also contains variation. Again the initial line is regular, but the lines that follow vary even more than those in the first stanza. Line four begins with a spondee, again for emphasis. And then the last line employs both pyrrhic and spondaic feet:

    Aňd lĭke | ă thún | děrbolt | hé fálls.

    The effect of the meter in this last line is to start weak and finish strong, the pyrrhic foot leading into the word *thunderbolt*, which is two iambs, and the line ending with a spondee, echoing the end of the first stanza. These concluding spondees center the action for the reader: the eagle "stands," the eagle "falls." All the other images cluster around these two essential actions, so it is appropriate that they receive double stress.

    Why not read the whole poem as though it were unrelieved iambic tetrameter? Aside from having to put emphasis on words that would not normally receive it ("to" in line 2, "with" in line 3), to read the meter in that way would give the poem a regularity and sing-song quality more fitting for a bubble gum jingle. Tennyson is describing an eagle, a bird of prey, not some predictable ordinary creature. The variation works.

2. The first line consists of four syllables. The caesura forces the reader to place the first three syllables into one foot composed of a weak stress followed by two strong ones on words that rhyme. The caesura ends the foot, and the line continues with a weak stress. Two elements stand out from this first line—the double stress and the caesura. The result is a syncopated, musical sound.

    Lines 2 through 7 are each composed of three syllables, spondee, caesura, weak stress. Given the strong beat of the poem, the reader expects the last line to be the same meter, but instead the poem ends with a single spondee, "Die soon." The shift in meter creates surprise and emphasis.

    It makes sense that the beat here is syncopated—not regular—that the meter does not fit neatly into a common form. The rhythm is that of jazz, street talk. And the last line emphasizes where these pool players are headed. The name of the bar—Golden Shovel—is as ironic as the speakers themselves in that being "real cool" doesn't cover up the emptiness of their lives anymore than gold can dress up a shovel.

Lesson 16—Distant Voices: Myth, Symbolism, and Allusion in Poetry

Matching exercises:

1. g (p. 986)
2. h (p. 941; Study Guide)
3. a (Study Guide)
4. j (pp. 945–946; Study Guide)
5. c (Study Guide)
6. d (p. 941; Study Guide)
7. f (pp. 992–993)
8. b (pp. 946–947; Study Guide)
9. k (p. 932; Study Guide)

Multiple choice:

1. c (p. 945; Study Guide)
2. c (p. 941; Study Guide)
3. a (Study Guide)
4. d (p. 983; Study Guide)
5. d (entire lesson)

Short essay sample answers:

1. In Greek myth, Circe ruled the island of Aeaea where she lived in her palace and, using her spells and power, turned men into swine. On his return from Troy, Odysseus, through the intervention of Hermes, escaped that fate but fell for her sexual charms and stayed with her a year. Olga Broumas's Circe is also a symbol of sexual power and lust, and she mixes Greek myth with Christian tradition to make her point.

    Broumas's Circe is also a caster of spells that entice men and turn them to swine. The poem is narrated by Circe, and its three sections set out "The Charm" itself, Circe's "Anticipation" of its working, and "The Bite," the result. The middle section, "The Anticipation," describes Circe as a spider that awaits its prey. The "they" who "weave even my web for me" are men who inadvertently prepare the trap through their rituals of courtship—their "courting hands." The "spell" in line 12 is, ironically, of their own making, their own lust. "Who could release them?" Circe asks. "Who / would untie the cord / with a cloven hoof?" The cloven hoof is an allusion to the devil, a reference that implies that the devil—Satan—is the power that binds the men to Circe.

2. The Odysseus made famous by Homer's *Iliad* and *Odyssey* is the Greek hero, noted for his wandering travels. King of Ithaca and leader of the Greeks during the Trojan war, he spent ten years at war and another ten getting back to his kingdom. Known for his wiliness, it was Odysseus who thought of the

strategy of the Trojan Horse that caused the downfall of Troy and ended the war. Having offended Poseidon, god of the sea, Odysseus finds his way home delayed again and again by natural and unnatural adventures. Merwin uses Odysseus's travels to show the effect of adventure, risk, and betrayal. Odysseus has become hollow and his life meaningless.

The Odysseus that Merwin shows us is tired, his adventures having become blurred by repetition. Even the love affairs he had, "the islands / Each with its woman,"—a reference to Circe and Calypso—blend together with his memories of his wife, Penelope, "the unraveling patience / He was wedded to," in a pattern of betrayal. This Odysseus has lost all meaning, so that "it was the same whether he stayed / Or went." At the end of the poem, lines 12–17, he cannot distinguish lover from wife, friend from enemy.

Lesson 17—Artful Resonance: Theme in Poetry

Matching exercises:

1. c (Study Guide)
2. a (Study Guide)
3. k (Study Guide)
4. m (Study Guide)
5. d (pp. 697–698, 968)
6. g (Study Guide)
7. f (Study Guide)
8. i (Study Guide)
9. e (pp. 1175–1176)
10. j (pp. 968–969, 1162; Study Guide)

Multiple choice:

1. b (pp. 802–803, 1175–1176, 639–640, 674–675)
2. c (pp. 1175–1176, 674–675, 802–803, 639–640)
3. b (Study Guide)
4. d (Study Guide)
5. c (Study Guide)

Short essay sample answers:

1. The speaker is an older woman who recalls a question posed "so many years ago" in an ethics class: "if there were a fire in a museum / which would you save, a Rembrandt painting / or an old woman who hadn't many / years anyhow?" The speaker concludes that "woman / and painting and season are almost one / and all beyond saving by children." The poem implies that for children the question is meaningless, for they lack the knowledge, maturity, and perspective to make a rational decision. Depending upon what the reader views as the subject of the poem, a variety of interpretations are possible. If, for instance, the subject is indeed ethics, then one possible theme is that moral choices require mature judgment. On the other hand, given the setting the subject could also be education, in which case a possible theme

may be that education in general and values in particular that do not relate to the experience of a child are meaningless, empty.

2. The end of the poem sets the present scene—it is fall, and the woman, grown old, is sanding in front of a Rembrandt painting in a museum. The scenes she remembers are the ones that begin the poem, the classroom for ethics where year after year every fall began with the poem's central question—Which to save, the Rembrandt or the woman? The students "caring little for pictures or old age" would play the game, one year choosing "life," the next opting for "art," but "always half-heartedly."

   As a child, the speaker would try to connect her own life to the hypothetical problem by imagining her grandmother as the woman in the museum, but since she had never been to a museum, the connection didn't work, the setting was too foreign. One year, she tried to foil the teacher by suggesting that the old woman make the choice. The teacher immediately pounced upon this cleverness by ridiculing it. The tone here is sarcastic, arch—"Linda . . . eschews / the burdens of responsibility."

   Education here seems more like an unspoken game than learning. The teacher poses a question that the children cannot relate to, but they know an answer is expected so they invent one. It has no meaning to them, nor does it respond adequately to the problem. But how could it? The point of the poem is that the kind of wisdom and knowledge needed to come to terms with the question are gained in maturity.

3. The allusion to Rembrandt works in several ways. First, it's readily recognizable, for Rembrandt's name is synonymous with the term "Old Master." While many would argue that Rembrandt is the greatest painter who ever lived, all would agree that he is the best and the most famous of 17th century Dutch painters. Then there's his subject matter and genius. Known for sympathetic yet realistic portrayals of the old and the poor, Rembrandt was a superb artist whose work with light was admired even by jealous contemporary rivals. By layering the oil paint, he made his dark colors rich and his highlights luminous, resulting in profound portrayals of humanity. Rembrandt is to art as Beethoven is to music or as Shakespeare is to literature.

   As the speaker in the poem stands before a Rembrandt painting, she notes the colors, "darker than autumn, / darker even than winter—the browns of earth, / though earth's most radiant elements burn / through the canvas." Looking, she finds that she, the painting, and the season—both in the sense of winter and of old age—"are almost one." They fuse in a way that school children could never understand. The kind of appreciation of life, age, and art that is necessary to make a moral decision in response to the dilemma posed by the teacher is beyond children.

Lesson 18—Image of Reality: The Elements of Drama

Matching exercises:

1. b (Study Guide)
2. g (Study Guide)
3. k (Study Guide)
4. h (Study Guide)
5. j (Study Guide)
6. c (Study Guide)
7. i (Study Guide)
8. l (Study Guide)
9. d (Study Guide)
10. f (Study Guide)

Multiple choice:

1. d (p. 1204; Study Guide)
2. a (Study Guide)
3. d (pp. 1268–1259; Study Guide)
4. c (pp. 1502–1504; Study Guide)
5. c (Study Guide)

Short essay sample answers:

1. The dialogue that precedes this short speech reveals that Horatio has seen the ghost, which Marcellus and Barnardo have also sighted. The dialogue also tells us that the ghost appeared in the form of the elder Hamlet, but fully armed, seeming to want to speak, and with "a countenance more in sorrow than in anger." In response to this news, Hamlet moves to immediate action, saying that he will take the watch that night. The short speech that follows, lines 244–246, indicates that the identity of the ghost is not established, that it may "assume [Hamlet's] noble father's person" and may not be him at all. In fact the ghost may be evil, there to tempt Hamlet into speaking to it and thereby condemning himself to hell. He is willing to risk that—"though hell itself should gape / And bid me hold my peace." In this few lines, Hamlet shows himself a man of courage and action.

2. Gertrude has just told Hamlet that "all that lives must die," and asks him—since death is common—"Why seems it so particular with thee?" Hamlet's response reveals both his state of mind and his intelligence. He responds first by a play on the word *seems*, then by using hyperbole and parallelism to point out the difference between one who "seems" to show grief and himself, who feels it deep inside. His opening pounce on "seems" reveals his bitterness and anger at his father's death and mother's swift remarriage. The tone here is sardonic, sarcastic, and his overstated listing of the signs of grief is driven in by his use of parallel phrases and repetition ("Nor . . . Nor . . . No . . . Nor"). These outward appearances, Hamlet says, "indeed seem, / For they are actions that a man might play." His grief is beyond all show, beyond anything the clothes of mourning might indicate. Do his words reveal depression that explains his later indecision? A grief so great that it tips him into madness? A

clever mind tainted by anger and suspicion? At this point in the play, any number of interpretations are possible.

3. In this speech, Hamlet commits himself to revenge his father's murder. The tone is emotionally charged yet earnest. At first, Hamlet swears by not only heaven and earth but also hell. He swears that not only will he remember the ghost (and his charge) as long as he has a memory but also that he will wipe away all that he has learned to dedicate himself to the ghost's "commandment," a word with important religious connotations. He has become born again.

But the ghost's charge is complex: he must revenge his father's murder and cleanse the state, yes, but he must do so without harming his mother (who will be left to her own conscience) and without corrupting himself—"Taint not thy mind." When Hamlet says "thy commandment all alone shall live / ... Unmixed with baser matter," he is pledging himself to divine retribution—not an easy undertaking for a mortal.

Hamlet also knows what he is up against. He is aware of Claudius's duplicty, "That one may smile, and smile, and be a villain." Hamlet ends his speech by taking the ghost's words as his motto, and swearing again to "remember" the commandment. The speech ends with the triple-stressed line—"I have sworn't"—a commitment emphasized by the stresses and the break from the predominant blank verse.

Lesson 19—Playing the Part: Character and Action

Matching exercises:

1. f (Study Guide)
2. i (Study Guide)
3. e (Study Guide)
4. k (p. 1321; Study Guide)
5. h (Study Guide)
6. g (Study Guide)
7. j (Study Guide)
8. d (Study Guide)
9. l (Study Guide)
10. c (Study Guide)

Multiple choice:

1. b (Study Guide)
2. d (Study Guide)
3. a (Study Guide)
4. d (p. 1268; Study Guide)
5. a (Study Guide)

Short essay sample answers:

1. The scene takes place in court, where Claudius addresses his Council and Polonius, his chief minister. What he says is a model of politic speech, and he appears to be intelligent, diplomatic, and judicious. He is both thoughtful and a man of action. His use of first person plural throughout the speech is purposely the royal "we," so that every pronoun reinforces his kingship.

    First Claudius speaks of his brother's death and his own and his subjects' grief over it—"our whole kingdom / To be contracted in one brow of woe." Then he brings up the subject of his marriage, acknowledging Gertrude as "our sometime sister, now our queen." He reminds the Council that they have supported this marriage, thus blunting the charge that the marriage was unseemly, even incestuous.

    Having acknowledged the death of the elder Hamlet and Gertrude's remarriage, Claudius then moves to action. He explains young Fortinbras's impending assault and motive and his response to it in the form of a letter to the King of Norway, informing him of the facts and asking for him to dismiss the army that, after all, is made up of the King's subjects, not Fortinbras's.

    Claudius gives the letter to two messengers, and it's interesting to note that he charges them with "no further personal power / To business with the king, more than the scope / Of these delated articles allow." Claudius is politic, diplomatic, intelligent, but also suspicious, concerned with power—qualities that rise closer to the surface as the play progresses.

2. Conscience is one of the key words in the play, and these lines reveal it at work within Claudius. The speech shows that Claudius is a Christian who is wrestling with his conscience. He is neither all evil nor an unsympathetic character, as he might have seemed up to this point in the play.

    The first few lines of the soliloquy reveal that Claudius knows how great a sin he has committed—Cain's sin with Cain's curse, the murder of a brother. In fact, he feels his guilt so strongly that he cannot pray. Claudius considers what is involved in forgiveness and mercy and knows that his sin can be forgiven. At the same time he knows that he cannot beg forgiveness unless he is willing to give up what he gained—crown, ambition, and queen. It's interesting that Claudius inserts "my" before each one of those achievements, thus unwittingly emphasizing the size of his ego.

    Claudius knows that evil may conquer justice in "the corrupted currents of this world . . . but 'tis not so above." Even so, he cannot repent and castigates himself for it, calling upon the angels for help. Yet he will try. The speech concludes with his commanding his knees to bend in prayer and his heart to soften, so that "All may be well." Hamlet comes upon him at prayer but does not kill him because Claudius's soul would go to heaven. The ultimate irony is that Claudius cannot pray—"My words fly up, my thoughts remain below."

414—*Literary Visions*

3. Fortinbras may be a flat character, indeed we don't see much of him, but he serves an important function in *Hamlet* by reinforcing the theme and the characters of Laertes and Hamlet. Although he does not see much action on stage, through other characters we can see him progress from a kind of Laertes to a kind of Hamlet.

Like Hamlet and Laertes, Fortinbras is the son of a murdered man whom he has sworn to avenge. His father, however, was killed honestly in battle. Even so, he responds with all the hotheadedness of a Laertes, vowing vengeance. Like Hamlet after the scene with Laertes at Ophelia's funeral, Fortinbras eventually cools down and repents his hasty reaction. Having already raised an army, he directs it against the Poles in a battle over disputed yet essentially useless land—"a little patch of ground / That hath in it no profit but the name" (IV.iv.18–19).

The motive for that impending battle appears to be Fortinbras's desire for fame, for Hamlet calls Fortinbras "a delicate and tender prince, / Whose spirit with divine ambition puffed . . . Even for an egg-shell" (IV.iv.48–54). The discrepancy between Fortinbras's ignoble motive and quick action and Hamlet's great motive and slow response inflames Hamlet and renews his resolve—"O from this time forth, / My thoughts be bloody, or be nothing worth" (IV.iv.65–66).

The Fortinbras we see at the end of the play is more like Hamlet than Laertes. In fact since Hamlet gives Fortinbras his vote for the crown of Denmark, there is reason to suspect that Hamlet's earlier assessment was based more on self-disgust than on knowledge. Fortinbras's assessment of Hamlet is not only accurate, it is spoken with the mature voice of a statesman—not a hothead.

Thus Fortinbras closes the play on a note both political and military. Fortinbras—now in charge—declares "Let four captains / Bear Hamlet like a soldier" and commands that he be given military honors. The state is cleansed of corruption, a proper succession is assured, and divine order is restored.

Lesson 20—Patterns of Action: Plot and Conflict in Drama

Matching exercises:

1. h (pp. 1279–1280; Study Guide)
2. c (pp. 1207–1209)
3. a (pp. 1207–1209)
4. b (Study Guide)
5. g (pp. 1207–1209; Study Guide)

Multiple choice:

1. b (Study Guide)
2. a (pp. 1322–1323; Study Guide)
3. d (pp. 1206–1207; Study Guide)
4. b (Study Guide)
5. d (Study Guide)

6. e (pp. 1206–1207; Study Guide)
7. m (pp. 1207–1209; Study Guide)
8. d (p. 1209; Study Guide)
9. j (pp. 1207–1209; Study Guide)
10. k (p. 1209; Study Guide)

Short essay sample answers:

1. The Sphinx had been plaguing Thebes with a riddle: What walks on four legs in the morning, two legs at noon, and three in the evening? Those who could not answer the riddle she killed. Oedipus, however, solved the riddle by answering "Man." The Sphinx then killed herself.

    The riddle is important in several ways. First, Oedipus's having solved it not only gains him the queen and crown but also reveals him to be courageous and clever. And it leads him later to suspect Tiresias's powers. Why didn't Tiresias solve the riddle, Oedipus asks.

    But probably the most important contribution the riddle makes is an ironic one, for the answer is also Oedipus. As a child, he had to crawl because his feet were injured. As a man, he walked proudly on two feet, but now that he is blind and knows the evil he has committed, he walks with a cane.

2. Another way of looking at the major conflict in *Oedipus the King* is to examine the play from the perspective of truth. If the characters are then lined up in terms of who does and who does not know the truth, it's possible to see the conflict as ignorance versus knowledge. On the side of ignorance, there are Oedipus, Jocasta, Creon, and the Theban elders; on the side of knowledge there are Tiresias and the Theban shepherd.

    The action of the play then follows Oedipus's progress along the path to knowledge. His first conflict is with Tiresias, for Tiresias knows the truth and, knowing it to be horrible, is reluctant to tell it. And when he does tell, Oedipus is too angry to hear. As for the shepherd, he too is reluctant. Oedipus has to threaten him with torture to get him to reveal his story. This time, the pieces of the puzzle fall in place, and Oedipus recognizes the truth. He blinds himself so that he cannot see what Tiresias calls his "guilt" (Fagles—line 419; Gould—line 418).

    Analyzing the conflict in this way exposes an irony that fits the overall dramatic irony of the play: Tiresias, who is blind, can see the truth; Oedipus can see but is blind to the truth. At the end of the play, Oedipus is blind but can see.

3. From Jocasta's first appearance to her last, she reminds us of the awful truth about Oedipus and thereby underscores the play's irony. At first, her actions are innocent of the knowledge of Oedipus's identity, but because the audience knows the truth, it can find clues about Oedipus in what she says and how she acts.

416—*Literary Visions*

For example, Jocasta first appears in a motherly role. Coming upon Creon and Oedipus trading insults, she responds as a mother might in speaking to two quarreling boys. She scolds them for arguing while the city suffers. To Oedipus she says, "Into the palace now. And Creon, you go home" (Fagles—line 713–714; Gould—line 642).

Then later, when Oedipus reports to Jocasta that Tiresias accused him of being the murderer of Laius, Jocasta responds with what she thinks is assurance. She tells Oedipus that Tiresias must be wrong because it was foretold that Laius would be killed by his son, yet he was murdered by robbers at a place where three roads meet. When Oedipus asks what Laius looked like, Jocasta answers "He had a figure not unlike your own." The irony here is striking.

As Oedipus begins to put the puzzle together, Jocasta tries to assure him that he could not be the murderer of Lauis. But after the appearance of the messenger and his tale of having received the infant Oedipus from a herdsman near Cithaeron, she realizes the truth. She begs Oedipus not to continue his search, but he takes her pleading to be evidence of shame at what may turn out to be his low birth. By the time Oedipus understands that her motive is quite different, it is too late, and Jocasta has hanged herself. The final irony is that Oedipus takes her brooches and uses them to blind himself.

Lesson 21—Perspectives on Illusion: Setting and Staging in Drama

Matching exercises:

1. m (Study Guide)
2. l (p. 1614; Study Guide)
3. a (Study Guide)
4. j (Study Guide)
5. b (p. 1212; Study Guide)
6. d (Study Guide)
7. c (pp. 1614–1615; Study Guide)
8. h (Study Guide)
9. f (Study Guide)
10. e (p. 1212; Study Guide)

Multiple choice:

1. b (Study Guide)
2. a (Study Guide)
3. b (pp. 1212–1214; Study Guide)
4. c (pp. 1616–1619; Study Guide)
5. d (p. 1619; Study Guide)

Short essay sample answers:

1. The limited space gives the play a rather claustrophobic atmosphere and lends credibility to the tensions within the family. As the stage directions

point out, the apartment really consists of two rooms, a living room and a dining room. Laura sleeps in the living room, and Tom writes in the dining room. Off stage is a "kitchenette." The door to the apartment opens onto a fire escape.

Since Laura does not work and Amanda's job is one she is able to carry out from the apartment, both spend a great deal of time in the apartment, particularly now that Laura is a dropout from the business school. Tom comes and goes, vanishing as often as possible to the movies and regularly to his job. And, of course, the family's financial pressures and unrealistic hopes exert a stress of their own that combine with the physical closeness forced by the apartment. The result is tension, conflict, and more pressure. The setting helps support the play's plot.

2. As Amanda launches forth into her often-told account of her days in Blue Mountain and her gentlemen callers, Tom, acting as stage director, signals for a "spot of light on Amanda" (page 1649). What follows is probably performed in a somewhat stylized manner, as though it is a set piece, rehearsed many times and delivered on cue. This impression is supported by Williams's description of Amanda: "Her eyes lift, her face glows, her voice becomes rich and elegiac" (page 1649).

Amanda's speech consists of a list of suitors and what happened to them, but how much of it is fiction we do not know. What does come through, however, is Amanda's belief that she had many gentlemen callers, and they were all headed for success or a romantic death. Her reverie is brought to a stop when she says, "But—I picked your *father*!" (page 1650). Laura immediately says to Mother, let me clear the table," as though to head off what may follow about her father. His desertion is a reality Amanda does not like to deal with.

The spotlight emphasizes Amanda's speech and strengthens the audience's belief in her belief (which may or may not be true) in the romantic life she led and could have continued. Obviously, it's a tale she likes to tell and tells often. As Laura says earlier, "She loves to tell it." Amanda lives on what is probably an illusion, but she believes it's real.

3. The fire escape figures large in the play. We are introduced to it in the stage directions (page 1647), where Williams points out that it is the entrance to the apartment and a "touch of accidental poetic truth, for all of these huge buildings are always burning with the slow and implacable fires of human desperation." Williams is using "Burning" in a metaphorical sense, and indeed the Wingfields in particular are burning with "human desperation."

But the fire escape is more than a general symbol. It is a very particular one for the Wingfield family. To Amanda it represents the ramshackle quality of their living quarters and also danger. In Scene 4, for instance, when Laura leaves the apartment and slips on the fire escape, Amanda bursts out with a tirade about the landlord and, by implication, the condition of the steps. For

418—*Literary Visions*

Laura, they represent one more hazard and one more reminder of her difficulty in walking—of her being "different."

For Tom, the fire escape represents an avenue of flight from the pressures exerted by his family. He uses it to relax with a cigarette (Scenes 5 and 6), and he uses it finally to escape from their lives. Yet—as he tells us in his role as narrator—he has not been able to escape. He cannot forget Laura. It's interesting to note that Tom introduces Scene 3 from the fire escape. Like the fire escape itself, he is part of *yet outside*—all that happens in the apartment. Thus the fire escape can also be said to symbolize Tom's dual role—as narrator and character.

Lesson 22—Speech and Silence: The Language of Drama

Matching exercises:

1. m (p. 1651; Study Guide)
2. d (p. 1321; Study Guide)
3. e (Study Guide)
4. f (p. 1685; Study Guide)
5. k (Study Guide)
6. l (Study Guide)
7. c (Study Guide)
8. a (Study Guide)
9. g (p. 1687; Study Guide)
10. i (Study Guide)

Multiple choice:

1. d (Study Guide)
2. b (Study Guide)
3. d (Study Guide)
4. a (Study Guide)
5. d (Study Guide)

Short essay sample answers:

1. One way to interpret that final silent scene is to see it as a reflection of Tom's memory. After all, Tom told us at the start that the play is memory. Using that idea as a key to the action, we are presented with the scene as Tom would like to see it—Amanda has "dignity and tragic beauty," and Laura, comforted, smiles. As though to validate Tom's escape and pursuit of his dream, Amanda glances at the picture of his father—another escapee. And then Laura blows out the candles, symbolically blotting out the family from Tom's mind.

   As the scene is described, there are none of the emotions one would expect—no recriminations, no anger, no tears. Nor is there the characterization the rest of the play would lead one to expect. This is not the desperate, fantasy-ridden, pathetic Amanda of the earlier scenes. And this Laura is capable of being comforted. In short, the characters are as Tom *wishes*. The irony is that although Laura blows out the candles, as Tom (in his roles as narrator and stage manager) directs her to do, he still cannot escape his memory of her.

2. The first exchange of dialogue sets a realistic tone for the language used in the rest of the play. The conversation—if you can call it that—has taken place in millions of American households belonging to millions of American families. Invariably, dinner is ready, but one member of the family has yet to appear. The nagging begins with a call of the guilty party's name, "Tom?" The question mark introduces the nagging tone that typifies this opening exchange. Not content with Tom's "Yes, Mother," which is said, one can imagine, in a tone of resignation, Amanda rubs it in: "We can't say grace until you come to the table!" Quite aside from the Wingfields, this little guilt-inducing dig too often characterizes the relationship between parent and child.

    What follows is almost predictable, a lesson in table manners. Again, Amanda is expert in hiding her criticism. In reality, she is nagging, but she disguises it with a mini-lecture on biology and tops that off with concern for her son's welfare, "Eat food leisurely, son, and really enjoy it." Tom's reaction is equally predictable; he strikes back. When Amanda retaliates with "Temperament like a Metropolitan star!" Tom rises and leaves the room only to be reprimanded with, "You're not excused from the table." Tom parries by saying that he's going to get a cigarette, but Amanda strikes again: "You smoke too much."

    In this short exchange, Williams manages to recrate the tensions and undercurrents that can characterize a family dinner. The difference is that one gets the impression that *every* Wingfield dinner is like this one. Seemingly innocuous remarks are really subtle thrusts, and seemingly rebellious actions are only blunted counterjabs. To some extent, duels like this one are part of every family's life, but to Tom and Amanda it is a *way* of life.

3. Act V opens on a note of death, as the grave-diggers finish what Hamlet does not realize is Ophelia's grave. Hamlet talks with them and then moves to the side as he sees the funeral group approaching. As he listens to the conversation between Laertes and the Doctor of Divinity, Hamlet realizes that the grave is for Ophelia and that she has committed suicide. Laertes blasts the Doctor for the brevity of the funeral rites and—in an outburst of grief—leaps into the grave.

    Laertes's speech reveals him to be hotheaded and overdramatic. He opens with hyperbole and curses the cause of her suicide:

O treble woe
Fall ten time treble on that cursed head
Whose wicked deed thy most ingenious sense
Deprived thee of.—(V.i.229–232)

He flings himself into the grave and asks to be buried with Ophelia under a mountain-high pile of dirt—hyperbole again. Hamlet, maddened by this excessive and therefore somewhat suspect show of grief, identifies himself and leaps into the grave as well. When Laertes tries to choke Hamlet, Hamlet warns him straightwardly that although he is not hot-tempered, he has reason to be dangerous.

After they are separated, Hamlet says simply that he will not have his grief topped by that of Laertes, for "I loved Ophelia." He goes on to mock Laerte's hyperbole in "forty thousand brothers / Could not with all their quantity of love / Make up my sum" (lines 252–254). He continues in this mocking tone, challenging Laertes to even more excessive displays of grief (lines 257–267). Then, after Gertrude calls Hamlet's behavior "mere madness," Hamlet cools down and reproves Laertes with, "What is the reason that you use me thus? / I loved you ever" (lines 272–273). Cryptically adding, "but it is no matter. / Let Hercules himself do what he may, / The cat will mew, and dog will have his day" (lines 273–275), Hamlet exits.

The speeches reveal Laertes's emotional impulsiveness and Hamlet's genuine love for Ophelia. They also show Hamlet's intellect. Mockery is almost guaranteed to ignite Laertes, and Hamlet mocks well. As for the speeches' contribution to action, they move Laertes to join Claudius in the plot to kill Hamlet. At the same time, Hamlet's last line foreshadows the inevitable destiny that awaits Claudius, Laertes, Gertrude, and Hamlet in the following scene.

Lesson 23—The Vision Quest: Myth and Symbolism in Drama

Matching exercises:

1. m (pp. 1210–1211; Study Guide)
2. g (pp. 1210–1211; Study Guide)
3. d (p. 1211; Study Guide)
4. j (Study Guide)
5. f (Study Guide)
6. b (Study Guide)
7. k (pp. 1210–1211; Study Guide)
8. i (Study Guide)
9. a (Study Guide)
10. c (Study Guide)

Multiple choice:

1. d (Study Guide)
2. b (Study Guide)
3. d (Study Guide)
4. a (Study Guide)
5. c (pp. 1210–1211; Study Guide)

Short essay sample answers:

1. Had Sophocles ended his play with Oedipus dying victoriously in battle, he would not have had a tragedy. A tragic hero must suffer, learn, and pay the price of knowledge. If Oedipus is to pay for his sins, he cannot die happily but must continue to carry the burden of his knowledge. Oedipus must also fully recognize his part in his fate. And that is what Sophocles's Oedipus does by blinding himself and obeying his own command by going into exile. The irony of blinding himself and of needing a staff or stick to find his way is powerful and in keeping with the controlling ironic tone of the play. Oedipus had sight but failed to see; now he is blind but sees the truth. Oedipus solved the riddle of the Sphinx; now he lives out the riddle by needing the staff usually associated with old age. Conflict, characterization, and tone make Sophocles's ending the only one possible.

2. "Blue Roses" is the name Jim had coined for Laura in high school. She had been ill and absent with pleurosis. When she returned and Jim asked her what had been the matter, he misheard her answer as "Blue Roses." For Laura, the term had special meaning and became a private symbol indicating she was something special, as opposed to being something odd.

    It is apparent from the conversation between Jim and Laura that Laura had idolized Jim. She had not only saved his yearbook but knew right where his "wonderful write-up" was. She had also heard him in the operetta three times and even remembered the name of his old girlfriend. Given Laura's vivid memories of Jim and his rather vague ones of her, it is probably also safe to assume that the name "Blue Roses" can also symbolize Laura's past and present fantasies about Jim, fantasies that, like most of those held by the Wingfield family, are based on little reality.

3. The context for the speech under consideration in Act III.ii.322–350 is the relationship among Rosencrantz and Guildenstern, Hamlet, and Claudius. Rosencrantz and Guildenstern are courtiers who were Hamlet's friends but earlier in the play agreed to spy on him for Claudius. As Act III.ii progresses, the play within the play ends with the desired result—Claudius reveals his guilt and thereby verifies the word of the Ghost. As Hamlet and Horatio compare notes on their observations of Claudius, Rosencrantz and Guildenstern enter; Hamlet calls for music.

    Rosencrantz and Guildenstern relay the concern of the King and Queen and try to pump Hamlet about his "distemper." Hamlet asks for a recorder and at first uses the language of the hunt to ask why they are pursuing him (lines 324–326). When Guildenstern responds that it is out of live, Hamlet says bluntly, "I do not well understand that," and asks him to play the recorder. Guildenstern says he cannot, he does not know how, and then after Hamlet has pointed out the instrument's stops and mouthpiece, Guildenstern adds that he lacks the skill to play.

Hamlet then uses the recorder as a symbol of himself, telling Rosencrantz and Guildenstern that "you would play upon me, you would seem to know my stops, you would pluck out the heart of my mystery . . . do you think I am easier to be played on than a pipe" (lines 343–348). He concludes with a pun on "fret" as a musical term and as a synonym for "worry": "Call me what instrument you will, though you can fret me, you cannot play upon me" (lines 348–350). Thus in this speech, Hamlet reveals that he is not as mad as he pretends to be, chides Rosencrantz and Guildenstern for their false concern, tips them off that he is onto them, gives them a neat mini-lesson in thinking by analogy, and does all of this by using the recorder as a symbol.

Lesson 24—A Frame for Meaning: Theme in Drama

Matching exercises:

1. f (Study Guide)
2. h (p. 1205)
3. l (Study Guide)
4. i (p. 1205)
5. g (Study Guide)
6. e (Study Guide)
7. m (Study Guide)
8. k (Study Guide)
9. j (Study Guide)
10. a (Study Guide)

Multiple choice:

1. a (Study Guide)
2. d (Study Guide)
3. d (Study Guide)
4. b (Study Guide)
5. a (Study Guide)

Short essay sample answers:

1. *The Glass Menagerie* raises many issues that can be stated as subjects: duty, family, unrealistic expectations, alienation, love, evil, guilt, class, fantasy. Of those, I find guilt the most interesting because it's one of those topics rarely talked about among families but deeply felt, and it's certainly a subject that the play explores in a perceptive way. Guilt is an emotion that all the characters feel. Amanda feels guilty for not being able to bring up her family in the tradition (real or imagined) she was brought up in. Laura feels guilty because she thinks she's a disappointment to Amanda. Tom feels guilty because he is torn between his own desires and his sense of responsibility towards his family. And even Jim feels guilty when he realizes he has led Laura to believe that he has more interest in her than he has. Of all these characters, only Jim is probably able to put

guilt behind him, for when he walks out of the Wingfields' door, he walks back into a reality that does not touch them, the world of his impending marriage, his job, and his classes. Amanda and Laura are left with no resolution in that they have not changed. Amanda can no more give up her attempts to gloss over the reality of their bare existence than Laura can overcome her shyness. As for Tom, he knows that he cannot rid himself of the image of Laura. His guilt accompanies him wherever he goes.

2. In *The Glass Menagerie*, the Wingfields' world of illusions, frustrations, and lack of communication leads to a sense of guilt that burdens everyone in the family. The antagonist in the play is Amanda. She refuses to acknowledge that the family's way of life has changed economically and socially, that Laura is "different," and that Tom has his own dreams that he must pursue. Instead she smooths over their financial and family hardships with tales of gentlemen callers and the better days of Blue Mountain. She never addresses problems directly, never talks about them. Her only open acknowledgement of the reality of their situation is the one she makes at the end of the play. She accuses Tom of having known that Jim was engaged and tells him "You live in a dream; you manufacture illusions" (page 1690). She's right, of course, but she fails to see the irony of her accusation, for she has raised Tom in a world of illusion.

When Tom responds by saying that he's going to the movies, Amanda lashes out at him:

> Don't think about us, a mother deserted, an unmarried sister who's crippled and has no job! Don't let anything interfere with your selfish pleasure! Just go, go, go—to the movies!
> —(page 1690)

Amanda's parting words are "Go then! Go to the moon—you selfish dreamer!" (page 1690). Her purpose here is not to face any kind of reality but to heap enough guilt on Tom so that he will keep on supporting the family. It doesn't work. Tom leaves and not just for the movies. But the guilt lingers. Tom is haunted by the image of Laura.

Guilt probably continues to haunt Laura, and Amanda probably continues unintentionally to encourage it by pretending that nothing is wrong—by not recognizing and talking about the reality of their lives. What makes the play poignant is that Amanda is no Claudius; the evil she does is not intentional. Nevertheless she has created an emotionally crippled family that is unable to talk about the things that matter and that lives in a world of fantasy ridden by guilt.

3. It's hard to settle the question of fate in *Oedipus the King* as the Greeks at that time might have, for within Greek religion both views are possible. The gods had foreknowledge, but they also interfered with the lives of mortals, as the tales of the Trojan wars show. But if the role of fate is determined on dramatic

424—*Literary Visions*

grounds alone, then predestination should be ruled out. If the gods controlled Oedipus's fate, the reader or viewer is left only with irony, and very cruel irony. It would be as though the gods were playing with Oedipus, making him take actions that lead to his own destruction.

The play is far more powerful if Oedipus controls his own destiny. Then the gods' role becomes benevolent in that they constantly warn Oedipus of the fate he is determining for himself by sending messages through the Delphic Oracle, the shrine of Apollo. True, Oedipus tries to heed the warnings in that he vows not to return to Corinth, which he believes to be the home of his parents. But the one act that he should have avoided is the one that counts: the murder of Laius. As Sophocles explains, Oedipus met up with a carriage whose driver tried to push him off the road. Oedipus "struck in anger" at the driver, knocked the older man out of the carriage, and then "killed them all—every mother's son" (Fagles—line 898; Gould—Line 818). Temper and pride are Oedipus's weaknesses, and they prove his downfall. He had a choice; he controlled his own destiny.

Lesson 25—Casting Long Shadows: The Power of Literature

Matching exercises:

1. f (pp. 697–698)
2. i (Study Guide)
3. h (Study Guide)
4. g (Study Gu ide)
5. j (pp. 802–803; Study Guide)
6. a (Study Guide)
7. b (Study Guide)
8. c (p. 1099; Study Guide)
9. e (pp. 586–590)

Multiple choice:

1. c (entire lesson)
2. a (Study Guide)
3. a (Study Guide)
4. c (entire lesson)
5. d (Study Guide)

Short essay sample answers:

1. If I were to imagine who is watching this show, I would probably come up with someone like Fran, a woman somewhere in her thirties. Unlike Fran, however, most of the show's viewers are probably white. As a character on the show, Fran is both African-American and a critical reader—someone who uses her background to help interpret what she reads. In many ways she is presented as a model for us: an interested informed reader who is knowledgeable but not so knowledgeable as the writers or critics. She is what we want to be—a critical reader.

Appendix B—425

2. Most of the writing I've done in the course has been formal, falling into the category of "academic essay," but I've written some informal pieces as well. If I look at myself as the narrator in both, a character of a sort, what surprises me is that I appear to be two people. In the formal essays, my diction level is a bit higher than I would use in speech and my sentences are certainly more crafted, less rambling. I've tried to recognize my assertions as assertions and always back them up with evidence from the texts. Thus the essays are more rational than emotional. The opposite is true for informal writing. There, my character is much closer to the way I am in conversation. I don't always back up my points; I let my imagination roam free, and I am more emotional. I also take more liberties with the rules of writing. My persona is much closer to the real me as opposed to putting on the persona of a student.
3. The dramatization that I found particularly effective was the one from "The Ballad of Birmingham." Fran reminds us beforehand that the poem is set at the time of civil rights demonstrations in the 1960s and that the particular event is the bombing of a church. The poem focuses on the mother of a child who was in the church when the bomb went off. Ironically, it was the mother who told the child she could not march in a demonstration because it was dangerous; instead, she could go to church to sing in the children's choir. The video presents us with the last two stanzas. Those are certainly the ones I would pick from the poem, for they are the most emotionally charged and present the mother's realization of what has happened.

Lesson 26—Continuing Vision: The Uses of Literature

Matching exercises:

1. d (video)
2. k (Study Guide)
3. f (pp. 333–343; Study Guide)
4. l (Study Guide)
5. b (Study Guide)
6. a (Study Guide)
7. i (Study Guide)
8. g (video)
9. j (pp. 586–590)
10. h (Study Guide)

Multiple choice:

1. a (Study Guide)
2. d (Study Guide)
3. a (Study Guide)
4. c (Study Guide)
5. b (Study Guide)

Short essay sample answers:

1. In a way, the video component of *Literary Visions* is a genre unto itself, although it shares a number of characteristics with the literary genres it

presents. First, it differs in that it is nonfiction and explanatory. The videos focus on various elements of literature to explain them. Literature, on the other hand, has enjoyment as its primary purpose. And though the videos deal with literature in the form of imaginative fiction, they deal with it as something tangible, real; in that sense the series is nonfiction. At the same time, like fiction, the series is created, has a distinct structure, uses various literary devices such as metaphor and symbolism, and has a theme. Like literature, the theme is implied rather than explicit. Put simply, the theme of the series is that literature is accessible, rewarding, and enjoyable.

2. Each title of the lessons for this course is presented as an image, followed by a colon and then the focus of the lesson. The point of the image is not only to get the reader's attention but also to set up the specific subject. "Continuing Vision: The Uses of Literature," the title of this lesson, for instance, carries out the central image announced by the title of the series—*Literary Visions*—while it provides more concrete ideas of what the lesson is about. In fact, all of the images announced in the titles either relate to the central idea of "vision" or to some aspect of language and literature. "Reflected Worlds," "Seeing Anew," and "Perspectives on Illusion" are all examples of images related to the controlling idea of vision; "The Story's Blueprint," "An Echo to the Sense," and "Playing the Part" suggest key elements of literature. In essence, the title of the series sets out a central metaphor that is followed through in the titles of individual lessons. And what could be more appropriate to literature than metaphor?

3. Taking the course by television may not give me much idea of what other students think, but it gives me a greater range of informed opinion. By listening to the critics, I can understand how they view various works and how they read. I'm also impressed that sometimes they disagree. Many teachers may tell you that there are equally valid yet different ways to interpret a work, but seeing is believing. Having critics give different interpretations helps me form my own interpretation of complex works such as *Hamlet*.

I also enjoyed hearing the writers and the drama professionals discuss the works. It gave me a sense of the people behind the texts and made the printed word more real. I've never been in a classroom that provided that sort of background directly, that presented the words and the voices and the images of the people involved.

And then there's Fran. I could identify with her because she's accessible, unintimidating. She presents a model of the informed yet not expert reader. I enjoyed the part she played as a kind of mediator between the works and the experts.

Perhaps most of all, I enjoyed seeing and hearing works come to life in the dramatizations. That's something that's hard to do in the classroom.